D1150911

# Economics Student Workbook

**Eighth Edition**

# Student Workbook

**Eighth Edition**

**Damian Ward**

**David Begg**

## The *McGraw·Hill* Companies

London · Boston · Burr Ridge, IL · Dubuque, IA · Madison, WI · New York
San Francisco · St. Louis · Bangkok · Bogotá · Caracas · Kuala Lumpur · Lisbon
Madrid · Mexico City · Milan · Montreal · New Delhi · Santiago · Seoul · Singapore
Sydney · Taipei · Toronto

Economics Student Workbook Eighth Edition
Damian Ward and David Begg
ISBN 10: 0-07-7107802
ISBN 13: 978-0077107802

Published by McGraw-Hill Education
Shoppenhangers Road
Maidenhead
Berkshire
SL6 2QL
Telephone: 44 (0) 1628 502 500
Fax: 44 (0) 1628 770 224
Website: www.mcgraw-hill.co.uk

British Library Cataloguing in Publication Data
A catalogue record for this book is available from the British Library

Library of Congress Cataloguing in Publication Data
The Library of Congress data for this book has been applied for from the Library of Congress

Acquisitions Editor: Kirsty Reade
Senior Development Editor: Caroline Howell
Senior Production Editor: Eleanor Hayes
Marketing Director: Petra Skytte


Text design by Claire Brodmann Book Designs, Lichfield, Staffs
Cover design by Ego Creative Ltd
Typeset by Northern Phototypesetting Co Ltd, Bolton
Printed and bound in the UK by Bell and Bain Ltd, Glasgow

Published by McGraw-Hill Education (UK) Limited an imprint of The McGraw-Hill Companies, Inc.,
1221 Avenue of the Americas, New York, NY 10020. Copyright © 2005 by McGraw-Hill Education (UK)
Limited. All rights reserved. No part of this publication may be reproduced or distributed in any form or by any
means, or stored in a database or retrieval system, without the prior written consent of The McGraw-Hill
Companies, Inc., including, but not limited to, in any network or other electronic storage or transmission, or
broadcast for distance learning.

ISBN 10: 0-07-70107802
ISBN 13: 978-0077107802
© 2005. Exclusive rights by The McGraw-Hill Companies, Inc. for manufacture and export. This book cannot be
re-exported from the country to which it is sold by McGraw-Hill.

# Contents

# Dedication

Mel, Lucy, Emily and inbound

# Preface

Economics is a topic of study, a topical media subject and of relevance to everyday life. But behind the headlines of 'Demise of the Dollar', 'Booming China' and 'Profits Plummet' there must be a means of understanding these issues in greater detail. Economics is that means.

Economics provides a structured framework of theories, approaches and terminology which enable a deeper understanding of interesting economic problems. However, the benefits to be gained from an economic understanding require students to gain competence in the use and application of economic theories and concepts. The purpose of this *Student Workbook* is to build your understanding of basic economic ideas and develop confidence in the use of data, theories and economic diagrams.

The eight edition of the *Student Workbook* has been revitalized with new data examples and real-world examples, helping you to engage in a deeper understanding of economics in a structured and practical manner. The workbook provides a series of exercises and triggers for thought that will supplement and guide your study of what we believe to be a most fascinating and challenging subject.

## Features of the *Student Workbook*:

The *Student Workbook* has a number of key features to provide a clear structure for your study. See the 'Guided tour' on pages x–xi for tips on making the most of the *Student Workbook* features.

- **Fresh, new design** The eighth edition of the workbook has been redesigned to enhance and clarify the text.
- **Learning objectives** These echo the corresponding chapter in *Economics, Eighth Edition* (the 'main text').
- **Key learning blocks** A new feature to draw together the aims of the chapter in a succinct and easily referenced manner.
- **Important concepts and technical terms** This provides a valuable checklist of key definitions, helping you to think carefully about important ideas and pieces of economic jargon. Many of the definitions reflect the wording of the main text for consistency and clarity.
- **Exercises** These put economics into action in a variety of carefully designed formats. Wherever possible the exercises use real-word data and allow you to carry out economic analysis of many day-to-day issues.
- **True/False** This section includes commentary on many common fallacies of economic life and readily facilitates revision.
- **Economics in action** This fascinating section uses up-to-date and topical extracts from the news and media to show how economics can be applied to real-world events happening all around us.
- **Questions for thought** These provide interesting topics for further discussion. Some of the exercises in this section extend the concepts of the chapter and introduce new ideas and applications.

## Answers and comments

The second half of the workbook comprises this vital section. The emphasis is on clear explanation of the questions posed in the first half of the book, especially in areas where students often encounter difficulty.

In many cases you may find it helpful to tackle the questions step by step alongside the commentary specially designed to enhance the learning experience.

In addition to the exercises and questions in the workbook, you can explore further resources available to you at **www.mcgraw-hill.co.uk/textbooks/begg**. For more information, see the section entitled 'Technology to enhance teaching and learning' (pages xii–xiii).

We hope you find using this *Student Workbook* an enjoyable and supportive experience.

# Guided tour

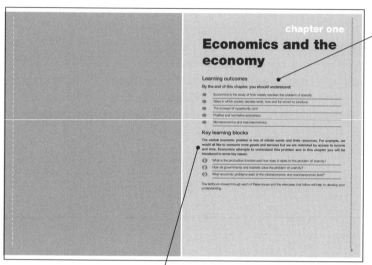

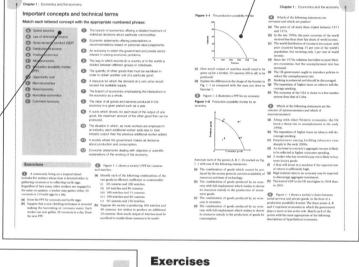

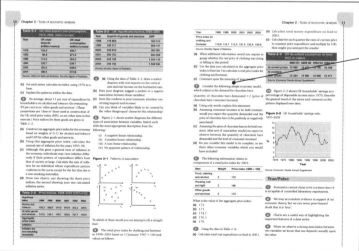

## Learning outcomes

Each chapter opens with a set of learning objectives, summarizing what readers should understand. They correspond with the chapters in the main textbook.

## Figures and tables

Each chapter provides a number of figures and tables to help you to visualize the various economic models and to illustrate and summarize important concepts.

## Key learning blocks

Structured into blocks, the workbook helps you to isolate the key learning points from each chapter in the main textbook. This should act as a useful checklist for your revision, helping you to focus on the most important points.

## Important concepts and technical terms

Match each term in the list with its corresponding definition. This exercise helps you to briefly review the technical terms and concepts you will have covered in the main textbook to ensure that you have acquired a solid understanding of the essential definitions in economics.

## Exercises

The variety of exercises on offer allows you to practise the techniques you have been taught and apply the economic methodology. They include graphical exercises as well as short answer style questions, supplementing the review questions from the main text.

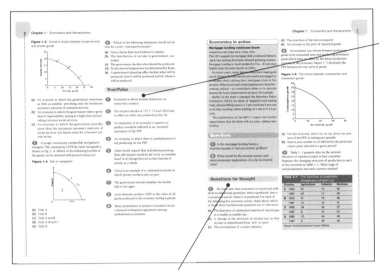

## True/False

These quick questions test your understanding of the basic concepts in economics.

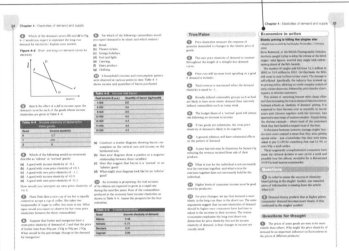

## Economics in action

The workbook features boxed examples which apply to the main economics concepts learned. Each case study has its own set of questions.

## Questions for thought

These questions encourage you to review and apply the knowledge you have acquired from each chapter. They may be useful revision questions prior to exams.

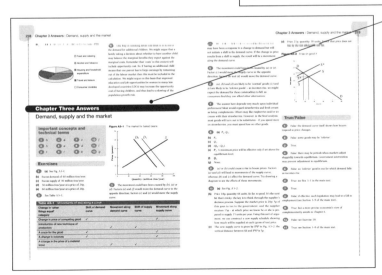

## Answers

The second section of the workbook provides the answers to the questions and exercises. Use it to check your workings as you progress.

# Technology to enhance learning and teaching

Visit www.mcgraw-hill.co.uk/textbooks/begg today

## Resources for students

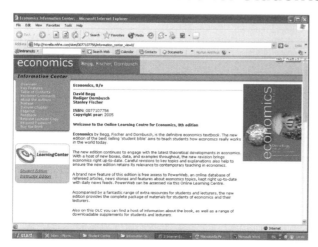

### Online Learning Centre (OLC)

After completing each chapter in the workbook, you can log on to the supporting Online Learning Centre website. Take advantage of the free study tools offered to reinforce the material you have read in the text, and to develop your knowledge of economics in a fun and effective way. A range of resources are offered providing revision tools and handy exam practice!

The new edition provides the complete package of materials for students of economics:

- **Additional case studies with exercises** – new cases in economics with questions enable students to apply and analyse concepts from the book.
- **Chapter-by-chapter student test questions** – to check understanding of key topics and ideas with progress tests online.
- **Interactive exercises including animated graphs** – to demonstrate how economic models work in practice.
- **Crossword quizzes** – to test knowledge of key terms in economics with interactive puzzles.
- **Web links** to a wealth of economics sources available online.
- **Learning objectives** – to check comprehension of the concepts explained in each chapter.
- **Glossary** of technical terms and more learning tools, all available with the book.

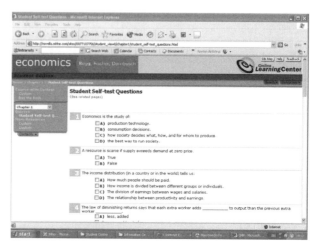

Visit the OLC at **www.mcgraw-hill.co.uk/textbooks/begg** for access to all these materials.

## PowerWeb

If you have also purchased the main textbook, *Economics, Eighth Edition*, you will have received a card with a password for PowerWeb. By entering the password into the Online Learning Centre, you will be able to access a subject-specific online database containing articles and daily news feeds about economics topics.

PowerWeb is perfect for researching essays and assignments, keeping in touch with current affairs and seeing how the topics you've learnt in class apply to economics in the real world. Ideal for expanding your knowledge of up-to-the-minute economics stories and issues – free of charge when you purchase *Economics, Eighth Edition*!

To find out more about *Economics Eighth Edition* by Begg, Fischer and Dornbusch, or to purchase a copy, go to **www.mcgraw-hill.co.uk**

## Study skills

Need help with exams, essays, assignments or research projects? Open University Press publishes guides to study, research and exam skills, to help undergraduate and postgraduate students through their university studies.

Visit **www.openup.co.uk/ss/** to see the full selection.

## Computing skills

If you'd like to brush up on your computing skills, we have a range of titles covering MS Office applications such as Word, Excel, PowerPoint, Access and more.

Get a £2 discount off these titles by entering the promotional code **app** when ordering online at **www.mcgraw-hill.co.uk/app**

# Resources for lecturers

### Online Learning Centre: Lecturer area

Lecturers can find a range of resources and tools to support the *Economics, Eighth Edition* textbook and workbook at the Online Learning Centre website. A test bank of questions is also available on CD-ROM.

- Access to PowerWeb, a topic-by-topic database of economics articles and news stories for access to regularly updated material for teaching and for students' independent research.
- Lecturer Manual of teaching tips for delivering a principles of economics module.
- Lecture presentations in PowerPoint for use in lectures, seminar or handouts, including all of the graphs and diagrams from the textbook.
- A variety of extra exercises, case materials and ideas for teaching principles of economics.

A CD-ROM test bank of questions is also available for use in generating multiple choice quizzes for progress tests and for creating more formal assessments.

To access all of the Online Learning Centre lecturer resources, and to contact your McGraw-Hill representative, simply visit the website at **www.mcgraw-hill.co.uk/textbooks/begg** and follow the instructions to register for a password.

### For lecturers: Primis Content Centre

Can't find the perfect book for your course? If you need to supplement your course with additional cases or content, create a personalized e-book for your students. Visit **www.primiscontentcenter.com** or e-mail **primis_euro@mcgraw-hill.com** for more information.

# Acknowledgements for the eighth edition

We would like to thank the following reviewers who provided helpful suggestions and comments on the previous edition of the workbook:

Steve Cook, University of Swansea
Tom Craven, University of Ulster at Jordanstown
Geoffrey Killick, University of Westminster
Jan Peter Madsen, Copenhagen Business School, Denmark
Thea Sinclair, University of Nottingham
Gerard Turley, National University of Ireland, Galway
Nalini Vittal, Royal Holloway, University of London

Thanks also to Richard Godfrey, University of Wales Institute, Cardiff, for carefully checking the book to ensure its accuracy.

# part one
# Introduction

# chapter one

# Economics and the economy

## Learning outcomes

**By the end of this chapter, you should understand:**

- Economics is the study of how society resolves the problem of scarcity
- Ways in which society decides what, how and for whom to produce
- The concept of opportunity cost
- Positive and normative economics
- Microeconomics and macroeconomics

## Key learning blocks

The central economic problem is one of *infinite wants* and *finite resources*. For example, we would all like to consume more goods and services but we are restricted by access to income and time. Economics attempts to understand this problem and in this chapter you will be introduced to some key issues:

**1** What is the production function and how does it relate to the problem of scarcity?

**2** How do governments and markets solve the problem of scarcity?

**3** What economic problems exist at the microeconomic and macroeconomic level?

The textbook moves through each of these issues and the exercises that follow will help to develop your understanding.

# Important concepts and technical terms

## Match each lettered concept with the appropriate numbered phrase:

**a** Scarce resource

**b** Law of diminishing returns

**c** Gross domestic product (GDP)

**d** Distribution of income

**e** Positive economics

**f** Microeconomics

**g** Production possibility frontier (PPF)

**h** Opportunity cost

**i** Macroeconomics

**j** Mixed economy

**k** Normative economics

**l** Command economy

**1** The branch of economics offering a detailed treatment of individual decisions about particular commodities.

**2** Economic statements offering prescriptions or recommendations based on personal value judgements.

**3** An economy in which the government and private sector interact in solving economic problems.

**4** The way in which income (in a country or in the world) is divided between different groups or individuals.

**5** The quantity of other goods that must be sacrificed in order to obtain another unit of a particular good.

**6** A resource for which the demand at a zero price would exceed the available supply.

**7** The branch of economics emphasizing the interactions in the economy as a whole.

**8** The value of all goods and services produced in the economy in a given period such as a year.

**9** A curve which shows, for each level of the output of one good, the maximum amount of the other good that can be produced.

**10** The situation in which, as more workers are employed in an industry, each additional worker adds less to total industry output than the previous additional worker added.

**11** A society where the government makes all decisions about production and consumption.

**12** Economic statements dealing with objective or scientific explanations of the working of the economy.

## Exercises

**1** A community living on a tropical island includes five workers whose time is devoted either to gathering coconuts or to collecting turtle eggs. Regardless of how many other workers are engaged in the same occupation, a worker may gather either 20 coconuts or 10 turtle eggs in a day.

**(a)** Draw the PPF for coconuts and turtle eggs.

**(b)** Suppose that a new climbing technique is invented making the harvesting of coconuts easier. Each worker can now gather 28 coconuts in a day. Draw the new PPF.

**2** Figure 1–1 shows a society's PPF for cameras and watches.

**(a)** Identify each of the following combinations of the two goods as efficient, inefficient or unattainable:
  (i)   60 cameras and 200 watches.
  (ii)  60 watches and 80 cameras.
  (iii) 300 watches and 35 cameras.
  (iv)  300 watches and 40 cameras.
  (v)   58 cameras and 250 watches.

**(b)** Suppose the society is producing 300 watches and 40 cameras, but wishes to produce an additional 20 cameras. How much output of watches must be sacrificed to enable these cameras to be made?

**Figure 1–1** The production possibility frontier

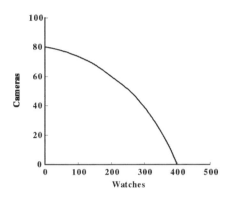

(c) How much output of watches would need to be given up for a further 20 cameras (80 in all) to be produced?

(d) Explain the difference in the shape of the frontier in Fig. 1–1 as compared with the ones you drew in Exercise 1.

**3** Figure 1–2 illustrates a PPF for an economy.

**Figure 1–2** Production possibility frontier for an economy

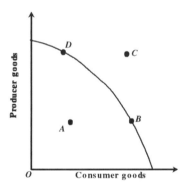

Associate each of the points (*A*, *B*, *C*, *D*) marked on Fig. 1–2 with one of the following statements:

(a) The combination of goods which cannot be produced by the society given its current availability of resources and state of technology.

(b) The combination of goods produced by an economy with full employment which wishes to devote its resources mainly to the production of investment goods.

(c) The combination of goods produced by an economy in recession.

(d) The combination of goods produced by an economy with full employment which wishes to devote its resources mainly to the production of goods for consumption.

**4** Which of the following statements are *normative* and which are *positive*?

(a) The price of oil more than tripled between 1973 and 1974.

(b) In the late 1990s, the poor countries of the world received less than their fair share of world income.

(c) The world distribution of income is too unjust, with poor countries having 35 per cent of the world's population, but receiving only 2 per cent of world income.

(d) Since the 1970s, inflation has fallen in most Western economies, but the unemployment rate has increased.

(e) The UK government ought to introduce policies to reduce the unemployment rate.

(f) Smoking is antisocial and should be discouraged.

(g) The imposition of higher taxes on tobacco will discourage smoking.

(h) The economy of the USA is closer to a free market system than that of Cuba.

**5** Which of the following statements are the concern of microeconomics and which of macroeconomics?

(a) Along with other Western economies, the UK faced a sharp rise in unemployment in the early 1990s.

(b) The imposition of higher taxes on tobacco will discourage smoking.

(c) Employment among building labourers rose sharply in the early 2000s.

(d) An increase in a society's aggregate income is likely to be reflected in higher consumer spending.

(e) A worker who has received a pay rise is likely to buy more luxury goods.

(f) A firm will invest in a machine if the expected rate of return is sufficiently high.

(g) High interest rates in an economy may be expected to discourage aggregate investment.

(h) The level of GDP in the UK was higher in 2004 than in 2001.

**6** Figure 1–3 shows a society's choice between social services and private goods, in the form of a production possibility frontier. The three points *A*, *B* and *C* represent economies in which the government plays a more or less active role. Match each of the points with the most appropriate of the following descriptions of hypothetical economies.

**Figure 1–3**  Society's choice between social services and private goods

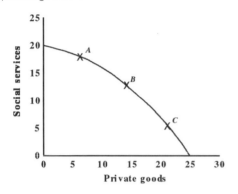

(a)  An economy in which the government intervenes as little as possible, providing only the minimum necessary amounts of essential services.

(b)  An economy in which the government takes a great deal of responsibility, taxing at a high level and providing extensive social services.

(c)  An economy in which the government provides more than the minimum necessary amounts of social services, but leaves room for a buoyant private sector.

**7**   A jungle community catches fish and gathers mangoes. The community's PPF for these two goods is shown in Fig. 1–4. Which of the following bundles of the goods can be attained with present resources?

**Figure 1–4**  Fish or mangoes?

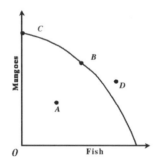

(a)  Only *A*.
(b)  Only *B*.
(c)  Only *A* and *B*.
(d)  Only *A*, *B* and *C*.
(e)  Only *D*.

**8**   Which of the following statements would not be true for a pure 'command economy'?

(a)  Firms choose how much labour to employ.
(b)  The distribution of income is government controlled.
(c)  The government decides what should be produced.
(d)  Production techniques are not determined by firms.
(e)  A government planning office decides what will be produced, how it will be produced and for whom it will be produced.

## True/False

**1**   Economics is about human behaviour, so cannot be a science.

**2**   The oil price shocks of 1973–74 and 2004 had no effect on what was produced in the UK.

**3**   An expansion of an economy's capacity to produce would be reflected in an 'outward' movement of the PPF.

**4**   An economy in which there is unemployment is not producing on the PPF.

**5**   Adam Smith argued that individuals pursuing their self-interest would be led 'as by an invisible hand' to do things that are in the interests of society as a whole.

**6**   China is an example of a command economy in which private markets play no part.

**7**   The government should subsidize the health bills of the aged.

**8**   Gross domestic product (GDP) is the value of all goods produced in the economy during a period.

**9**   Many propositions in positive economics would command widespread agreement among professional economists.

## Economics in action

### Mortgage lending continues boom

(Adapted from BBC Online News, 24 May 2004)

The UK's appetite for mortgage debt continued rising in April, but existing borrowers showed growing caution. Mortgage lending in April totalled £25 bn – 25 per cent higher than the same month in 2003.

In recent years, many homeowners have made good use of historically low interest rates and remortgaged to a cheaper deal, cutting their mortgage costs in the process. Others have used remortgaging as a cheap borrowing vehicle – to consolidate debts or to provide finance for home improvement projects, for example.

Earlier in the week it emerged the Monetary Policy Committee (MPC), the Bank of England's rate-setting body, debated lifting rates to 4.5 per cent from 4 per cent at its May meeting, before settling on a rise to 4.25 per cent.

The publication of the MPC's report has fuelled expectations that the Bank will act soon, raising rates further.

## Questions

**1** Is the mortgage lending boom a macroeconomic or microeconomic problem?

**2** What would be the microeconomic and macroeconomic implications of a rise in interest rates?

## Questions for thought

**1** We have seen that economics is concerned with three fundamental questions: *what* is produced, *how* it is produced and *for whom* it is produced. For each of the following five economic events, think about which of these three fundamental questions are of relevance:

(a) The discovery of substantial reserves of natural gas in a readily accessible site.

(b) A change in the structure of income tax, so that income is redistributed from 'rich' to 'poor'.

(c) The privatization of a major industry.

(d) The invention of the microcomputer.

(e) An increase in the price of imported goods.

**2** An economy can choose between producing goods to be consumed now and producing *investment goods* which have an effect on the future productive capacity of the economy. Figure 1–5 illustrates the PPF between the two sorts of goods.

**Figure 1–5** The choice between consumption and investment goods

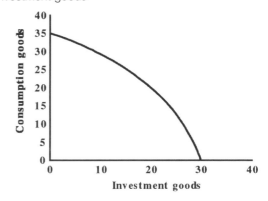

(a) For this economy, what can we say about the position of the PPF in subsequent periods?

(b) How is your answer to (a) affected by the particular choice point selected in a given period?

**3** Table 1–1 presents data on the sectoral structure of national output in four countries. Examine the changing structure of production in each of the countries in Table 1–1. What stage of industrialization has each country reached?

| Table 1–1 | The structure of production (Distribution of GDP (%)) | | |
|---|---|---|---|
| **Country** | **Agriculture** | **Industry** | **Services** |
| **A** 1965 | 52 | 13 | 35 |
| 1997 | 44 | 17 | 39 |
| **B** 1965 | 51 | 13 | 36 |
| 1997 | 16 | 42 | 41 |
| **C** 1965 | 38 | 25 | 37 |
| 1997 | 6 | 43 | 51 |
| **D** 1965 | 10 | 44 | 46 |
| 1997 | 2 | 38 | 60 |

*Source: World Development Report 1998/99.*

# chapter two

# Tools of economic analysis

## Learning outcomes

**By the end of this chapter, you should understand:**

- Why theories are deliberate simplifications of reality

- Time-series and cross-section data

- How to construct index numbers

- Nominal and real variables

- How to build a simple theoretical model

- How to plot data and interpret scatter diagrams

- How to use 'other things equal' to ignore, but not forget, important influences

## Key learning blocks

**You will have now realized that economics is a little different from other subjects that you may have studied. Economists have their own language, like to use diagrams and, as with many natural sciences, seek to match numerical data with theories. The key issues that you need to be familiar with are:**

1 Economists like to build models which are *simple*: why? In part, the answer to this question is because simple models with simple relationships can be examined using simple numerical data, so the next two issues are:

2 What kind of *data* do economists use?

3 How do economists *use* these data to *test* their theories? Graphs are a simple approach, economic models are more advanced.

The textbook moves through all of these issues in detail and you can use the questions that follow to build your understanding around these key learning blocks.

# Important concepts and technical terms

## Match each lettered concept with the appropriate numbered phrase:

a  Growth rate

b  Index number

c  Model

d  Nominal variable

e  Purchasing power of money

f  Real price

g  Time series

h  Positive relationship

i  Retail price index

j  Other things equal

k  Cross-section

l  Econometrics

m  Negative relationship

n  Real variable

1  A sequence of measurements of a variable at different points in time.

2  A situation in which higher values of one variable are associated with lower values of another variable.

3  The price of a commodity relative to the general price level for goods.

4  A simplifying assumption which enables the economist to focus on key economic relationships.

5  A deliberate simplification of reality based on a series of simplifying assumptions from which it may be deduced how people will behave.

6  An index of the prices of goods purchased by a typical household.

7  A variable measured in money terms at current prices.

8  The percentage change in a variable per period (typically per year).

9  Measurements of an economic variable at a point in time for different individuals or groups of individuals.

10  An index of the quantity of goods that can be bought for £1.

11  A way of expressing data relative to a given base value.

12  A situation in which higher values of one variable are associated with higher values of another variable.

13  A variable measured at constant prices, or after adjustment has been made for inflation.

14  The branch of economics devoted to measuring relationships using economic data.

## Exercises

1  Which of the following data sets would be *time series* and which would relate to a *cross-section*?

(a) Consumers' expenditure on durable goods, annually in 1990–2004.

(b) Households' expenditure on housing in urban areas in 2004.

(c) Monthly price index for potatoes in 2004.

(d) Gross domestic product of the UK for each quarter in 2004.

(e) Average weekly earnings for a sample of 350 individuals first interviewed in 1990 and reinterviewed in 1993, 1996, 1999, 2002 and 2005.

(f) Unemployment categorized by area, 14 October 2004.

2  Table 2–1 presents information on UK steel consumption and imports between 1976 and 2004.

(a) From observation of the figures (i.e. without reaching for your calculator), comment on the trend in steel imports and total consumption.

**Table 2–1** UK steel imports and consumption, 1976–2004, million tonnes

| Year | UK steel imports (million tonnes) | UK steel consumption (million tonnes) |
|---|---|---|
| 1976 | 103.6 | 498.7 |
| 1982 | 96.2 | 271.4 |
| 1988 | 114.4 | 364.8 |
| 1994 | 126.7 | 336.1 |
| 2000 | 162.6 | 298.0 |
| 2004 | 168.0 | 272.8 |

*Source: Office for National Statistics, Monthly Digest of Statistics.*

**(b)** For each series, calculate an index, using 1976 as a base.

**(c)** Explain the patterns within the data.

**3** On average, about 11 per cent of expenditure by households is on alcohol and tobacco; the remaining 89 per cent is on 'other goods and services'. (These proportions are 'close to' those used in construction of the UK retail price index (RPI), as are other data in this exercise.) Price indices for these goods are given in Table 2–2.

**(a)** Construct an aggregate price index for the economy based on weights of 0.11 for alcohol and tobacco and 0.89 for other goods and services.

**(b)** Using this aggregate price index, calculate the annual rate of inflation for the years 1995–98.

**(c)** Although this gives a general view of inflation in the economy, individuals may view inflation differently if their pattern of expenditure differs from that of society at large. Calculate the rate of inflation for an individual whose expenditure pattern conforms to the norm except for the fact that she is a non-smoking teetotaller.

**(d)** Draw two charts, one showing the three price indices, the second showing your two calculated inflation series.

**Table 2–2** Price indices, 1994–2003 (1987=100)

| Year/Price index | 1998 | 1999 | 2000 | 2001 | 2002 | 2003 |
|---|---|---|---|---|---|---|
| Alcohol and tobacco | 192.3 | 202.6 | 210.3 | 216.9 | 222.3 | 228.0 |
| All other goods and services | 147.6 | 148.1 | 149.7 | 160.0 | 151.7 | 154.4 |
| Aggregate price index | | | | | | |
| Inflation | | | | | | |
| Inflation for non-smoking teetotaller | | | | | | |

**Table 2–3** UK imports and income, 1998–2003

| Year | Imports of goods and services | GDP |
|---|---|---|
| 1998 | 185 869 | 858 616 |
| 1999 | 195 217 | 903 167 |
| 2000 | 220 912 | 950 561 |
| 2001 | 230 703 | 994 309 |
| 2002 | 233 192 | 1 044 145 |
| 2003 | 235 136 | 1 099 896 |

*Source: Monthly Digest of Statistics.*

**4** **(a)** Using the data of Table 2–3, draw a scatter diagram with real imports on the vertical axis and real income on the horizontal axis.

**(b)** Does your diagram suggest a *positive* or a *negative* association between these variables?

**(c)** Does this conform to your economic intuition concerning imports and income?

**(d)** Can you think of variables likely to be covered by the 'other things equal' clause for this relationship?

**5** Figure 2–1 shows scatter diagrams for different types of association between variables. Match each with the most appropriate description from the following:

(i) A negative linear relationship.

(ii) A positive linear relationship.

(iii) A non-linear relationship.

(iv) No apparent pattern of relationship.

**Figure 2–1** Patterns of association

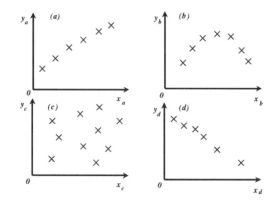

To which of these would you *not* attempt to fit a straight line?

**6** The retail price index for clothing and footwear in 1998–2003 based on 13 January 1987 = 100 took values as follows:

| Year | 1998 | 1999 | 2000 | 2001 | 2002 | 2003 |
|------|------|------|------|------|------|------|
| Price index for clothing and footwear | 119.9 | 116.7 | 112.3 | 107.5 | 102.4 | 100.8 |

*Source: Monthly Digest of Statistics.*

**(a)** What additional information would you require to gauge whether the *real* price of clothing was rising or falling in this period?

**(b)** Use the data you calculated as the aggregate price index in Exercise **3** to calculate a real price index for clothing and footwear.

**(c)** Comment upon the meaning of your results.

**7** Consider the following simple economic model, which relates to the demand for chocolate bars:

Quantity of chocolate bars demanded = ƒ {price of chocolate bars; consumer incomes}

**(a)** Using only words, explain this statement.

**(b)** Assuming consumer incomes to be held constant, would you expect the quantity demanded and the price of chocolate bars to be positively or negatively associated?

**(c)** Assuming the price of chocolate bars to be held constant, what sort of association would you expect to observe between the quantity of chocolate bars demanded and the level of consumer incomes?

**(d)** Do you consider this model to be complete, or are there other economic variables which you would have included?

**8** The following information relates to components of a retail price index for 2003:

| Item | Weight | Price index (1995 = 100) |
|------|--------|--------------------------|
| Food, catering and alcohol | 3 | 170 |
| Housing, fuel and light | 2 | 186 |
| Other goods and services | 5 | 173 |

What is the value of the aggregate price index?

**(a)** 172

**(b)** 173

**(c)** 174.7

**(d)** 176.3

**(e)** 178.

**9** Using the data in Table 2–4:

**(a)** Calculate total real expenditure on food in 2003.

**(b)** Calculate total money expenditure on food in 2003.

**(c)** Calculate for each quarter the ratio of current price to constant price expenditure and multiply by 100. How might you interpret the results?

**Table 2–4    UK household expenditure on food, 2003 (£ million)**

| | 2003 Q1 | 2003 Q2 | 2003 Q3 | 2003 Q4 |
|---|---------|---------|---------|---------|
| At current prices | 15 960 | 16 470 | 16 190 | 16 298 |
| At constant 2001 prices | 15 224 | 15 686 | 15 396 | 15 471 |

*Source: Economic Trends Annual Supplement.*

**10** Figure 2–2 shows UK households' savings as a percentage of disposable income since 1970. Describe the general trend of the series and comment on the pattern displayed over time.

**Figure 2–2    UK households' savings ratio, 1970–2003**

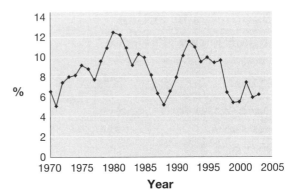

*Source: Economic Trends Annual Supplement.*

## True/False

**1** Economics cannot claim to be a science since it is incapable of controlled laboratory experiments.

**2** We may accumulate evidence in support of an economic theory, but we can never prove beyond doubt that it is 'true'.

**3** Charts are a useful way of highlighting the important features of a data series.

**4** When we observe a strong association between two variables we know that one depends causally upon the other.

**5** Cross-section data are more often used in microeconomics because they deal with individuals.

**6** Invoking 'other things equal' enables us to ignore the complicated parts of an economic model.

**7** Economic models deal with straight line relationships between variables.

**8** If you look hard enough at the facts, you will inevitably discover the correct theory.

**9** Index numbers are an invaluable device if we wish to compare two variables measured in different units.

**10** A positive economic relationship is one that supports our model.

**11** Inflation is measured by the price level.

**12** Real wage rates are calculated by adjusting nominal wage rates for changes in the cost of living.

## Economics in action

### Nationwide house price index

(Adapted from Nationwide press release, May 2004)

| | April | March |
|---|---|---|
| Monthly index (seasonally adjusted) Q1 1993=100 | 291.0 | 284.9 |
| Annual change | 18.9% | 16.7% |
| Average price | £145 918 | £142 584 |

Commenting on the figures Alex Bannister, Nationwide's group economist, said:

Having peaked at 26.5 per cent in early 2003, UK annual house price inflation slowed to 14.3 per cent in January 2004 before pushing back up to 18.9 per cent in April. Underlying the average price rise, the UK housing market remains regionally polarised with prices continuing to rise rapidly in the cheaper North and more slowly in the South East.

However, the pace of price growth we are expecting this year is clearly unsustainable given that affordability has become so stretched. The 15 per cent rise in prices we are expecting during 2004 partly reflects buyers taking on higher levels of debt in response to lower nominal interest rates. In the current low inflation environment, real debt burdens will be slow to erode. Given this, borrowers need to take a prudent approach to the amount of debt they take on.

## Questions

**1** Is the monthly house price index time-series or cross-sectional data?

**2** What was the percentage price rise between March and April?

**3** Since 1993 house price growth has been 191 per cent: why? Is this growth real or nominal?

## Questions for thought

**1** Which of the following represents the weighted index number of prices for year *Y* based on the information in Table 2–5?

(a) 94.6
(b) 105.7
(c) 113.3
(d) 131.0
(e) Cannot be determined from the above, because one needs to know the total expenditure on each item.

| Table 2–5 | Components of a price index | | |
|---|---|---|---|
| Commodity | Price in base year (p) | Price in year *Y* (p) | Weights |
| 1 | 10 | 12 | 2 |
| 2 | 100 | 80 | 5 |
| 3 | 50 | 70 | 3 |
| | | | 10 |

**2** Devise a simple economic model to analyse the demand for school lunches.

**3** Table 2–6 contains data on the various weights assigned to different expenditure categories when calculating the RPI. Graphically, how would you go about illustrating the data within the table?

**4** How might economic analysis help us to explain family size?

| Table 2–6 | Retail price index weights per expenditure group, 2004 | | | | | |
|---|---|---|---|---|---|---|
| Year | Food and catering | Alcohol and tobacco | Housing and household expenditure | Travel and leisure | Consumer durabales | Total |
| 2004 | 160 | 97 | 339 | 283 | 121 | 1000 |

*Source: Monthly Digest of Statistics.*

# chapter three

# Demand, supply and the market

## Learning outcomes

By the end of this chapter, you should understand:

- The concept of a market
- Demand and supply curves
- Equilibrium price and equilibrium quantity
- How price adjustment reconciles demand and supply in a market
- What shifts demand and supply curves
- Free markets and markets with price controls
- How markets determine what, how and for whom to produce

## Key learning blocks

In Chapter 1 you were introduced to the concept of *scarcity* and the need to find a *resource allocation mechanism*. In this chapter you will begin to study the market as one such mechanism. The key blocks which you need to understand are:

1. What is supply and what is demand?
2. What factors might cause demand and supply to change?
3. What is the market equilibrium and how might the market fail?

The textbook discusses each of these issues in turn and the exercises that follow will help to develop your understanding.

# Important concepts and technical terms

## Match each lettered concept with the appropriate numbered phrase:

**a** Market

**b** Equilibrium price

**c** Normal good

**d** Excess supply

**e** Comparative-static analysis

**f** Market price

**g** Demand

**h** Inferior good

**i** Free market

**j** Excess demand

**k** Supply

**l** Price controls

**1** The price at which the quantity supplied equals the quantity demanded.

**2** A good for which demand falls when incomes rise.

**3** The price prevailing in a market.

**4** The study of the effect (on equilibrium price and quantity) of a change in one of the 'other things equal' factors.

**5** A set of arrangements by which buyers and sellers are in contact to exchange goods and services.

**6** Government rules or laws that forbid the adjustment of prices to clear markets.

**7** A good for which demand increases when incomes rise.

**8** The situation in which quantity supplied exceeds quantity demanded at a particular price.

**9** The quantity of a good that sellers wish to sell at each conceivable price.

**10** The situation in which quantity demanded exceeds quantity supplied at a particular price.

**11** A market in which price is determined purely by the forces of supply and demand.

**12** The quantity of a good that buyers wish to purchase at each conceivable price.

## Exercises

**1** Suppose that the data of Table 3–1 represent the market demand and supply schedules for baked beans over a range of prices.

**Table 3–1** Demand and supply of baked beans

| Price (p) | Quantity demanded (million tins/year) | Quantity supplied (million tins/year) |
|---|---|---|
| 8 | 70 | 10 |
| 16 | 60 | 30 |
| 24 | 50 | 50 |
| 32 | 40 | 70 |
| 40 | 30 | 90 |

(a) Plot on a single diagram the demand curve and supply curve, remembering to label the axes carefully.

(b) What would be the excess demand or supply if price were set at 8p?

(c) What would be the excess demand or supply if price were set at 32p?

(d) Find the equilibrium price and quantity.

(e) Suppose that, following an increase in consumers' incomes, the demand for baked beans rises by 15 million tins/year at each price level. Find the new equilibrium price and quantity.

**2** The distinction between shifts of the demand and supply curves and movements along them is an important one. Place ticks in the appropriate columns of Table 3–2 to show the effects of changes in the 'other things equal' categories detailed in the first column. (Two ticks are required for each item.)

*(Please note that in Exercises **3–8** more than one answer is possible.)*

**3** In Fig. 3–1 the demand curve for pens has

| Table 3–2 | Movements of and along a curve | | | | |
|---|---|---|---|---|---|
| Change in 'other things equal' category | Shift of demand curve | Movement along demand curve | Shift of supply curve | Movement along supply curve |
| Change in price of competing good | | | | |
| Introduction of new technique of production | | | | |
| A craze for the good | | | | |
| A change in incomes | | | | |
| A change in the price of a material input | | | | |

moved from $D_0$ to $D_1$. Which of the following could have brought about the move?

**Figure 3–1** The demand for pens

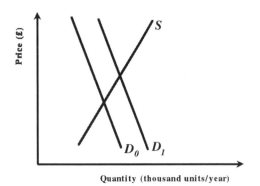

Quantity (thousand units/year)

(a) A fall in the price of a substitute for pens.
(b) A fall in the price of a complement to pens.
(c) A fall in the price of a raw material used to produce pens.
(d) A decrease in consumers' incomes (assume that a pen is an inferior good).
(e) A decrease in the rate of value added tax (VAT).
(f) A decrease in consumers' incomes (assume that a pen is a normal good).

**4** Which of the following would probably lead to a shift in the demand curve for cameras?

(a) A decrease in the price of cameras.

(b) An increase in real incomes.
(c) A decrease in the price of film.

**5** In Fig. 3–2 the supply curve for tents has moved from $S_0$ to $S_1$. Which of the following could have brought about this move?

**Figure 3–2** The supply of tents

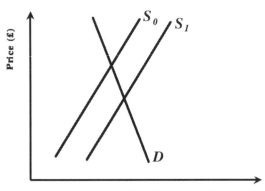

Quantity (thousand units/year)

(a) The introduction of a new improved method of producing tents.
(b) A fall in the price of a complement to tents.
(c) An increase in the wage rate paid to tent workers.
(d) An increase in consumers' incomes (assume that a tent is a normal good).
(e) A fall in the price of a tent component.

**6** Which of these goods would you expect to be 'normal' goods and which 'inferior'?

(a) Colour television.
(b) Coffee.
(c) Rice.
(d) 3G phone.
(e) Bus journey.

**7** Which of these goods might be regarded as 'substitutes' for strawberries and which 'complements'?

(a) Raspberries.
(b) Fresh cream.
(c) Petrol.
(d) Ice cream.
(e) Roast beef.
(f) Bus journey.
(g) Lap-top computer.

**8** Suppose that Fig. 3–3 depicts the market for eggs and that the government decides to safeguard egg production by guaranteeing producers a minimum price for eggs. Thus, if eggs are left unsold to households, the government promises to buy up the surplus at the set price.

**Figure 3–3**  The market for eggs

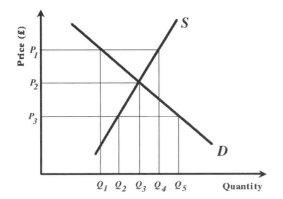

(a)  What would be the equilibrium price and quantity in the absence of intervention?

(b)  What would be the market price if the government were to guarantee a price of $P_1$?

(c)  What would be the quantity demanded by households at this market price?

(d)  How many eggs would need to be purchased by the government at this price?

(e)  What would be the market price if the government were to guarantee a price of $P_3$?

(f)  What would be the quantity demanded by households at this market price?

(g)  How many eggs would need to be purchased by the government at this price?

**9**   Which of the following could cause a rise in house prices?

(a)  A decline in house-building.

(b)  An increase in lending by building societies.

(c)  A rise in mortgage interest rates.

(d))  An increase in the willingness of local authorities to sell council houses to tenants.

**10**   Suppose that the data of Table 3–3 represent the (linear) market demand and supply schedules for commodity $X$ over a range of prices.

(a)  Plot the demand curve and supply curve.

(b)  Find the equilibrium price and quantity.

Suppose that a tax of 5p per unit is imposed on firms supplying this commodity. Thus, if a firm charges 20p per unit to buyers, the government takes 5p and the firm receives 15p.

**Table 3–3    Demand and supply of good X**

| Price (p) | Quantity demanded (units/year) | Quantity supplied (units/year) |
|---|---|---|
| 15 | 50 | 35 |
| 16 | 48 | 38 |
| 17 | 46 | 41 |
| 18 | 44 | 44 |
| 19 | 42 | 47 |
| 20 | 40 | 50 |
| 21 | 38 | 53 |
| 22 | 36 | 56 |

(c)  Draw the supply curve after the tax is imposed – i.e. the relation between quantity supplied and the price paid by consumers.

(d)  Find the equilibrium price and quantity.

## True/False

**1**   A change in the price of a good will cause a shift in its demand curve.

**2**   An increase in consumers' incomes will cause an expansion in the demand for all goods.

**3**   A poor potato harvest will result in higher prices for chips, other things being equal.

**4**   The price charged for a good is the equilibrium price.

**5**   An inferior good is one that has been badly produced.

**6**   Mad cow disease led to an increase in the price of pork.

**7**   If the demand for a good rises following an increase in consumers' incomes (other things being equal), that good is known as 'normal'.

**8**   The imposition of a minimum legal wage will lead to an increase in employment.

**9**   In everyday parlance, two goods $X$ and $Y$ are known as complements if an increase in the price of $X$, other things being equal, leads to a fall in demand for good $Y$.

**10**   The imposition of a £1 per unit tax on a good will lead to a £1 increase in the price of the good.

**11**   When the Pope gave permission for Catholics to eat meat on Fridays, the equilibrium price and quantity of fish fell.

## Economics in action

### BA outbid for Heathrow slots

(Adapted from an article by David Gow, *The Guardian*, 21 January 2004)

Qantas and Virgin Atlantic have trumped British Airways by paying record sums for scarce take-off and landing slots at London's congested Heathrow airport. The Australian flag carrier, a BA partner, has paid £20 million – up to twice the normal rate – for two pairs of daily slots, industry sources said. Virgin has paid a similar sum for four pairs.

'They've certainly paid top dollar, in fact a shedload of money,' said sources. The moves by Qantas and Virgin are seen as underlining a more optimistic future for sales and growth in an industry ravaged by falling passenger numbers and revenues.

## Questions

**1** Explain how an expectation of higher passenger numbers would shift the demand curve for Heathrow landing slots and explain the impact of such a shift on the equilibrium price.

**2** Late in 2003, the government decided to block the proposed building of a third runway at Heathrow. How will this impact the equilibrium price for slots?

## Questions for thought

**1** Sketch a diagram showing the demand and supply curves for a commodity. Suppose that the price of the commodity is set at a level which is above the market clearing price. How will producers and consumers perceive this market situation? How are they likely to react? How would your analysis differ if the market price were to be set below the equilibrium level?

**2** How would you expect the market for coffee to react to a sudden reduction in supply, perhaps caused by a poor harvest? Would you expect the revenue received by coffee-growers to fall or rise as a result?

**3** Discuss some of the ways in which a change in the demand or supply conditions in a market may spill over and affect conditions in another market. Provide some examples of such spill-over effects.

**4** Suppose you are trying to observe the demand curve for a commodity. When you collect price and quantity data for a sequence of years, you find that they suggest a *positive* relationship. What line of reasoning and additional information would you need to use in order to make an interpretation of the data?

# part two

# Positive microeconomics

# chapter four

# Elasticities of demand and supply

## Learning outcomes

**By the end of this chapter, you should understand:**

- How elasticities measure responsiveness of demand or supply
- The price elasticity of demand
- How the price elasticity of demand affects the revenue effect of a price change
- Why bad harvests may help farmers
- The fallacy of composition
- How cross-price elasticity relates to complements and substitutes
- Income elasticity of demand
- Inferior, normal and luxury goods
- Elasticity of supply
- How supply and demand elasticities affect tax incidence

## Key learning blocks

In Chapter 3 we discussed the factors which led to demand and supply changing. In this chapter we examine the idea of *elasticity*, which simply addresses the question, 'by how much does demand and supply change?' The issues which you need to be familiar with are:

1. Demand elasticity.
2. Income elasticity.
3. Cross-price elasticity.
4. Supply elasticity.

The textbook covers these issues in detail and working through the questions that follow will reinforce your understanding.

# Important concepts and technical terms

## Match each lettered concept with the appropriate numbered phrase:

a  Cross-price elasticity of demand

b  Inelastic demand

c  Long run

d  Normal good

e  Necessity

f  Substitutes

g  Unit elastic demand

h  Short run

i  Income elasticity of demand

j  Elastic demand

k  Inferior good

l  Complements

m  Luxury good

n  Own-price elasticity of demand

1  The percentage change in quantity demanded divided by the corresponding percentage change in income.

2  The quantity demanded is insensitive to price changes: elasticity is between 0 and −1.

3  A good with a positive income elasticity of demand.

4  A good with a negative income elasticity of demand.

5  A measure of the responsiveness of demand for a good to a change in the price of another good.

6  A good having an income elasticity of demand less than 1.

7  The percentage change in the quantity of a good demanded divided by the corresponding change in its price.

8  Two goods for which a rise in the price of one is generally associated with an increase in demand for the other.

9  A good having an income elasticity of demand greater than 1.

10  The quantity demanded is highly responsive to price changes: elasticity is more negative than −1.

11  Expenditure is unchanged when price falls: elasticity is equal to −1.

12  The period necessary for complete adjustment to a price change.

13  Two goods for which an increase in the price of one is generally associated with a fall in demand for the other.

14  The period during which consumers are still in the process of adjusting to a price change.

## Exercises

| Table 4–1 The demand for rice popsicles | | | |
| --- | --- | --- | --- |
| Price per packet (£p) | Quantity demanded (000) | Total spending (revenue) (£ 000) | Own-price elasticity of demand |
| 2.10 | 10 | | |
| 1.80 | 20 | | |
| 1.50 | 30 | | |
| 1.20 | 40 | | |
| 0.90 | 50 | | |
| 0.60 | 60 | | |
| 0.30 | 70 | | |

**Table 4–2   Cross-price and own-price elasticities of demand in Mythuania**

| % change in quantity demanded of: | In response to 1% change in price of: | | |
|---|---|---|---|
| | **Food** | **Wine** | **Beer** |
| Food | −0.25 | 0.06 | 0.01 |
| Wine | −0.13 | −1.20 | 0.27 |
| Beer | 0.07 | 0.41 | 0.85 |

**1**   Table 4–1 presents the quantity of rice popsicles demanded at various alternative prices.

**(a)** Draw the demand curve on graph paper, plotting price on the vertical and quantity on the horizontal axis.

**(b)** Suppose price were £1.20. What would be the change in quantity demanded if price were to be reduced by 30p? Would your answer be different if you started at any other price?

**(c)** Calculate total spending on rice popsicles at each price shown.

**(d)** Calculate the own-price elasticity of demand for prices between 60p and £2.10.

**(e)** Draw a graph showing total revenue against sales. Plot revenue on the vertical axis and quantity demanded on the horizontal axis.

**(f)** At what price is revenue at its greatest?

**(g)** At what price is the demand elasticity equal to −1?

**(h)** Within what ranges of prices is demand
  (i)   Elastic?
  (ii)  Inelastic?

**2**   Answer the following questions using the estimated elasticities presented in Table 4–2.

**(a)** Comment on the own-price demand elasticities of the three goods, identifying for which goods demand is elastic and for which it is inelastic.

**(b)** What is the effect of a change in the price of food on the consumption of wine and of beer? What does this suggest about the relationship between food and the other commodities?

**(c)** Figure 4–1 shows the demand curve for wine $(D_w)$ Sketch in the effect on the demand curve of an increase in the price of:
  (i)   Food
  (ii)  Beer.

**Figure 4–1**   The demand for wine in Mythuania

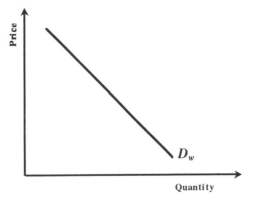

**3**   Table 4–3 presents the total spending and income of a household in two years.

**(a)** Calculate the budget shares in each year for each good.

**(b)** Calculate the income elasticity of demand for each good.

**(c)** Classify each of the goods as either 'normal' or 'inferior'.

**(d)** Classify each of the goods as either a 'luxury' or a 'necessity'.

**Table 4–3   Total spending and income of a household**

| Good | Income Year 1 £100 | Income Year 2 £200 | Budget share (year 1) | Budget share (year 2) | Income elasticity of demand | Normal (No) or inferior (I) good | Luxury (L) or necessity (Ne) |
|---|---|---|---|---|---|---|---|
| A | £30 | £50 | | | | | |
| B | £30 | £70 | | | | | |
| C | £25 | £20 | | | | | |
| D | £15 | £60 | | | | | |

**4**   Which of the demand curves **DD** and **dd** in Fig. 4–2 would you expect to represent the long-run demand for electricity? Explain your answer.

**Figure 4–2**   Short- and long-run demand curves for electricity

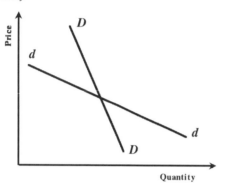

**5**   Sketch the effect of a *fall* in income upon the demand curve for each of the goods whose income elasticities are given in Table 4–4.

| Table 4–4 | Income elasticity of demand for three goods |
|---|---|
| **Good** | **Income elasticity** |
| X | 1.7 |
| Y | –0.8 |
| Z | 0 |

**6**   Which of the following would an economist describe as 'inferior' or 'normal' goods?

(a)   A good with income elasticity of –0.1.
(b)   A good with cross-price elasticity of +0.3.
(c)   A good with own-price elasticity of –1.1.
(d)   A good with income elasticity of +0.9.
(e)   A good with own-price elasticity of –0.2.

How would you interpret an own-price elasticity of +0.3?

**7**   Flora Teak likes a nice cup of tea but is equally content to accept a cup of coffee. She takes two teaspoonsful of sugar in coffee, but none in tea. What signs would you expect to observe for her cross-price elasticities between the three commodities?

**8**   Suppose that butter and margarine have a cross-price elasticity of demand of 2 and that the price of butter rises from 80p per 250g to 90p per 250g. What would be the percentage change in the demand for margarine?

**9**   For which of the following commodities would you expect demand to be *elastic* and which *inelastic?*

(a)   Bread.
(b)   Theatre tickets.
(c)   Foreign holidays.
(d)   Fuel and light.
(e)   Catering.
(f)   Dairy produce.
(g)   Clothing.

**10**   A household's income and consumption pattern were observed at various points in time. Table 4–5 shows income and quantities of bacon purchased.

| Table 4–5 | Income and bacon |
|---|---|
| **Real income (£ p.a.)** | **Quantity of bacon (kg/month)** |
| 4 000 | 2.0 |
| 6 000 | 3.0 |
| 8 000 | 3.5 |
| 10 000 | 4.0 |
| 12 000 | 4.3 |
| 14 000 | 4.4 |
| 16 000 | 4.5 |

(a)   Construct a scatter diagram showing bacon consumption on the vertical axis and income on the horizontal axis.
(b)   Does your diagram show a positive or a negative relationship between these variables?
(c)   Does this suggest that bacon is a 'normal' or an 'inferior' good?
(d)   What might your diagram look like for an 'inferior' good?

**11**   An economy is prospering; the real incomes of its citizens are expected to grow at a rapid rate during the next five years. Four of the commodities produced in the economy have income elasticities as shown in Table 4–6. Assess the prospects for the four industries.

| Table 4–6 | Income elasticities |
|---|---|
| **Good** | **Income elasticity of demand** |
| Milples | 0.46 |
| Nohoes | –1.73 |
| Bechans | 2.31 |
| Zegroes | 0.00 |

## True/False

**1**  Price elasticities measure the response of quantity demanded to changes in the relative price of goods.

**2**  The own-price elasticity of demand is constant throughout the length of a straight-line demand curve.

**3**  Price cuts will increase total spending on a good if demand is inelastic.

**4**  Total revenue is maximized when the demand elasticity is equal to –1.

**5**  Broadly defined commodity groups such as food are likely to have more elastic demand than narrowly defined commodities such as rump steak.

**6**  The budget share of a 'normal' good will always rise following an increase in income.

**7**  If two goods are substitutes, the cross-price elasticity of demand is likely to be negative.

**8**  A general inflation will have substantial effects on the pattern of demand.

**9**  A poor harvest may be disastrous for farmers by reducing the revenue received from sale of their produce.

**10**  What is true for the individual is not necessarily true for everyone together, and what is true for everyone together does not necessarily hold for the individual.

**11**  Higher levels of consumer income must be good news for producers.

**12**  For price changes, we say that demand is more elastic in the long run than in the short run. The same arguments suggest that income elasticities of demand should be higher once consumers have had time to adjust to the increase in their incomes. The reason economists emphasize the long-run/short-run distinction for price elasticity, but not for income elasticity of demand, is that changes in income are usually small.

## Economics in action

### Elastic pricing is killing the singles star

(Adapted from an article by Paul Murphy, *The Guardian*, 11 February 2004)

Steve Redmond, of the British Phonographic Industry, has been caught trying to delay the release of the latest singles' sales figures, worried they might look embarrassing ahead of the Brit Awards.

The number of singles sold fell from 52.5 million in 2002 to 35.9 million in 2003. On this basis, the Brits will cease to exist in three to four years. The damage is self-inflicted. Specifically, the industry has screwed up its pricing policy, allowing an overly complex system of early release discounts, followed by price rises for chart-toppers, to alienate customers.

This system of attracting interest with cheap offers and then increasing the cost as demand rises is known in business schools as 'elasticity of demand' pricing. It is supposed to have become ever so scientific in recent years and, thrown together with the Internet, has spawned a new range of business models – EasyJet being the obvious example – where most of the customers think they have landed a bargain most of the time.

In the music business, however, teenage singles' buyers have never enjoyed a sense that they were getting special value – just a knowledge that they were being asked to pay £3.99 for something that cost £1.99, or even 99p, a week earlier.

These supposedly unsophisticated consumers have made the rational decision to save up for a week and possibly buy the album, available for a discounted £9.99 in their nearest supermarket.

### Questions

**1**  In order to assess the success of elasticity-based pricing in the singles' market, one essential piece of information is missing from the article: what is it?

**2**  Demand theory predicts that at higher prices, consumers' demand becomes more elastic. Is this confirmed in the singles' market?

### Questions for thought

**1**  The prices of some goods are seen to be more volatile than others. Why might the price elasticity of demand be an important influence on fluctuations in the prices of different products?

**2**    Explain why each of the following factors may influence the own-price elasticity of demand for a commodity.

(a) Consumer preferences: that is, whether consumers regard the commodity as a 'luxury' or a 'necessity'.
(b) The narrowness of definition of the commodity.
(c) The length of the period under consideration.
(d) The availability of substitutes for the commodity.

**3**    The coffee market is subject to volatility caused by weather conditions in key supplying countries such as Brazil. What *other* factors are likely to influence this market?

**4**    Imagine that you are responsible for running a bus company and you have access to the following information about the elasticities of demand for coach travel:

(a) Income elasticity –0.4.
(b) Own-price elasticity –1.2.
(c) Cross-elasticity with respect to rail fares +2.1.

How might this information be of use to you in circumstances when your company is running a service which is currently making a loss?

# chapter five

# Consumer choice and demand decisions

## Learning outcomes

By the end of this chapter, you should understand:

- How to derive a budget line
- Diminishing marginal utility
- Diminishing marginal rate of substitution
- How to represent tastes as indifference curves
- How indifference curves and budget lines explain consumer choice
- How consumer income affects quantity demanded
- Income and substitution effects
- How a price change affects quantity demanded
- The market demand curve

## Key learning blocks

This chapter provides a more theoretical treatment of demand theory. It relies upon a technical representation known as *indifference curve analysis*. You should try to build your understanding around the following topics:

1. What is utility?
2. What are indifference curves?
3. What is the budget line?
4. What are the income and substitution effects?
5. How can you use all of these concepts to derive a demand curve?

The textbook discusses each of these topics in turn and the exercises that follow will help to develop your understanding.

# Important concepts and technical terms

## Match each lettered concept with the appropriate numbered phrase:

**a** Utility

**b** Income expansion path

**c** Budget constraint

**d** Indifference curve

**e** Substitution effect

**f** Individual demand curve

**g** Marginal rate of substitution

**h** Utility maximization

**i** Income effect

**j** Market demand curve

**k** Complementarity

**l** Giffen good

**1** A curve showing how the chosen bundle of goods varies with consumer income levels.

**2** The sum of the demand curves of all individuals in that market.

**3** The quantity of one good that the consumer must sacrifice to increase the quantity of the other good by one unit without changing total utility.

**4** A situation where goods are necessarily consumed jointly.

**5** An inferior good where the income effect outweighs the substitution effect, causing the demand curve to slope upwards to the right.

**6** That part of a consumer's response to a price change arising from the change in her purchasing power.

**7** That part of a consumer's response to a price change arising from the change in relative prices.

**8** A curve showing all the consumption bundles that yield the same utility to the consumer.

**9** The assumption that the consumer chooses the affordable bundle that yields the most satisfaction.

**10** The set of different consumption bundles that the consumer can afford, given income and prices.

**11** The satisfaction a consumer derives from a particular bundle of goods.

**12** A curve showing the amount demanded by a consumer at each price.

## Exercises

**1** Ashley, a student living at home, has a weekly allowance of £60, which he spends on two goods: food and entertainment. Draw Ashley's budget line for each of the following situations, using the vertical axis for food and the horizontal axis for entertainment:

**(a)** The price of food *(Pf)* is £1.50 per unit; the price of entertainment *(Pe)* is £1.50 per unit.

**(b)** *Pf* is £1.50; *Pe* is £2.

**(c)** *Pf* is £2; *Pe* is £1.50.

**(d)** *Pf* is £1; *Pe* is £1.

**(e)** *Pf* is £1.50; *Pe* is £1.50, but Ashley's allowance is increased to £75 per week.

Comment on the budget lines of *(d)* and *(e)* compared with *(a)*.

**2** Table 5–1 summarizes part of Ashley's preferences for food (*F*) and entertainment (*E*), by showing various combinations of the two goods between which he is indifferent. Each of the three sets of bundles represents a different utility level.

| Table 5–1 | Ashley's preferences for food and entertainment | | | | |
|---|---|---|---|---|---|
| Utility | set 1: IC1 | Utility | set 2: IC2 | Utility | set 3: IC3 |
| E | F | E | F | E | F |
| 2 | 40 | 10 | 40 | 12 | 45 |
| 4 | 34 | 12 | 35 | 14 | 39 |
| 8 | 26 | 14 | 30 | 16 | 34 |
| 12 | 21 | 17 | 25 | 18 | 30 |
| 17 | 16 | 20 | 20 | 21 | 25 |
| 22 | 12 | 25 | 16 | 27 | 20 |
| 30 | 8 | 30 | 13 | 37 | 15 |
| 40 | 5 | 38 | 10 | 44 | 13 |
| 50 | 4 | 50 | 8 | 50 | 12 |

(a) Use the information from Table 5–1 to sketch three indifference curves, plotting food on the vertical axis and entertainment on the horizontal axis.

(b) Which of the three indifference curves represents the highest level of utility?

(c) Which of the three indifference curves represents the lowest level of utility?

(d) Consider the following bundles of goods:

    **A:** $50(E), 8(F)$

    **B:** $45(E), 4(F)$

    **C:** $12(E), 45(F)$

    **D:** $25(E), 16(F)$

    **E:** $21(E), 11(F)$.

Rank the five bundles in *descending* order of satisfaction.

(e) Can the information in this exercise be used to find Ashley's optimal choice point?

(f) Superimpose on your graph the budget line from part (a) of Exercise 1. Can you now find the consumption bundle that maximizes Ashley's utility?

**3**  Which of the following statements is *not* valid? A utility-maximizing consumer chooses to be at a point at a tangent between his budget line and an indifference curve because:

(a) This is the highest indifference curve that can be attained.

(b) At any point to the left of the budget line some income would be unused.

(c) All combinations of goods that lie to the right of his budget line are unreachable, given money income.

(d) This point represents the most favourable relative prices.

(e) At any other point on the budget line he will gain less utility.

**4**  Barbara is choosing how to allocate her spending between CDs and clothes. Figure 5–1 shows her budget line and an indifference curve. Match each lettered point on the diagram with the appropriate numbered phrase.

**Figure 5–1** Barbara's choice between CDs and clothes

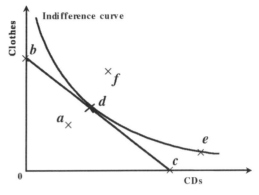

(1) The point at which Barbara maximizes her utility.

(2) The point at which Barbara buys only CDs and no clothes.

(3) A consumption bundle which would not exhaust Barbara's budget for these goods.

(4) A point yielding the same satisfaction as at *d* but which Barbara cannot afford.

(5) The point at which Barbara buys only clothes and no CDs.

(6) A consumption bundle preferred to point *d* but which Barbara cannot afford.

**5**  Christopher is choosing between two goods **X** and **Y**. Figure 5–2 shows some of his indifference curves between these goods. $BL_1$ represents his budget line, given his income and the prices of the goods.

**Figure 5–2** Christopher's preferences between goods X and Y

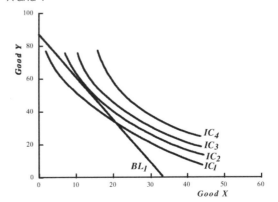

**(a)** Suppose that Christopher's tastes and the prices of X and Y remain constant, but his income varies. Plot the income expansion path.

**(b)** Classify goods X and Y as being either 'normal' or 'inferior'.

**(c)** What form would the income expansion path take if both X and Y were 'normal' goods?

**(d)** Is it possible to draw an income expansion path to depict the case where both X and Y are 'inferior' goods?

**6**    Christopher is still choosing between goods X and Y. Figure 5–3 is the same as Fig. 5–2. Suppose that Christopher's tastes, his income and the price of good Y remain fixed, but the price of good X varies.

**(a)** Show on the diagram the way in which Christopher's demand for X varies as the price of X varies.

**(b)** Is it possible to derive Christopher's demand curve for X from this analysis?

**(c)** Comment on the cross-price effect – that is, the way in which the demand for good Y changes as the price of X changes.

**Figure 5–3**   Christopher's preferences between goods X and Y

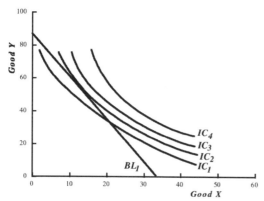

**7**    A consumer begins at point P in Fig. 5–4 with the budget line as depicted. Which of the following could have transpired if the consumer later chooses to be at Q?

**(a)** A change in tastes.

**(b)** A small increase in the price of X and a larger percentage decrease in the price of Y.

**(c)** An increase in the price of X and a smaller percentage increase in the price of Y.

**(d)** A fall in real income.

**(e)** Equal percentage increases in money income and both prices.

**Figure 5–4**   A change in a customer's choice point

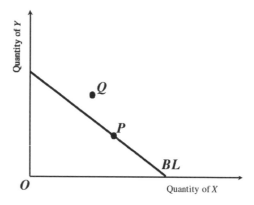

**8**    Figure 5–5 shows how Debbie reacts to a fall in the price of beefburgers, in her choice between beefburgers and pork chops.

**Figure 5–5**   Debbie's choice between beefburgers and pork chops

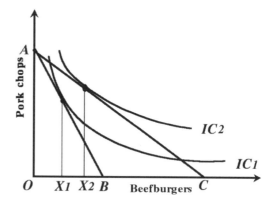

AB represents the original budget line and $OX_1$ the quantity of beefburgers bought by Debbie. After the price fall, the budget line moves to AC, and Debbie now consumes $OX_2$ beefburgers.

**(a)** Illustrate the real income and substitution effects involved in Debbie's reaction to the price fall. (*Hint:* You will need to be careful, because the discussion of this topic in the main text (Section 5–3) is in terms of a price *increase*. A price fall must be treated a little differently.)

**(b)** Does your analysis reveal beefburgers to be a 'normal' or an 'inferior' good?

**(c)** Do the income and substitution effects reinforce each other or work in opposite directions?

**(d)** Under what circumstances would your answer to (c) be different?

**9** In reality, we cannot observe indifference curves. However, we can observe prices and income, and in some situations we can make inferences about consumer preferences. Suppose we observe Eliot in two different circumstances. He is choosing between goods *X* and *Y* and has constant money income, but faces different prices in two situations. His budget lines are shown in Fig. 5–6.

**Figure 5–6** Eliot's preference

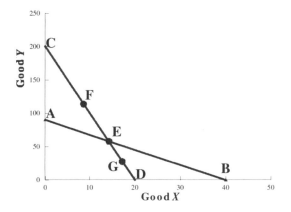

*AB* is Eliot's initial budget line and *CD* the new one after an increase in the price of *X* and a fall in the price of *Y*. His initial choice point was at *E*. All questions relate to his subsequent choice.

**(a)** If Eliot's tastes do *not* change, is it possible that he would choose to be at point *F*? Explain your answer.

**(b)** If Eliot's tastes do *not* change, is it possible that he would choose to be at point *G*? Explain your answer.

**(c)** If Eliot's tastes do *not* change, in what section of the budget line *CD* would you expect his choice to lie?

**(d)** What would you infer about Eliot's tastes if he *does* choose point *G*?

**10** *Please note that this exercise is based on material in the Appendix to Chapter 5 in the main text and assumes that utility can be measured.*

Frank reads magazines and listens to cassettes. Table 5–2 shows the utility he derives from consuming different quantities of the two commodities, given consumption of other goods. The price of magazines is £1.50 and the price of cassettes is £7.50. Suppose that Frank has a fixed budget of £30 to spend on these goods and is currently buying 2 cassettes and 10 magazines. The issue to consider is whether he is maximizing his utility for a given expenditure.

**(a)** How much utility does Frank receive from his current combination of goods?

**(b)** Calculate the *marginal* utility that Frank derives from magazines and cassettes.

**(c)** Sketch Frank's marginal utility schedule for cassettes.

**(d)** Can we yet pronounce on whether Frank is maximizing utility?

**(e)** What is Frank's utility if he spends his entire budget on cassettes?

**(f)** Calculate the ratios of marginal utility to price for each of the commodities.

**(g)** What combination of the two commodities maximizes Frank's utility, given his budget?

**Table 5–2** Frank's utility from magazines and cassettes

| Number consumed | Magazines | | | Cassettes | | |
|---|---|---|---|---|---|---|
| | (1)<br>Utility<br>(utils) | (2)<br>Marginal<br>utility | (3)<br>MUm/Pm | (4)<br>Utility<br>(utils) | (5)<br>Marginal<br>utility | (6)<br>MUc/Pc |
| 1 | 60 | | | 360 | | |
| 2 | 111 | | | 630 | | |
| 3 | 156 | | | 810 | | |
| 4 | 196 | | | 945 | | |
| 5 | 232 | | | 1050 | | |
| 6 | 265 | | | 1140 | | |
| 7 | 295 | | | 1215 | | |
| 8 | 322 | | | 1275 | | |
| 9 | 371 | | | 1350 | | |
| 10 | 371 | | | 1350 | | |

## True/False

**1**    Indifference curves always slope downwards to the right if the consumer prefers more to less of a good.

**2**    Indifference curves never intersect if the consumer has consistent preferences.

**3**    The slope of the budget line depends only upon the relative prices of the two goods.

**4**    The budget constraint shows the maximum affordable quantity of one good given the quantity of the other good that is being purchased.

**5**    An individual maximizes utility where his budget line cuts an indifference curve.

**6**    A change in money income alters the slope and position of the budget line.

**7**    All Giffen goods are 'inferior' goods.

**8**    All 'inferior' goods are Giffen goods.

**9**    The income expansion path slopes upwards to the right if both goods are 'normal' goods.

**10**    The substitution effect of an increase in the price of a good unambiguously reduces the quantity demanded of that good.

**11**    If following an increase in the price of $X$, the substitution effect is exactly balanced by the income effect, then $X$ is neither a 'normal' nor an 'inferior' good.

**12**    The theory of consumer choice demonstrates that consumers prefer to receive transfers in kind rather than transfers in cash.

## Economics in action

### First Choice drops Costa Brava
(Adapted from BBC News Online, 6 April 2004)

Spain's Costa Brava, the area that launched the package holiday phenomenon, has been dropped by a leading holiday company. The company says the decision is down to 'destination fatigue' and a lack of adequate hotels. First Choice product director, Tim Williamson, said: 'Our sales have declined to the Costa Brava. Book-ings are almost 25 per cent down this year compared with the same time in 2003.'

The decline has been blamed on soaring prices, the strengthening Euro and the rise of low-cost airlines. Other tour operators are also reducing capacity to Spain in summer 2005, with Cosmos axing Ibiza from its 2005 summer brochures and Club 18-30 dropping Benidorm.

## Questions

**1**    What evidence is there for a substitution effect behind the falling sales to Spain's Costa Brava?

**2**    If holidaymakers are instead taking more long-haul holidays, how would you explain this using consumer choice theory?

## Questions for thought

**1**    The market demand curve has been portrayed as the horizontal sum of the individual demand curves, under the assumption that individual preferences are independent. However, suppose this assumption is not valid; for instance, it might be that consumers will demand more of a good if they think that 'everyone is buying it' – or they may demand more if they think it is exclusive because few can afford it. How would these interdependencies affect the relationship between the individual and market demand curves?

**2**    So far, we have always assumed that indifference curves are downward-sloping: this follows from the assumptions that we made about consumer preferences. For instance, we assumed that there is always a diminishing marginal rate of substitution between the goods and that more is always better. If an individual has preferences which do not fit these rules, then the indifference curves can turn out to have quite a different pattern. In Fig. 5–7 some indifference curves reflecting different assumptions about preferences are shown.

In each case, utility increases from $IC_1$ to $IC_2$ to $IC_3$. For each set of indifference curves, explain the nature of consumer preferences and suggest examples of pairs of commodities which might illustrate these preferences.

**Figure 5–7** Unconventional preferences

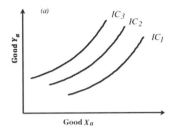

(a)

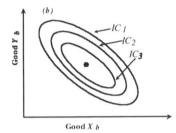

(b)

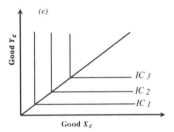

(c)

3  Will an increase in the hourly wage rate induce an individual worker to work longer or shorter hours? On the face of it, this seems an alien concept in the context of this chapter. However, an individual has preferences about other things than goods – for instance, between income and leisure (that is, hours not working). We can thus draw indifference curves between income (on the vertical axis) and hours of leisure (on the horizontal axis). If the individual gives up an hour of leisure, she receives an income, dependent upon the wage rate; so we can draw a budget line whose slope depends upon the wage rate. The higher the wage rate, the steeper the budget line. Use this framework to think about the question posed.

4  Felicity gains utility from listening to CDs and from watching videos. If she wishes to maximize her utility, which of the following conditions must be met?

(a) The marginal utility from CDs must be equated with the marginal utility from videos.

(b) She must receive the same total utility from each of the two commodities.

(c) The price of CDs multiplied by the marginal utility obtained from CDs must be equal to the product of price and marginal utility of videos.

(d) The ratio of the marginal utility of CDs to the price of CDs must be equated to the ratio of marginal utility of videos to the price of videos.

(e) The ratio of the total utility of CDs to the price of CDs must be equated to the ratio of total utility of videos to the price of videos.

# chapter six

# Introducing supply decisions

## Learning outcomes

**By the end of this chapter, you should understand:**

- The legal forms in which businesses are owned and run
- Revenue, cost, profit and cash flow
- Accounts for flows and for stocks
- Economic and accounting definitions of cost
- Whether a firm chooses output to maximize profits
- How this choice reflects marginal cost and marginal revenue

## Key learning blocks

**This chapter addresses some very basic questions about firms:**

1. What types of firms exist?
2. Why do firms exist – is it that they seek to maximize profits?
3. If they do seek to maximize profits, then how do they manage their supply in order to achieve this?

The textbook moves through each of these topics and the exercises that follow will help to develop your understanding.

# Important concepts and technical terms

## Match each lettered concept with the appropriate numbered phrase:

a Total revenue

b Assets

c Profits

d Total cost

e Marginal cost

f Opportunity cost

g Accounting cost

h Liabilities

i Depreciation

j Marginal revenue

k Inventories

l Dividends

m Supernormal profits

n Hostile takeover

o Principal–agent problem

1 That part of profits that the firm does not wish to reinvest and is thus paid to shareholders.

2 The profit over and above the return which the owners could have earned by lending their money elsewhere at the market rate of interest.

3 Goods held in stock by the firm for future sales.

4 A situation in which a company is bought out although uninvited by existing managers.

5 The increase in total revenue when output is increased by one unit.

6 The loss in value resulting from the use of machinery during the period.

7 The increase in total cost when output is increased by one unit.

8 What the firm owns.

9 All expenses of production including both fixed costs and those costs which vary with the level of output (and including opportunity cost).

10 What the firm owes.

11 The receipts of a business from sale of its output, equal to total expenditure by consumers on the firm's product.

12 The excess of total revenue over total cost.

13 The actual payments made by a firm in a period.

14 A situation which arises from conflict of interest between owners and managers.

15 The amount lost by not using a resource in its best alternative use.

## Exercises

1 Set out below are descriptions of four hypothetical firms. Identify each as being a sole trader, a partnership or a company.

(a) Count & Balance is a firm of chartered accountants. The five qualified accountants who work for the firm share the profits between them and are jointly responsible for any losses, as the firm does not have limited liability.

(b) Will Mendit & Son is a small family business. Will does electrical repair work while his son helps with the paperwork and assists with some repairs; they each take their share of the earnings. If the firm were to go bankrupt, Will would have to sell his car and his son his motorbike.

(c) D. Harbinger Limited supplies communication equipment to the military. Profits are distributed among the shareholders, who have limited liability. The original founder of the firm has now retired, leaving management in the hands of the board of directors.

**(d)** Connie Fection runs a sweet shop, living in a flat over the premises with her daughter, who is paid to work the till on four afternoons a week. Connie does not have limited liability and in case of difficulty would have to sell her possessions.

**2**    The following items represent the expenditures and receipts of Lex Pretend & Sons Limited during 2004. Prepare the income statement for the firm and calculate profits before and after tax on the assumption that the firm is liable only for corporation tax of 30 per cent on its profits.

**(a)** Rent £25 000.

**(b)** Proceeds from sale of 5000 units of good X at £40 each.

**(c)** Travel expenses £19 000.

**(d)** Stationery and other office expenses £15 000.

**(e)** Wages £335 000.

**(f)** Telephone £8000.

**(g)** Proceeds from sale of 4000 units of good Y at £75 each.

**(h)** Advertising £28 000.

**3**    Fiona Trimble is a sole trader operating in the textile industry. During the past year, revenue received amounted to £55 000 and she incurred direct costs of £27 000. Fiona had £25 000 of financial capital tied up in the business during the whole year. Had she chosen to work for the large company round the corner, she could have earned £21 000. Calculate the following items (you will need to know that the going market rate of interest was 10 per cent):

**(a)** Accounting cost.

**(b)** Accounting profit.

**(c)** Opportunity cost of Fiona's time.

**(d)** Opportunity cost of financial capital.

**(e)** Total economic cost.

**(f)** Economic profit (supernormal).

**4**    The following items comprise the assets and liabilities of GSC Limited (the Great Spon Company) as at 31 March 2004. Incorporate them into a balance sheet for the firm and calculate the net worth of the company. Note that the company has been in operation for just one year and that buildings and other physical capital are assumed to depreciate at the rate of 20 per cent p.a.

**(a)** Wages payable £25 000.

**(b)** Inventories held £80 000.

**(c)** Bank loan payable £50 000.

**(d)** Buildings, original value £300 000.

**(e)** Cash in hand £30 000.

**(f)** Accounts receivable £55 000.

**(g)** Accounts payable £40 000.

**(h)** Mortgage £180 000.

**(i)** Salaries due to be paid £30 000.

**(j)** Physical capital other than buildings, original value £250 000.

**5**    Table 6–1 contains data which represent the cost and revenue situation of a firm.

**(a)** Calculate marginal cost as output rises.

**(b)** Calculate marginal revenue as output rises. (*Hint*: You will need first to calculate total revenue.)

**(c)** At what level of output would profits be maximized?

**(d)** Calculate profit at each level of output.

| Table 6–1    Costs and revenue for a firm | | |
|---|---|---|
| **Total production (units/week)** | **Price received (£)** | **Total costs (£)** |
| 1 | 25 | 10 |
| 2 | 23 | 23 |
| 3 | 20 | 38 |
| 4 | 18 | 55 |
| 5 | 15 | 75 |
| 6 | 12 | 98 |

**6**    Mr Smith owns a small factory. Every Thursday one of his lorry drivers spends the morning driving Mrs Jones round the shops. The lorry driver is, of course, paid his normal wage and Mrs Jones gives him an extra £5. Which of the following identifies the opportunity cost to Mr Smith of the lorry driver's chauffeuring?

**(a)** The £5 plus the wage he would normally earn.

**(b)** The work he would have done if not taken away from the factory.

**(c)** The wage he would normally earn.

**(d)** The £5 Mrs Jones pays him.

**7**    Table 6–2 summarizes marginal revenue and marginal cost for a firm.

**(a)** Plot marginal revenue and marginal cost schedules, associating each marginal value with the midpoint of the quantity interval (i.e. place the marginal cost of the first unit midway between 0 and 1, etc.).

**(b)** At what (approximate) level of output would the

firm choose to operate if it wanted to maximize *profits*?

(c) At what (approximate) level of output would the firm choose to operate if it wanted to maximize *revenue*? (*Hint*: You will need to extend your *MR* line a little.)

(d) If marginal cost were to increase by £30, at each level of output at what point would profits be maximized?

(e) Given the original level of marginal cost, at what level of output would the firm maximize profits if marginal revenue were to increase by £34 at each level of output?

| Table 6–2 | Marginal revenue, marginal costs for a firm | |
|---|---|---|
| **Total production (units/week)** | **Marginal revenue (£)** | **Marginal cost (£)** |
| 0 | 72 | 17 |
| 1 | 56 | 15 |
| 2 | 40 | 25 |
| 3 | 24 | 40 |
| 4 | 8 | 60 |
| 5 | | |

**8** Which of the following might describe the motivation for a firm in setting output and (where appropriate) price?

(a) The wish to maximize profits.

(b) The wish to maximize sales.

(c) The wish to obtain as large a market share as possible.

(d) The wish to obtain enough profit to keep the shareholders content.

(e) The wish to see the firm grow as quickly as possible.

Which of these do you consider to be most important?

## True/False

**1** Small traders are the most numerous form of business organization in the UK, but companies are, on average, the most profitable.

**2** The balance sheet of a firm summarizes information concerning the flow of receipts and expenditures during a given year.

**3** To avoid the possibility of having to sell their possessions, shareholders should be careful to buy shares in thriving firms.

**4** Firms that show an accounting profit must be thriving.

**5** Opportunity cost plus accounting cost equals economic cost.

**6** The net worth of a firm as revealed by the balance sheet does not necessarily reflect the true worth, which should take notice of 'goodwill' factors.

**7** Firms maximize profits by selling as much output as they can.

**8** When a firm's demand curve slopes down, marginal revenue will fall as output rises.

**9** Long-term profitability is all that matters; cash flow is unimportant.

**10** Any firm wanting to maximize profits will minimize cost for any given level of output.

**11** A fall in marginal revenue will cause profits to be maximized at a lower output level.

**12** Inventories are produced by mad scientists.

**13** When the firm's demand curve slopes down, marginal revenue must be less than the price for which the last unit is sold.

**14** More than 90 per cent of UK corporate investment is financed from retained profits.

## Economics in action

### Sainsbury chairman is forced out

(Adapted from BBC News Online, 1 July 2004)

Key shareholders have forced Sainsbury's chairman Sir Peter Davis to resign with immediate effect. They were angry that Sir Peter had been awarded a £2.4 million bonus at a time when profits and market share were falling. Sainsbury's also warned that its profits for this year would be 'significantly below' expectations, causing its shares to drop sharply. Sainsbury's has lost ground to both Tesco and Asda and in May it reported a 2.9 per cent fall in annual profits.

Sir Peter became Sainsbury's chairman only in May, having been chief executive for four years. Sainsbury's thanked Sir Peter for 'all his hard work on behalf of the company'.

### Questions

**1** In this article, identify the principals and the agent.

**2** Was there a separation of ownership from control problem at Sainsbury's?

## Questions for thought

**1** Why might marginal cost be falling at low levels of output? What might cause marginal cost to rise?

**2** What do you consider to be the opportunity cost that you are incurring by thinking about this question?

**3** Suppose that you own shares in a computer software company, but you do not become directly involved in the running of the company as your activities as a rock star keep you fully occupied. Your hope is that the firm will maximize profits, although you know that this is a tough and competitive market. In thinking about the following questions, you may find it helpful to read them in conjunction with the commentary provided in the main text.

**(a)** Are the managers of the company likely to share your enthusiasm for profit maximization?

**(b)** Is it possible for you to impose profit maximization and to monitor the actions of the managers?

**(c)** Would the threat of a hostile takeover be a help or a hindrance in this instance?

**(d)** How might the threat of a hostile takeover affect the long-term position of the firm?

**(e)** What steps might you take to safeguard your interests?

# chapter seven

# Costs and supply

## Learning outcomes

**By the end of this chapter, you should understand:**

- A production function
- Technology and a technique of production
- How the choice of technique depends on input prices
- Total, average and marginal cost, in the long run and short run
- Returns to scale and their relation to average cost curves
- Fixed and variable factors in the short run
- The law of diminishing returns
- How a firm chooses output level, in the long run and short run

## Key learning blocks

**In this chapter we are interested in knowing what influences the firm's level of costs. The answer is broadly related to three areas:**

1. What the production technology employed by the firm is and what the factor mix is.
2. In the long run, the firm's costs are influenced by so-called returns to scale.
3. In the short run, costs are influenced by the law of diminishing returns.

The textbook moves through each of these issues and you should try to build your understanding around these three points. The exercises that follow will aid your understanding.

# Important concepts and technical terms

## Match each lettered concept with the appropriate numbered phrase:

**a** Production function

**b** Fixed cost

**c** Constant returns to scale

**d** Long-run average cost

**e** Law of diminishing returns

**f** Short-run marginal cost

**g** Economies of (increasing returns to) scale

**h** Long run

**i** Variable costs

**j** Long-run marginal cost

**k** Short run

**l** Long-run total cost

**m** Minimum efficient scale

**n** Diseconomies of (decreasing returns to) scale

**1** The specification of the maximum output that can be produced from any given amount of inputs.

**2** The total cost of producing a given output level when the firm is able to adjust all inputs optimally.

**3** The period long enough for the firm to adjust all its inputs to a change in conditions.

**4** The output level at which further economies of scale become unimportant for the individual firm and the average cost curve first becomes horizontal.

**5** The situation in which long-run average costs increase as output rises.

**6** The increase in short-run total costs (and in short-run variable costs) as output is increased by one unit.

**7** The cost per unit of producing a given output level when the firm is able to adjust all inputs optimally.

**8** Costs that change as output changes.

**9** The situation where, beyond some level of the variable input, further increases in the variable input lead to a steadily decreasing marginal product of that input.

**10** The increase in long-run total costs if output is permanently raised by one unit.

**11** Costs that do not vary with output levels.

**12** The situation when long-run average costs are constant as output rises.

**13** The situation when long-run average costs decrease as output rises.

**14** The period in which the firm can make only partial adjustment of its inputs to a change in conditions.

## Exercises

**1** A firm making toffees has a choice between three production techniques, each using different combinations of labour input and capital input, as shown in Table 7–1.

Suppose labour costs £200 per unit/week and capital input costs £400 per unit/week.

**(a)** Calculate total cost for each level of output.

**(b)** For each level of output, state which production technique should be adopted by the firm.

**(c)** Suppose that the price of labour input increases to £300 per unit/week, but the price of capital remains constant. In what way would you expect the firm's choice of technique to be affected by this change in relative prices?

**(d)** With the new labour cost, state which production technique should be adopted for each output level and calculate total cost.

**Table 7–1    Production techniques for toffee**

| Output | Technique A L | K | Technique B L | K | Technique C L | K |
|---|---|---|---|---|---|---|
| 1 | 9 | 2 | 6 | 4 | 4 | 6 |
| 2 | 19 | 3 | 10 | 8 | 8 | 10 |
| 3 | 29 | 4 | 14 | 12 | 12 | 14 |
| 4 | 41 | 5 | 18 | 16 | 16 | 19 |
| 5 | 59 | 6 | 24 | 22 | 20 | 25 |
| 6 | 85 | 7 | 33 | 29 | 24 | 32 |
| 7 | 120 | 8 | 45 | 38 | 29 | 40 |

Note: L denotes labour; K denotes capital.

All measured in units per week.

**Table 7–2    Output and long-run total cost**

| Output (units/week) | Total cost (£) | Long-run average cost | Long-run marginal cost |
|---|---|---|---|
| 0 | 0 | | |
| 1 | 32 | | |
| 2 | 48 | | |
| 3 | 82 | | |
| 4 | 140 | | |
| 5 | 228 | | |
| 6 | 352 | | |

**2**    A firm faces long-run total cost conditions as given in Table 7–2.

**(a)** Calculate long-run average cost (LAC) and long-run marginal cost (LMC).
**(b)** Plot LAC and LMC curves.
    (Hint: Remember to plot LMC at points halfway between the corresponding output levels.)
**(c)** At what output level is LAC at a minimum?
**(d)** At what output level does LMC equal LAC?

**3**    Look at the diagram you drew in Exercise 2.

**(a)** Within what range of output does this firm experience economies of scale (increasing returns to scale)?
**(b)** Within what range of output does the firm experience diseconomies of scale (decreasing returns to scale)?

**(c)** What is the minimum efficient scale for this firm?
**(d)** Suppose that you could measure returns to scale at a particular point on the LAC curve, what would characterize the point where LAC is at a minimum?

**4**    Which of the following statements describes the law of diminishing returns? Suppose in each case that labour is a variable factor, but capital is fixed.

As more labour is used:

**(a)** Total output will fall because the extra units of labour will be of poorer quality than those previously employed.
**(b)** The relative shortage of capital will eventually cause increases in total product to become progressively smaller.
**(c)** The cost of the product will eventually be forced up because the wage rate will rise as labour becomes more scarce.
**(d)** After a while fewer units of labour will be needed in order to produce more output.
**(e)** The marginal revenue obtained from each additional unit produced will decline.

**5**    Which of the following conditions is (are) necessary before the law of diminishing returns to a factor can be said to operate?

**(a)** Other factors are held constant.
**(b)** The state of technical knowledge does not change.
**(c)** All units of the variable factor are homogeneous.

**6**    A firm faces fixed costs of £45 and short-run average variable costs (SAVC) as shown in Table 7–3.

**Table 7–3** Short-run costs of production

| Output (units/week) | Short-run average variable cost (SAVC) |
|---|---|
| 1 | 17 |
| 2 | 15 |
| 3 | 14 |
| 4 | 15 |
| 5 | 19 |
| 6 | 29 |

(a) From the figures in Table 7–3, calculate short-run average fixed cost (SAFC), short-run average total cost (SATC), short-run total cost (STC) and short-run marginal cost (SMC).

(b) Plot SAVC, SATC and SMC; check that SMC goes through the minimum points of the other two curves.

(c) If the firm were to increase production from five to six units/week, the short-run marginal cost would be high. Explain why this should be so, being sure to describe the role played by the marginal product of labour.

**7** In the short run, a firm can vary labour input flexibly but cannot change the level of capital input. Table 7–4 shows how output changes as only labour input is varied.

(a) Calculate the marginal product of labour (MPL) and the average product of labour (APL).

(b) Plot MPL and APL.

(c) At approximately what level of labour input do diminishing returns set in?

(d) At approximately what level of labour input does MPL cut APL?

(e) How would you expect the MPL curve to be affected by a change in the level of capital input?

**8** Which of the following statements about the short-run marginal cost curve are not true?

(a) Marginal cost equals average cost when average cost is at a minimum.

(b) When average cost is falling, marginal cost will be below average cost.

(c) Marginal cost is greater than average cost when the number of units produced is greater than the optimum technical output.

(d) Marginal cost will be rising under conditions of diminishing returns.

(e) Marginal cost is unaffected by changes in factor prices.

(f) Marginal cost depends in part upon fixed costs.

**9** Each of the four separate short-run average total cost curves in Fig. 7–1 represents a different scale of operation of a firm.

**Figure 7–1** Short-run average cost

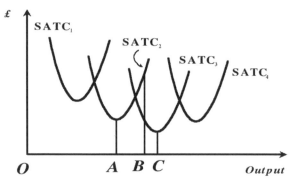

(a) On the basis of Fig. 7–1, what would be the most efficient level of output for the firm to produce?

(b) If the firm were to expand its scale of operation beyond this point, what would be the nature of the returns to scale?

**Table 7–4** Output and labour input

| Labour input (workers/week) | Output (goods/week) | Marginal product of labour | Average product of labour |
|---|---|---|---|
| 0 | 0 | | |
| 1 | 35 | | |
| 2 | 80 | | |
| 3 | 122 | | |
| 4 | 156 | | |
| 5 | 177 | | |
| 6 | 180 | | |

**Table 7–5**    Short- and long-run decisions

| Price (£) | Short-run decision | | | Long-run decision | | |
|---|---|---|---|---|---|---|
| | Produce at a profit | Produce at a loss | Close down | Produce at a profit | Produce at a loss | Close down |
| 18.0 | | | | | | |
| 5.0 | | | | | | |
| 7.0 | | | | | | |
| 13.0 | | | | | | |
| 11.50 | | | | | | |

(c) Which of the four scales of operation would be appropriate if the firm wished to produce *OA* output?

(d) If the firm then wanted to expand to produce *OB* output, what would be the chosen scale of operation in the short run and in the long run?

(e) Sketch in the long-run average cost curve for the firm.

**10**    A firm has selected the output level at which it wishes to produce. Having checked the marginal condition, the firm is now considering the average condition as it applies in the short run and the long run. Cost conditions are such that *LAC* is £12; *SATC* is £17 (made up of *SAVC* £11 and *SAFC* £6). In Table 7–5, tick the appropriate short- and long-run decisions for the firm at each stated market price.

## True/False

**1**    Capital and labour are the only two factors of production which the firm needs to consider when making its output decision.

**2**    The typical U-shape often assumed for the long-run average cost curve is valid only for a firm facing economies of scale at low levels of output, changing to diseconomies as output expands.

**3**    Specialization (the division of labour) can lead to economies of scale.

**4**    Small firms are always less efficient than large ones.

**5**    Firms who make losses are 'lame ducks' who should be closed down at once.

**6**    A firm will close down in the short run if price is less than average revenue.

**7**    The long-run supply decision is determined by finding the level of output at which long-run marginal cost is equal to marginal revenue.

**8**    Holding labour constant while increasing capital input will lead to diminishing returns.

**9**    *LAC* is falling when *LMC* is less than *LAC* and rising when *LMC* is greater than *LAC*; *LAC* is at a minimum at the output level at which *LAC* and *LMC* cross.

**10**    Empirical evidence suggests that if there were more than one refrigerator manufacturer in the UK, it would be impossible for every firm in that industry to be producing at minimum efficient scale.

**11**    The decision whether to continue to produce should be taken regardless of how much money has been devoted to the project in the past.

**12**    The long-run average cost curve passes through the lowest point of each short-run average cost curve.

## Economics in action

### Toyota shifts gears to foreign plants

(Adapted from an article by Khozem Merchant, *Financial Times*, 30 June 2004)

Toyota's Indian gearbox plant, located near Bangalore, is one of five around the world that are manufacturing components for a family of vehicles that will undergo final assembly in several countries.

Under the plan, India and the Philippines will supply gearboxes; Thailand diesel engines; Indonesia petrol-engines; and Latin America other parts. The product range will include vans, SUVs and trucks based on a single new platform, replacing two existing ones. They will be exported to some 38 countries.

Toyota's overall strategy is to try to get closer to demand centres such as China and India while using global sourcing to create economies of scale. The Indian market is growing rapidly but remains too small on its own for a local manufacturing and assembly base to be very profitable for a multinational company such as Toyota. If that base is also used to provide components for the company's global operations, however, the numbers begin to add up.

## Questions

**1** What key steps have Toyota undertaken in order to exploit economies of scale?

**2** What problems might Toyota face by operating in this way?

## Questions for thought

**1** Explain why large firms in some industries are able to produce at lower average cost than small firms. Name some industries with this characteristic. In what sorts of activity might the reverse be true, and why?

**2** Is it possible for an industry to experience economies of scale and diminishing returns to labour simultaneously?

**3** It has been suggested that in practice firms do not know all the details of the various cost curves that we have discussed. If this is so, how relevant is all this analysis?

**4** Think about how you would expect economies of scale to have changed in recent years in each of the following activities. What effects might these changes have on the way that these markets might be expected to operate?

**(a)** Satellite TV.
**(b)** Banking.
**(c)** Motor vehicles.
**(d)** Textiles.
**(e)** Opticians.
**(f)** Water supply.

# chapter eight

# Perfect competition and pure monopoly

## Learning outcomes

By the end of this chapter, you should understand:

- Perfect competition
- Why a perfectly competitive firm equates marginal cost and price
- How profits and losses lead to entry and exit
- The industry supply curve
- Comparative-static analysis of a competitive industry
- A market in which international competition occurs
- Pure monopoly
- Why a monopolist equates *MC* and *MR*
- How output compares under monopoly and perfect competition
- How price discrimination affects a monopolist's output and profits

## Key learning blocks

Following Chapters 3–7 you should now be familiar with the issues relating to the costs and revenues of a firm. The concepts of perfect competition and monopoly take the analysis on to the next stage, where we consider how the level of competition determines the *profitability* of the firm. The key blocks of understanding stem from the following questions:

1. What is perfect competition and what are its main outcomes?
2. What is monopoly and what are the main outcomes of such a market structure?
3. If we compare monopoly and perfect competition, which is the better form of market?

The textbook goes through each of these blocks and provides a wide-ranging discussion. The exercises that follow will reinforce your understanding.

# Important concepts and technical terms

## Match each lettered concept with the appropriate numbered phrase:

**a** Perfectly competitive market

**b** Industry supply curve

**c** Natural monopoly

**d** Shutdown price

**e** Law of One Price

**f** Monopoly

**g** Marginal firm

**h** Normal profit

**i** Supernormal profits

**j** Firm's supply curve

**k** Monopsony

**l** Free entry or exit

**1** A market in which both buyers and sellers believe that their own buying or selling decisions have no effect on the market price.

**2** The curve showing the quantity that the firm wants to produce at each price.

**3** The least efficient firm in a perfectly competitive industry, just making normal profits.

**4** A market structure in which there is only one buyer or potential buyer of the good in that industry.

**5** A situation in which firms can leave or join an industry without hindrance.

**6** A market structure in which there is only one seller or potential seller of the good in that industry.

**7** A situation in which the price of a given commodity would be the same all over the world if there were no obstacles to trade and no transport costs.

**8** An industry in which the firm faces such substantial economies of scale that long-run average cost falls over the entire range of output, making it difficult for more than one firm to operate.

**9** The price below which the firm reduces its losses by choosing not to produce at all.

**10** That level of profits which just pays the opportunity cost of the owners' money and time.

**11** An excess of total revenue over total cost.

**12** The curve showing the total quantity that firms in (or potentially in) an industry want to supply at each price.

## Exercises

**1** A firm operating in a perfectly competitive industry faces the cost curves shown in Fig. 8–1. *OP* is the going market price.

**(a)** Mark on the diagram the profit-maximizing level of output.

**(b)** Mark on the diagram the area representing the profits made by the firm at this level of price and output.

**(c)** If you were told that this industry was in equilibrium, would you judge it to be a short-run or a long-run equilibrium? Justify your answer.

**Figure 8–1** A firm under perfect competition

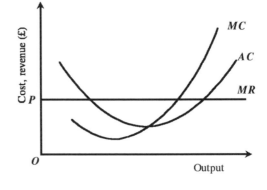

**(d)** How would you expect the firm to be affected by a decrease in the market demand for the commodity produced by this industry?

**2** Figure 8–2 shows the short-run cost curves for a perfectly competitive firm.

**Figure 8–2** Short-run cost curves for a perfectly competitive firm

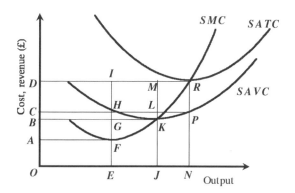

**(a)** What is the shutdown price for the firm?
**(b)** At what price would the firm just make normal profits?
**(c)** What area would represent total fixed cost at this price?
**(d)** Within what range of prices would the firm choose to operate at a loss in the short run?
**(e)** Identify the firm's short-run supply curve.
**(f)** Within what range of prices would the firm be able to make short-run supernormal profits?

**3** A monopolist faces the cost and revenue conditions shown in Fig. 8–3.

**Figure 8–3** A monopolist's cost and revenue conditions

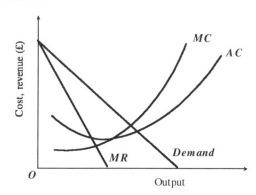

**(a)** Mark on the diagram the profit-maximizing level of output.

**(b)** Mark on the diagram the price at which the monopolist would choose to sell this output.
**(c)** Identify the area representing the level of monopoly profits at this price and output.
**(d)** How would you expect the monopolist to be affected by a decrease in the market demand for the commodity?

**4** Figure 8–4 shows the long-run cost and revenue situation facing a monopolist.

**Figure 8–4** The long-run position of a monopolist

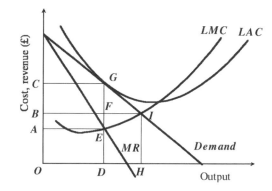

**(a)** What is the profit-maximizing level of output?
**(b)** At what price would the monopolist choose to sell the good?
**(c)** What level of supernormal profits would be made in this situation?
**(d)** How much output (and at what price) would the monopolist produce if forced to set price equal to marginal cost?

**5** Table 8–1 represents the demand curve faced by a monopolist.

| Table 8–1 | A monopolist's demand curve | | |
|-----------|------------|------------|------------|
| **Demand (000/week)** | **Price (£)** | **Total revenue** | **Marginal revenue** |
| 0 | 40 | | |
| 1 | 35 | | |
| 2 | 30 | | |
| 3 | 25 | | |
| 4 | 20 | | |
| 5 | 15 | | |
| 6 | 10 | | |
| 7 | 5 | | |

(a) Calculate total revenue and marginal revenue.
(b) Plot average revenue and marginal revenue.
(c) On a separate graph, plot total revenue.
(d) At what level of demand is total revenue at a maximum?
(e) At what level of demand is marginal revenue equal to zero?
(f) At what level of demand is there unit own-price elasticity of demand?

**6** Figure 8–5 shows a firm's cost and revenue position. At which output level would the firm be:

(a) Maximizing profits?
(b) Maximizing total revenue?
(c) Producing the technically optimum output?
(d) Making only normal profits?

**Figure 8–5** Cost and revenue for a firm

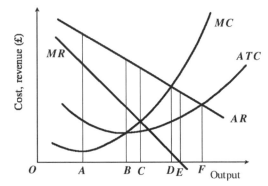

**7** Under which of the following conditions will a profit-maximizing, perfectly competitive firm close down in the short run?

(a) Price is less than marginal cost.
(b) Average revenue is less than average cost.
(c) Average fixed cost is greater than price.
(d) Average revenue is less than average variable cost.
(e) Total cost is greater than total revenue.

**8** Which of the following situations characterize a perfectly competitive market, and which relate to a monopoly (or to both)? Assume that firms are aiming to maximize profits.

(a) Price exceeds marginal cost (MC).
(b) Price equals marginal revenue (MR).
(c) Marginal revenue equals marginal cost.
(d) Abnormal profit is zero in long-run equilibrium.
(e) New firms are excluded from the market.
(f) A firm chooses its price–output combination.
(g) There are no barriers to entry.

(h) Average revenue exceeds marginal revenue.
(i) Price equals marginal cost.

**9** Which of the following corresponds most closely to the economists' notion of 'normal profit'?

(a) The level of profits a firm makes by setting MC = MR.
(b) The level of profits made by the typical firm in the industry.
(c) The level of profits a firm would tend to make under normal conditions of trade.
(d) The level of profits needed to persuade a firm to stay in its current line of business.
(e) The rate of profits that ensures a comfortable standard of living for the entrepreneur.

**10** A perfectly competitive industry is taken over by a monopolist who intends to run it as a multi-plant concern. Consequently, the long-run supply curve of the competitive industry (LRSS) becomes the monopolist's long-run marginal cost curve (LMCm); in the short run the SRSS curve becomes the monopolist's SMCm. The position is shown in Fig. 8–6.

**Figure 8–6** The monopolization of a perfectly competitive industry

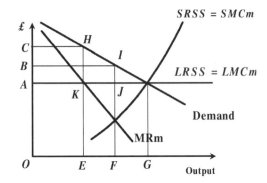

(a) What was the equilibrium price and industry output under perfect competition?
(b) At what price and output would the monopolist choose to operate in the short run?
(c) At what price and output would the monopolist maximize profits in the long run?
(d) What would be the size of these long-run profits?

**True/False**

**1** Price is equal to marginal revenue for a firm under perfect competition.

**2**    The short-run supply curve for a perfectly competitive firm is flatter than the long-run supply curve.

**3**    A firm making economic profits is said to be making normal profits.

**4**    An industry in which long-run average costs fall throughout the relevant range of output is ideally suited for a perfectly competitive market.

**5**    The supply curve of an industry is obtained by a horizontal aggregation of the quantities supplied by firms in the industry at each price.

**6**    A monopolist will always produce on the inelastic part of the demand curve.

**7**    Other things being equal, an increase in variable costs will cause a monopolist to increase output and reduce price.

**8**    A monopolist makes supernormal profits because it is more efficient than a competitive industry.

**9**    Total revenue is maximized when average revenue is at a maximum.

**10**    A monopolist may increase total profits by charging different prices in different markets.

**11**    A perfectly competitive firm will be selling at a price equal to marginal cost, but a monopolist can set a price above marginal cost.

**12**    Very small firms typically do little research and development, whereas many larger firms have excellent research departments.

## Economics in action

### EasyJet nose dives

(Adapted from 'Webster Ponders the "Branson Solution"', *The Observer*, 9 May 2004)

EasyJet shares took a two-day pummelling on the markets, losing 25 per cent of their value on Wednesday. 'This is quite a setback for us and our staff,' said company boss Webster.

The shares dived, but the company's half-year figures were good – the airline flew more passengers, had more planes and the planes were fuller. But comments about 'unprofitable and unrealistic pricing' from airlines throughout Europe, combined with remarks about the

54 low-cost operators crowding into the European market must lie behind the fall.

However, in the near future, 'a lot of the capacity is going to exit'. Aircraft leasing costs for those without strong balance sheets are creeping up in the uncertain market and without the economies of scale on group-wide costs, such as fuel and insurance, many can't hope to compete long-term.

## Questions

**1**    Assess whether the no-frills airline market is perfectly competitive by benchmarking the industry against the key characteristics of a perfectly competitive market.

**2**    If 'a lot of the capacity is going to exit' in the short term, will long-term profit levels return to a supernormal level?

## Questions for thought

**1**    We have seen that a monopolist wishing to maximize profits will tend to restrict output and increase price. Can you think of circumstances in which a monopolist might choose not to take full advantage of these potential profits?

**2**    Explain why it is said that the firm under perfect competition operates at the technically optimum point of production in the long run. Can any conclusions be drawn about the efficient allocation of resources in the industry?

**3**    The monopoly producer of a commodity supplies two separate markets. The commodity is one that cannot be resold – in other words, it is not possible for a consumer to buy in market 2 and resell in market 1. Figure 8–7 shows the demand and marginal revenue curves in the two markets and in the combined market. Note that the *MR* curve for the combined market has a 'jump' in it at the point where price falls sufficiently for the monopolist to make sales in market 2.

This question extends the analysis in the main text: you may wish to tackle it slowly, with the help of the comments provided in the 'Answers and Comments' section of this box. Throughout the analysis, the monopolist's output level is decided by reference to marginal cost and revenue in the *combined* market.

**Figure 8–7** A discriminating monopolist

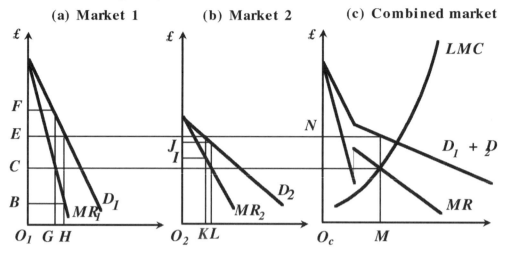

You can draw lines across to the submarket diagrams to find *MR* and *AR*.

**(a)** What level of output will the monopolist produce to maximize profits?

**(b)** If the monopolist sets a common price to all customers, what will that price be?

**(c)** How much will the monopolist sell in each of the two submarkets?

**(d)** At this selling price, what is marginal revenue in each of the two markets?

**(e)** If the monopolist now finds that price discrimination is possible, how could profits be increased? (*Hint*: Your answer to part *(d)* is important here.)

**(f)** With price discrimination, what prices would the monopolist set in each market, and how much would be sold?

**4** This question extends the discussion of Fig. 8–6 (Exercise **10**), in which we were looking at the case of a perfectly competitive industry being taken over by a monopolist. We saw that under perfect competition, equilibrium would be at output *OG*, price *OA*, whereas the profit-maximizing monopolist would restrict output in the short run to *OF* and raise price to *OB*, and in the long run move to *OE*, *OC*. We will consider the two long-run equilibrium positions. An amended version of Fig. 8–6 appears as Fig. 8–8.

However, first think a bit about the demand curve. What does a point on the demand curve really represent? At a point such as *I*, consumers are jointly prepared to pay a price *OB* for *OF* output. In a sense, *OB* is the consumers' valuation of a marginal unit of the good. Indeed, on this argument we might describe the demand curve as representing the 'marginal social benefit' function. Notice that

at the higher price *OC* there are still consumers prepared to purchase *OE* units of the good. When the price is only *OB*, those consumers pay less at the margin than they would have been prepared to pay for at least some of the units. We could argue that this implies that they receive a 'surplus' above what they actually pay at point *I*. This is sometimes known as the *consumer surplus*; it is represented in Fig. 8–6 by the area under the demand curve. For example, at point *I*, consumers' total valuation of the good they consume is the area *OMIF*; they pay *OBIF*, and receive consumer surplus of *BMI*. This was a long preamble to a very short question! However, the concept of consumer surplus will reappear later in the book, and it is good for you to be prepared. Three short questions to see whether this discussion has made sense to you:

**(a)** What is the consumer surplus at the perfect competition long-run equilibrium?

**(b)** What is the consumer surplus at the monopoly long-run equilibrium?

**(c)** So what has happened to the 'lost' consumer surplus?

**Figure 8–8** The monopolization of a perfectly competitive industry revisited

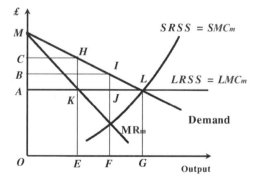

# chapter nine

# Market structure and imperfect competition

## Learning outcomes

By the end of this chapter, you should understand:

- How cost and demand affect market structure
- How globalization changes domestic market structure
- Monopolistic competition
- Oligopoly and interdependence
- The kinked demand curve model
- Game theory and strategic behaviour
- Commitment and credibility
- Reaction functions and Nash equilibrium
- Cournot and Bertrand competition
- Stackleberg leadership
- Contestable markets
- Innocent and strategic entry barriers

## Key learning blocks

The concept of *oligopolistic markets* with a small number of large players is readily identifiable in the banking and supermarket industries. The issues for economists are threefold:

1. Which factors are likely to lead to a market being oligopolistic?

2. Using game theory, how can we understand current-period strategic interaction between rivals in oligoplistic markets?

3. How might long-term competition be affected by strategic or natural entry barriers?

The textbook covers each of these areas in turn and the questions that follow will help you to explore the important issues.

# Important concepts and technical terms

## Match each lettered concept with the appropriate numbered phrase:

**a** Oligopoly

**b** Imperfect competition

**c** Contestable market

**d** Credible threat

**e** Dominant strategy

**f** Product differentiation

**g** Pre-commitment

**h** Monopolistic competition

**i** Predatory pricing

**j** Game theory

**k** Kinked demand curve

**l** Prisoners' Dilemma

**m** Innocent entry barrier

**n** Nash equilibrium

**o** Cournot model

**p** Bertrand model

**q** Reaction function

**1** A market structure in which firms recognize that their demand curves slope downwards and that output price will depend on the quantity of goods produced and sold.

**2** An industry with only a few producers, each recognizing that its own price depends not merely on its own output but also on the actions of its important competitors in the industry.

**3** A tactic adopted by existing firms when faced by a new entrant, involving deliberately increasing output and forcing down the price, causing all firms to make losses.

**4** How a firm's optimal output varies with each possible action by its rival.

**5** The analysis of the principles behind intelligent interdependent decision-making.

**6** The demand curve perceived by an oligopolist who believes that competitors will respond to a decrease in his price but not to an increase.

**7** An industry having many sellers producing products that are close substitutes for one another and in which each firm has only a limited ability to affect its output price.

**8** A model of oligopoly where each firm assumes that the prices of rivals are given.

**9** Actual or perceived differences in a good compared with its substitutes, designed to affect potential buyers.

**10** A situation in which a player's best strategy is independent of that adopted by other players.

**11** An arrangement entered into voluntarily which restricts a firm's future options.

**12** A game between two players, each of whom has a dominant strategy.

**13** A model of oligopoly where firms assume that the output of rivals is a given.

**14** A barrier to entry not deliberately erected by firms.

**15** The threat of a punishment strategy which, after the fact, a firm would find it optimal to carry out.

**16** A situation where each player chooses the best strategy, given the strategies followed by the other players.

**17** A market characterized by free entry and free exit.

## Exercises

**1**    For each of the situations listed below, select the market form in the list which offers the best description.

*Market forms*    **A** Perfect competition
**B** Monopoly
**C** Oligopoly
**D** Monopolistic competition
**E** Monopsony

**(a)** A fairly large number of firms, each supplying branded footwear at very similar prices.
**(b)** A sole supplier of telecommunication services.
**(c)** A large number of farmers supplying carrots at identical prices.
**(d)** A few giant firms supplying the whole of the market for car tyres.
**(e)** A single buyer of coal-cutting equipment.
**(f)** A sole supplier of rail transport.

**2**    Table 9–1 presents some hypothetical concentration ratios and information about scale economies in a number of industries.

| Table 9–1 | Concentration and scale economies in Hypothetica | |
|---|---|---|
| **Industry** | **3-firm concentration ratio (CR)** | **Number of plants at min. efficient scale allowed by market size (NP)** |
| **A** | 100 | 1 |
| **B** | 11 | 221 |
| **C** | 81 | 3 |
| **D** | 49 | 5 |
| **E** | 21 | 195 |

**(a)** Which industry is most likely to be operated as a monopoly?
**(b)** Which industry(ies) would you expect to find operating under conditions of perfect competition?
**(c)** In which industry(ies) would conditions be conducive to oligopoly?
**(d)** In which industry(ies) would oligopoly be unlikely to arise? Explain your answer.

**3**    Which of the following characteristics are typical of an industry operating under monopolistic competition in long-run equilibrium? (*Note*: There may be more than one valid response.)

**(a)** Individual firms in the industry make only small monopoly profits.
**(b)** Individual firms in the industry would be keen to sell more output at the existing market price.
**(c)** There is product differentiation.
**(d)** Each firm faces a downward-sloping demand curve.
**(e)** Firms operate below full capacity output.
**(f)** Firms maximize profits where marginal cost equals marginal revenue.
**(g)** There is collusion among firms in the industry.
**(h)** The profits accruing to firms are just sufficient to cover the opportunity cost of capital employed.

**4**    Figure 9–1 shows a profit-maximizing firm in monopolistic competition.

**Figure 9–1**    A firm in monopolistic competition

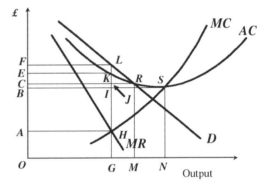

**(a)** How much output will be produced by the firm?
**(b)** At what price will the output be sold?
**(c)** Will the firm make supernormal profits in this situation? If so, identify their extent.
**(d)** Would you consider this to be a long-run or short-run equilibrium for the firm?
**(e)** Explain your answer to (*d*) and describe how the situation might differ in the 'other run'.

**5**    In an oligopolistic market, which of the following conditions tend to favour collusion and which are more likely to encourage non-cooperation?

| Influence | Encourages collusion | Favours non-cooperation |
|---|---|---|
| | **(Tick one column)** | |
| Barriers to entry | | |
| Product is non-standard | | |
| Demand and costs are stable | | |
| Collusion is legal | | |
| Secrecy about price and output | | |

| Collusion is illegal |
| --- |
| Easy communication of price and output |
| Standard product |

**6**   Figure 9–2 shows the demand curve (*DD*) for the output of an individual firm, as perceived by that firm. The firm is currently producing the amount *OQ* at a price *OP*. Assess the likely validity of each of the following inferences that may be drawn concerning conditions in the industry of which this firm is a part.

**Figure 9–2**   A firm's perceived demand curve

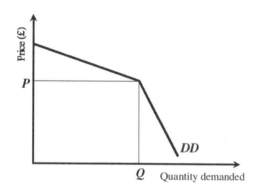

(a)   The firm may be slow to change price, even if faced by a change in cost conditions.

(b)   The firm is a discriminating monopolist, charging different prices in two separated markets.

(c)   The industry is a non-cooperative oligopoly in which the individual firm must take into consideration the likely behaviour of the few rival firms.

(d)   The firm faces production difficulties at levels of output above *OQ* as a result of labour shortages.

**7**   Suppose that there are two firms (**X** and **Y**) operating in a market, each of which can choose to produce either 'high' or 'low' output. Table 9–2 summarizes the range of possible outcomes of the

firms' decisions in a single time period. Imagine that you are taking the decisions for firm **X**:

(a)   If firm **Y** produces 'low', what level of output would maximize your profit in this time period?

(b)   If you (firm **X**) produce 'high', what level of output would maximize profits for firm **Y**?

(c)   If firm **Y** produces 'high', what level of output would maximize your profit in this time period?

(d)   Under what circumstances would you decide to produce 'low'?

(e)   Suppose you enter into an agreement with firm **Y** that you both will produce 'low': what measures could you adopt to ensure that **Y** keeps to the agreement?

(f)   What measures could you adopt to convince **Y** that you will keep to the agreement?

(g)   Suppose that the profit combinations are the same as in Table 9–2, except that if both firms produce 'high' each firm makes a loss of 8. Does this affect the analysis?

**8**   Which of the following entry barriers are 'innocent' and which are strategic?

(a)   Exploiting the benefits of large-scale production.

(b)   Undertaking a research and development (R&D) project to develop new techniques and products.

(c)   Holding a patent on a particular product.

(d)   Producing a range of similar products under different brand names.

(e)   Extensive multi-media advertising.

(f)   Installing more machinery than is required for normal (or current) levels of production.

(g)   Holding an absolute cost advantage.

**9**   A crucial characteristic of a monopoly is the existence of barriers to entry. One type of such barrier is patent protection. Suppose the monopolist's patent on a good expires. How is the market likely to adjust?

**10**   Think about some of the firms that operate in your own neighbourhood. Classify them according to market structure – i.e. as perfect competition, monopoly, oligopoly or monopolistic competition.

**11**   Figure 9–3 shows the reaction functions for a Cournot oligopoly.

| Table 9–2   The Prisoner's Dilemma game | | | | |
| --- | --- | --- | --- | --- |
| **Profits** | **Firm Y chooses:**   **High output** | | | |
| | **Low output** | | | |
| | | **X** | **Y** | **X**   **Y** |
| Firm **X** chooses:   Low output | | 15 | 15 | 2   20 |
| High output | | 20 | 2 | 8   8 |

**Figure 9–3**　Reaction functions for a Cournot oligopoly

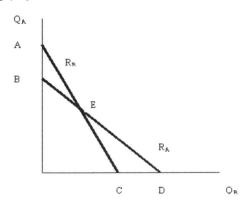

(a)　The reaction function of firm *A*, $R_A$, indicates that there is what type of relationship between the output of firm *B* and the output of firm *A*?

(b)　Is the relationship between firm *A*'s and firm *B*'s output one for one?

(c)　Which point on the diagram depicts a Nash equilibrium?

(d)　If firm *A* suddenly acquired new productive technology, how would Fig. 9–3 change?

(e)　What would a reaction function look like for a perfectly competitive firm?

**12**　Can you think of any examples in your own lives where first mover advantages might apply?

## True/False

**1**　The firm under imperfect competition has some influence over price, evidenced by the downward-sloping demand curve for its product.

**2**　A key aspect of an oligopolistic market is that firms cannot act independently of each other.

**3**　An industry where diseconomies of scale set in at a low level of output is likely to be a monopoly.

**4**　A firm in long-run equilibrium under monopolistic competition produces at an output below the technically optimum point of production.

**5**　A feature of the kinked oligopoly demand curve model is that price may be stable when costs for a single firm change, but may change rapidly when the whole industry is faced with a change in cost conditions.

**6**　Firms under oligopoly face kinked demand curves.

**7**　A player holding a dominant strategy always wins.

**8**　Cartels may be made workable if their members are prepared to enter into binding pre-commitments.

**9**　A cartel member's announcement of intent to adopt a punishment strategy will maintain a cartel.

**10**　A monopolist always maximizes profits by setting marginal cost equal to marginal revenue.

**11**　Free exit from a market implies that there are no sunk or irrecoverable costs.

**12**　Fixed costs may artificially increase scale economies and help to deter entry by firms new to the industry.

**13**　The equilibrium under a Bertrand type oligopoly is identical to that under perfect competition.

**14**　In a Cournot type model the two players will share the market equally.

**15**　A firm's reaction function is based on the potential actions of its rivals, not is own costs.

## Economics in action

### EU probes memory price-fixing charge

(Adapted from an article by Michael Kanellos, CNET News.com, 2 March 2004)

The European Union is investigating whether the world's largest memory makers conspired to raise chip prices in 2001. The probe focuses on whether memory manufacturers such as Micron, Samsung and Infineon colluded. In 2001, the PC market was shrinking, but prices for DRAM and double data rate DRAM were skyrocketing. Even in good times, memory prices often drop because of excess manufacturing capacity worldwide. At various times in the past five years, some memory manufacturers have had to sell chips at below manufacturing costs.

### Questions

**1**　What factors within the memory chip market are likely to promote collusion?

**2**　How might a PC manufacturer combat a memory chip cartel?

## Questions for thought

**1**    Exercise **8** listed various sorts of entry barriers. Can you think of examples of British industries in which they appear to be operative?

**2**    Figure 9–4 shows the trading conditions for a two-firm cartel. Panels *(a)* and *(b)* show, respectively, the conditions facing the two firms *A* and *B*; panel *(c)* shows the combined cartel position. $D = ARc$ in panel *(c)* shows the market demand curve, and *MRc* is the associated marginal revenue curve. Notice that firm *A* has a cost advantage over firm *B*.

(a)    If the two firms collude to maximize profits in the combined market, what joint output level will they choose?

(b)    At what price will the cartel sell the good?

(c)    If each firm accepts the cartel *MR* level, how much output will each produce?

(d)    Identify profit levels in each of the firms.

(e)    Suppose that firm *B* imagined that it was a price-taker at the price set by the cartel. What would be its perceived profit-maximizing output level?

(f)    If firm *B* were to set output at this level, what would be the effect on market price?

**3**    For many years the only information that tobacco manufacturers were allowed to include in their advertising was that smoking is harmful. Why should they bother?

**4**    If oligopoly is so common in the real world, and perfect competition is so rare, why do we bother with the theory of perfect competition?

**Figure 9–4**  A two-firm cartel

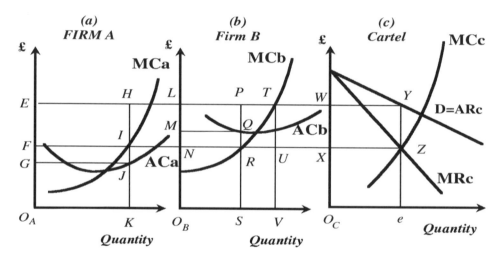

# chapter ten

# The labour market

## Learning outcomes

**By the end of this chapter, you should understand:**

- A firm's demand for inputs in the long run and in the short run

- Marginal value product, marginal revenue product and marginal cost of a factor

- The industry demand for labour

- Labour supply decisions

- Transfer earnings and economic rent

- Labour market equilibrium and disequilibrium

- How minimum wages affect employment

- Isoquants and the choice of production technique

## Key learning blocks

The labour market is one of the most important markets in an economy and it is perhaps the one that is most different from all other markets. In order to develop your understanding of this key market you will need to be familiar with the following issues:

1. What factors determine a firm's demand for labour?

2. What factors determine an individual's willingness to work?

3. Why might labour markets struggle to return to equilibrium?

The textbook covers each of these topics in detail and the exercises that follow will help to develop your understanding.

# Important concepts and technical terms

## Match each lettered concept with the appropriate numbered phrase:

**a** Insider-outsider distinctions

**b** Efficiency wage theory

**c** Economic rent

**d** Derived demand

**e** Poverty trap

**f** Minimum wage

**g** Participation rate

**h** Involuntary unemployment

**i** Equalizing wage differential

**j** Transfer earnings

**k** Marginal cost of labour

**l** Labour mobility

**1** The demand for a factor of production – not for its own sake, but for the output produced by the factor.

**2** A condition that may result in effective barriers to entering employment in existing firms.

**3** The monetary compensation for differential non-monetary characteristics of the same job in different industries, so that workers with a particular skill have no incentive to move between industries.

**4** The cost of an additional unit of labour.

**5** A legal constraint imposed on firms establishing the lowest wage payable to workers.

**6** The minimum payments required to induce a factor to work in a particular job.

**7** The ability of workers to leave low-paying jobs and join other industries where rates of pay are higher.

**8** A condition that occurs when workers are prepared to work at the going wage rate but cannot find jobs.

**9** The extra payment a factor receives over and above that required to induce the factor to supply its services in that use.

**10** The percentage of a given group of the population of working age which decides to enter the labour force.

**11** A theory which argues that firms may pay existing workers a wage which on average exceeds the wage for which workers as a whole are prepared to work.

**12** A situation in which unskilled workers are offered such a low wage that they lose out by working.

### Exercises

**1** Table 10–1 reproduces some information used (and calculated) in Exercise 7 of Chapter 8: we are now in a position to carry the analysis further.

A new column in Table 10–1 shows the price which must be charged by the firm to sell the output produced. The firm is a 'wage-taker' and must pay £280 per unit of labour input however much labour is hired. The only other cost to the firm is capital, for which the firm incurs a fixed cost of £200.

**(a)** Calculate the marginal value product of labour (*MVPL*).

**(b)** Calculate the marginal revenue product of labour (*MRPL*).

**(c)** Plot *MVPL* and *MRPL* curves.

**(d)** At what level of labour input will profits be maximized in the short run?

**(e)** Calculate the level of short-run profits.

**Table 10–1    Output and labour input**

| Labour input (workers/week) | Output (goods/week) | Marginal physical product of labour (MPL) | Price (£) | Total revenue | Marginal revenue per unit output | Marginal value product of labour (MVPL) | Marginal revenue product of labour (MRPL) |
|---|---|---|---|---|---|---|---|
| 0 | 0 | | | | | | |
| 1 | 35 | 35 | 12 | | | | |
| 2 | 80 | 45 | 10 | | | | |
| 3 | 122 | 42 | 8 | | | | |
| 4 | 156 | 34 | 6 | | | | |
| 5 | 177 | 21 | 4 | | | | |
| 6 | 180 | 3 | 2 | | | | |

**2** Figure 10–1 shows marginal cost, marginal product of labour curves and the wage rate for a firm. Identify the profit-maximizing level of output for each of the following firms:

(a) A perfectly competitive firm facing a perfectly competitive situation in the labour market.
(b) A firm having no influence on the price of its output but acting as a monopsonist in the labour market.
(c) A firm facing a downward-sloping demand curve for its product and acting as a monopsonist in the labour market.
(d) A firm facing downward-sloping demand for its product but a perfectly competitive labour market.
(e) What is the effect of monopoly and monopsony power on the firm's labour demand?

**Figure 10–1** Monopoly and monopsony power

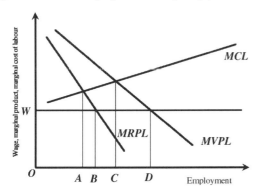

**3** Figure 10–2 shows George's indifference curves between income and leisure. Suppose that George faces no fixed costs of working and receives £50 unearned income whether or not he chooses to work.

**Figure 10–2** George's supply of labour

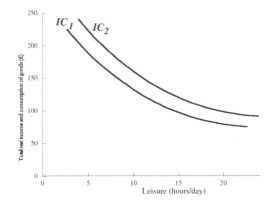

(a) Add to the diagram his budget line if he can work at the rate of £5 per hour.
(b) How many hours will George choose to work?
(c) Suppose the wage rate increases to £7.50, show how this affects the budget line.
(d) How many hours will George now choose to work?
(e) Does George regard leisure as a normal or an inferior good?

**4** An industry's demand for clerical workers is shown in Fig. 10–3, together with its supply curve.

**Figure 10–3** Equilibrium in an industry labour market

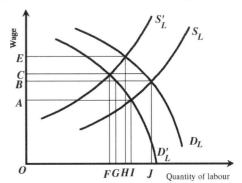

(a) Initially the industry demand curve is $D_L$ and it faces the supply curve $S_L$. What is the equilibrium wage and employment level?

(b) Suppose the industry faces a decline in the demand for its output: what would be the new equilibrium wage and employment level? Explain your answer.

(c) Beginning again at $D_L$, $S_L$, the industry now finds that an increase in the demand for clerical workers in another industry has affected their wages elsewhere. How would the equilibrium wage and employment level be affected for this industry?

(d) From $D_L$, $S_L$ the industry demand for labour moves to $D'_L$, but the clerical workers' trade union resists a wage cut, maintaining the wage rate at its original level. Identify the nature and extent of the disequilibrium.

**5** Figure 10–4 represents a monopsonistic labour market in which employees are not organized into a union.

**Figure 10–4** A monopsonistic labour market

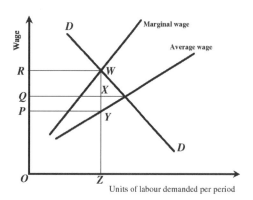

(a) What is the wage rate that will be paid by the employer?

(b) What is the employer's wage bill?

(c) What is the surplus that accrues to the employer?

(d) What would the wage rate have been if the employer had not been a monopsonist, but was a 'wage-taker' in the labour market?

**6** Figure 10–5 illustrates the demand and supply situation in a particular labour market. Suppose the market to be in equilibrium:

(a) Which area represents the amount of transfer earnings?

(b) Identify the amount of economic rent.

(c) How would the relative size of economic rent and transfer earnings differ if the supply of labour were more inelastic?

**Figure 10–5** Supply and demand in a labour market

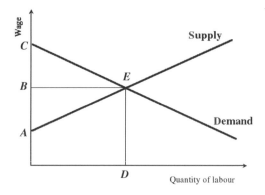

**Figure 10–6** An individual's labour supply

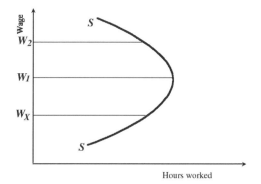

**7** Figure 10–6 shows the amount of labour supplied by an individual at different wage rates. Which of the following statements concerning the reaction to a move from $W_1$ to $W_2$ is *not* valid?

(a) The individual's employer fails to induce an increase in hours worked by this move.

(b) The firm substitutes capital for labour.

(c) The employer could have induced the same amount of hours worked by offering a wage rate $W_x$.

(d) The individual demands more leisure.

(e) In the choice between income and leisure, the 'income effect' dominates the 'substitution effect'.

**8** A firm is seeking the cost-minimizing method of producing a good. Various combinations of labour and capital can be used to produce a particular level of output, as shown in Table 10–2.

(a) Draw the isoquants for these three levels of output.

(b) Draw the isocost line showing the combinations of capital and labour input which the firm could purchase for £1000 if capital costs £20 per unit and labour costs £2 per unit.

| Table 10–2 | Production techniques available to a firm | | | | |
| --- | --- | --- | --- | --- | --- |
| 10 units of output capital | Labour | 20 units of output capital | Labour | 30 units of output capital | Labour |
| 35 | 80 | 42 | 100 | 45 | 170 |
| 28 | 100 | 30 | 150 | 35 | 210 |
| 20 | 134 | 25 | 170 | 30 | 230 |
| 16 | 160 | 20 | 200 | 27 | 245 |
| 13 | 200 | 16 | 240 | 21 | 295 |
| 10 | 248 | 12 | 300 | 18 | 350 |
| 7 | 300 | 10 | 350 | 16 | 400 |
| 5 | 350 | 8 | 400 | 14 | 450 |

(c) What is the maximum amount of output which the firm could produce in these conditions? How much capital and labour is used in producing this output?

(d) Draw the isocost line if the firm still spends £1000, but the cost of labour increases to £3 per unit.

(e) What is the maximum output which could now be produced? How much capital and labour would now be used?

(f) Calculate the percentage change in the use of capital and labour in (e) compared with (c). Is this what you would expect to happen?

(g) How much output could be produced by the firm if it spends only £800? (Capital still costs £20 per unit and labour £3 per unit.)

**9** Which of the following may cause involuntary unemployment?

(a) Minimum wage legislation intended to protect the lower-paid.

(b) The payment of higher-than-average wage rates by employers wishing to discourage quits.

(c) Economies of scale.

(d) Entry barriers confronting outsiders being implemented by insiders.

(e) Action taken by a strong trade union to increase rates of pay for its members.

**10** Examine theories which have been advanced to explain inflexibility in a labour market. Which of these do you find plausible in the current UK situation?

## True/False

**1** The labour market ensures that a helicopter pilot is paid the same money wage in whatever industry he is employed.

**2** Following an increase in labour cost, a firm will employ more capital input.

**3** For a firm operating under perfect competition in both output and labour markets, profits are maximized by employing labour up to the point where the marginal value product of labour equals the money wage rate.

**4** For a firm operating under perfect competition in both output and labour markets, profits are maximized by employing labour up to the point where the marginal physical product of labour equals the real wage rate.

**5** A firm with monopsony power is not a price-taker in its input markets.

**6** For a firm with a downward-sloping demand curve, the marginal revenue product of labour is greater than the marginal value product of labour.

**7** For a competitive industry, the industry labour demand curve is the horizontal aggregation of the firms' MVPL curves.

**8** An individual's labour supply curve is always upward-sloping – a higher real wage induces the individual to work longer hours.

**9** The participation rate is higher for unmarried than for married women.

**10** Labour mobility provides a crucial link between industry labour markets.

**11** Economic rent reflects differences in individuals' supply decisions, not in their productivity.

**12** Involuntary unemployment arises from inflexibility in the labour market.

## Economics in action

### Want to know what you're really worth?

(Adapted from an article in *The Guardian*, 8 May 2004)

Finding out whether the person sitting at the next desk is being paid more than you isn't always easy. Headline salaries in job adverts were once the first and last stop on the evidence trail. But some recruitment ads now omit salary details while others list a vague salary band. Plus, you may work in an area that recruits rarely or you may find that a comparable job to yours in another organization has a different title, making it difficult to pinpoint a position matching your own.

Janine Broom searched a website by her occupation as a risk analyst and by her location, and was amazed that people doing the same job as her in a sister company were earning up to £10 000 more. She quickly negotiated a pay rise in line with the other workers.

## Questions

**1** What was Janine Broom's economic rent after negotiating her pay rise?

**2** What evidence is there to suggest that the marginal revenue product theory of labour demand and wage determination is flawed?

## Questions for thought

**1** In Chapter 8 we saw that a firm operating under perfect competition would maximize profits in the short run by producing at the point where $SMC = MR$. Now it transpires that the firm should employ labour up to the point where $W = MVPL$. Can you reconcile these two methods?

**2** Figure 10–7 shows Helen's indifference curves between income and leisure. Helen receives £10 per day unearned income only if she does not work. She never chooses to work more than 12 hours per day, so the diagram focuses on only the relevant 12 hours.

(a) Mark on the diagram the point where Helen would be if she chooses not to work.

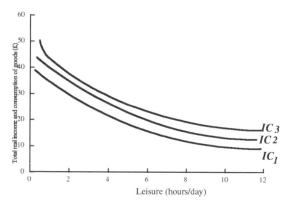

**Figure 10–7**   Labour supply with overtime

(b) Add to the diagram Helen's budget line if she can work at £2.50 per hour.

(c) Assuming Helen has complete flexibility on hours of work, how many hours will she choose to work at that rate of pay?

(d) Amend the budget line to conform to a situation in which Helen earns 'treble time' for hours worked in excess of eight hours a day.

(e) How many hours will Helen now choose to work?

**3** Figure 10–8 shows a production function for a good: *1X*, *2X*, *3X*, etc. are isoquants showing the various combinations of capital and labour that can be used to produce different levels of output of the good; *C0*, *C1*, *C2*, etc. are isocost lines, whose slope represents the current relative prices of capital and labour.

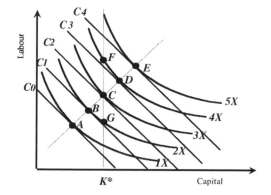

**Figure 10–8**   Isoquants and isocost lines

**(a)** Which isocost line represents the least-cost method of producing three units of output (*3X*)?

**(b)** Suppose that in the short run the amount of capital input available is fixed at K*. Consider how labour input must change if output is increased from *2X* to *3X* and then to *4X*. What does this suggest for the return to labour?

**(c)** Given the technology embedded in the isoquants, the path *ABCDE* shows least-cost ways of producing different output levels under the assumptions that both capital and labour inputs can be varied and that relative factor prices remain unchanged. What do these points imply for the shape of the long-run average cost curve?

# chapter eleven

# Different types of labour

## Learning outcomes

By the end of this chapter, you should understand:

- The results of differences in workers' abilities
- Investment in human capital
- How signalling reveals differences in workers
- Forms of discrimination
- How trade unions raise wages and improve conditions for workers

## Key learning blocks

The labour market is not homogeneous. That is, we see individuals with different sets of skills and firms paying different levels of wages. We need to have some understanding of these issues. As an initial analysis three central areas are explored:

1. *Education* may increase the productivity of labour and hence its value to employers and employees.

2. *Discrimination* by employees may diminish the value of particular workers to employers.

3. Trade unions may restrict the *supply* of particular workers, thus pushing up the price.

Now use the textbook and the questions that follow to build your understanding of the issues associated with each area.

# Important concepts and technical terms

## Match each lettered concept with the appropriate numbered phrase:

**a** Human capital

**b** Cost-benefit analysis

**c** Trade union

**d** Firm-specific human capital

**e** Signalling

**f** Compensating wage differentials

**g** Age–earnings profile

**h** General human capital

**i** Discrimination

**j** Closed shop

**1** A procedure for making long-run decisions by comparing the present value of the costs with the present value of the benefits.

**2** The stock of expertise accumulated by a worker, valued for its income-earning potential in the future.

**3** A situation in which a group of workers is treated differently from other groups because of the personal characteristics of that group, regardless of qualifications.

**4** Differences in wage rates reflecting non-monetary aspects of working conditions.

**5** An agreement that all a firm's workers will be members of a trade union.

**6** The skills which a worker acquires that can be transferred to work for another firm.

**7** The theory that educational qualifications indicate a worker's worth even when not directly relevant to his or her productivity.

**8** The skills which a worker acquires that cannot be transferred to work for another firm.

**9** A schedule showing how the earnings of a worker or group of workers vary with age.

**10** A worker organization designed to affect pay and working conditions.

## Exercises

**1** Ian, a teenager, is considering whether or not to undertake further education. Having studied A level Economics, he decides to apply cost-benefit analysis to evaluate his decision. After applying appropriate discount rates, he arrives at the following valuations (the units are notional):

| Books, fees | Present value |
|---|---|
| | 3000 |
| Benefits (non-monetary) of student life | 2500 |
| Income forgone (net) | 7000 |
| Additional future expected income due to qualification | 9000 |

**(a)** Given these valuations, would Ian decide upon further education?

**(b)** How would Ian's calculations be affected if he were not confident of passing his examinations at the end of his course?

**(c)** Ian's friend Joanne shares Ian's views about the economic value of education, but is much less keen on the idea of university life. How would her calculations differ?

**(d)** Keith subscribes to the 'eat, drink, and be merry, for tomorrow we die' philosophy, and is keen to enjoy life in the present. How would his calculations differ from Ian's?

**2** Below are figures showing how pre-tax earnings vary with age for three groups of male workers in full-time employment in the economy of Hypothetica. Average gross weekly earnings are measured in Hypothetical dollars.

| Group | A | B | C |
|---|---|---|---|
| Age: | | | |
| 20–29 | 236 | 180 | 200 |
| 30–39 | 310 | 200 | 250 |
| 40–49 | 370 | 195 | 280 |
| 50–64 | 425 | 185 | 235 |

(a) Plot the age–earnings profile for each group of workers.

(b) The distinguishing characteristic of each group is the level of highest educational attainment. Using your knowledge of similar groups in the UK, associate each of the following with the appropriate age–earnings profile:

(i) Workers with A levels or their equivalent.

(ii) Workers with no formal qualifications.

(iii) Workers with a university degree or equivalent.

**3**    In the economy of Elsewhere, the following observations are made. Which of them would provide strong evidence of discrimination?

(a) Women earn less than men.

(b) Female trainee accountants earn less than male trainee accountants.

(c) Black workers earn less than white workers.

(d) Black machine tool-fitters earn less than white machine tool-fitters.

**4**    Figure 11–1 shows the position in a labour market. *OA* represents the economy-wide wage rate. *DD* is the initial demand curve for labour.

(a) Identify the initial equilibrium for the industry.

(b) Suppose that a trade union restricts the supply of labour to *OE*. What is the equilibrium wage in the industry?

**Figure 11–1**  Unions, wages and employment

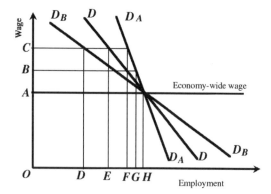

(c) In the long run, this industry faces increased competition from overseas suppliers, who face lower labour costs. Which of the demand curves in Fig. 11–1 might represent the industry's new (derived) demand for labour?

(d) What is the new equilibrium for the industry?

(e) What wage rate would the union need to accept to maintain employment at *OE*?

**5**    Data on wages, salaries and earnings all seem to indicate that in the labour force as a whole, men tend to receive higher pay than women. Which of the following may contribute to this overall earnings differential?

(a) Female workers are more likely to work part-time.

(b) Men work in different industries and occupations.

(c) Companies promote women more slowly and offer them less training.

(d) Women choose different subjects at school.

(e) Fewer women choose to undertake higher education.

(f) Women are biologically different from men.

(g) Employers discriminate against women.

**6**    In some professions, it is necessary to undertake several years of training in order to qualify for entry. However, the returns to such training are perceived to be high in terms of future earnings potential.

(a) What is the opportunity cost of undertaking professional training?

(b) How is this likely to be seen relative to the potential returns?

(c) If the manufacturing sector of the economy is in relative decline, and the economy is also in recession, how will this affect the demand for professional training?

(d) Examine the long-term prospects for earnings in the professions.

**7**    Explain how each of the following situations may influence the bargaining position of a trade union in negotiating with employers:

(a) There is excess demand for labour.

(b) There is a 'closed shop'.

(c) The marginal revenue product of labour is less than the wage rate.

(d) Unemployment is at an historically high level.

(e) The demand for labour is highly inelastic.

(f) The union faces a monopsony buyer of labour.

**Table 11–1**  Estimated rates of return to education

| Country group | Social return | | Private return | |
|---|---|---|---|---|
| | Secondary | Higher | Secondary | Higher |
| Africa | 17 | 13 | 26 | 32 |
| Asia | 15 | 13 | 15 | 18 |
| Latin America | 18 | 16 | 23 | 23 |
| Industrial | 11 | 9 | 12 | 12 |

*Source: George Psacharopoulos, 'Education and development: a review', World Bank Research Observer, 3(1), 1988.*

**8**  Table 11–1 shows estimated private and social rates of return to education at different levels in various parts of the world.

(a) How do these rates of return compare with those of other types of investment?

(b) Why should the rate of return be so much higher for some parts of the world?

(c) At what level of education are private returns maximized?

(d) At what level of education are social returns maximized?

(e) How is this apparent conflict likely to be resolved?

(f) Will all groups in society perceive these returns in the same way?

## True/False

**1**  The human capital approach assumes that wage differentials reflect differences in the productivity of different workers.

**2**  Workers in firms receiving general training will be offered high but shallow age–earnings profiles.

**3**  Reading Classics at university does nothing to improve productivity; it is more profitable to leave school and go straight into industry.

**4**  Free schooling between 16 and 18 means that children from poor families can stay on in education as easily as children from wealthy families.

**5**  The perceived return from higher education is less for women than for men, so fewer women than men decide to invest in higher education.

**6**  Black workers earn less than white workers; therefore employers are racist.

**7**  Differences in the occupational structure of the employment of men and women do not suffice to explain differences in earnings.

**8**  By 1980, more than two-thirds of the civilian labour force in the UK belonged to trade unions.

**9**  Since many low-paid workers belong to a trade union, this proves that unions have little effect on improving pay and conditions for their members.

**10**  The largest rise in wages would be achieved by restricting labour supply in the industry where the demand for labour was most inelastic.

**11**  The UK is the most strike-prone economy in the world.

## Economics in action

### CV fibbers warning for employers

(Adapted from BBC News Online, 14 May 2004)

Employers are being warned to be on their guard as most people lie in their job applications, a survey has found. Research shows two-thirds of more than 3000 CVs submitted by applicants contained inaccuracies. They ranged from gaps in employment to outright lies about qualifications and fraud committed against past bosses. Women in their early 30s were the worst offenders with 77 per cent of CVs showing discrepancies, while men in their early 20s were the most honest group.

Under 'Employment', people might say they left a project when they were made redundant, or worked somewhere they did not. In their personal details, applicants sometimes concealed previous addresses because of court judgements registered against them. And concerning education, it was found: 'There is a great temptation to inflate their academic record.'

**Questions**

**1** Explain how the article highlights the issues of informational asymmetry and adverse selection.

**2** Why are women in their early 30s likely to be the worst offenders?

## Questions for thought

**1** Would society find it worthwhile to invest in a higher education system if degree training provides only a signalling device and has no effect on the productivity of workers?

**2** If strikes benefit neither employers nor employees, why do they ever happen?

**3** A firm that has been operating without trade unions becomes unionized. Is it necessarily the case that employment in that firm will fall?

**4** We have shown equilibrium in a labour market in Fig. 11–2.

It has been argued that a trade union may attempt to gain higher wages for its members by restricting employment. How might the union select the desired wage–employment combination? (*Hint*: Try to think of the trade union as a monopoly seller of labour, and look back to the analysis of monopoly in Chapter 8 to see how it could be applied in this case.)

**5** Suppose there is a significant structural change in an economy, away from manufacturing activity and towards services. What effect would you expect this to have on the gender balance of the labour force and the level of unemployment?

**Figure 11–2**  Equilibrium in a labour market

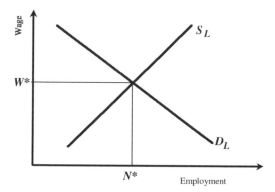

# chapter twelve

# Factor markets and income distribution

## Learning outcomes

**By the end of this chapter, you should understand:**

- The markets for capital and land
- How incomes of factors are determined
- Functional and personal distributions of income
- Flows over time and stocks at a point in time
- The markets for capital services and for new capital assets
- The concept of present value
- Nominal and real interest rates
- How saving and investment determine the real interest rate
- How land is allocated between competing uses

## Key learning blocks

**This chapter examines the employment of productive capital. The central issues which you need to understand are:**

1. What determines the price of capital?
2. What determines the demand for capital?
3. What factors influence the market equilibrium for capital?

The textbook covers each of these issues and the exercises that follow will help you to develop your understanding.

# Important concepts and technical terms

## Match each lettered concept with the appropriate numbered phrase:

**a** Land

**b** Personal income distribution

**c** Physical capital

**d** Capital–labour ratio

**e** Asset price

**f** Wage–rental ratio

**g** Required rental

**h** Nominal rate of interest

**i** Saving

**j** Financial capital

**k** Real rate of interest

**l** Present value

**m** Opportunity cost of capital

**n** Functional income distribution

**1** The stock of produced goods that contribute to the production of other goods and services.

**2** The factor of production that nature supplies.

**3** The value today of a sum of money due at some time in the future.

**4** The difference between current income and current consumption.

**5** The rate of return available on funds in their best alternative use: may be represented by the real interest rate.

**6** Shows the division of national income between the different factors of production.

**7** The return on a loan measured as the increase in goods that can be purchased, not as the increase in the money value of the loan fund.

**8** A measure of relative factor prices: the price of labour relative to the price of capital.

**9** Shows how national income is divided between different individuals, regardless of the factor services from which these individuals earn their income.

**10** Describes the relative importance of inputs of capital and labour in the production process.

**11** The sum for which a capital asset can be purchased outright.

**12** The return on a loan measured in money terms.

**13** Assets such as money or bank deposits which may be used to buy factors of production.

**14** The rental rate that just allows the owner of capital to cover the opportunity cost of owning it.

## Exercises

**1** Identify each of the following as being either a 'stock' or a 'flow':

**(a)** Vans owned by Rent-a-Van Limited.
**(b)** Land available for planting wheat.
**(c)** Use of truck for delivery.
**(d)** Railway lines.
**(e)** A TV programme as viewed by the consumer.
**(f)** Use of office space.

**2** A 10 per cent government bond with a nominal value of £100 sells on the stock exchange for £62.50.

**(a)** What is the prevailing rate of interest?
**(b)** What would the rate of interest be if the price of the bond were £75?
**(c)** If the rate of interest fell to 8 per cent, for what price would you expect the bond to sell?

**3** Lucy has £100 to save or spend. If she loans out the money she will receive £112 in a year's time. Inflation is ocurring at 14 per cent p.a.

**(a)** What is the nominal rate of interest which Lucy faces?
**(b)** What is the real rate of interest?
**(c)** Financially, would Lucy be advised to save or spend?
**(d)** How would your answer be affected if the inflation rate were 10 per cent, with the nominal interest rate at the same level?

**4** A machine is expected to be productive for three years, bringing earnings of £2000 in each year and being worth £6000 as scrap at the end of the third year. Using present value (PV) calculations, what would be the 'break-even' price for the machine if:

**(a)** The interest rate is 8 per cent?
**(b)** The interest rate is 10 per cent?
**(c)** The interest rate is 8 per cent and it is realized that no account has been taken of inflation, which is expected to be 7 per cent p.a.?

**5** An economy has two sectors: agriculture and industry. Figure 12–1 shows their demand schedules for land ($DA_1$ and $DI$ respectively). $SS$ represents the total fixed supply of land.

**Figure 12–1** Allocating land between alternative uses

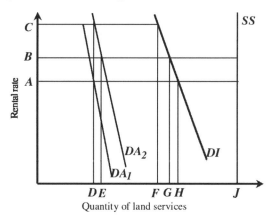

**(a)** Identify the equilibrium rental rate and each sector's demand for land.

Suppose that the government is concerned about the level of food imported into the economy and decides to encourage domestic food production by subsidizing agricultural land. This has the effect of shifting the demand curve for agricultural land to $DA_2$.

**(b)** How will land be allocated between agriculture and industry in the short run?
**(c)** What will be the rental rates in the two sectors in the short run?
**(d)** What will be the equilibrium position in the long run?

**6** A firm is considering the purchase of a piece of capital equipment, to be funded by a bank loan. (For simplicity, assume that both capital good and loan last for ever.) The cost of the equipment is £25 000 and the interest on the bank loan is fixed at 10 per cent p.a. Maintenance and depreciation amount to 12 per cent of the cost of the machine each year. Inflation is occurring at an annual rate of 8 per cent.

**(a)** What is the required rental on the capital equipment?
**(b)** What would be the required rental if inflation increased to 10 per cent p.a.?

**7** Figure 12–2 shows the demand for capital services and short- and long-run supply curves. Suppose that workers in the industry agree to accept a wage cut.

**Figure 12–2** Capital adjustment

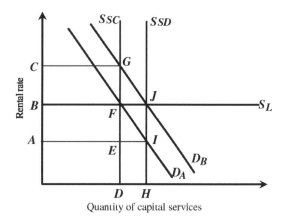

Quantity of capital services

**(a)** Identify the initial equilibrium position before the wage cut is implemented.
**(b)** What does the rental rate here represent – i.e. how is it determined?
**(c)** Identify the short-run position after the wage cut.
**(d)** Can this position be sustained? If not, why not?
**(e)** What is the long-run equilibrium position?
**(f)** How do we normally describe the adjustment process that has taken place between (c) and (e)?

**8**    Which of the following statements could validly be applied to the UK?

**(a)**    There has been little change in the shares of factors of production in pre-tax earnings since the 1980s.
**(b)**    Labour receives the greatest portion of national income.
**(c)**    Wealth is less equally distributed than income.
**(d)**    Capital stock grew much more rapidly than the labour force between 1981 and 1996.
**(e)**    Inequality in the distribution of wealth contributes to inequality in the distribution of income.

**9**    Table 12–1 shows information concerning the distribution of 'original' and 'disposable' household income in the UK in 2000. 'Original' income represents income before account is taken of any taxes, benefits, etc. 'Disposable' income adds in transfer payments and deducts direct tax payments. Complete columns (5) and (6) of Table 12–1 to show amounts of income accruing to the bottom 20, 40, 60, etc. per cent of households.

Economists sometimes try to illustrate such data on distribution using 'Lorenz curves'. Construct a diagram plotting the figures from column (4) on the horizontal axis and those from column (5) on the vertical axis. Joining the points gives a Lorenz curve. The closer the curve to a straight line joining (0,0) to (100,100), the more even the distribution. Draw a second Lorenz curve using the figures in column (6): the difference between the two should give an impression of the redistributive effect of UK taxation and benefits.

In 1995 in Brazil, the poorest 20 per cent of the population received 2.5 per cent of income, the next 20 per cent received 5.7 per cent, the next 20 per cent, 9.9 per cent, the next 20 per cent, 17.7 per cent and

the richest 20 per cent received 64.2 per cent of total income. Construct a Lorenz curve showing this distribution and compare it with that for the UK. (Data are taken from the *World Development Report 1998/99*.)

**10**    Figure 12–3 shows an economy in equilibrium, with the single consumer choosing between current and future consumption.

**(a)**    Identify the equilibrium point.
**(b)**    How much is saved at this point?
**(c)**    If all current resources were invested in new capital goods, what would be the maximum attainable future consumption level?
**(d)**    How would you measure the rate of return on investment?
**(e)**    What determines the slope of the price line?

**Figure 12–3**    Current and future consumption

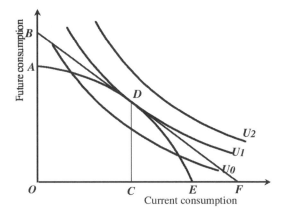

**11**    Back in Chapter 6, we saw that a consumer's reaction to a price change can be analysed in terms of *real income* and *substitution effects*. Explain how the same sort of decomposition can be used to analyse the effect on savings of a change in the interest rate. What

| **Table 12–1**    UK income distribution, 2000 | | | | | |
|---|---|---|---|---|---|
| **(1)** Proportion of households (%) | **(2)** Original income | **(3)** Disposable income | **(4)** Cumulative households | **(5)** Cumulative original income | **(6)** Percentages disposable income |
| Bottom 20 | 2 | 8 | 20 | | |
| Next 20 | 7 | 12 | 40 | | |
| Next 20 | 15 | 16 | 60 | | |
| Next 20 | 25 | 23 | 80 | | |
| Top 20 | 51 | 42 | 100 | | |
| *Source: Economic Trends.* | | | | | |

would you expect to be the net effect on savings of an increase in the interest rate?

**12** Consider a movement of a production possibility frontier (PPF) between current and future consumption. Which of the following factors would cause the new PPF to have a steeper slope at each output of current consumption? (*Note*: More than one answer may be valid.)

**(a)** An increase in thriftiness of members of society.
**(b)** An increase in the productivity of new capital equipment.
**(c)** A fall in the rate of interest.
**(d)** A rise in the rate of interest.
**(e)** An increase in investment.
**(f)** A technological break-through improving efficiency in production.

## True/False

**1** Tangible wealth includes land, machinery, factory buildings, vehicles and government bonds.

**2** Since people cannot be bought and sold, there can be no asset price for labour.

**3** The present value of a capital asset is the sum of future rental payments that asset will provide.

**4** Inflation makes nominal interest rates go up. This must reduce the present value of future income.

**5** The real interest rate can be negative.

**6** The flow of capital services can be varied in the long run but is rigidly fixed in the short run.

**7** Differences in rental rates can lead to the transfer of capital between industries or even nations.

**8** Equilibrium in the market for land demands that rents be equal in all sectors.

**9** The main feature distinguishing between the three factors of production (land, capital and labour) is the speed of adjustment of their supply.

**10** In the long run the supply of labour is less elastic than the supply of capital.

**11** Labour's share in UK national income increased markedly between 1981–89 and 1998.

**12** The distribution of wealth is even more unequal than that of income.

## Economics in action

### Wealth hotspots 'outside London'

(Adapted from BBC News Online, 7 July 2004)

The UK's top five areas for growth in high-earning residents are all outside the South East, a survey has found. The number of people earning more than £60 000 a year in High Peak in Derbyshire rose by 68 per cent last year. Monmouth, Cardiff North, Manchester Withington and Keighley also saw a huge increase in their number of top earners. Steven Mendel, a business development director for Barclays, said the UK's economic slowdown had not been matched by a slowdown in already affluent people getting richer.

Overall, 29 areas in England and Wales have more than 1 in 10 people earning over £60 000 a year, compared to only 1 in 8 in 2003. But in terms of absolute wealth – rather than growth – Kensington and Chelsea continues to have the highest proportion of residents in the top earning bracket.

### Questions

**1** Is High Peak or Chelsea and Kensington the UK wealth hotspot?

**2** Why do you think the rich keep getting richer?

## Questions for thought

**1** Distinguish between economic rent and transfer earnings. With reference to examples, explain what determines the economic rent received by factors of production.

**2** Examine the extent to which it is helpful to treat energy as a fourth factor of production.

# chapter thirteen

# Risk and information

## Learning outcomes

**By the end of this chapter, you should understand:**

- Risk-aversion and diminishing marginal utility
- Risk-pooling and risk-spreading
- How inside information leads to moral hazard and adverse selection
- How an asset return reflects its cash income and its capital gain (loss)
- How correlation of asset returns affects risk-pooling
- Asset market efficiency
- Spot and forward markets
- How hedging shifts the burden of risk

## Key learning blocks

*Risk* is an important issue in economics and particularly finance. In this chapter you are introduced to a number of basic ideas associated with risk and you need to develop your understanding around the following issues:

**1** Differing attitudes to risk such as risk-averse, risk-neutral or risk-lover.

**2** Reduction in risk through transfer to insurance companies.

**3** Reduction in risk via portfolio diversification and hedging.

The textbook explores the more complex issues which surround these core concepts and the exercises that follow will help to develop your understanding.

# Important concepts and technical terms

## Match each lettered concept with the appropriate numbered phrase:

**a** Risk-pooling

**b** Risk-neutral

**c** Beta

**d** Speculative bubble

**e** Hedgers

**f** Moral hazard

**g** Spot price

**h** Adverse selection

**i** Risk-averse

**j** Forward market

**k** Risk-sharing

**l** Theory of efficient markets

**m** Risk-lover

**n** Speculators

**1** A measurement of the extent to which a share's return moves with the return on the whole stock market.

**2** The reduction of uncertainty about the average outcome by spreading the risk across many individuals who independently face that risk.

**3** A view of a market as a sensitive processor of information, quickly responding to new information to adjust prices correctly.

**4** A person who will accept a bet even when a strict calculation reveals that the odds are unfavourable.

**5** A trader in a forward market who expects to earn profits by taking risks.

**6** The spreading of risk among insurance companies, thus reducing the stake of each individual company.

**7** A situation where the act of insuring increases the likelihood of the occurrence of the event against which insurance is taken out.

**8** A market in contracts made today for delivery of goods at a specified future date at a price agreed today.

**9** A person who ignores the dispersion of possible outcomes, but is concerned with the average outcome.

**10** A market in which everyone believes the price will rise tomorrow, even if the price has already risen a lot.

**11** Traders who use a forward market to reduce their risk by making contracts about future transactions.

**12** The price for immediate delivery of a commodity.

**13** A person who will refuse a fair gamble, requiring sufficiently favourable odds that the probable monetary profit outweighs the risk.

**14** The situation faced by insurance companies in which the people wishing to insure against a particular outcome are also those most likely to require a payoff.

## Exercises

**1** Maureen, Nora and Olga are each offered the opportunity of buying a sketch, allegedly by a famous artist, for £500. If genuine, the value of the sketch would be £1000; if phoney it would be totally worthless. There is a 50:50 chance of each alternative. Maureen rejects the idea outright, Nora jumps at the chance and Olga flips a coin to decide.

(a) Characterize each attitude to risk.

(b) Would you buy the sketch?

(c) What does this imply about your own attitude to risk?

(d) Would your attitude differ if you had recently won £1 million on the pools?

**2**    In which of the following circumstances are risks being pooled?

(a) Insurance for David Beckham's legs (or those of some other top footballer of your choice).
(b) Car insurance.
(c) Insurance for contents of a freezer.
(d) Insurance against an accident at a nuclear power station.
(e) Medical insurance for a holiday abroad.

**3**    Which of the following situations illustrate moral hazard, and which adverse selection?

(a) Paula never locks her car, knowing it is adequately insured.
(b) Having taken out life insurance in favour of his family, Quentin continues to smoke heavily.
(c) Rosemary takes out life insurance, knowing that her heavy smoking has given her terminal lung cancer.
(d) Having insured against rain, Simon makes advance payments to cricket stars for his Easter single-wicket competition.
(e) Tessa takes out extra health insurance shortly before going on a skiing holiday.

**4**    Suppose you wish to invest £200 in shares. Two industries, chemicals and computers, have shares on offer at £100 each. The return expected from the two industries are independent. In each case, there is a 50 per cent chance that returns will be good (£12) and a 50 per cent chance that returns will be poor (£6).

(a) If you buy only chemicals shares, and times are good, what return will you earn?
(b) If you buy only computers shares, and times are bad, what return will you earn?
(c) If you put all your funds in one industry, what is your average expected return?
(d) If you put all your funds in one industry, what is the chance of a poor return?
(e) What is your average return if you diversify?
(f) If you diversify, what is the chance of a poor return (i.e. the same level as in *(b)*)?

**5**    Match each lettered definition with the numbered term (suppose that contracts are established for one year hence and that today's date is 1 July 2005):

(a) The price of gold on 1 July 2005 for delivery and payment on 1 July 2005.
(b) The price in the forward market on 1 July 2005 at which gold is being traded for delivery and payment on 1 July 2006.
(c) Today's best guess about what the spot price will be on 1 July 2006.
(d) The price of gold being traded in the spot market on 1 July 2005.
(e) The differences between the expected future spot price and the current forward price.

(1) Risk premium.
(2) Future spot price.
(3) Today's spot price.
(4) Forward price.
(5) Expected future spot price.

**6**    Which of the following offers the best chance of a better-than-average return in the stock market?

(a) Careful reading of the financial press.
(b) Sticking a pin into the financial pages of the newspaper.
(c) Employing a financial adviser.
(d) Computer analysis of past share price movements.
(e) Being the first agent to react to news.

**7**    Which of the following statements is/are correct?

(a) A share with beta = 1 moves independently of the rest of the market.
(b) A share with a high beta moves with the market, but more sluggishly.
(c) A share with a negative beta decreases the riskiness of a portfolio.
(d) A share with a negative beta increases the riskiness of a portfolio.
(e) Most shares have a beta close to 1.

**8**    Which of the following statements concerning unit trusts is/are true?

(a) They allow small savers to diversify their risks.
(b) They normally give a fixed rate of interest and re-invest surpluses so as to give unit trust holders capital appreciation.
(c) Their price remains constant so that unit trust holders can never lose their savings in monetary terms.
(d) They are especially attractive to risk-lovers.

## True/False

**1**    A risk-lover is indifferent to risk.

**2**    The principle of diminishing marginal utility of wealth makes most people risk-averse.

**3**    Insurance companies often do not insure against acts of God because these risks cannot be pooled.

**4**    In purely economic terms, life insurance premia should be lower for women than for men because women live longer than men on average.

**5**    Treasury bills are more risky than company shares.

**6**    A risk-averse financial investor prefers higher average return on a portfolio but dislikes higher risk.

**7**    Diversification means not putting all your eggs in one basket.

**8**    Diversification fails when share returns are negatively correlated.

**9**    In equilibrium, low beta shares will have below average prices.

**10**    Speculative bubbles are less likely the larger the share of the total return that comes in the form of dividends rather than capital gains.

**11**    A forward market in cars would help to stabilize prices.

**12**    A trader buying forward in the hope of a higher future spot price is hedging.

## Economics in action

### Rough and ready beats market

(Adapted from an article by Chris Dillow, *Investors Chronicle*, 8 June 2004)

Diversification pays. It's easy to spread risk without sacrificing returns by holding just two or three stocks. A simple rule of thumb – 'hold stocks that seem to have little in common' – can therefore work well. Many stocks really do have nothing in common, as their movements are unrelated to each other.

By the same token, the big portfolios of professional investors might not be much better diversified than those of amateur investors – because in holding dozens of stocks they hold highly correlated assets, which add to the volatility of a portfolio.

## Questions

**1**    What formal terminology would we use to describe 'stocks that seem to have little in common'?

**2**    Why does 'hold[ing] stocks that seem to have little in common' reduce risk?

**3**    Why might holding a very large portfolio of stocks not reduce risk?

## Questions for thought

**1**    Explain why the occurrence of large positive or negative returns on shares in particular years was probably unanticipated.

**2**    Discuss whether the stock market most resembles a casino or an efficient market. What sort of evidence helps your decision?

**3**    Regardless of how you believe the stock market does work, which is the more desirable method if we are concerned that funds are appropriately allocated between firms?

**4**    Discuss whether moral hazard or adverse selection might influence the markets for insurance against unemployment or bad health in a situation where there is no state provision of such insurance.

# chapter fourteen

# The information economy

## Learning outcomes

By the end of this chapter, you should understand:

- Key attributes of information products
- Why e-products have high fixed costs/low marginal costs
- Why e-commerce fosters monopolies that want to price discriminate
- Price discrimination, versioning and bundling
- Why strategic alliances arise
- Competition to set standards and competition between networks
- The boom and bust in share prices of dot.com companies

## Key learning blocks

The popularity and importance of the Internet is evidenced by the significant use of this new technology by consumers and firms. Naturally economists are interested in trying to understand why such a market has developed and how it might look in the future. The core issues for economists are:

1. Why do consumers require information?

2. What advantages does new technology bring to the distribution of information?

3. Given the new characteristics of the market place, how will competition develop in the future?

The textbook builds on these core ideas and the exercises that follow will help you to explore the issues further.

# Important concepts and technical terms

## Match each lettered concept with the appropriate numbered phrase:

**(a)** Switching cost

**(b)** E-product

**(c)** Network externality

**(d)** Standard

**(e)** Bundling

**(f)** Experience good

**(g)** Niche market

**(h)** Versioning

**(i)** Price discrimination

**(j)** Two-part tariff

**(k)** Strategic alliance

**(l)** Information overload

**(1)** A product that can be digitally encoded then transmitted rapidly, accurately and cheaply.

**(2)** A good (or service) that must be sampled before the user knows its value.

**(3)** The deliberate creation of different qualities in order to facilitate price discrimination.

**(4)** The joint supply of more than one product in order to reduce the need for price discrimination.

**(5)** Costs that arise when existing costs are sunk, so that changing supplier incurs additional costs.

**(6)** A situation that arises when the volume of available information is large, but the cost of processing it is high, so that screening devices become very valuable.

**(7)** The technical specification that is common throughout a particular network.

**(8)** A situation that arises when an additional network member conveys benefits to those already on the network.

**(9)** A pricing arrangement in which an annual charge is levied to cover fixed costs, together with a small price per unit related to marginal costs.

**(10)** A blend of cooperation and competition in which a group of suppliers provides a range of products that partly complement one another.

**(11)** A situation in which a supplier is able to charge different prices to different customers for the same product.

**(12)** A market based on the specialist preferences of a group of consumers.

## Exercises

**1** Which of the following goods or services may be classified as information products?

**(a)** Music

**(b)** Pencil

**(c)** Today's issue of *The Guardian*

**(d)** A dictionary

**(e)** Refrigerator

**(f)** Computer

**(g)** Web page

**(h)** Lever arch file

**(i)** A football match.

**2** You receive an email from a company offering a tutoring service for economics students. For £100 per month, you can have access to a website that provides advice on aspects of economic theory.

**(a)** Would you subscribe?

**(b)** Given that this is an 'experience good', and you would probably not subscribe without some assurance that the product will be useful to you, which of the following might make you more likely to

respond favourably to the invitation to subscribe?
(i)   The website is run by one of the top university economics departments in the UK.
(ii)  The firm is offering a free preview of part of the website – the section on game theory.
(iii) You are familiar with the firm, having used one of its other websites in the past.
(iv)  The firm offers you a week's free trial of the whole site.
(v)   You have an end-of-semester examination next week.

**3**    The delivery of an information product entails the following sorts of costs:

A    Production costs
B    Reproduction costs
C    Distribution costs.

(a)  Classify each of these cost items as a fixed or variable cost.
(b)  Evaluate the likely relative magnitude of these items.
(c)  What do your answers imply for the overall cost structure for the product in terms of returns to scale?

**4**    Figure 14–1 shows the market for a good which has network externalities associated with it. $D_1$ represents the initial demand curve and $P_1$ is the initial price being charged.

**Figure 14–1**  Demand with a network externality

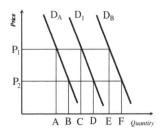

(a)  What is the initial equilibrium quantity demanded?

Suppose the firm reduces price from $P_1$ to $P_2$:

(b)  What is the new equilibrium quantity demanded in the short run?
(c)  What effect might this have on the attractiveness of the network?
(d)  Which is the new (short-run) demand curve and equilibrium quantity demanded?
(e)  Sketch in the long-run demand curve (i.e. the demand curve recognizing the existence of the network externality).

**5**    Which of the following products are subject to versioning?

(a)  Books
(b)  Railways
(c)  Sausages
(d)  Computer software
(e)  Air travel.

**6**    Which of the following are important characteristics of an information product – and why do they matter?

(a)  You cannot know its value until you have it.
(b)  Once you have it, you don't need it again.
(c)  More of it may reduce utility.
(d)  Once you have chosen a particular product, you may be stuck with it.
(e)  The more other people who have it, the more useful it is to you.

**7**    You have developed some specialist computer software that will offer an improved service for potential clients who currently use *Package X*, which is produced by a rival company, Comp.or. To set up an account for a typical new customer will cost you £30, but will entail hassle to the customer that she values at £65.

(a)  What are the total switching costs?
(b)  If the present value of the expected future stream of profit from a customer is £90, do you proceed with the new product?
(c)  Would your decision be different if the expected profit stream is £200?
(d)  What steps might you take to attract customers in this situation?
(e)  What action might Comp.or take to protect its own market position?

**8**    Table 14–1 sets out the willingness to pay (WTP) for two goods of three supermarket customers.

**Table 14–1    Willingness to pay (£)**

|  | Pizza | Treacle tart |
|---|---|---|
| Anna | 3 | 0 |
| Bob | 0 | 3 |
| Caroline | 2 | 2 |

(a)  What would the supermarket's revenue be if it set prices of £3 for pizza and for treacle tart?
(b)  What would the supermarket's revenue be if it set prices of £2 for pizza and for treacle tart?

**(c)** What would revenue be if it set prices at £3 for pizza, £3 for treacle tart, but with the option of buying both for £4?

**(d)** How could the supermarket find out how to reach the pricing strategy expressed in *(c)*?

**9**    Could a market for an information product be perfectly competitive? What alternative market structures are likely, and why?

## True/False

**1**    Revenues from e-commerce are forecast to rise almost fivefold in Western Europe between 1999 and 2005.

**2**    It took Yahoo! only five years to overtake General Motors in terms of its market capitalization.

**3**    The problem with information is that once you have it, you do not need to buy it.

**4**    Search engines are among the most popular websites because they help users to cope with information overload.

**5**    The fixed costs of learning a new word processor or other software packages are high, so there is a strong incentive to stick with what you know.

**6**    The more people that join a network, the more people will want to join it.

**7**    The typical cost structure of an information product leads us to expect that a perfectly competitive market will develop.

**8**    The production of 'student' and 'professional' versions of computer software packages is an attempt by the producers to introduce a form of price discrimination.

**9**    Bundling beats uniform pricing across users, but is usually less effective than perfect price discrimination.

**10**    Strategic alliances are good for the consumer.

**11**    European firms lagged behind their American counterparts in developing a standard for mobile telephony.

**12**    The information revolution has required a revolution in economic analysis in order to understand what is happening.

### Economics in action

**Qjump rail ticket outfit hits buffers**

(Adapted from an article by Heather Tomlinson, *The Guardian*, 10 February 2004)

The two leading online train ticket retailers, TheTrainline and Qjump, are to merge with the potential loss of 300 jobs. In the year to the beginning of March, the company made a pre-tax loss of £12.3 million on turnover of £22.3 million, according to the accounts of TheTrainline holdings filed at Companies House. Cost savings of £8 million a year will be produced when the companies merge, TheTrainline said in a statement . TheTrainline said the new company should make a profit and would have annual sales of £300 million, just under 10 per cent of all rail tickets sold. Around a half of those sales came from Qjump.

### Questions

**1**    Given the cost nature of e-products, why was the merger of TheTrainline and Qjump likely?

**2**    What do you think the commercial implications would be of moving from 10 per cent to a 20 per cent share of all rail tickets sold?

### Questions for thought

**1**    The Internet was originally developed by academics in different universities and countries wanting to exchange information freely. What does economics have to say about the market equilibrium here? To put it another way, should access to the Internet remain free?

**2**    Why should firms like Microsoft and Intel choose to form a strategic alliance rather than undergo a full merger?

**3**    Microsoft became embroiled in a lengthy and costly battle with the US Justice Department over the bundling of its Internet Explorer, which was competing with the well-established Netscape

Navigator. Netscape argued that Microsoft was being predatory in pricing the Internet Explorer at zero, whereas Microsoft countered by saying that Internet Explorer was part of a larger integrated package. Use the concepts introduced in this chapter to come to your own view of Microsoft's strategy.

# part three

# Welfare economics

# chapter fifteen

# Welfare economics

## Learning outcomes

**By the end of this chapter, you should understand:**

- What we mean by welfare economics
- Horizontal and vertical equity
- The concept of Pareto efficiency
- How the Invisible Hand may achieve efficiency
- The concept of market failure
- Why partial removal of distortions may be harmful
- The problem of externalities and possible solutions
- How monopoly power causes market failure
- Distortions from pollution and congestion
- Why missing markets create distortions

## Key learning blocks

Welfare economics is where positivist meets normative economics (see Chapter 1 for a review), but essentially positivist economics tries to be *value free* while normative economics is not. The topic of welfare economics thus creates controversy. However, there are some central ideas which you need to build your understanding around:

1. What is Pareto efficiency?
2. What is market failure and what creates market failure?
3. What are some of the solutions to market failure?

The textbook provides a detailed analysis of these topics and the exercises that follow will help you to broaden your understanding.

# Important concepts and technical terms

## Match each lettered concept with the appropriate numbered phrase:

a  Horizontal equity

b  Resource allocation

c  Property rights

d  Welfare economics

e  Second-best

f  Free-rider problem

g  Market failure

h  Allocative efficiency

i  Externality

j  Pareto-efficient

k  Vertical equity

l  Distortion

1  The branch of economics dealing with normative issues, its purpose being not to describe how the economy works but to assess how well it works.

2  The identical treatment of identical people.

3  A list or complete description of who does what and who gets what.

4  Circumstances in which equilibrium in free unregulated markets will fail to achieve an efficient allocation.

5  The different treatment of different people in order to reduce the consequences of these innate differences.

6  A situation causing society's marginal cost of producing a good to diverge from society's marginal benefit from consuming that good.

7  A situation in which an individual has no incentive to pay for a good which is costly to produce, as she can consume it anyway.

8  A theory by which the government may increase the overall efficiency of the whole economy by introducing new distortions to offset distortions that already exist.

9  A situation where an economy is getting the most out of its scarce resources and not squandering them.

10  A situation arising whenever an individual's production or consumption decision directly affects the production or consumption of others, other than through market prices.

11  An allocation of resources such that, given consumer tastes, resources and technology, it is impossible to move to another allocation which would make some people better off and nobody worse off.

12  The legal right to compensation for infringement of vested rights.

## Exercises

1  Suppose that Ursula and Vince judge their utility in terms of the goods they receive. Figure 15–1 shows a number of alternative allocations of goods between the two of them.

(a)  Which allocations are superior to *A*?

(b)  Which allocations are inferior to *A*?

(c)  Are there any allocations which you have not mentioned in your answers to *(a)* and *(b)*? If so, explain why you have not been able to judge them either superior or inferior to *A*. Is society indifferent between such points?

Suppose that the quantity of goods available is 20:

(d)  Which allocations are inefficient?

(e)  Which allocations are efficient?

(f)  Which allocations are infeasible?

**Figure 15–1** Allocation of goods between Ursula and Vince

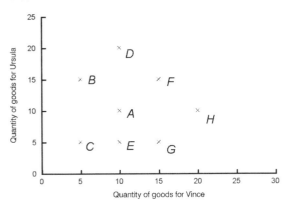

**Figure 15–2** A commodity tax and second best

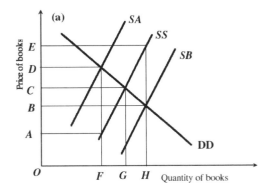

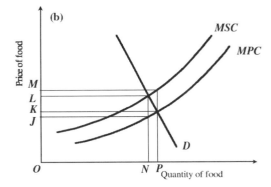

**2** Suppose that an economy has many producers and consumers, but only two goods, food and books. Both markets are unregulated and perfectly competitive. The equilibrium price of food is £20 and that of books is £10. Labour is the variable factor of production, and workers gain equal job satisfaction from working in each of the two sectors. The economy is in equilibrium.

(a) How much additional utility (in money value) did consumers obtain from the last book produced?

(b) How many books would consumers exchange for one unit of food if their utility were to remain constant?

(c) What was the marginal cost of the last book and last unit of food produced? Justify your answer.

(d) What can be said about relative wage rates in the two sectors?

(e) What is the ratio of the marginal physical product of labour in production of books to that in production of food?

(f) How many additional books could be produced if one less unit of food is produced?

(g) Bearing in mind your answers to parts *(b)* and *(f)*, what can be said about the allocation of resources in this economy?

**3** Panel *(a)* of Fig. 15–2 shows the demand curve for books *(DD)* in the economy of Exercise **2**. *SS* shows the supply curve for books.

(a) Identify equilibrium price and quantity.

(b) Suppose the authorities impose a tax on books: identify the tax-inclusive supply curve and the new equilibrium consumer price and quantity. What is the amount of the tax?

(c) At this equilibrium, what is the marginal social cost of books? What is the marginal consumer benefit?

Given that the books tax is imposed as in part *(b)*, now consider the market for food, shown in panel *(b)* of Fig. 15–2. *D* represents the demand curve, *MPC* the marginal private cost of food and *MSC* the marginal social cost of producing food.

(d) Identify equilibrium price and quantity in the market for food.

(e) Does this equilibrium ensure a satisfactory resource allocation? Explain your answer.

(f) Explain the divergence between *MPC* and *MSC*.

(g) Given that the tax on books must remain, what is the preferred output of the food industry? How could the authorities bring about this production level?

**4** Which of the following would be indicative of market failure? (*Note:* More than one response may be appropriate.)

(a) Traffic congestion.

(b) The existence of a collusive oligopoly.

(c) The absence of a forward market for cars.

(d) The presence of a market in which marginal social benefit exceeds marginal private benefit.

(e) A situation in which a firm is free to pollute the atmosphere around its factory (a residential area) without cost.

**5** A dog-owner daily allows his dog to foul the pavement. In what sense is this an externality? In the absence of a realistic charge to dog-owners, would you expect there to be too many or too few dogs for social efficiency? Should the authorities tackle this problem by raising the dog licence fee or by restricting the number of licences issued – or should they leave things as they are?

**6** Two neighbouring factories in a remote rural area operate independently. One is a branch of a company *(XYZ plc)* which has incurred the cost of improving and maintaining the main road linking the two factories with the motorway. The other factory makes no contribution towards the road, but shares its advantages. Figure 15–3 illustrates the position facing *XYZ plc*, which is assumed (for simplicity) to be a price-taker in this market, with a demand curve horizontal at *DD*. *MPC* represents the marginal private cost faced by *XYZ plc*.

**Figure 15–3**   The effect of a production externality

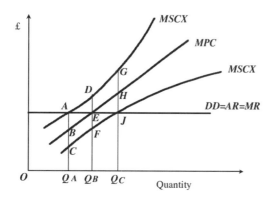

(a) At what point will the firm produce?
(b) Taking account of the externality of the road, identify the marginal social cost curve *(MSCX* or *MSCY)*. Explain your answer.
(c) What would be the socially efficient point of production? Why?
(d) What is the social cost of producing at *(a)* rather than at *(c)*?

**7** A factory emits smoke during the production process, which imposes an external diseconomy upon the environment. The following data describe the situation.

| Output (units) | Marginal private cost (£) | Marginal revenue (£) | Marginal social cost of air pollution (£) |
|---|---|---|---|
| 1 | 12 | 24 | 4 |
| 2 | 12 | 22 | 6 |
| 3 | 12 | 20 | 8 |
| 4 | 12 | 18 | 10 |
| 5 | 12 | 16 | 12 |
| 6 | 12 | 14 | 14 |
| 7 | 12 | 12 | 16 |
| 8 | 12 | 10 | 18 |

Initially, the firm maximizes profits without regard to the social cost of air pollution. If, subsequently, the authorities levy pollution tax on the firm equal to marginal social cost, which of the following describes what happens to output?

(a) Falls by 4 units.
(b) Falls by 2 units.
(c) Falls by 1 unit.
(d) Remains constant.
(e) Rises by 1 unit.

**8** Which of the following describes a situation in which resource allocation may be said to be efficient?

(a) Production processes use as little energy as is possible.
(b) No one can be made better off without someone else being made worse off.
(c) There is no need to trade with other countries.
(d) The balance of payments is in surplus.
(e) The production of one commodity cannot be increased without reducing the production of another commodity.
(f) All private companies within the economy are producing at an equilibrium level of output in order to maximize profits.
(g) Gross national income grows at a planned percentage rate every year.

**9** A local government councillor said: 'The authority is short of revenue and the roads into the town centre are congested; therefore, we should double car parking charges.' If this is the aim of the policy, which of the following assumptions is/are implicitly being made?

(a) The elasticity of demand for car parking in the town centre is less than unity.

(b) The social costs of driving to the town centre outweigh the social benefits.

(c) The local authority has no substantial competition in the provision of car parking facilities in the town centre.

**10** Explain the sense in which some pollution might be socially desirable.

(*Hint*: You may find it helpful to draw a diagram to show the effects of pollution in a market. For example, imagine that you live in a flat overlooking the sea, but that offshore there is an oil refinery. This means that you have to spend extra time cleaning the floor and must wash your clothes more frequently. The oil refinery is imposing costs on to you and your neighbours (i.e. society) that it does not have to pay for. Draw a diagram to show the firm's production decision and then compare this with the optimal position for society as a whole. The question is whether the optimum position requires zero pollution.)

## True/False

**1** Welfare economics deals with normative issues.

**2** An allocation of resources in which it is impossible to make any one individual better off without making somebody else worse off is Pareto-efficient.

**3** If every market in the economy but one is a perfectly competitive free market, the resulting equilibrium throughout the economy will be Pareto-efficient.

**4** If a distortion is unavoidable in a particular sector, the best action for the government to take is to ensure that the other sectors are distortion-free.

**5** Under imperfect competition, marginal revenue is different from average revenue: this causes market failure.

**6** The formal establishment of property rights can help to achieve socially efficient allocation by internalizing externalities.

**7** River pollution represents a situation where private cost exceeds social cost.

**8** Private cost exceeds social cost whenever a firm fails to make a profit.

**9** Pollution still exists; therefore past pollution control has been ineffective.

**10** An important problem which inhibits the development of forward and contingent markets is the provision of information.

**11** Human life is beyond economic calculation and must be given absolute priority, whatever the cost.

**12** Estimates for the implicit social marginal benefit from saving life in the UK range from £50 to £20 million.

---

## Economics in action

### Welfare reform: The tasks ahead

(Adapted from BBC Business News)

Tony Blair has said that completing welfare reform is one of the key tasks for his second term of government. As he arrived at Number 10 Downing Street after his historic second-term victory, the Prime Minister made it clear that he was determined to press on with the reform of the welfare system. 'We need to separate very clearly those who cannot work, who need security and protection, and those who can work but at present don't, who we must try to help off a life on benefit and into productive work,' Mr Blair said. 'We are increasingly looking at tightening up conditionality, so that people get their rights, but there is a tighter regime to make sure people can and actually do help themselves.' But in doing so, the government will have to tackle some of the more difficult issues that it dodged during its first term of office.

### Making work pay

There will be more changes in the tax system, designed to make work pay. The working families tax credit, which boosts the income of low-income heads of household in work, will be extended to other people in the workforce. This employment tax credit – introduced in 2003 – could cost the government up to £1 bn, according to the Institute for Fiscal Studies (IFS). And the Chancellor's plan to combine the child tax credit with child payments made to people on benefit – which would also increase incentives to work – could be even more costly, if no one is to be made worse off, according to the IFS.

### Housing benefit reform

Housing benefit is the payment made to millions of households to help with the cost of their rent payments. From the point of view of the government, housing benefit as it is currently structured is a major disincentive to people moving from benefits to work. However, any reform of the system to improve 'tapers' – so that people lose less housing benefit as their income goes up – is likely to be expensive. So the government might opt for a simplification, giving people on benefit a fixed sum to help with their housing costs (with some regional variations).

But the government also faces a broader choice on welfare reform, relating both its ambitions and means.

- Should it target narrowly defined groups of the socially excluded, such as teenage mothers or rough sleepers, or should it target broad groups, such as families with children?
- Are targeted means-tests ineffective in delivering benefits and stigmatizing for the poor?
- How far can it attack poverty through increasing means-tested benefits, such as the pensioners' minimum income guarantee, without encouraging real redistribution through the tax and benefits system?

## Questions

**1** Does the welfare system tackle vertical or horizontal inequity in UK society?

**2** Does the welfare system support market failures?

## Questions for thought

**1** The nuclear accident at Chernobyl created widespread radioactive pollution. Discuss how you would assess the costs and benefits of nuclear energy.

**2** Discuss how the granting of property rights could help to internalize externalities suffered by people living near football grounds or having noisy neighbours.

# chapter sixteen

# Government spending and revenue

## Learning outcomes

**By the end of this chapter, you should understand:**

- Different kinds of government spending
- Why public goods cannot be provided by a market
- Average and marginal tax rates
- How taxes can compensate for externalities
- Supply-side economics
- Why tax revenue cannot be raised without limit
- How cross-border flows limit national economic sovereignty
- The political economy of how governments set policy

## Key learning blocks

**This chapter recognizes the role of *government* in providing goods and services. The key areas to understand are:**

**1** Why should the government provide goods and services?

**2** What factors at the national level might impede the government's ability to provide goods and services?

**3** At an international level, how else might the government be prevented from delivering public services?

The textbook covers all of these issues in detail and the exercises that follow will help to develop your understanding.

# Important concepts and technical terms

## Match each lettered concept with the appropriate numbered phrase:

**a** Council tax

**b** Progressive tax structure

**c** Corporation tax

**d** Indirect tax

**e** Incidence of a tax

**f** Merit good

**g** Laffer curve

**h** Direct tax

**i** Marginal tax rate

**j** Tiebout model

**k** Benefits principle

**l** Deadweight tax burden

**m** Wealth tax

**n** Regressive tax structure

**1** A tax structure in which the average tax rate rises with an individual's income level.

**2** The waste caused by a distortionary tax leading to a misallocation of resources.

**3** A description of the relationship between tax rates and tax revenue.

**4** A tax on asset holdings or transfers rather than the income from asset holding: examples in the UK are rates and capital transfer tax (CTT).

**5** A tax structure in which the average tax rate falls as income level rises.

**6** The principle underlying a tax structure in which people who receive more than their share of public spending pay more than their share of tax revenues.

**7** The percentage taken by the government of the last pound that an individual earns.

**8** A tax levied on expenditure on goods and services.

**9** An important model of local government, sometimes called the model of the 'invisible foot'.

**10** A tax with a mixture of property, income and household tax components.

**11** Tax paid by UK companies based on their taxable profits after allowance for interest payments and depreciation.

**12** Tax levied directly on income.

**13** A good that society thinks everyone ought to have regardless of whether it is wanted by each individual.

**14** A measure of the final tax burden on different people once we have allowed for the indirect as well as the direct effects of the tax.

## Exercises

**1** **(a)** Use the data from Table 16–4 of the main text to draw pie-charts showing the shares of the major categories of government expenditure and tax revenue.

**(b)** Since 1997, Gordon Brown has proposed a policy of fiscal prudence; how would you expect this policy to be evident in the pie-charts?

**(c)** In a global economic slowdown, how would you expect the sectors of the pie-charts to change?

**2** Assume that income tax is levied at a standard rate of 30 per cent on all income over £5000.

**(a)** Calculate the marginal and average tax rates at the following income levels:
   (i)   £3000.
   (ii)  £9000.

(iii) £12 000.

(iv) £20 000.

**(b)** Is the tax progressive or regressive?

Suppose the tax structure is revised so that income over £5 000 is taxed at 30 per cent as before, but the rate increases to 50 per cent for income over £10 000.

**(c)** Calculate the marginal and average tax rates at the same income levels as in *(a)*.

**(d)** Is the tax more or less progressive than before?

**③** This exercise is concerned with the market for a pure public good. In Fig. 16–1, $D_1$ and $D_2$ represent the demand curves for the good of two individuals: we assume that for each individual the demand curve shows the marginal private benefit of the last unit of the public good. The line *MC* shows the private and social marginal cost of producing the public good.

**Figure 16–1** Demand curves for a pure public good

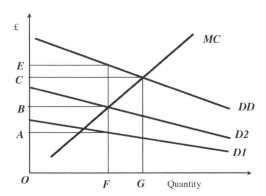

**(a)** If *DD* is to represent the marginal social benefit obtained from the good, what should be the relationship between *DD* and $D_1$ and $D_2$?

**(b)** If the quantity produced is given by *OF*, what valuation per unit is placed upon the good by individual 1?

**(c)** If individual 1 actually pays this amount for the provision of the good, what will individual 2 have to pay?

**(d)** What is the marginal social benefit of *OF* units of this good?

**(e)** How does marginal social benefit compare with marginal social cost in this situation?

**(f)** What is the socially efficient quantity of this good?

**④** Figure 16–2 shows the market for a good in which there is a negative production externality such that marginal social cost *(MSC)* is above marginal

private cost *(MPC)*. *MSB* represents the marginal social benefit derived from consumption of the good.

**Figure 16–2** Market for a good in which there is a negative production externality

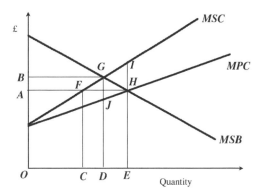

**(a)** If this market is unregulated, what quantity of this good will be produced?

**(b)** What is the socially efficient quantity?

**(c)** What is the amount of the deadweight loss to society if the free market quantity is produced?

**(d)** What level of tax on the good would ensure that the socially efficient quantity is produced?

**(e)** Suggest an example of a situation in which this analysis might be relevant.

**⑤** A firm engaged in producing a certain good has private costs which are not equal to social costs. Which of the following steps could the government take to increase economic welfare?

**(a)** Tax the firm if social costs are less than its private costs.

**(b)** Subsidize the firm if social costs exceed its private costs.

**(c)** Tax the firm if social costs exceed its private costs.

**(d)** Subsidize other firms in the same industry if their private costs are less than social costs.

**⑥** Figure 16–3 (overleaf) shows the position in a labour market. *DD* is the demand curve for labour; *SSa*, *SSb* and *SSc* are labour supply curves – but ignore *SSc* for the moment. The 'wage' here is to be regarded as the gross wage. Suppose a tax on wages is imposed.

**(a)** Of *SSa* and *SSb*, which represents labour supply without the tax, and which shows the post-tax situation?

**(b)** What is the labour market equilibrium without the tax?

**(c)** What effect does the tax have on hours worked?

**Figure 16–3**   A tax on wages

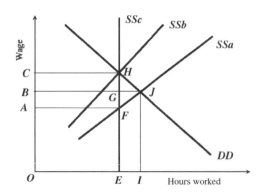

(d)   In this situation, what is the wage paid by firms?

(e)   What is the wage received by workers?

(f)   What area represents tax revenue?

(g)   What area represents the deadweight loss?

(h)   Identify the areas which represent the incidence of the tax on workers and employers.

Suppose now that the supply of labour is perfectly inelastic at *SSc*, and a tax of *AC* is levied:

(i)   What is the wage paid by firms?

(j)   What is the wage received by workers?

(k)   What area represents tax revenue?

(l)   What area represents the deadweight loss?

(m)  Identify the areas which represent the incidence of the tax on workers and employers.

**7**    The provision of some public services is delegated by central government to local authorities, together with some responsibility for raising finance to fund those activities. The Tiebout model recommends local government jurisdiction areas, but the externalities argument suggests that the geographical jurisdiction areas should be relatively large. Which of the following arguments favour the Tiebout model?

(a)   People are different and do not want to be treated the same.

(b)   Public goods are non-exclusive.

(c)   Differential pricing for residents and non-residents for facilities such as art galleries is difficult to implement.

(d)   People feel that central government is remote from their needs.

(e)   Residents mainly consume the public services provided by their own local authorities.

(f)   Larger jurisdictions enable externalities to be internalized.

(g)   Smaller jurisdictions maximize people's choices.

**8**    Table 16–1 shows the sources of tax revenues in a range of countries around the world. Examine these data. What do they reveal about the way that governments in different parts of the world seek to raise revenue?

## True/False

**1**    Government spending on transfer payments has risen faster than national income since 1956, and continues to do so.

**2**    Income tax is progressive because the marginal tax rate is greater than the average tax rate.

**3**    The largest government revenue-raiser in the UK in 2004 was taxes on goods.

**4**    A football match is a public good.

**5**    Social security payments damage social efficiency by pre-empting resources that would be more productively used in the private sector.

**6**    Income tax was not introduced in peacetime in the UK until the 1840s.

**7**    Public goods must be produced by the government.

| **Table 16–1**   Sources of tax revenue, 2004 (% of total) | | | | | | | |
|---|---|---|---|---|---|---|---|
| | **UK** | **Bolivia** | **Cameroon** | **India** | **Malaysia** | **S. Korea** | **Zambia** |
| Income, profits, capital gains | 38.9 | 3.8 | 23.5 | 29.2 | 45.6 | 35.9 | 35.4 |
| Social security contributions | 18.6 | 9.9 | 0.0 | 0.0 | 1.5 | 8.7 | 0.0 |
| Property | 7.0 | 15.4 | 1.6 | 0.1 | 0.6 | 2.6 | 0.2 |
| Domestic goods and services | 35.3 | 59.7 | 34.8 | 38.5 | 31.8 | 37.0 | 51.6 |
| International trade | 0.1 | 10.1 | 38.1 | 32.0 | 15.1 | 7.4 | 12.8 |
| Other | 0.1 | 1.1 | 2.0 | 0.2 | 5.4 | 8.4 | 0.0 |

*Source: Government Financial Statistics Yearbook 2003.*

**8** The underlying principle of income tax is the 'benefits principle'.

**9** The tax on tobacco tends to be regressive in its effect.

**10** The Laffer curve demonstrates that, for many 'big government–big tax' countries, a cut in tax rates would increase tax revenues.

**11** Cigarettes are a merit bad.

**12** Closer economic integration with other countries undermines the sovereignty of nation-states.

## Economics in action

### Brown rejects pre-election spree

(Adapted from BBC News Online, 6 July 2004)

Gordon Brown has warned ministers he will not go on 'an irresponsible pre-election spending spree'.

Mr Brown told the CBI president's dinner in London: 'It has been in the past at times like this in the political and economic cycle – and I recall the mid-1970s, the mid-1980s, and the early 1990s – governments of both parties have relaxed their fiscal disciplines and gone on to raise the rate of spending in an unaffordable pre-election spree.'

'In next week's Spending Review, there will be no short-termist quick fixes, no irresponsible pre-election spending sprees, a ruthless focus on priorities and no relaxation of our fiscal discipline. We will – over this cycle and the next – continue to meet our strict fiscal rules. So current spending will grow no more than an average of 2.5 per cent in real terms between 2006 and 2008.'

## Questions

**1** Is this speech by Gordon Brown an example of the importance of commitment and credibility in policy setting?

**2** Which do you think is the greater priority, the control of spending or the amount of spending on health and education?

## Questions for thought

**1** How would you expect a switch in policy from direct to indirect taxation to affect income distribution?

**2** In looking to correct an externality, the authorities have a choice of policies. One possibility is to take action on the quantity side of the market, perhaps by direct regulation, or by selling licences. As an alternative, they may choose to influence market price, either by taxation or by direct price-setting. This question explores the circumstances under which this choice is significant, when the authorities have imperfect knowledge of market conditions. First consider Fig. 16–4.

**Figure 16–4** Price or quantity control: 1

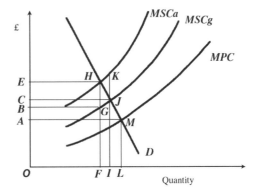

Here, **D** represents the market demand curve and **MPC** marginal private cost. Suppose the authorities know the location of **D**, and that marginal social costs (**MSC**) are higher than **MPC**, but are uncertain about the position of **MSC**. Specifically, suppose that they perceive **MSC** to be at **MSCg**, although in fact **MSCa** represents the actual level.

**(a)** Which combination of price and quantity is socially desirable?

**(b)** At which combination will the government aim?

**(c)** What would be the deadweight loss if the policy adopted is to set price?

**(d)** What would be the deadweight loss if the policy adopted is to set quantity?

**(e)** Does it matter which policy is adopted?

Suppose now that the government knows the 'true' level of marginal social cost (*MSC* in Fig. 16–5), but is uncertain about market demand. *Da* in Fig. 16–5 is the actual market demand, but the government perceives it to be at *Dg*.

**(f)** Which combination of price and quantity is socially desirable?

**(g)** At which combination will the government aim?

**(h)** What would be the deadweight loss if the policy adopted is to set price?

**(i)** What would be the deadweight loss if the policy adopted is to set quantity?

**(j)** Does it matter which policy is adopted?

**Figure 16–5** Price or quantity control: 2

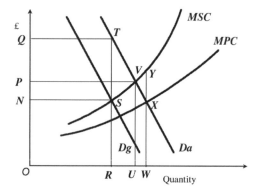

# chapter seventeen

# Industrial policy and competition policy

## Learning outcomes

By the end of this chapter, you should understand:

- Competition policy and industrial policy to offset market failures

- How patents boost investment in R&D

- Market failures in sunrise and sunset industries

- Locational externalities

- Consumer surplus and producer surplus

- The social cost of monopoly

- The principles behind UK competition policy

- Types of merger and why merger booms occurred

- Regulation of potential mergers

## Key learning blocks

Following Chapters 8 and 9 on market structures we now need to examine how the government might develop policies to *aid or control the competitive process*. Three broad areas require your attention:

1. What is industrial policy?

2. What are the undesirable consequences of monopoly?

3. What is competition policy?

The textbook discusses each of these topics in turn and the exercises that follow will help to develop your understanding.

# Important concepts and technical terms

## Match each lettered concept with the appropriate numbered phrase:

**a** Competition Commission

**b** Horizontal merger

**c** Industrial concentration

**d** Deadweight burden

**e** Vertical merger

**f** Locational externality

**g** Takeover bid

**h** R&D

**i** Conglomerate merger

**j** Competition policy

**k** 'Cream-skimming'

**l** Patent system

**m** Industrial policy

**n** Consumer surplus

**o** Producer surplus

**1** A governmental body set up to investigate whether or not a monopoly lessens competition.

**2** A voluntary union of two firms whose production activities are essentially unrelated.

**3** A situation in which one firm offers to buy out the shareholders of the second firm.

**4** A part of government economic policy which aims to enhance economic efficiency by promoting or safeguarding competition between firms.

**5** A situation in which a new entrant into a former monopoly market takes over only the profitable parts of the business, thereby undermining scale economies elsewhere.

**6** A union of two firms at different production stages in the same industry.

**7** The loss to society resulting from the allocative inefficiency of imperfect competition.

**8** Government economic policy aiming to offset externalities that affect production decisions by firms.

**9** A situation in which activity in an industry becomes focused in a few firms.

**10** The excess of consumer benefits over spending.

**11** Activity undertaken by private and public sector organizations to discover and develop new products, processes and technologies.

**12** A union of two firms at the same production stage in the same industry.

**13** A situation in which one firm's cost curve depends upon the proximity of other similar firms.

**14** The excess of revenue over total costs.

**15** A temporary legal monopoly awarded to an inventor who registers the invention.

## Exercises

**1** Identify each of the following as vertical, horizontal or conglomerate mergers:

**(a)** The union of a motor vehicle manufacturer with a tyre producer.

**(b)** The union of a motor vehicle manufacturer with a retail car distributor.

**(c)** The union of a tobacco company with a cosmetic firm.

**(d)** The union of two firms producing man-made fibres.

**2** In Fig. 17–1, **DD** represents the market demand curve for a commodity. If organized as a competitive market, *BY* would represent the long-run marginal cost curve. However, a monopolist would face the long-run marginal (and average) cost curve *AX*.

**Figure 17–1** Monopoly and competition

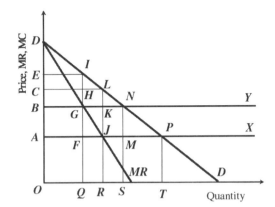

(a) What would be the price and output of the competitive industry?

(b) What would be the price and output under monopoly?

(c) What is the deadweight loss to consumers from the monopoly as compared with the competitive industry?

(d) What area represents the cost-savings of the monopoly?

(e) What area represents monopoly profits?

(f) Explain why the monopolist and competitive industry might face different cost conditions.

**3**  Figure 17–2 shows an industry operated as a monopoly, with long-run marginal cost given by *LMC*.

**Figure 17–2** Monopoly and consumer surplus

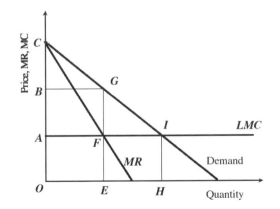

(a) Identify the profit-maximizing price and output.

(b) What is the area representing consumer surplus in this position?

(c) What is the area representing producer surplus?

(d) What is the social surplus?

(e) What would the price–output combination have been in a fully competitive market (assuming that the industry still faced the same cost conditions)?

(f) What would the consumer surplus be in this situation?

(g) What would producer surplus be?

(h) What is the social surplus?

(i) What position would maximize total social surplus?

**4**  Which is the 'odd one out' of the following proposed mergers?

(a) Air France/Sabena.

(b) Alcatel/Telettra.

(c) Aerospatiale/Alenia/De Havilland.

(d) Renault/Volvo.

(e) Courtaulds/SHIA.

**5**  Which of the following might explain why a firm wished to embark on a conglomerate merger?

(a) A wish to retain its share of the market for its main product.

(b) A wish to gain control of its supplies of raw materials.

(c) The desire to eliminate competition from foreign firms.

(d) The desire to diversify and extend its product range.

(e) A wish to reduce its dependence on supplies of skilled labour.

Why was there an increase in the number of conglomerate mergers relative to other forms in the late 1980s?

**6**  Which of the following might explain why a firm wished to embark on a horizontal merger?

(a) The wish to acquire or extend monopoly power.

(b) The desire to exploit external economies of scale.

(c) The desire to diversify and extend its product range.

(d) The desire to gain control of its supplies of raw materials.

**7**  Which of the following would tend to increase the degree of monopoly power of a firm?

(a) The concentration of production into a smaller number of industrial plants.

(b) The expiry of a patent.

(c) Diversification into a broader range of product lines.

(d) An increase in monopoly profits.

(e) A reduction in advertising expenditure.

**(f)** A fall in the cross-price elasticity of demand for the firm's product.

**8** A market has been operating as a monopoly for many years, with the protection of a barrier to entry. The market situation is shown in Fig. 17–3.

**Figure 17–3** Monopoly and X-inefficiency

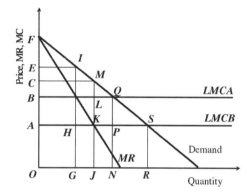

**(a)** Which of the *LMC* curves is most likely to be effective?

**(b)** What is the profit-maximizing price–output combination?

**(c)** Identify the consumer surplus in this situation.

Suppose the market is now opened up to competition:

**(d)** How might this affect costs?

**(e)** What price–output combination might then result under competition?

**(f)** What is consumer surplus in this new situation?

**(g)** In what ways is society better off?

**9** Which of the following factors might be seen to affect the social cost of monopoly?

**(a)** The elasticity of demand for the good.

**(b)** The steepness of marginal cost.

**(c)** The resources used in erecting and maintaining barriers to entry, by advertising, holding excess capacity and so on.

**(d)** The political influence that accrues to a large company with monopoly power.

**(e)** The effect of monopoly profits on the distribution of resources.

**10** Below are listed a number of policy actions. Identify each as belonging either to competition policy or to industrial policy.

**(a)** Referral to the Competition Commission of a firm supplying more than 25 per cent of the total market for a particular commodity.

**(b)** The promotion of R&D.

**(c)** Assistance for a national firm involved in strategic international competition.

**(d)** Subsidization of an emerging hi-tech industry.

**(e)** A patent system.

**(f)** The restriction of excessive non-price competition (e.g. advertising).

**(g)** The subsidization of 'lame duck' industries in areas of high unemployment.

**(h)** The outlawing of explicit price-fixing agreements between firms in an industry.

**(i)** Nationalization.

## True/False

**1** Each firm in an imperfectly competitive market enjoys a degree of monopoly power.

**2** The social cost of monopoly in the UK is probably equivalent to more than one-tenth of national income.

**3** Competition policy in the UK is more pragmatic than that in the USA.

**4** Monopoly may allow social gain through the exploitation of economies of scale.

**5** One of the potential benefits of merger activity is that it allows an inspired management to show its worth.

**6** We would expect that the law allowing mergers to be referred to the Competition (Monopolies and Mergers) Commission would discourage mergers from taking place.

**7** The cost conditions of a firm are always independent of location and the presence of other firms.

**8** Consumer surplus is what you have left over at the end of the month.

**9** Pre-emptive patenting can be used as an effective strategic barrier to entry.

**10** Government expenditure on R&D in the UK is aimed mainly at the advancement of knowledge (via the universities) and at developing new products and processes in the industrial sector.

**11** An important part of industrial policy is to subsidize sunrise industries.

**12** It is silly to spend money on dole payments; a much better policy is to subsidize declining industries to protect employment.

## Economics in action

### The curse of the clever

(Adapted from *Investors Chronicle*, 7 May 2004)

New research confirms what investors should have learned from the bursting of the tech bubble – that innovative companies are not great investments. The profits to be made from innovations are tiny. 'Only a minuscule fraction of the social returns from technical advances over the 1948–2001 period was captured by producers,' concludes Yale University's William Nord-haus in a recent paper. He calculates that just 2.2 per cent of the discounted present value of the social returns to innovations go to innovators. The rest flows to consumers, in the form of newer, cheaper products.

This is because the profits to be made from new ideas are small and get competed away quickly. For example, at the peak of the bubble, Etoys.com – an online toy retailer – seemed a good idea. But Toys-R-Us quickly imitated it. Both have since faced financial difficulties.

## Questions

**1** Given the findings provided by William Nordhaus, what are the implications for competition policy?

**2** In light of these findings, assess the likely impact of current UK industrial policy, which seeks to promote enterprise and innovation.

## Questions for thought

**1** Which do you think is more serious for society – concentration or collusion?

**2** In 2003, the EU Commission accused the Football Premier League and Sky of acting as a cartel in live Premiership football rights. Do you think that consumers would benefit from a free market in this instance?

**3** Think about the town where you live. If you wanted to buy a house, where in town would you go? If you wanted a newspaper, where would you go? Comment on the difference.

**4** Imagine it is a hot and sunny day in mid-summer. Figure 17–4 represents a beach, on which there are sunbathers, evenly distributed along the beach. At point *K*, there is a kiosk selling ice-cream. Just arriving on the beach is an ice-cream seller with a mobile stall, who aims to maximize profits by selling as many ice-creams as possible. Her ice-creams are the same brand and quality as those on sale in the kiosk, and she is selling at the same price. Where will she choose to locate her mobile stall on the beach? How would your answer differ if instead of a fixed kiosk, there were two sellers with mobile stalls – where would they choose to be?

**Figure 17–4** Imagine a beach on a hot sunny day . . .

# chapter eighteen

# Natural monopoly: public or private?

## Learning outcomes

**By the end of this chapter, you should understand:**

- The problem of natural monopoly
- Nationalization as a solution to the problem of natural monopoly
- Social marginal cost pricing
- Social cost–benefit analysis of investment decisions
- Two-part tariffs and peak-load pricing
- Privatization and the Private Finance Initiative (PFI)
- Regulation of a private natural monopoly
- How globalization reduces natural monopoly

## Key learning blocks

**This chapter covers a well-defined set of learning blocks:**

1. What is a natural monopoly?
2. How effective is public ownership in dealing with public monopolies?
3. How effective is private ownership in dealing with public ownership?

The textbook covers each in turn and the exercises that follow will aid your understanding.

# Important concepts and technical terms

## Match each lettered concept with the appropriate numbered phrase:

**a** Regulation

**b** Privatization

**c** Employee buyout

**d** Allocative efficiency

**e** Private Finance Initiative

**f** Production efficiency

**g** Marginal cost-pricing

**h** Nationalization

**i** Discount rate

**j** Offer price

**k** Regulatory capture

**l** Natural monopoly

**1** The acquisition of private companies by the public sector.

**2** The sale of public sector companies to the private sector.

**3** An industry having enormous economies of scale such that only one firm can survive.

**4** The price at which shares in an enterprise to be privatized are initially sold to investors: this often turns out to be below the free market price established on the first day of trading on the stock market.

**5** Measures adopted to ensure that privatized companies do not misuse their market situation.

**6** The interest rate used in calculating present values of future streams of benefits or costs.

**7** A state in which firms are on the lowest possible cost curve so there is no slack or waste.

**8** A state in which the balance of activities in the economy is Pareto-efficient such that no reallocation of resources can increase social welfare.

**9** A way of drawing on private sector expertise to finance and manage public projects.

**10** A situation in which a regulator gradually comes to identify with the interests of the firm it regulates, eventually becoming its champion rather than its watchdog.

**11** A price system where users pay a price equal to marginal production costs: a system that is not viable for a private natural monopoly, as the firm would incur losses.

**12** A privatization with all shares being sold to employees of the enterprise, e.g. National Freight Corporation.

## Exercises

**1** Which of the following have been advanced as reasons for the nationalization of an industry?

(a) A natural monopoly situation exists, with large economies of scale meaning that average cost lies above marginal cost.

(b) Externalities exist, such that the social gains from the provision of a commodity exceed the private benefits for which direct users are prepared to pay.

(c) There is a need to protect the interests of some members of society who might lose out if profit maximization were the sole criterion for the provision of a service.

(d) Certain basic industries should be under state control.

Which of these reasons do you consider to be valid?

**2** Which of the following effects is/are not claimed as being associated with privatization?

(a) An increase in competition – and hence a lowering of costs and prices.

(b) A reduction in political interference.

(c) An increase in the efficiency of management.

(d) A reduction in the money that the government needs to borrow to finance its expenditure programme.

(e) A reduction of deadweight burden.

(f) A widening of consumer choice, as private firms must be more sensitive to market demand.

**3**    Figure 18–1 illustrates an industry which is a natural monopoly, with long-run average costs falling continuously over the relevant range of output.

**Figure 18–1**    A natural monopoly

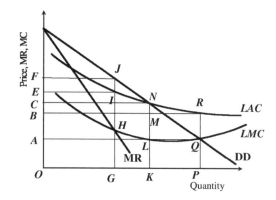

(a) If the industry is operated by an unregulated profit-maximizing monopolist, what price and output would be chosen?

(b) What would be the deadweight loss to society of this decision?

(c) What would be the level of monopoly profits?

(d) What would be the socially efficient levels of price and output?

(e) How would the monopolist act if allowed to produce only at the socially efficient point?

**4**    Suppose that you are in authority and are contemplating the privatization of an industry currently within your responsibility. The following thoughts run through your mind. Identify each as being in favour of or against privatization and assess their validity.

(a) The industry has consistently incurred losses over a period of many years and thus is a drain on the government's coffers.

(b) The industry enjoys substantial economies of scale and is a natural monopoly, so losses are to be expected. Society as a whole benefits from the scale economies, which would be sacrificed if the industry were to be broken up into a number of smaller firms.

(c) In the absence of competition, the industry has been operating less efficiently than it could have done.

(d) If the industry were to be privatized, the shareholders would be such a diverse group of people that they would be no spur to efficiency.

(e) Privatization would enable the industry to be freed from interference by the government in its pursuit of various political objectives.

(f) Keeping the industry under public control would be a safeguard, ensuring that needy groups in society were protected from a withdrawal of service.

(g) The proceeds from the sale of the industry can be used to finance necessary capital investment in other parts of the public sector.

What other arguments might influence your thinking on this matter? On balance, would you decide to privatize or to maintain the status quo?

**5**    Assess whether the telecommunications, gas, electricity and water industries should be nationalized.

**6**    Suppose that you are the manager of a firm in the private sector considering a capital investment project. Three plans have been submitted for your consideration (all figures are in £ million).

| Project | Private benefits | Private costs | Externalities Favourable | Unfavourabe |
|---------|---------|---------|---------|---------|
| A | 400 | 380 | 20 | 80 |
| B | 320 | 350 | 120 | 20 |
| C | 350 | 300 | 70 | 80 |

(a) If your aim is to maximize financial profits for your firm, which project do you choose?

(b) Suppose you know that your shareholders are keen to see successful sales figures rather than large profits (so long as there is no financial loss). Which project do you now choose?

(c) Suppose now that the same projects are submitted to the manager of a nationalized industry. Which project would maximize economic welfare for society as a whole?

**7**    Exercise 3 explored the situation facing a private natural monopoly if it were forced to produce at the socially efficient point. Let us now extend the analysis to see how the industry might operate if nationalized.

(a) If the nationalized industry produces at the socially efficient point (*OP* in Fig. 18–1), what subsidy is necessary?

**(b)** Under a two-part tariff pricing scheme, what fixed charge would be needed if the subsidy is to be replaced by user charges?

**(c)** What variable charge would be needed?

**(d)** At what price and output would the industry just break even?

**(e)** What would be the deadweight loss to society in this break-even position?

**(f)** Would the managers of this industry face appropriate incentives to maintain efficiency in production? If not, how is this likely to affect the situation shown in Fig. 18–1?

**8** This exercise considers the relative merits of two alternative schemes for public housing policy: the provision of council housing and rent vouchers. Figure 18–2 summarizes demand and supply conditions for the schemes. Initial equilibrium in the housing market is shown by demand curve **DD** and supply curve **SS**.

**Figure 18–2** Council housing or rent vouchers?

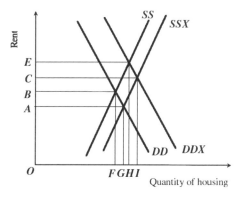

**(a)** In this 'without-policy' state, identify equilibrium rent and quantity of housing.

**(b)** Suppose that the local authority now issues rent vouchers to needy families. Using Fig. 18–2, describe the response in the housing market and identify the new equilibrium rent and quantity of housing.

**(c)** Suppose that, instead of issuing rent vouchers, the local authority provides council housing. How will the market now respond, and what are the new equilibrium levels of rent and quantity of housing?

**(d)** Which of the two schemes has the greatest effect on the quantity of housing? Why should this be?

**(e)** Assess the relative merits of the two schemes.

**9** Comment on the economic arguments relevant to these characteristics of the Private Finance Initiative (PFI).

**(a)** The PFI is a natural extension to the transfer of opportunities and assets from the public to the private sector that has been taking place since the 1980s.

**(b)** The PFI attempts to introduce competition into the provision of social infrastructure previously seen as the sole responsibility of the public sector.

**(c)** The aim is to reduce the amount of X-inefficiency entailed in the provision of public goods.

**(d)** The PFI alters the government's role in the provision of public goods from owner of assets and direct provider of services to that of purchaser of services from the private sector.

**(e)** The PFI enables more rapid completion of infrastructure projects.

**(f)** The private sector tends to view risk differently from their counterparts in Whitehall.

## True/False

**1** The deadweight burden of a natural monopoly can be eliminated by forcing the firm to set price equal to long-run average cost.

**2** Experience with deregulation of airlines in the USA shows that the removal of legal barriers to entry encourages competition and leads to lower prices and higher usage.

**3** To ensure efficiency, investment decisions made by nationalized industries should be made with reference to market rates of interest.

**4** Peak-load pricing is a system of price discrimination.

**5** Privatized industries subject to regulation spend considerable resources in trying to influence the regulator.

**6** Incentives for private managers to be efficient are strong because actual and potential shareholders monitor their performance carefully.

**7** Private industries are immune from government interference in the pursuit of political aims.

**8** Selling off state assets mortgages the country's future.

**9**    In the period up to 1986, all privatization share offers were under-priced.

**10**    The most successful of the early privatizations were those involving companies which faced significant competition after privatization.

## Economics in action

### 118 gays tell it to you straight: twins give you the runaround

(Adapted from an article by Richard Wray, *The Guardian*, June 19 2004)

Gay men and women get the best service out of the new 118 telephone directory enquiry services that have sprung up since the market opened to competition last summer. 118-GAY – or the queen of directory enquiries, as manager Keyth Rickards refers to it – scored joint highest with Telegate's 118355 for their 96 per cent accuracy in providing the correct residential or business telephone number. Overall roughly one in 10 callers to 118 services receives incorrect information.

The research also highlighted widespread confusion among consumers about what the new numbers cost and a worrying fall in the number of people using the service. Ofcom's mystery shopper research showed there is still wide disparity in price, with calls costing from 27p to 65p. Almost half of consumers believe the services are more expensive than the 40p it cost to call BT's old 192 number. As a result, consumers are deserting 118.

## Questions

**1**    Increased competition has been a key objective behind many privatizations and deregulations; do you think increased competition for directory enquiries was a good idea?

**2**    How else could you introduce competition in the directory enquiries market?

## Questions for thought

**1**    Discuss the incentives facing managers in public and private sector enterprises. Think about their relative effectiveness and the potential for improvement.

**2**    It has been argued that privatization not only raises revenue in the short run, but may also lead to social benefits if improved incentives lead to greater efficiency. Evaluate these arguments, and discuss whether these and other benefits will be maintained in the long run.

# chapter nineteen

# Introduction to macroeconomics

## Learning outcomes

**By the end of this chapter, you should understand:**

- Macroeconomics as the study of the whole economy

- Internally consistent national accounts

- The circular flow between households and firms

- Why leakages always equal injections

- More comprehensive measures of GDP and GNP

## Key learning blocks

**This is a fairly simple chapter which develops the context for the more theoretical chapters which follow. The key learning blocks are as follows:**

1. What is macroeconomics?

2. The circular flow of income as an intuitive representation of the economy.

3. How can we measure economic activity?

The textbook deals with each of these issues in turn. The exercises that follow will help to develop your understanding.

# Important concepts and technical terms

## Match each lettered concept with the appropriate numbered phrase:

**a** Inventories

**b** Exports

**c** Saving

**d** Depreciation

**e** Current prices

**f** Constant prices

**g** Open economy

**h** Closed economy

**i** Gross national product (GNP)

**j** Personal disposable income

**k** Value added

**l** GNP deflator

**m** Investment

**n** Imports

**o** Gross domestic product (GDP)

**p** Net income from abroad

**1** Goods that are produced abroad but purchased for use in the domestic economy.

**2** The total income earned by domestic citizens, regardless of the country where their factor services were supplied.

**3** The output produced by factors of production located in the domestic economy, regardless of who owns those factors.

**4** The excess of inflows of income from factor services supplied abroad over the outflows of income arising from the supply of factor services by foreigners in the domestic economy.

**5** The purchase of new capital goods by firms.

**6** A valuation of expenditures or output using the prices prevailing at some base year.

**7** A valuation of expenditures or output using the prices prevailing at the time of measurement.

**8** Goods that are domestically produced but sold abroad.

**9** That part of income which is not spent buying goods and services.

**10** The increase in the value of goods as a result of the production process.

**11** A measurement of the rate at which the value of the existing capital stock declines per period as a result of wear and tear or of obsolescence.

**12** Household income after direct taxes and transfer payments: the amount that households have available for spending and saving.

**13** An economy which does not transact with the rest of the world.

**14** Goods currently held by a firm for future production or sale.

**15** An economy which has transactions with other countries.

**16** The ratio of nominal GNP to real GNP expressed as an index.

## Exercises

Some of the relevant techniques and issues which you will need in the exercises in this chapter were first introduced in Chapter 2.

**1** Table 19–1 presents consumer price indices (CPIs) for the UK, the USA and Spain.

**(a)** Calculate the annual inflation rate for each of the countries.

(b) Plot your three inflation series on a diagram against time.

(c) By what percentage did prices increase in each country over the whole period – i.e. between 1992 and 2002?

(d) Which economy has experienced most stability of the inflation rate?

(e) Which economy saw the greatest deceleration in the rate of inflation between 1998 and 2000?

Table 19–2 presents some data relating to national output (real GDP) of the same three economies over a similar period, expressed as index numbers.

(f) Calculate the annual growth rate for each of the countries.

(g) Plot your three growth series on a diagram against time.

(h) By what percentage did output increase in each country over the whole period?

(i) To what extent did growth follow a similar pattern over time in these three countries?

**2** In a hypothetical closed economy with no government, planned consumption is 150, planned investment is 50 and total production is 210.

(a) How much is total planned expenditure?

## Table 19–1 Consumer prices, 1992–2002

|  | UK | | USA | | Spain | |
|---|---|---|---|---|---|---|
|  | Consumer price index | Inflation rate (%) | Consumer price index | Inflation rate (%) | Consumer price index | Inflation rate (%) |
| 1992 | 92.9 | | 92.1 | | 87.2 | |
| 1993 | 94.4 | | 94.8 | | 91.2 | |
| 1994 | 96.7 | | 97.3 | | 95.5 | |
| 1995 | 100.0 | | 100.0 | | 100.0 | |
| 1996 | 102.4 | | 102.9 | | 103.6 | |
| 1997 | 105.7 | | 105.3 | | 105.6 | |
| 1998 | 109.3 | | 107.0 | | 107.5 | |
| 1999 | 112.1 | | 108.2 | | 115.4 | |
| 2000 | 114.6 | | 109.0 | | 120.3 | |
| 2001 | 117.2 | | 111.5 | | 123.5 | |
| 2002 | 121.0 | | 112.8 | | 126.0 | |

*Source: International Financial Statistics.*

## Table 19–2 National production, 1992–2002

|  | UK | | USA | | Spain | |
|---|---|---|---|---|---|---|
|  | GDP index | Growth rate (%) | GDP index | Growth rate (%) | GDP index | Growth rate (%) |
| 1992 | 91.4 | | 92.3 | | 96.3 | |
| 1993 | 93.3 | | 94.5 | | 95.2 | |
| 1994 | 97.3 | | 97.8 | | 97.4 | |
| 1995 | 100.0 | | 100.0 | | 100.0 | |
| 1996 | 102.6 | | 103.4 | | 102.4 | |
| 1997 | 106.2 | | 107.5 | | 106.0 | |
| 1998 | 108.5 | | 111.7 | | 110.1 | |
| 1999 | 111.9 | | 117.4 | | 111.8 | |
| 2000 | 115.3 | | 121.8 | | 115.7 | |
| 2001 | 117.8 | | 122.1 | | 120.6 | |
| 2002 | 119.9 | | 125.1 | | 125.8 | |

*Source: International Financial Statistics.*

(b) Calculate unplanned stock changes.

(c) How much is savings in this situation?

(d) What is actual investment?

(e) How would you expect producers to react to this situation in the next period?

**3** Table 19–3 lists a number of components of UK GNP from both income and expenditure sides of the account for 2002. All quantities are measured in £ million at current prices and are taken from ONS, *United Kingdom National Accounts* (2003 edition).

Using the expenditure side of the accounts, calculate the following:

(a) GDP at market prices.

(b) GNP at market prices.

(c) GDP at basic prices.

(d) Net national product at market prices.

(e) Net national income at basic prices.

(f) GDP at market prices from the income side of the accounts.

(g) Can you explain why your answers to (a) and (f) are not identical?

**4** Consider five firms in a closed economy: a steel producer, rubber producer, machine tool-maker, tyre producer and bicycle manufacturer. The bicycle manufacturer sells the bicycles produced to final customers for £8000. In producing the bicycles, the firm buys tyres (£1000), steel (£2500) and machine tools (£1800). The tyre manufacturer buys rubber (£600) from the rubber producer and the machine tool-maker buys steel (£1000) from the steel producer.

(a) What is the contribution of the bicycle industry to GDP?

(b) Calculate total final expenditure.

| Table 19–3 | Components of GNP in the UK, 2002 | | | |
|---|---|---|---|---|
| Final consumption expenditure* | 545 124 | | Capital consumption | 88 771 |
| Subsidies | 7 453 | | Stock changes | 3 621 |
| Other indirect taxes** | 17 619 | | Fixed investment | 148 202 |
| Net income from abroad | 11 737 | | Exports | 224 202 |
| Government final consumption | 153 564 | | Employment income | 463 398 |
| Taxes on products*** | 103 634 | | Mixed income | 43 379 |
| Profits and rent | 223 212 | | Imports | 232 714 |

Notes      * By households and non-profit institutions serving households.

           ** Taxes on production, which register on the income side of the accounts only.

           *** Taxes on products, which register on both expenditure and income sides of the accounts.

| Table 19–4 | Household savings in the UK, 1992–2003 |
|---|---|
| Year | Households savings ratio |
| 1992 | 11.6 |
| 1993 | 10.8 |
| 1994 | 9.3 |
| 1995 | 10.0 |
| 1996 | 9.3 |
| 1997 | 9.5 |
| 1998 | 6.4 |
| 1999 | 5.3 |
| 2000 | 5.5 |
| 2001 | 7.0 |
| 2002 | 5.8 |
| 2003 | 6.0 |

**5** Table 19–4 lists the UK household savings ratio for the period 1992–2003.

(a) Why do you think the savings ratio has fallen?

(b) What will the impact of a falling savings ratio be on the circular flow of income?

**6** According to the ONS, *United Kingdom National Accounts* (2003 edition), GDP at current market prices was £994 309 in 2001 and £1 099 896 in 2003. The implicit GDP deflator was 100.0 in 2001 and 106.3 in 2003. Calculate real and nominal growth in GDP for 2002 and 2003.

**7** The following table illustrates the domestic expenditure and national income of an economy during three consecutive years:

|  | Year 1 (£ bn) | Year 2 (£ bn) | Year 3 (£ bn) |
|---|---|---|---|
| National income | 500 | 250 | 200 |
| Government expenditure | 200 | 250 | 200 |
| Private expenditure | 250 | 300 | 250 |
| Investment | 50 | 200 | 200 |

For each of the three years, evaluate the balance of trade situation facing the economy.

**8** The following table refers to one country in two consecutive years:

|  | Index of GNP | Retail price index | Index of population | Average working week (hours) |
|---|---|---|---|---|
| Year 1 | 105 | 102 | 102 | 44 |
| Year 2 | 110 | 106 | 103 | 44 |

On the basis of these figures, evaluate each of the following statements as a description of the changes that took place between year 1 and year 2.

(a) Real GNP increased.
(b) Real GNP per capita increased.
(c) The standard of living of all people within the country fell.
(d) The working population increased in size.

**9** Which of the following items are included in the calculation of GNP in the UK, and which are excluded?

(a) Salaries paid to schoolteachers.
(b) Tips given to taxi drivers.
(c) Expenditure on social security benefits.
(d) The income of a second-hand car salesman.
(e) Work carried out in the home by a housewife.
(f) Work carried out in the home by a paid domestic helper.
(g) The value of pleasure from leisure.
(h) Free-range eggs sold in the market.
(i) Blackberries picked in the hedgerows.

## True/False

**1** The increase in the quantity of goods and services which the economy as a whole can afford to purchase is known as economic growth.

**2** In the period 1990–2004, Japan grew significantly faster than European countries such as the UK, Switzerland or France.

**3** During the 1980s and 1990s, the UK suffered the highest price inflation in the world.

**4** Unemployment in the UK decreased tenfold between 1990 and 2004.

**5** Given full and accurate measurement, we should get the same estimate of total economic activity whether we measure the value of production output, the level of factor incomes or spending on goods and services.

**6** A closed economy is one with excessive levels of unemployment.

**7** The calculation of value added is a way of measuring output without double-counting.

**8** In a closed economy with no government, savings are always equal to investment.

**9** Gross domestic product at basic prices is equal to GDP at market prices plus net indirect taxes.

**10** Depreciation is an economic cost because it measures resources being used up in the production process.

**11** Gross national product at current prices is a measure of real economic activity.

**12** Gross national product at constant prices is a useless measure of economic welfare because it fails to measure so many important ingredients of welfare.

## Economics in action

### United Kingdom in the near term

(Adapted from *OECD Economic Outlook*, June 2004)

With the housing market picking up and the labour market strong, private consumption is likely to expand vigorously. The recent appreciation of sterling may dampen exports. The government deficit exceeded the golden rule of 3 per cent so some tightening of taxation may be expected.

## Questions

**1** How does the OECD expect leakages and injections into the UK economy to develop over the near term?

**2** How might rising interest rates impact on the UK circular flow of income?

## Questions for thought

**1** Reconsider the items listed in Exercise 9 of this chapter. Which of these should be included in a measure of national economic welfare? What additional items (positive or negative) should be incorporated if the measure is to reflect the quality of life?

**2** In many less developed countries, much economic activity is concentrated in small-scale subsistence agriculture. How would you expect this to affect comparisons of living standards based on GNP measurements? What other difficulties would you expect to encounter in making international comparisons of living standards?

**3** Why is it so important to distinguish between real and nominal national income measures?

# chapter twenty

# Output and aggregate demand

## Learning outcomes

**By the end of this chapter, you should understand:**

- Actual output and potential output
- Why output is demand-determined in the short run
- Short-run equilibrium output
- Consumption and investment demand
- How aggregate demand determines short-run equilibrium output
- The marginal propensity to consume (MPC)
- How the size of the multiplier affects the MPC
- The paradox of thrift

## Key learning blocks

**In this chapter we move on from the circular flow of income and begin to develop a more formal model of the economy. You are required to understand the following central issues:**

**1** The difference between planned and actual output.

**2** The determinants of aggregate demand.

**3** The multiplier effect.

The textbook provides an in-depth treatment of the more complex issues surrounding these topics and the exercises that follow will help you to develop your understanding.

# Important concepts and technical terms

## Match each lettered concept with the appropriate numbered phrase:

**a** Investment demand

**b** Autonomous consumption

**c** Potential output

**d** Short-run equilibrium output

**e** Marginal propensity to save

**f** Consumption function

**g** Savings function

**h** Aggregate demand schedule

**i** Marginal propensity to consume

**j** Paradox of thrift

**k** Unplanned inventory change

**l** Multiplier

**1** The part of consumption expenditure which is unrelated to the level of income.

**2** Firms' desired or planned additions to their physical capital (factories and machines) and to inventories.

**3** An unanticipated increase or decrease in the level of stocks held by firms.

**4** A relationship showing the level of planned savings at each level of personal disposable income.

**5** A curve which shows the amount that firms and households plan to spend on goods and services at each level of income.

**6** The level of output the economy would produce if all factors of production were fully employed.

**7** The ratio of the change in equilibrium output to the change in autonomous spending that causes the change in output.

**8** The situation whereby a change in the amount households wish to save at each income level leads to a change in the equilibrium level of income but no change in the equilibrium level of savings, which must still equal planned investment.

**9** The fraction of each extra pound of disposable income that households wish to use for saving.

**10** The fraction of each extra pound of disposable income that households wish to use to increase consumption.

**11** The level of output in an economy when aggregate demand or planned aggregate spending just equals the output that is actually produced.

**12** A relationship showing the level of aggregate consumption desired at each level of personal disposable income.

## Exercises

**1** Table 20–1 presents data on real consumers' expenditure and personal disposable income for the UK.

**(a)** Calculate real savings in each year during the period and the percentage of income saved.

**(b)** Plot a scatter diagram with real consumption on the vertical axis and real personal disposable income on the horizontal axis.

**(c)** Draw a straight line passing as close as possible to these points on the diagram and measure the approximate slope of the line.

**(d)** Under what conditions would you regard this slope as a reasonable estimate of the marginal propensity to consume?

**(e)** Plot a scatter diagram of real savings against income.

**(f)** If you were to draw a straight line through these points, how would you expect it to relate to the one

| Table 20–1 | UK consumption and income, 1992–2002, £ bn, at constant 1995 prices | |
|---|---|---|
| Year | Households' final consumption expenditure | Real households' disposable income |
| 1992 | 476 834 | 522 915 |
| 1993 | 490 594 | 537 310 |
| 1994 | 505 711 | 545 269 |
| 1995 | 514 042 | 557 940 |
| 1996 | 532 735 | 571 440 |
| 1997 | 552 138 | 595 043 |
| 1998 | 573 873 | 596 745 |
| 1999 | 599 185 | 616 235 |
| 2000 | 626 537 | 654 649 |
| 2001 | 645 981 | 685 263 |
| 2002 | 668 994 | 695 183 |

*Source: Economic Trends Annual Supplement, UK National Accounts.*

you drew in *(c)?* Do it, and measure its approximate slope.

(g) Assuming this to be a sensible estimate of the marginal propensity to save, what does this imply for the value of the multiplier?

**2** Table 20–2 shows some data on consumption and income (output) for the economy of Hypothetica. Planned investment is autonomous and occurs at the rate of H$60 bn per period.

(a) Calculate savings and aggregate demand at each level of income.

(b) For each level of output, work out the unplanned change in inventory holdings and the rate of actual investment.

(c) If, in a particular period, income turned out to be H$100 bn, how would you expect producers to react?

(d) If, in a particular period, income turned out to be H$350 bn, how would you expect producers to react?

(e) What is the equilibrium level of income?

(f) What is the marginal propensity to consume?

(g) If investment increased by H$15 bn, what would be the change in equilibrium income?

**3** (a) Using the data of Exercise **2**, use graph paper to plot the consumption function and aggregate demand schedule.

(b) Add on the 45° line and confirm that equilibrium occurs at the same point suggested by your answer to **2***(e)* above.

(c) Show the effect on equilibrium of an increase in investment of $15 bn.

**4** (a) Again using the data on Hypothetica from Exercise **2**, use graph paper to plot how savings vary with income.

(b) Add on the investment line and confirm that equilibrium again occurs at the same income level.

(c) Show that an increase in investment of $15 bn leads to a new level of equilibrium income.

(d) Explain the process by which this new equilibrium is attained.

**5** Figure 20–1 (overleaf) shows the aggregate demand schedule for an economy, together with the 45° line.

(a) Suppose output is *OG*: identify the level of aggregate demand and specify whether there is excess demand or excess supply.

(b) What is the size of the unplanned inventory change with output *OG*?

| Table 20–2 | Income and consumption in Hypothetica (all in Hypothetical $ bn) | | | | | |
|---|---|---|---|---|---|---|
| Income (output) | Planned consumption | Planned investment | Savings | Aggregate demand | Unplanned inventory change | Actual investment |
| 50 | 35 | | | | | |
| 100 | 70 | | | | | |
| 150 | 105 | | | | | |
| 200 | 140 | | | | | |
| 250 | 175 | | | | | |
| 300 | 210 | | | | | |
| 350 | 245 | | | | | |
| 400 | 280 | | | | | |

**Figure 20–1** The income–expenditure diagram

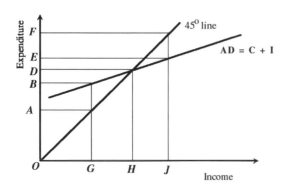

**(c)** How will firms respond to this situation?

**(d)** Identify equilibrium income and expenditure.

**(e)** Suppose output is *OJ*: identify the level of aggregate planned expenditure and specify whether there is excess demand or excess supply.

**(f)** What is the size of the unplanned inventory change with output *OJ* – and how will firms react to it?

**6** Figure 20–2 shows autonomous investment for an economy, together with the savings function showing how savings vary with income. $I_B$ is the initial level of investment.

**Figure 20–2** Savings and investment

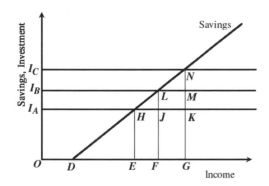

**(a)** Identify the initial equilibrium levels of income and savings.

**(b)** Which level of investment represents the effect of an increase in business confidence – a surge in optimistic animal spirits?

**(c)** What is the new equilibrium level of income?

**(d)** What is the multiplier?

**(e)** Which level of investment shows an increase in pessimism on the part of firms?

**(f)** What would be the new equilibrium level of income?

**7** Consider a closed economy with no government sector in which consumption *(C)* is related to income *(Y)* by the equation:

$$C = A + cY$$

**(a)** What is the marginal propensity to consume?

**(b)** How is the level of savings related to income in this economy?

Suppose that $A = 400$, $c = 0.75$ and the level of investment is 500:

**(c)** At what level of national income would savings be zero?

**(d)** What would be the equilibrium level of income?

**8** Figure 20–3 represents a closed economy with no government sector. At the equilibrium level of income, how would you interpret:

**(a)** *XY/UX*

and

**(b)** *WY/OW?*

**Figure 20–3** A closed economy with no government

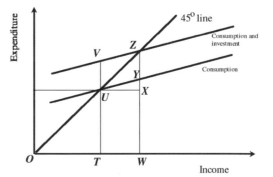

**9** Figure 20–4 shows an economy which initially has an aggregate demand schedule given by *AK*.

**Figure 20–4** Equilibrium and the marginal propensity to consume

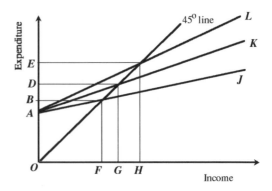

(a) What is the initial equilibrium level of income?

(b) Suppose there is an increase in the marginal propensity to save: which is the new aggregate demand schedule?

(c) What is the new equilibrium level of income?

(d) Suppose that, instead, the marginal propensity to consume had increased: what would be the new aggregate demand schedule?

(e) What is the new equilibrium level of income?

**10** For the last exercise of this chapter we return to the economy of Hypothetica. Initially, consumption is determined (as before) as 70 per cent of income. Investment is again autonomous and occurs at the rate of H$90 bn per period.

(a) What is the equilibrium level of income? (If it helps, you might create a table similar to Table 20–2 in Exercise **2**, for values of output between, say, 250 and 600.)

(b) What would be the equilibrium level of income if investment increased by H$15 bn?

(c) Calculate the value of the multiplier.

Suppose that our Hypothetical consumers become more spendthrift, spending 80 cents in the dollar rather than 70. With investment again at H$90 bn per period:

(d) Calculate the equilibrium level of income.

(e) Calculate the equilibrium level of income if investment increased by H$10 bn.

(f) Calculate the value of the multiplier.

## True/False

**1** Potential output includes an allowance for 'normal unemployment'.

**2** The Keynesian model suggests that output is mainly demand-determined.

**3** Consumption is linearly related to income.

**4** The marginal propensities to consume and save sum to unity.

**5** Investment is autonomous.

**6** The purpose of the aggregate demand schedule is to separate out the change in demand directly induced by changes in income.

**7** Short-run equilibrium occurs when spending plans are not frustrated by a shortage of goods and when firms do not produce more output than they can sell.

**8** Unplanned inventory changes are the signal to firms that there is disequilibrium.

**9** Planned savings always equals planned investment.

**10** The slope of the aggregate demand schedule depends only on the level of autonomous consumption.

**11** The multiplier in our simple model tells us how much output changes when aggregate demand shifts.

**12** If only people saved more, investment would increase and we could get the economy moving again.

## Economics in action

### Study casts cold light on pace of Japan's recovery

(Adapted from an article by David Pilling, *Financial Times*, May 2004)

Japan is growing at less than half the speed suggested by official data because of problems in calculating deflation and seasonal adjustments. Instead of growing at a real rate of 5.6 per cent, the Japanse economy expanded by only 2.5 per cent in 2003, according to HSBC.

There are two issues with real GDP estimation. The first is a technical problem linked to calculating the GDP deflator, which leads to an over-estimation of price falls. That is important because the headline figure for real growth appears bigger when the number for deflation is large. The second problem is simply that the adjustment for seasonality is far too crude, according to HSBC.

### Questions

**1** What do the problems highlighted in the article mean for the estimation of actual and potential GDP?

**2** Is the Japanese economy operating above or below the potential level of GDP?

## Questions for thought

**1**    In a closed economy with no governmental economic activity, savings and investment are always equal. How, then, does it make sense for economists to talk about situations in which they take different values?

**2**    Think about the consumption expenditures undertaken by your household. Is income the only factor influencing the aggregate amount? What other factors may help to determine aggregate consumption?

**3**    Suppose that equilibrium output for an economy entails high levels of unemployment. Does the analysis of this chapter suggest any action which the authorities might take to mitigate the effects of unemployment?

# chapter twenty-one

# Fiscal policy and foreign trade

## Learning outcomes

**By the end of this chapter, you should understand:**

- How fiscal policy affects aggregate demand
- How short-run equilibrium output is determined in this extended model
- The balanced budget multiplier
- Automatic stabilizers
- The structural budget and the inflation-adjusted budget
- How budget deficits add to national debt
- The limits to discretionary fiscal policy
- How foreign trade affects equilibrium output

## Key learning blocks

In this chapter you will be introduced to the workings and issues relating to *fiscal policy*. The central areas which you need to be familiar with are:

1. How can the government influence aggregate demand?
2. What is the budget deficit, and how does it relate to economic activity?
3. What is the national debt, and how does it relate to economic activity?

The textbook discusses each of these topics in turn. The exercises that follow will help to develop your understanding.

# Important concepts and technical terms

## Match each lettered concept with the appropriate numbered phrase:

**a** Automatic stabilizers

**b** National debt

**c** Marginal propensity to import

**d** Stabilization policy

**e** Discretionary fiscal policy

**f** Code for Fiscal Stability

**g** Balanced budget multiplier

**h** Budget deficit

**i** Fine-tuning

**j** The structural budget

**k** Fiscal policy

**l** Inflation-adjusted government deficit

**1** The government's decisions about spending and taxes.

**2** Mechanisms in the economy that reduce the response of GNP to shocks.

**3** Government actions to control the level of output in order to keep GNP close to its full-employment level.

**4** The government deficit adjusted for the difference between real and nominal interest rates.

**5** The excess of government outlays over government receipts.

**6** The process by which an increase in government spending, accompanied by an equal increase in taxes, results in an increase in output.

**7** A commitment by the government to a medium-run objective of financing current government spending out of current revenues.

**8** The fraction of each additional pound of national income that domestic residents wish to spend on imports.

**9** The government's total stock of outstanding debts.

**10** Frequent discretionary adjustments to policy instruments.

**11** A calculation of the government budget deficit under the assumption of full employment: a cyclically adjusted indicator of fiscal stance.

**12** The use of active fiscal policy in response to economic conditions.

## Exercises

**1** Table 21–1 carries us back to the kingdom of Hypothetica, which we visited in Chapter 20. As then, planned consumption is 70 per cent of disposable income, but now the government imposes net taxes amounting to 20 per cent of gross income. Planned investment is still H$60 bn and the government plans to spend H$50 bn.

**(a)** For each level of income in Table 21–1, calculate disposable income, planned consumption, savings and net taxes.

**(b)** Calculate aggregate demand, showing it at each level of aggregate supply.

**(c)** If, in a particular period, income turned out to be

H$350 bn, how would you expect producers to react?

**(d)** What is the equilibrium level of income?

**(e)** Calculate the government budget deficit at equilibrium income.

Suppose that government expenditure is increased by H$22 bn:

**(f)** What is the new equilibrium income?

**(g)** Calculate the government budget deficit at this new equilibrium position.

**(h)** What is the value of the multiplier?

**2** **(a)** Using the data of Exercise 1, plot the consumption function and aggregate demand schedule.

**(b)** Add on the 45° line and confirm that equilibrium

**Table 21–1 Government comes to Hypothetica (all values in Hypothetical $ bn)**

| Income/output | Disposable income | Planned consumption | Planned investment | Government spending | Savings | Net taxes | Aggregate demand |
|---|---|---|---|---|---|---|---|
| 50 | | | | | | | |
| 100 | | | | | | | |
| 150 | | | | | | | |
| 200 | | | | | | | |
| 250 | | | | | | | |
| 300 | | | | | | | |
| 350 | | | | | | | |
| 400 | | | | | | | |

occurs at the same point suggested by your answers to **1**(d) above.

(c) Show the effect on equilibrium income of an increase in government spending of H$22 bn.

**3** This exercise concerns the multiplier under different circumstances in a closed economy with and without government. Consumption is determined as 80 per cent of the income available to households. Investment is autonomous at a level of 450, as shown in Table 21–2.

(a) Calculate consumption 1 and aggregate demand 1, assuming there is no government.
(b) What is the equilibrium level of income?
(c) What would be equilibrium income if investment increased by 50?
(d) Calculate the value of the multiplier.

Suppose now that the government levies direct taxes of 10 per cent of income and undertakes expenditure of 250, with investment back at 450:

(e) Calculate disposable income, consumption 2 and aggregate demand 2.
(f) What is the equilibrium level of income?
(g) What is the size of the government budget deficit?
(h) Use your answers to parts (b), (e) and (f) to explain the balanced budget multiplier.

(i) What would equilibrium income be if investment increased by 70?
(j) Calculate the value of the multiplier.

**4** The government in an economy undertakes expenditure on goods and services of £100 million and makes transfer payments amounting to 10 per cent of national income. The rate of direct taxation is 30 per cent.

(a) Draw a diagram showing autonomous government expenditure and the way in which net taxes vary with national income.
(b) At what level of income does the government have a balanced budget?
(c) Within what range of income does the government run a budget deficit?
(d) Within what range of income does the government run a budget surplus?
(e) What would be the government deficit/surplus if equilibrium income were £400 million?
(f) If full-employment income is £750 million, what is the full-employment budget?

**5** A government has £100 bn of outstanding debt, on which it must make interest payments at the current nominal rate of 8 per cent. Inflation is running at 6 per cent p.a.

**Table 21–2 The multiplier with and without government**

| Income/output | Consumption 1 | Investment | Aggregate demand 1 | Disposable income | Consumption 2 | Government spending | Aggregate demand 2 |
|---|---|---|---|---|---|---|---|
| 2000 | | 450 | | | | | |
| 2250 | | 450 | | | | | |
| 2500 | | 450 | | | | | |
| 2750 | | 450 | | | | | |
| 3000 | | 450 | | | | | |

(a) Nominal interest payments are included in government expenditure and thus contribute to the government deficit. What is the nominal interest burden?

(b) What is the real interest rate? (*Note*: This was discussed in Chapter 12.)

(c) What is the real interest burden?

(d) If you have followed this line of reasoning through, you may feel suspicious that we have just been manipulating the figures. After all, holders of government bonds must be paid their (nominal) 8 per cent return. How in practice will the government be able to meet the payments?

**6** An economy exports £150 million worth of goods each period, this quantity being autonomous. Imports, however, vary with national income such that imports always comprise 20 per cent of income.

(a) Draw a diagram which shows imports and exports against national income.

(b) What is the trade balance when income is £1000 million?

(c) What is the trade balance when income is £500 million?

(d) At what level of income are imports equal to exports?

(e) If full-employment income is £1000 million, explain how the balance of trade may act as a constant on government policy.

**7** This exercise explores the balanced budget multiplier in a closed economy. Investment expenditure is fixed at 450, consumption is 80 per cent of disposable income. Initially, government expenditure is 250 and direct taxes are 10 per cent of income.

(a) Identify the initial equilibrium income for the economy.

(b) Calculate the amount of consumption expenditure, tax revenue and the government budget deficit/surplus.

Suppose now that government expenditure is increased by 500 and the tax rate raised from 10 to 25 per cent.

(c) Before output has had time to adjust, by how much is disposable income reduced?

(d) Calculate the resulting change in consumption expenditure and the net effect on aggregate demand, remembering the increase in government expenditure.

(e) What is the new equilibrium income level for the economy?

(f) What is the government budget deficit/surplus?

(g) Calculate the balanced budget multiplier.

**8** Figure 21–1 shows aggregate demand schedules with and without foreign trade, together with the 45° line.

**Figure 21–1**    Equilibrium in an open economy

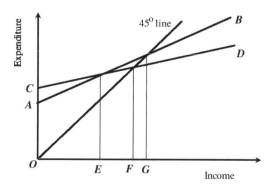

(a) *AB* and *CD* represent aggregate demand schedules with and without foreign trade. (Assume that imports are proportional to income, but exports are autonomous.) Which is aggregate demand with, and without, foreign trade?

(b) Identify equilibrium income in the absence of foreign trade.

(c) Identify equilibrium income when there is foreign trade.

(d) At what level of income is there a zero trade balance?

(e) Explain whether the presence of foreign trade increases or reduces the size of the multiplier.

**9** Figure 21–2 shows the ratio of national debt to GDP in the UK for each year since 1975.

**Figure 21–2**    UK national debt as a percentage of GDP, 1975–2005

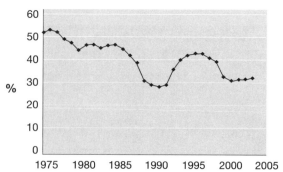

(a) What is meant by the 'national debt'?

(b) Discuss the time-path followed by the national debt in this period, paying especial attention to the changes in the 1990s.

(c) Should the government have been concerned at the size of the national debt in the 1990s?

**10** Explain why each of the following items may constitute an obstacle to the use of active fiscal policy.

(a) Monitoring the economy's performance.

(b) Implementing changes in the spending pro-gramme.

(c) Timing the multiplier process.

(d) Uncertainty concerning the operation of the multi-plier.

(e) Uncertainty concerning future aggregate demand.

(f) The possibility of indirect policy effects.

(g) Danger to other policy objectives.

(h) Uncertainty about the level of full employment.

## True/False

**1** In the 1990s, direct purchases by government comprised about half of national output in most European countries.

**2** The effect of net taxes is to make the relationship between consumption and national income steeper.

**3** An increase in government spending accompanied by an equal increase in taxes results in an increase in output.

**4** The effect of net taxes is to reduce the multiplier.

**5** For a given level of government spending, an increase in the tax rate reduces both the equilibrium level of national income and the size of the budget deficit.

**6** The size of the budget deficit is a good measure of the government's fiscal stance.

**7** The structural budget shows the state of the government deficit/surplus if the other components of aggregate demand were such as to ensure the economy were at full-employment output.

**8** In a world with significant inflation, it is sensible to count only the real interest rate times the outstanding government debt as an item of expenditure contributing to the overall government deficit.

**9** Income tax, VAT and unemployment benefit are important automatic stabilizers.

**10** In recent times, the debt–GDP ratio has been rising in France and Germany.

**11** Net exports in the UK amount to nearly 30 per cent of GDP.

**12** Direct import restrictions are always good for domestic output and employment as they allow the economy to reach full employment without hitting the constraint of the trade balance.

## Economics in action

### Germany falls deeper into stability pact breach

(Adapted from an article by Mark Milner, *The Guardian*, 14 May 2004)

Germany looks likely to become a serial offender against the eurozone's budget rules after the finance ministry yesterday revealed a bigger than expected black hole in the country's public finances.

However, 'tax hikes and more rigorous spending cuts would be the wrong answers to this development. They would be poison for the recovery which has not yet firmly taken root, a recovery we need for our savings efforts to succeed', said the finance minister.

Germany's hopes that economic recovery will bolster its finances received little comfort yesterday, with growth of 1.4 per cent expected for 2004.

### Questions

**1** Why would tax hikes and spending cuts be poison for a recovery?

**2** The German government is proposing to privatize the German telecommunications and train industries: why?

**3** What impact, if any, will privatization have on the German budget deficit in the long run?

## Questions for thought

**1** Examine the effect on the multiplier of the existence of government activity and international trade. Discuss the problem of timing the multiplier process and explore reasons why this model may not provide an adequate explanation of how an economy 'really' works.

**2** Discuss the importance of automatic stabilizers. To what extent may imports be regarded as one such automatic stabilizer?

**3** What do you regard as the principal shortcomings of the national income determination model as developed so far?

# chapter twenty-two

# Money and banking

## Learning outcomes

**By the end of this chapter, you should understand:**

- The medium of exchange as the key attribute of money
- Other functions of money
- How banks create money
- The monetary base, the money multiplier and the money supply
- Different measures of money in the UK
- How banks compete for deposits and loans
- Motives for holding money
- How money demand depends on output, prices and interest rates

## Key learning blocks

For monetary economists the *money side* of the economy is central to understanding how the economy works. In this chapter you are required to understand the following central areas:

**1** What are the key characteristics of money?

**2** How do banks create money?

**3** What factors determine the demand for money?

The latter two of these key learning blocks have some complexity associated with them and the textbook covers them in detail. The exercises that follow will help to further your understanding of the topics.

# Important concepts and technical terms

## Match each lettered concept with the appropriate numbered phrase:

**a** Medium of exchange

**b** Financial intermediary

**c** Money

**d** Near money

**e** Financial panic

**f** M0

**g** Money supply

**h** Store of value

**i** Liquidity

**j** Reserve ratio

**k** Money multiplier

**l** Unit of account

**m** Monetary base

**n** Barter economy

**1** Any generally accepted means of payment for the delivery of goods or the settlement of debt.

**2** The function of money by which it enables the exchange of goods and services.

**3** The function of money by which it provides a unit in which prices are quoted and accounts are kept.

**4** The function of money by which it can be used to make purchases in the future.

**5** The quantity of notes and coin in private circulation plus the quantity held by the banking system, sometimes known as the stock of high-powered money.

**6** An economy with no medium of exchange, in which goods are traded directly or swapped for other goods.

**7** The change in the money stock for a £1 change in the quantity of the monetary base.

**8** An institution that specializes in bringing lenders and borrowers together.

**9** Assets that are 'almost' as good as money: stores of value that can readily be converted into money but are not themselves a means of payment.

**10** A self-fulfilling prophecy by which people believe that a bank will be unable to pay and, in the stampede to get their money, thereby ensure that the bank cannot pay.

**11** Notes and coin in circulation plus bankers' operational deposits with the Bank of England.

**12** The value of the total stock of money, the medium of exchange, in circulation.

**13** The speed and certainty with which an asset can be converted into money.

**14** The ratio of reserves to deposits.

## Exercises

**1** Eight individuals in a barter economy have and want the following goods:

- Alice has some haddock but would like some apples
- Barry has some gin but fancies blackcurrant jam
- Carol is in possession of doughnuts but wants coconuts
- Daniel has obtained some jellied eels but really wants doughnuts
- Eleanor has some figs but would prefer jellied eels
- Felix fancies figs but has only blackcurrant jam
- Gloria has coconuts but yearns for gin
- Henry has apples but would like haddock.

(a) Can you work out a series of transactions which would satisfy all concerned?

(b) Can you now understand how money is so helpful in making the world go round?

**2** Identify each of the following items as legal, token, commodity or IOU money – or, indeed, as not-money:

(a) Gold.
(b) £1 coin.
(c) Cigarettes.
(d) Cheque for £100.
(e) Petrol.
(f) Camera accepted in part-exchange.
(g) A building society deposit.
(h) Pigs, turkeys and cocoa nuts.

**3** This exercise shows how the banks can create money through their loan policy. For simplicity, assume that there is a single commercial bank, which aims to hold 10 per cent of its deposits as cash. The public is assumed to have a fixed demand for cash of £10 million. We begin in equilibrium with the following situation.

Consider the sequence of events that follows if the central bank autonomously supplies an extra £10 million cash which finds its way into the pockets of Joe Public:

(a) How will Joe Public react? (Remember the fixed demand for cash.)
(b) How does this affect the cash ratio of the commercial bank?
(c) How will the commercial bank react to this 'disequilibrium'?
(d) How much cash does Joe Public now hold?
(e) What will Joe Public do with the excess cash?
(f) How does this affect the behaviour of the commercial bank?
(g) At what point will the system settle down again, with both bank and public back in equilibrium?
(h) How does money stock alter as this process unfolds?

*Note*: If this sequence of questions does not make any sense to you, you are recommended to tackle them again in conjunction with the commentary provided in the 'Answers and comments' section in the book.

**4** Which of the following characteristics are necessary for an asset to function as money?

(a) Backed by a precious metal.
(b) Authorized as legal tender by the monetary authorities.
(c) Generally acceptable as a medium of exchange.
(d) Having value in future transactions.

**5** The commercial banks in an economy choose to hold 5 per cent of deposits in the form of cash reserves. The general public chooses to hold an amount of notes and coin in circulation equal to one-quarter of its bank deposits. The stock of high-powered money in the economy is £12 million.

(a) Calculate the value of the money multiplier from the data in the table below.
(b) What is the size of the money stock if both public and banks are holding their desired amounts of cash?
(c) Suppose the banks now decide that they need to hold only 4 per cent of deposits as cash. Calculate the value of the money multiplier.
(d) What is now the size of 'equilibrium' money stock?
(e) Suppose that the banks again choose to hold 5 per cent of deposits as cash, but the public increases its cash holdings to 30 per cent of its bank deposits. Now what is the value of the money multiplier?
(f) What is now the size of 'equilibrium' money stock?
(g) Does this analysis provide any clues to how the monetary authorities might try to influence the size of the money stock?

**6** Suppose that the clearing banks maintain a minimum cash ratio of 12 per cent, then:

(a) If an individual bank receives a cash deposit of £1000, what additional deposits would the bank feel able to create?
(b) What difference would it have made if the cash ratio had been only 10 per cent?

| Commercial bank balance sheet (£ million) | | | | | | |
| Liabilities | | Assets | | Cash ratio | Public cash holdings | Money stock |
| --- | --- | --- | --- | --- | --- | --- |
| Deposits | 100 | Cash | 10 | | | |
| | | Loans | 90 | | | |
| | 100 | | 100 | 10% | 10 | 110 |

**(c)** Under what circumstances might a bank choose to hold a higher cash ratio than is required by government regulations?

**7** In Table 22–1 are listed a number of components of the monetary aggregates in the UK, as at May 2004. (These data were taken from the Bank of England's website at http://www.bankofengland.co.uk/mfsd/) Calculate M0 and M4.

| Table 22–1    Some components of UK monetary aggregates, May 2004 | |
| --- | --- |
| | **£ million** |
| Notes and coin in circulation outside the Bank of England | 40 596 |
| Banks' cash and balances at Bank | 72 000 |
| Banks' retail deposits | 612 877 |
| Building society retail shares and deposits | 146 951 |
| Wholesale deposits | 289 769 |

**8** Assess the liquidity and likely return of each of the following financial assets:

**(a)** Cash.
**(b)** Equities.
**(c)** Bonds.
**(d)** Bills.
**(e)** Industrial shares.
**(f)** Perpetuities.

**9** In what way would you expect each of the following items to affect the demand for real money balances?

**(a)** An increase in real income.
**(b)** An increase in confidence about the future.
**(c)** An increase in the opportunity cost of holding money.
**(d)** A fall in nominal interest rates.
**(e)** An increase in the price level.
**(f)** An increase in the interest differential between risky assets and time deposits.
**(g)** An increase in uncertainty concerning future transactions.
**(h)** A fall in the frequency of income payments – for example, a switch from weekly to monthly payment.
**(i)** An increase in the stock of high-powered money brought about by open market operations by the Bank of England.

## True/False

**1** Dogs' teeth have been used as money.

**2** Trading is expensive in a barter economy.

**3** Money in current accounts in banks is legal tender.

**4** Financial panics are rare in present-day Britain because of the actions of the Bank of England.

**5** If the goldsmiths insisted that all transactions were backed by equal amounts of gold in the vaults, then their actions could not cause growth in the money supply.

**6** Banks are the only financial intermediaries.

**7** The clearing system represents one way in which society reduces the costs of making transactions.

**8** The more liquid an asset, the higher the return received.

**9** The modern fractional reserve banking system is an intrinsic part of the process of money creation.

**10** The monetary base is the quantity of notes and coin in circulation with the non-bank private sector.

**11** The more cash that the public wishes to hold, the higher is money supply.

**12** Building society deposits are so liquid that they ought to be included in the definition of money.

**13** The transactions motive for holding money falls with a rise in income.

**14** The precautionary motive for holding money reflects a need for liquid assets.

**15** The speculative motive for holding money will fall when interest rates fall.

## Economics in action

### Get the most out of rate hikes

(Adapted from *Investors Chronicle*, 2 July 2004)

Interest rates are now firmly set on an upward curve. It may seem like an age since rates last went up in the late 1990s but, since November 2003 when the Bank of England nudged up the base rate by 0.25 per cent, the trend has bedded in. The base rate has now risen a full 1 per cent – to 4.5 per cent – from the summer 2003 low. And, with US rates expected to rise this week, we can expect that upwards momentum to continue.

Generally, though, rising interest rates mean a more difficult time for fixed-interest investments, such as gilts and investment-grade corporate bonds, and these have already seen some capital depreciation in the first few months of 2004.

## Questions

**1** Explain what is meant by a capital depreciation of fixed-interest securities.

**2** What do you expect to happen to the demand for fixed-interest securities following the capital depreciation?

## Questions for thought

**1** Discuss why you think that people want to hold money rather than using the funds to earn a return.

**2** How do you expect the increased use of credit cards to affect the money supply?

# chapter twenty-three

# Interest rates and monetary transmission

## Learning outcomes

**By the end of this chapter, you should understand:**

- How a central bank can affect the money supply
- The central bank's role as lender of last resort
- Money market equilibrium
- An intermediate target for monetary policy
- The transmission mechanism of monetary policy
- How a central bank sets interest rates
- How interest rates affect consumption and investment demand

## Key learning blocks

This chapter examines the role of *money and the central bank* in economic activity. The central issues are as follows:

1. To understand the role and actions of the central bank.

2. To understand the means by which the central bank can attempt to control the money supply.

3. To understand money market equilibrium.

The textbook discusses each of these topics in detail. The exercises that follow will help to develop your understanding.

# Important concepts and technical terms

## Match each lettered concept with the appropriate numbered phrase:

a Monetary instruments

b Central bank

c Repo rate

d Investment demand schedule

e Open market operations (OMOs)

f Wealth effect

g Lender of last resort

h Life-cycle hypothesis

i Gilt repo

j Permanent income hypothesis

1 The most important bank in a country, usually having official standing in the government, having responsibility for issuing banknotes and acting as banker to the banking system and to the government.

2 A sale and repurchase agreement: a bank sells a gilt with a simultaneous agreement to buy it back at a specified price on a particular future date.

3 Action by the central bank to alter the monetary base by buying or selling financial securities in the open market.

4 The role of the central bank whereby it stands ready to lend to banks and other financial institutions when financial panic threatens the financial system.

5 The interest rate that the central bank charges when the commercial banks want to borrow money.

6 The variables over which the central bank exercises day-to-day control.

7 A function showing how much investment firms wish to make at each interest rate.

8 The upward (downward) shift in the consumption function when household wealth increases (decreases) and people spend more (less) at each level of personal disposable income.

9 A theory about consumption developed by Ando and Modigliani which argues that people form their consumption plans by reference to their expected lifetime income.

10 A theory about consumption developed by Friedman which argues that consumption depends not on current disposable income but on average income in the long run.

## Exercises

1 The items in the adjacent column comprise the assets and liabilities of the Bank of England in May 2004. Identify each item as an asset or a liability and complete the balance sheets for the two departments of the Bank.

2 In a given economy, the public chooses to hold an amount of cash equal to 40 per cent of its bank deposits. The commercial banks choose to hold 5 per cent of deposits in the form of cash in order to service

| Item | £ bn |
|---|---|
| Government securities (Issue Department) | 13.5 |
| Public deposits | 0.7 |
| Advances | 7.3 |
| Government securities (Banking Department) | 1.8 |
| Notes in circulation | 34.5 |
| Bankers' deposits | 1.9 |
| Reserves and other accounts | 14.5 |
| Other securities (Issue Department) | 20.9 |
| Other assets (Banking Department) | 13.7 |

Source: http://www.bankofengland.co.uk

their customers. The stock of high-powered money is £12 million.

**(a)** What is the size of the money supply?

Each of the following four situations represents an attempt by the monetary authorities to reduce the size of money supply. In each case, assume that the banking system is initially as described above.

**(b)** What would be the size of money supply if the central bank imposed a 10 per cent cash ratio on the commercial banks?

**(c)** What would be the size of money supply if the central bank raised its discount rate to such a penalty rate that the banks choose to hold an extra 5 per cent of deposits as cash?

**(d)** What would be the size of money supply if the central bank called for Special Deposits of an amount corresponding to 5 per cent of bank deposits?

**(e)** What would be the reduction in money supply if the central bank undertook open market operations (OMOs) to reduce the stock of high-powered money by £1 million?

**3** Figure 23–1 plots the growth rate in M4. It also plots the growth rates of the component parts of M4.

**(a)** Explain what has led to the growth in M4.

**(b)** Why do you think growth rates in M4 wholesale deposits are more volatile than M4 lending and retail deposits?

**(c)** How might the UK housing market boom lead to an increase in M4?

**Figure 23–1** M4 growth rates, 12-monthly, and components of M4, 2001–04

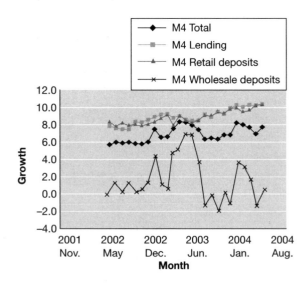

**4** Figure 23–2 shows conditions in the money market. $LL_0$ and $LL_1$ are money demand schedules; $MS_0$ and $MS_1$ represent alternative real money supply schedules. In the initial state, the money market is in equilibrium with the demand for money $LL_0$ and money supply $MS_0$.

**Figure 23–2** Short-run cost curves for a perfectly competitive firm

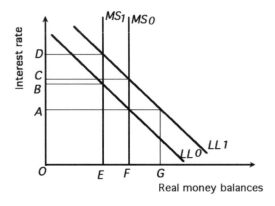

**(a)** Identify equilibrium money balances and rate of interest.

**(b)** Suggest why it might be that the money demand schedule shifted from $LL_0$ to $LL_1$.

**(c)** Given the move from $LL_0$ to $LL_1$, suppose that no adjustment has yet taken place: what is the state of excess demand/supply in the bond market?

**(d)** How does this disequilibrium in the bond market bring about adjustments in the money market?

**(e)** Identify the new market equilibrium.

**(f)** Suppose that money demand remains at $LL_1$: what measures could the authorities adopt to move money supply from $MS_0$ to $MS_1$?

**(g)** Identify the new market equilibrium.

**5** Which of the following situations would entail an increase in the transactions demand for money?

**(a)** A general rise in consumer prices.

**(b)** An expected general rise in consumer prices.

**(c)** The extension of value added tax (VAT) to goods which were previously zero-rated.

**(d)** An increase in the level of real income.

**(e)** An increase in the standard rate of income tax.

**(f)** A fall in interest rates.

**6** In which of the following circumstances would a rise in interest rates be expected?

**(a)** A fall in money supply.

**(b)** An increase in money demand.
**(c)** A rise in liquidity preference.
**(d)** A fall in the price of bonds.
**(e)** An increase in consumer prices.

**7** Use a diagram to explain how the authorities may attempt to control money stock through interest rates. Comment on the problems of this procedure.

**8** Explain how the authorities may attempt to influence interest rates by controlling money stock. Comment on the problems of this procedure.

**9** Figure 23–3 depicts income and consumption during the life-cycle. The path *ACDFG* represents the pattern of disposable income, increasing through the individual's working life and then reducing to pension level on retirement. *OB* represents long-run average, or 'permanent', income. The individual aims at a steady level of consumption through life so as just to exhaust total lifetime income.

**Figure 23–3** Consumption and the life-cycle

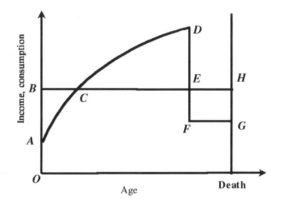

**(a)** What level of consumption will be chosen?
**(b)** What does the area *ABC* represent?
**(c)** How is the area *ABC* to be financed?
**(d)** The area *CDE* represents an excess of current income over consumption. Why does the individual 'save' during this period?
**(e)** What does the area *EFGH* (during pension years) represent?
**(f)** How is *EFGH* financed?
**(g)** How will consumption behaviour be affected if the individual begins life with a stock of inherited wealth?
**(h)** Discuss the effect of an increase in interest rates upon the present value of future income and upon consumption.

**10** This exercise concerns the transmission mechanism of monetary policy in a closed economy with fixed prices. Suppose that there is a fall in the interest rate.

**(a)** What effect does this policy have on the bond market?
**(b)** Outline the effect that this will have on consumption and investment.
**(c)** What does this imply for aggregate demand?
**(d)** How does this change in aggregate demand affect equilibrium output?
**(e)** How does this then affect money demand?
**(f)** What is implied for the rate of interest, and what further effects may follow?
**(g)** What do you expect to be the net effect on equilibrium output?

*Please note*: If you find that any links in this chain are obscure, you are advised to work through the question in conjunction with the commentary provided in the 'Answers and comments' section in the book.

## True/False

**1** There is no possibility that the Bank of England can go bankrupt because it can always meet withdrawals by its depositors by printing new banknotes a little more quickly.

**2** The central bank can reduce the money supply by reducing the amount of cash that the commercial banks must hold as reserves.

**3** Open market operations (OMOs) are a means by which the Bank alters the monetary base, banks' cash reserves, deposit lending and the money supply.

**4** A reverse repo is where you repossess your car from the loan shark.

**5** The initiation of the London repo market increased M4 by about £6 bn in early 1996.

**6** When you've tried everywhere else to get money for your holidays, you go to the lender of last resort.

**7** Money is a nominal variable, not a real variable.

**8** The existence of uncertainty increases the demand for bonds.

**9** The best measure of the opportunity cost of holding money is the real interest rate.

**10** The central bank can control the real money supply with precision more easily than the nominal money supply.

**11** An excess demand for money must be exactly matched by an excess supply of bonds: otherwise people will be planning to hold more wealth than they actually possess.

**12** The central bank can fix the money supply and accept the equilibrium interest rate implied by the money demand equation, or it can fix the interest rate and accept the equilibrium money supply implied by the money demand equation; but it cannot choose both money supply and interest rate independently.

## Economics in action

### Bank staves off interest rate rise

(Adapted from an article by Charlotte Moore, *The Guardian*, 9 July 2004)

The City warned industry and homeowners last night that they had only been granted a temporary reprieve after the Bank of England left interest rates on hold at 4.5 per cent.

Although the Bank's nine-member monetary policy committee decided against a third successive rise in the cost of borrowing, analysts believe a fifth upward move since November is in prospect next month.

Data over the past month have shown that Britain's economy is steaming ahead, annualized GDP growth may have accelerated to 4 per cent, above the sustainable rate of growth of 2.5–3 per cent.

The authorities are now likely to stick to raising rates gradually, with the next increase in the cost of borrowing expected in August when the latest inflation report will be published. The decision to leave rates at 4.5 per cent was welcomed by the manufacturing sector.

## Questions

**1** Explain how the transmission mechanism of monetary policy is likely to develop in the UK with successive interest rate rises.

**2** Why was the decision to hold interest rates at 4.5 per cent welcomed by the manufacturing sector?

## Questions for thought

**1** Imagine that you have a stock of wealth to be allocated between money and bonds, your main concern being to avoid the capital losses which might ensue if the price of bonds falls when you are holding bonds. Suppose that you expect the rate of interest to be at a particular level $Rc$.

**(a)** How would you allocate your wealth between money and bonds if the current rate of interest were below $Rc$?

**(b)** How would you allocate your wealth between money and bonds if the current rate of interest were higher than $Rc$?

**(c)** What would be implied for the aggregate relationship between money holdings and the rate of interest if different individuals have different expectations about future interest rates?

**2** Discuss whether monetary policy has any meaning in an economy where we cannot clearly define money supply, and cannot control it even if we can define it.

**3** According to the permanent income hypothesis, individuals would not be expected to alter their consumption plans in response to a purely transitory change in income.

**(a)** How would you expect individuals to react to a temporary reduction in income? Under what circumstances might they be unable to respond in this way?

**(b)** Suppose the government runs a budget deficit by introducing tax cuts, with the policy being funded by borrowing. How would you expect rational consumers to react?

**4** **(a)** How may a firm compare alternative investment projects with different capital costs, different expected income streams and different expected economic lives?

**(b)** How would a rise in the rate of interest affect firms' decisions to invest?

# chapter twenty-four

# Monetary and fiscal policy

## Learning outcomes

**By the end of this chapter, you should understand:**

- Different forms of monetary policy
- A Taylor rule
- A monetary target
- *IS* and *LM* curves
- Equilibrium in both the output and money market
- The effect of a fiscal expansion
- The effect of a monetary expansion
- The mix of monetary and fiscal policy
- How expected future taxes affect current demand

## Key learning blocks

This chapter develops your understanding of *aggregate demand management policies*. The core learning blocks are:

1. How is monetary policy managed?
2. What is *IS–LM* analysis and how is it used to evaluate policy?
3. How might fiscal and monetary policy be mixed?

The textbook moves through these areas and it is advisable to pay particular attention to *IS–LM* analysis. The exercises that follow will help to aid your understanding.

# Important concepts and technical terms

## Match each lettered concept with the appropriate numbered phrase:

**a**  Wealth effect

**b**  Investment demand schedule

**c**  *IS* schedule

**d**  Crowding-out

**e**  Transmission mechanism

**f**  *LM* schedule

**g**  Demand management

**h**  Ricardian equivalence

**i**  Taylor rule

**j**  Inflation target

**k**  Monetary target

**1**  A function showing how much investment firms wish to make at each interest rate.

**2**  The upward (downward) shift in the consumption function when household wealth increases (decreases) and people spend more (less) at each level of personal disposable income.

**3**  The route by which a change in money supply affects aggregate demand.

**4**  The use of monetary and fiscal policy to stabilize the level of income around a high average level.

**5**  A curve which shows the different combinations of interest rates and income compatible with equilibrium in the money market.

**6**  The reduction in private demand for consumption and investment caused by an increase in government spending, which increases aggregate demand and hence interest rates.

**7**  Targeting nominal money stocks with interest rate policies.

**8**  The correlated relationship between central bank interest rate decisions and expected changes in inflation and output.

**9**  A curve which shows the different combinations of income and interest rates at which the goods market is in equilibrium.

**10**  A situation in which a reduction in direct taxation has no effect on aggregate demand because individuals realize that tax cuts now will be balanced by higher future taxes.

**11**  Targeting of an inflation rate by the use of monetary policies.

## Exercises

**1**  Figure 24–1 is a fan chart of forecasted inflation by the Bank of England. The forecast was made in May 2004 and forecasts forward to 2006.

(a) Explain why the lines fan out over time?

(b) If the Bank of England follows a Taylor rule when setting interest rates and the target inflation rate is 2 per cent, how do you expect the interest rate path to develop over the period 2004–06?

**2**  This exercise concerns the crowding-out effects of fiscal policy in a closed economy with fixed prices. We begin this time with a cut in the rate of direct taxation. As with Exercise **1**, if the chain does not make sense to you, follow the question in conjunction with the commentary in the book.

(a) How will the policy change initially affect disposable income and aggregate demand?

(b) What is the subsequent effect on equilibrium output?

**Figure 24–1** Bank of England inflation forecast fan chart, May 2004

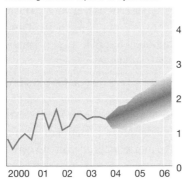

Percentage increase in prices on a year earlier

*Source: www.bankofengland.co.uk*

(c) What implications does this have for the demand for real money balances?

(d) Given fixed money supply, how will this affect bond prices and interest rates?

(e) How will this feed through to affect aggregate demand?

(f) What is the effect on equilibrium output?

(g) Under what circumstances will this crowding-out effect be complete?

**3** Figure 24–2 shows the *IS* and *LM* schedules for a closed economy with fixed prices.

**Figure 24–2** Equilibrium in the goods and money markets

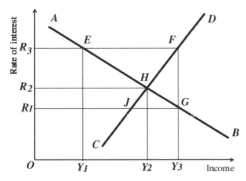

(a) *AB* and *CD* are the *IS* and *LM* schedules – but which is which?

(b) Comment on the equilibrium/disequilibrium states of the goods and money markets at each of the points *E, F, G, H* and *J*.

(c) How would you expect the economy to react if it is at point *J*?

(d) For each of the following items, identify whether the *IS* or *LM* schedule is likely to shift – and in which direction (assume *ceteris paribus* in each case):

(i) An increase in business confidence.

(ii) An increase in nominal money supply.

(iii) A reduction in government spending.

(iv) A once-for-all increase in the price level.

(v) A redistribution of income from rich to poor.

(vi) An increase in the wealth holdings of households.

**4** Figure 24–3 illustrates the effects of fiscal policy on equilibrium income and the interest rate under alternative assumptions about the slope of the *LM* function. In each case, fiscal policy is represented by a movement of the *IS* curve from $IS_0$ to $IS_1$.

**Figure 24–3** Fiscal policy

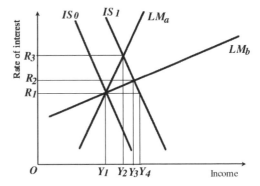

(a) What is the initial equilibrium income and interest rate?

(b) What could have caused the move from $IS_0$ to $IS_1$?

(c) What would be the 'full multiplier' effect of the fiscal policy – that is, if the interest rate remains unchanged?

(d) If the fiscal policy is bond-financed and the *LM* schedule is relatively elastic, what is the effect of the fiscal policy on the equilibrium position?

(e) If the fiscal policy is bond-financed and the *LM* schedule is relatively inelastic, what is the effect of the fiscal policy on the equilibrium position?

(f) Identify the extent of crowding-out in each of these situations.

(g) What determines the elasticity of the *LM* schedule?

(h) How could the authorities arrange policy in order to achieve the 'full multiplier' effect?

**5** Figure 24–4 (overleaf) illustrates the effects of a restrictive monetary policy on equilibrium income and interest rate under alternative assumptions about the slope of the *IS* schedule. Monetary policy is here represented by a movement of the *LM* schedule from $LM_0$ to $LM_1$.

**Figure 24–4** Monetary policy

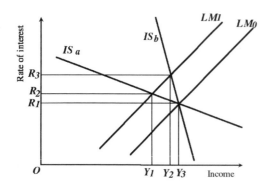

(a) What is the initial equilibrium income and interest rate?

(b) What could have caused the move from $LM_0$ to $LM_1$?

(c) What is the effect of monetary policy on the equilibrium when the *IS* schedule is relatively steep?

(d) What is the effect when *IS* is relatively flat?

(e) What factors determine the steepness of the *IS* curve, and hence the effectiveness of monetary policy?

**6** It has been argued that individuals realize that reductions in direct taxation in the present will have to be offset by higher taxes in the future, which will have to be paid by them or by their children. This means that tax cuts do not really affect real income in the long run, so consumption plans should not be affected. This argument is known as 'Ricardian equivalence'. A number of objections have been raised to this line of argument, some of which are listed below. Which of them may have some validity?

(a) Ricardian equivalence implies that government spending on roads has no effect, which is obviously false.

(b) Future higher taxes may be imposed only after present taxpayers are dead.

(c) There may be breakdowns in intergeneration transfers.

(d) Marginal taxes drive distortionary wedges between the price paid and the price received, which may have supply-side effects.

(e) There are capital market imperfections which effectively ensure that the government can borrow at a lower interest rate than private citizens.

**7** Suppose you are given the following information.

It is estimated that individuals who receive an increase in disposable income will treat 80 per cent of the increase as being likely to be sustained into the future, and the other 20 per cent as transitory. The marginal propensity to consume out of permanent income is 0.93. Consumption at a zero level of permanent income is estimated to be zero.

(a) Give an algebraic expression for consumption.

(b) Last year permanent income was £15 000. This year disposable income rose to £25 000. What is this year's estimate of permanent income?

(c) What is the marginal propensity to consume out of current income?

(d) What do these marginal propensities imply about the Keynesian multiplier for government expenditure and the effectiveness of fiscal policy? (Ignore taxes and the foreign sector.)

### True/False

**1** The use of monetary targets is impeded by the difficulties of measuring the money supply.

**2** Inflation targeting is a common policy pursued by many economies.

**3** Targeting of inflation diminishes the importance of GDP targeting.

**4** Under a Taylor rule, the central bank is concerned about current and future inflation.

**5** An increase in the target rate of inflation will lead to a higher long-run interest rate.

**6** Changes in the rate of interest affect the position of the aggregate demand schedule in the income–expenditure model.

**7** When we take into account the money market and interest rate effects, the multiplier on government spending is enhanced.

**8** Movements along the *IS* schedule tell us about shifts in equilibrium income caused by shifts in the aggregate demand schedule as a result only of changes in interest rates.

**9** The position of the *LM* schedule depends on the price level.

**10** Monetary and fiscal policy affect aggregate demand through different routes, but have very similar effects.

**11** The Keynesian model developed so far is deficient because it overemphasizes the demand side of the economy, holds prices fixed and relies on the existence of spare capacity.

## Economics in action

### The Greenspan putt

(Adapted from *The Economist*, 2 July 2004)

America's Federal Reserve (the Fed) has raised interest rates for the first time in over four years. Much tightening remains to be done – real interest rates are still negative – but the Fed likes to move step-by-step. The Fed's task is difficult. Not only are policy-makers unsure about the precise impact their instrument – the Fed-funds rate – will have, they are also uncertain about what they are aiming for. To preserve price stability, the Fed must let the economy fulfil, but not stretch, its potential. But the economy's 'potential' output is not something the Fed can observe.

The Fed's pace will also depend on how America's households respond to its putting. By cutting rates so savagely from 2001 to 2003, it openly invited households to borrow, and they heartily accepted. Their debts now total about 115 per cent of their disposable income. One of the most important sources of demand for the American economy, the uninhibited spending of unearned money, may thus begin to dwindle. Unless earned income or foreign demand replaces it, the economy will slow.

## Questions

**1** Explain what is meant by 'real interest rates are still negative'. Also explain the impact of real negative interest rates on the level of borrowing.

**2** 'The difficulties of controlling aggregate demand through monetary policy are little different from the difficultites associated with fiscal policy.' Discuss.

## Question for thought

**1** This question requires some facility with simple algebra. Suppose that the following equations represent behaviour in the goods and money markets of a fixed price closed economy:

*Goods market*
Consumption: $C = A + c(Y - T) - dR$
Investment: $I = B - iR$
Taxes: $T = tY$
Equilibrium: $Y = C + I + G$
*Money market*
Money supply: $Ms = M$
Money demand: $Md = kPY + N - mR$
Equilibrium: $Ms = Md$

where $A$ = autonomous consumption, $B$ = autonomous investment, $C$ = consumption, $G$ = government expenditure, $I$ = investment, $M$ = real money, $N$ = autonomous money demand, $P$ = price level, $R$ = rate of interest (per cent), $T$ = net taxes, $Y$ = income, output. Lower-case letters denote parameters of the model.

**(a)** Derive an expression for the *IS* curve – i.e. use the equations for the goods market to find a relationship between $Y$ and $R$.

**(b)** Derive an expression for the *LM* curve.

**(c)** Suppose the variables and parameters in the model take the following values: A = 700; B = 400; c = 0.8; d = 5; G = 649.6; i = 15; k = 0.25; M = 1200; m = 10; N = 200; P = 1; t = 0.2. Plot *IS* and *LM* curves and read off the approximate equilibrium values of income and the rate of interest.

**(d)** For these equilibrium values, calculate consumption and investment, and confirm that the goods market is in equilibrium.

**(e)** Check that the money market is also in equilibrium.

**(f)** Calculate the government budget deficit or surplus.

# chapter twenty-five

# Aggregate supply, prices and adjustment to shocks

## Learning outcomes

By the end of this chapter, you should understand:

- The macroeconomic demand schedule (MDS)

- Aggregate supply in the classical model

- The equilibrium inflation rate

- Complete crowding-out in the classical model

- Why wage adjustment may be slow

- Short-run aggregate supply

- Temporary and permanent supply shocks

- How monetary policy reacts to demand and supply shocks

- Flexible inflation targets

## Key learning blocks

This chapter moves on from the demand-side analysis of the economy to the *supply side*. The key areas which you need to be familiar with are:

1. What determines aggregate supply in the long and short run?

2. How is the labour market linked to the supply of the economy?

3. What are economic shocks and how can they be accommodated?

The textbook discusses each of these issues in turn and the exercises that follow will help to further your understanding.

# Important concepts and technical terms

## Match each lettered concept with the appropriate numbered phrase:

**a** Aggregate supply schedule

**b** Business cycle

**c** Overtime and short-time working

**d** Job acceptance schedule

**e** Voluntary unemployment

**f** Money illusion

**g** Involuntary unemployment

**h** Real balance effect

**i** Short-run aggregate supply schedule

**j** Registered unemployment

**k** Labour force schedule

**l** Lay-off

**m** Price level

**n** The natural rate of unemployment

**1** The average price of all the goods produced in the economy.

**2** A schedule showing how many people choose to be in the labour force at each real wage.

**3** A temporary separation of workers from a firm.

**4** The increase in autonomous consumption demand when the value of consumers' real money balances increases.

**5** A schedule which shows the prices charged by firms at each output level, given the wages they have to pay.

**6** A schedule which shows the quantity of output that firms wish to supply at each price level.

**7** A situation in which people confuse nominal and real variables.

**8** The percentage of the labour force that is unemployed when the labour market is in equilibrium.

**9** A schedule showing how many workers choose to accept jobs at each real wage.

**10** The number of people without jobs who are registered as seeking a job.

**11** Devices used by firms to vary labour input without affecting numbers employed.

**12** The tendency for output and employment to fluctuate around their long-term trends.

**13** A situation in which some people have chosen not to work at the going wage rate.

**14** A situation in which some people would like to work at the going real wage but cannot find a job.

## Exercises

**1** This exercise explores the relationship between price and aggregate demand. Figure 25–1 (overleaf) shows an economy's *IS* and *LM* schedules. The economy begins in equilibrium, with $IS_0$ and $LM_0$ being the relevant schedules.

**(a)** Identify equilibrium income, interest rate and aggregate demand.

Suppose the price level rises to a new level:

**(b)** Which of the *LM* schedules is appropriate?

**(c)** In the absence of the real balance effect, identify the new equilibrium levels of income, interest rate and aggregate demand.

**(d)** Explain and identify the influence of the real balance effect.

**(e)** Repeat parts *(b)*, *(c)* and *(d)* for a fall in price level from its original level.

**(f)** Explain why the price level affects the position of the *LM* curve.

**(g)** Draw a diagram to illustrate the macroeconomic demand schedule with and without the real balance effect.

**Figure 25–1**   Price and aggregate demand

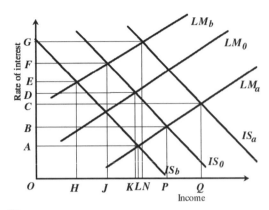

**2**   Which of the following characteristics are valid for all points along the macroeconomic demand schedule? (*Note*: More than one response may be valid.)

(a)  Planned spending equals actual output.
(b)  Planned demand for real money balances is equal to nominal money supply divided by the price level.
(c)  Demanders of goods receive the quantities they want to buy.
(d)  The money market is in equilibrium.
(e)  There is no disequilibrium in the goods market.

**3**   Figure 25–2 shows the labour market of an economy. *LD* is labour demand, *AJ* is the job acceptances schedule and *LF* the labour force schedule.

**Figure 25–2**   The labour market

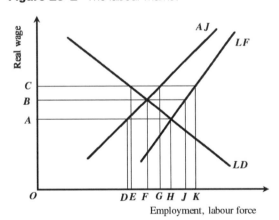

(a)  What is the equilibrium real wage?
(b)  Identify the level of employment and registered unemployment.
(c)  In this situation, what is the natural rate of unemployment, and what is the quantity of involuntary unemployment?

Suppose the real wage is at *OA*:

(d)  Identify the level of unemployment, registered unemployment and the quantity of involuntary unemployment.
(e)  How will the market react?

Suppose now the real wage is at *OC*:

(f)  Identify the level of employment, registered unemployment and the quantity of involuntary unemployment.
(g)  How will the market react?
(h)  Explain why there should be a connection between employment and aggregate supply.
(i)  What are the implications for aggregate supply if the labour market is always in equilibrium?

**4**   This exercise examines monetary and fiscal policy, using the *MDS* and the aggregate supply schedule. Figure 25–3 shows two macroeconomic demand schedules (*MDS$_a$* and *MDS$_b$*) and the aggregate supply schedule (*AS*). First, we consider the effects of monetary policy in the classical model – specifically, an increase in nominal money supply.

(a)  Identify the 'before' and 'after' *MDS*.
(b)  What was the original equilibrium price and output?
(c)  What is equilibrium price and output after the policy is implemented?

Next, consider fiscal policy – again in the classical model. Suppose there is a reduction in government expenditure.

(d)  Identify the 'before' and 'after' *MDS*.
(e)  What was the original equilibrium price and output?
(f)  What is the equilibrium price and output after the policy is implemented?

**Figure 25–3**   Macroeconomic equilibrium

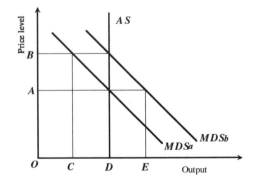

The Keynesian model is characterized by sluggish adjustment. Consider the period *after* the policy but *before* adjustment begins.

**(g)** Identify price and output.

**(h)** The *MDS* represents points at which goods and money markets are in equilibrium. In the position you have identified in *(g)*, adjustment has still to take place – so in what sense is the goods market in 'equilibrium'?

**5** Consider the following factors. Explore which of them encourage and which discourage rapid adjustment in the labour market. For each of the factors, state whether you expect firms or workers mainly to be affected.

**(a)** The costs of job search.

**(b)** Lack of redundancy agreement.

**(c)** Predominantly unskilled workforce.

**(d)** Production process well suited to short-time or overtime working.

**(e)** Concern of firm for its reputation as an employer.

**(f)** Unemployment at low level.

**(g)** Acquisition of firm-specific skills.

**6** The following symptoms describe the response of an economy to a leftward movement of either the demand or the supply schedule, in a situation where adjustment is not instantaneous. In each case, deduce whether the shock was to the demand side or the supply side.

**(a)** A short-run fall in the price level.

**(b)** Lower long-run output.

**(c)** No short-run change in price.

**(d)** Price lower in the long run.

**(e)** A short-run fall in output.

**(f)** No long-run change in output.

**(g)** Price higher in the long run.

**(h)** Output unchanged in the short run.

**7** Which of the following factors would you expect to affect the demand side of the economy and which the supply side? State whether each leads to an increase or a decrease in demand (or supply).

**(a)** An increase in the number of married women going out to work.

**(b)** An increase in the price of a vital imported raw material.

**(c)** An increase in business confidence.

**(d)** An autonomous increase in money wages.

**(e)** A fall in nominal money supply.

**(f)** A shift in the distribution of income from rich to poor.

**(g)** An increase in the demand for leisure.

**8** Consider an economy in which the aggregate supply curve is perfectly inelastic. Which of the following would result from an increase in aggregate demand?

**(a)** An increase in production.

**(b)** A decrease in production.

**(c)** An increase in prices.

**(d)** An increase in real income.

**(e)** An increase in money income.

**9** Consider an economy in which all resources are fully employed. Which of the following would result in a rise in the general level of prices?

**(a)** An increase in demand for the country's exports.

**(b)** An increase in government expenditure.

**(c)** An increase in personal consumption.

**(d)** A fall in the productivity of labour.

**10** This exercise explores the effects on price and output of a once-for-all increase in nominal money supply in the short, medium and long run. These effects are examined using Fig. 25–4, in which *AS* is aggregate supply, $SAS_{a,b,c}$ are short-run aggregate supply schedules and $MDS_{a,b}$ are macroeconomic demand schedules.

**Figure 25–4** An increase in nominal money supply

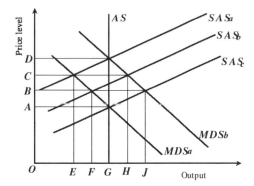

**(a)** If Fig. 25–4 is to be used to analyse the policy described, and if the economy begins in equilibrium, what are the initial levels of price and output?

**(b)** How would the economy react to the increase in nominal money supply according to a classical model?

Assume that adjustment is sluggish:

(c) Identify the initial reaction of price and output and explain how it comes about.

(d) Using Fig. 25–4, describe how adjustment begins and identify the position of the economy in the medium term.

(e) What is the final position of the economy when all adjustment is complete?

(f) Draw a diagram showing how the adjustment process is mirrored in the labour market.

(g) Do you expect adjustment to this change to be slower or more rapid than adjustment to a decrease in nominal money supply?

(h) If the increase in nominal money supply were 10 per cent, what would be the eventual percentage increase in the price level?

## True/False

**1** The position of the *MDS* depends upon the nominal money supply, government spending and all other variables relevant to the level of aggregate demand.

**2** The real balance effect is the decrease in autonomous consumption demand when the value of consumers' real money balances decreases.

**3** Full employment is achieved when there is no unemployment.

**4** Money illusion is when people are tricked by forged banknotes.

**5** The labour market is in equilibrium anywhere on the classical aggregate supply schedule.

**6** In the classical model a change in nominal money supply leads to an equivalent percentage change in nominal wages and the price level.

**7** Fiscal policy in the classical model leads mainly to an increase in price and only to a modest increase in output.

**8** Sluggish wage adjustment is the most likely cause of a slow adjustment of price to changes in aggregate demand.

**9** In the short run firms adjust to an increase in labour demand by hiring additional workers.

**10** In the model developed in this chapter, the labour market bears the brunt of any short-run disequilibrium.

**11** An increase in full-capacity output resulting from a favourable supply shift leads to a higher price and output.

**12** The technology boom of the late 1990s led to a positive supply side shock and an increase in GDP.

## Economics in action

### Reasons to be cheerful

(Adapted from an article by Martin Wolf, *Financial Times*, 30 June 2004)

It is increasingly evident that a fundamental driver of growth – rising productivity – is operating strongly in favour of long-term growth.

A two-year moving average of growth in US output per hour in the non-farm business sector has been rising almost without pause since 1994 to reach just under 5 per cent a year. Output per hour rose at a 4.5 per cent annual rate during the slowdown of 2001–03, against only 2 per cent in the slowdown of 1990–92.

What might this imply for the future? Estimates of steady-state growth of US labour productivity range from a low of 1.3 per cent a year to a high of 3 per cent. This demonstrates considerable uncertainty. But a reasonable view would be that the trend has improved by close to a percentage point a year since the mid-1990s. If so, US output per hour should be more than 20 per cent higher by 2015 than it would have been if the pre-1995 trend had continued.

### Questions

**1** Is rising productivity in the USA a temporary or a permanent supply shock?

**2** Under an inflation target, what are the implications for interest rate policy following a change in the productivity growth rate?

## Questions for thought

**1** **(a)** Explain how cuts in money wages lead to higher output if real wages are initially set at too high a level.

Suppose an economy is in *IS–LM* equilibrium, as shown in Fig. 25–5. $LM_a$ shows the initial *LM* schedule, $LM_b$ shows how the *LM* schedule moves when the price level falls. **IS** is the *IS* schedule, $Y_0$ is equilibrium income, $R_0$ the equilibrium interest rate and $Y_{fe}$ represents full employment.

**Figure 25–5** The liquidity trap

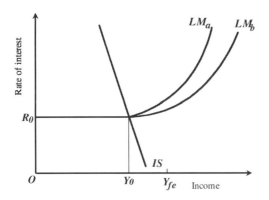

**(b)** Re-examine the story you told in *(a)*. Why might the cut in money wages fail to restore full employment?

**(c)** How might the story be affected if account is taken of the real balance effect?

**(d)** Would you expect fiscal policy to be more or less effective than monetary policy in this situation?

**2** The Keynesian concept of the 'liquidity trap' refers to which of the following?

**(a)** The inability of businesses with poor profit performances to obtain funds on loan for investment.

**(b)** The international problems of insufficient funds to finance any growth in world trade and payments.

**(c)** The downward inflexibility of interest rates as the money supply expands above a certain level.

**(d)** The disincentive of high income tax rates on savers depositing money with commercial banks or building societies.

**3** Can the liquidity trap explain the large US fiscal deficit in the mid-2000s?

# chapter twenty-six

# Inflation, expectations and credibility

## Learning outcomes

**By the end of this chapter, you should understand:**

- The quantity theory of money

- How nominal interest rates reflect inflation

- Seigniorage, the inflation tax and why hyperinflations occur

- When budget deficits cause money growth

- The Phillips curve

- The costs of inflation

- Central bank independence and inflation control

- How the Monetary Policy Committee (MPC) sets UK interest rates

## Key learning blocks

**This chapter builds an understanding of inflation. This has been a central issue of economics for the last 20 years. The key areas which you need to understand are:**

1. How is inflation linked to the money supply and the concept of expectations?

2. What are the costs of inflation?

3. How might inflation be controlled?

The textbook provides a discussion of these topics. The exercises that follow will help to develop your understanding.

# Important concepts and technical terms

## Match each lettered concept with the appropriate numbered phrase:

**a** Fiscal drag

**b** Hyperinflation

**c** Shoe-leather costs

**d** Inflation tax

**e** Phillips curve

**f** Menu costs

**g** Fisher hypothesis

**h** Inflation illusion

**i** Quantity theory of money

**j** Indexation

**k** Stagflation

**l** Inflation

**m** Inflation accounting

**n** Seigniorage

**1** A rise in the average price of goods over time.

**2** The costs imposed by inflation because physical resources are required to reprint price tags, alter slot machines and so on.

**3** A theory which states that changes in the nominal money supply lead to equivalent changes in the price level but do not have effects on output and employment; sometimes summarized in the equation $MV = PY$.

**4** The increase in real tax revenue when inflation raises nominal incomes and pushes people into higher tax brackets in a progressive income tax system.

**5** A period of both inflation and high unemployment, often caused by an adverse supply shock.

**6** The costs imposed by inflation because high nominal interest rates induce people to economize on holding real money balances, so that society must use a greater quantity of resources in undertaking transactions.

**7** The adoption of definitions of costs, revenue, profit and loss that are fully inflation-adjusted.

**8** A means of raising finance for government spending via the price rises that follow the printing of money.

**9** A situation in which people confuse nominal and real changes, although their welfare depends on real variables, not nominal variables.

**10** Periods when inflation rates are extremely high.

**11** A theory by which a 1 per cent increase in inflation would be accompanied by a 1 per cent increase in nominal interest rates.

**12** A process by which nominal contracts are automatically adjusted for the effects of inflation.

**13** The value of real resources acquired by the government through its ability to print money.

**14** A relationship showing that a higher inflation rate is accompanied by a lower unemployment rate, and vice versa. It suggests we can trade off more inflation for less unemployment, or vice versa.

## Exercises

**1** The long-run position of an economy is described by the quantity theory of money:

$M/P = L(Y,r)$

where $M$ = nominal money stock
$\quad$ $P$ = price level
$\quad$ $Y$ = real income
$\quad$ $r$ = interest rate

This economy does not immediately adjust to equilibrium, so we can distinguish both *short-run* and *long-run* effects. The economy begins in equilibrium.

Suppose there is a demand shock – namely, a 10 per cent increase in nominal money supply used to finance an increase in government expenditure:

**(a)** By what percentage will nominal income change?
**(b)** Describe the effects upon real income and the price level in the short run.
**(c)** Describe the effects upon real income and the price level in the long run.

Suppose now that the economy, again from equilibrium, experiences a supply shock, say, an increase in the cost of a vital raw material:

**(d)** Describe the short-run effect of the supply shock.
**(e)** How would the government be likely to act if its primary concern was the level of unemployment?
**(f)** What effect would this policy have on the long-run equilibrium position?
**(g)** How would the government be likely to act if its primary concern was the rate of inflation?
**(h)** What effect would this policy have had on the long-run equilibrium position?

**2** An alternative specification for the quantity theory of money is $MV = PY$, where $V$ is the velocity of circulation. In an economy with nominal GDP ($PY$) of £10 bn and a nominal money supply of £1 bn, then the money supply has to circulate 10 times, so $V = 10$.

In the following example assume $V = 4$.

| Item | Year 1 | Year 2 |
|---|---|---|
| Nominal interest rate | 9 | 9 |
| Nominal money supply | 2000 | 2000 |
| Real income | 4000 | 4065 |

**(a)** Calculate the growth rate of nominal money supply.
**(b)** What was the rate of inflation between year 1 and year 2?
**(c)** Calculate the real interest rate in year 2.
**(d)** Calculate real money demand in each of the two years.

**3** This exercise shows how taxing capital is complicated by the presence of inflation. Initially, suppose there is no inflation, a nominal interest rate of 3 per cent and income tax levied at 30 per cent on earnings from interest. Being a money-lender, this fact is of interest to you!

Suppose you lend £5000 to a client for the purchase of a car:

**(a)** Calculate your gross earnings from this transaction in the year.
**(b)** For how much tax are you liable?
**(c)** Calculate net earnings and the after-tax real rate of return on the deal.

Suppose now that the same deal goes through when inflation is 10 per cent p.a., but that institutions have adapted, so the market nominal interest rate is 13 per cent (i.e. the real pre-tax interest rate is still 3 per cent):

**(d)** Calculate gross earnings and tax liability.
**(e)** Calculate net earnings and the after-tax real rate of interest on the deal.

| Table 26–1 | UK inflation and unemployment, 1990–2003 | |
|---|---|---|
| **Year** | **Inflation rate** | **Unemployment rate** |
| 1990 | 8.1 | 7.0 |
| 1991 | 6.7 | 8.6 |
| 1992 | 4.7 | 9.8 |
| 1993 | 3.0 | 10.5 |
| 1994 | 2.3 | 9.7 |
| 1995 | 2.9 | 8.8 |
| 1996 | 3.0 | 8.3 |
| 1997 | 2.8 | 7.2 |
| 1998 | 2.6 | 6.2 |
| 1999 | 2.3 | 6.1 |
| 2000 | 2.1 | 5.6 |
| 2001 | 2.1 | 4.9 |
| 2002 | 2.2 | 5.2 |
| 2003 | 2.8 | 5.0 |

*Source: ONS, www.statistics.co.uk*

**4** Table 26–1 presents data on inflation and unemployment in the UK for the period 1990–2003.

**(a)** Plot a scatter diagram with inflation on the vertical axis and unemployment on the horizontal axis. You will find it helpful to mark each point with the year.

**(b)** To what extent does your diagram support the idea of a trade-off between inflation and unemployment?

**5** Figure 26–1 shows two short-run Phillips curves ($SRPC_0$ and $SRPC_1$). $SRPC_0$ corresponds to a situation in which workers expect no inflation.

**Figure 26–1** Government policy and the Phillips curve

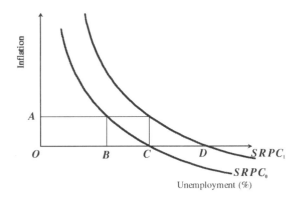

**(a)** What is the natural rate of unemployment?

**(b)** What is the expected rate of inflation if the Phillips curve is $SRPC_1$?

Suppose that the economy begins in long-run equilibrium with zero inflation and that the authorities adopt a policy of constant monetary growth because they wish to reduce unemployment below its existing level:

**(c)** Identify the short-run effect on inflation and unemployment.

**(d)** Explain why this new position for the economy is untenable in the long run.

**(e)** Towards what long-run equilibrium position will the economy tend?

Suppose that the government now wishes to return to zero inflation and holds money supply constant:

**(f)** Identify the short-run impact on inflation and unemployment.

**(g)** Identify the long-run equilibrium position.

**(h)** Under what conditions will this long-run equilibrium be attained?

**(i)** Can you see a role for incomes policy in this process?

**6** Which of the following initial causes of inflation stem from the demand side of the economy and which from the supply side?

**(a)** An increase in government expenditure on goods and services financed by printing money.

**(b)** An increase in the price of oil.

**(c)** An increase in value added tax (VAT).

**(d)** An increase in the income tax allowances for individuals.

**(e)** An increase in money wage rates.

**(f)** A decrease in the marginal propensity to save of households.

**7** Which of the following would result from a rise in the supply of money relative to its demand in an economy operating at full employment under the Quantity Theory of money?

**(a)** A reduction in the velocity of circulation.

**(b)** An increase in the level of real output.

**(c)** An increase in the price level.

**(d)** An increase in money income.

**8** Which of the following items is most likely to have caused the move from $PC_0$ to $PC_1$ in Fig. 26–2?

**Figure 26–2** Inflation and unemployment

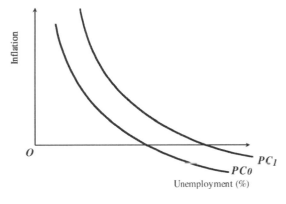

**(a)** A decrease in the natural rate of unemployment.

**(b)** An increase in wage inflation.

**(c)** The expectation of a future increase in the rate of unemployment.

**(d)** The expectation of a future increase in the rate of inflation.

**(e)** An increase in labour supply.

**9** State whether each of the following costs of inflation are real or illusory and whether they apply to anticipated or only to unanticipated inflation.

**(a)** Fiscal drag.

**(b)** A redistribution of income affecting those on fixed incomes.

**(c)** All goods becoming more expensive.

**(d)** Shoe-leather and menu costs.

**(e)** An increase in uncertainty.

**(f)** A fall in the real wage arising from the inflation set off by the monetary expansion following a supply shock.

**10** Incomes policy has, and has had, many critics. Explain why each of the following items has been a problem area in the past, and whether it nullifies the potential use of incomes policy in the future.

**(a)** The lack of support from other policy instruments.

**(b)** Multiplicity of objectives.

**(c)** The temporary nature of incomes policy.

**(d)** Inflexibility in a changing employment structure.

**(e)** Inappropriate incentive structures.

## True/False

**1** The UK price level was no higher in 1950 than it was in 1920.

**2** Sustained inflation is always and everywhere a monetary phenomenon.

**3** The simple Quantity Theory says that the inflation rate always equals the rate of nominal money growth.

**4** According to the Fisher hypothesis, an increase in the rate of money growth will lead to an increase in the inflation rate and to an increase in nominal interest rates.

**5** The German hyperinflation of the 1920s was so severe that the government had to buy faster printing presses to print money quickly enough.

**6** A large budget deficit necessarily leads to inflation by forcing the government to print money.

**7** The velocity of circulation is the speed at which the outstanding stock of money is passed round the economy as people make transactions.

**8** The Phillips curve shows that a decrease in unemployment can be achieved at the expense of higher inflation.

**9** The menu costs of inflation reflect the fact that the faster the inflation rate, the more frequently menus have to be reprinted if real prices are to remain constant.

**10** There are no costs to inflation so long as it can be fully anticipated.

**11** In order to incur the permanent benefits of lower inflation, the economy must first undergo a period of low output and employment.

**12** Indexation may make inflation tolerable in the long run.

## Economics in action

### Who to blame now it's payback time?

(Adapted from an article by Ashley Seager, *The Guardian*, 9 August 2004)

Official data from the Bank of England in late July showed that UK total indebtedness had topped the £1 trillion level for the first time, doubling in only seven years. Some experts have warned for years that the easy availability of credit, combined with falling interest rates, would lead to trouble in the end.

The Bank of England released a little-noticed report into unsecured, or non-mortgage, debt late in 2003, which concluded, interestingly, that the biggest holders of unsecured debt were the wealthier households rather than the poorest. While a typical mortgage might be between £50 000 and £100 000, some individual unsecured store card debt can be as high as £50 000.

### Questions

**1** Using the Quantity Theory of money, assess whether a doubling of indebtedness to £1 trillion would be problematic for the UK economy.

**2** Why do you think unsecured debt is rising amongst the more affluent households?

## Questions for thought

**1** Given the relationship between inflation and unemployment outlined in this chapter, which do you think should be the prime target of economic policy?

**2**   The simple Quantity Theory assumes that the velocity of circulation is constant. What factors might lead velocity to vary in the short and long run?

**3**   Discuss the costs of inflation. Which of these cost items is likely to have encouraged Western governments in their adoption of inflation as public enemy number one?

**4**   Figure 26–3 shows the way in which the demand for real money balances varies with the rate of interest. Notice that we regard the nominal rate of interest as the opportunity cost of holding money in this context. In Fig. 26–3, the real rate of interest is given by *OA*. Remember that the real interest rate is equal to the nominal rate less the inflation rate. Suppose initially that there is zero inflation.

**(a)**   Identify the level of real money demand.

Now suppose that the government attempts to finance a deficit by printing money, allowing inflation to rise to *AB*.

**(b)**   Identify the nominal rate of interest.
**(c)**   What is the demand for real money balances?
**(d)**   What area represents the real revenue from the inflation tax?
**(e)**   What costs does society bear in this situation?
**(f)**   What would you expect to happen to revenue from the inflation tax as the government deficit increases and the economy heads for hyperinflation?

**Figure 26–3**   The inflation tax

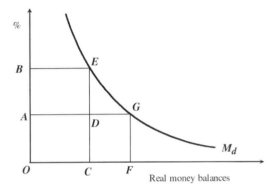

# chapter twenty-seven

# Unemployment

## Learning outcomes

**By the end of this chapter, you should understand:**

- Classical, frictional and structural unemployment
- Voluntary and involuntary unemployment
- Determinants of unemployment
- How supply-side policies reduce equilibrium unemployment
- Private and social costs of unemployment
- Hysteresis

## Key learning blocks

In the last five years unemployment has become an economic backwater, where 15–20 years ago it was a significant area of analysis. The reason is simple: people are now back in work; but with recession looming, unemployment could soon again move to centre stage. The key issues which you need to be familiar with are:

1. What are the different types of unemployment?

2. How can we explain changes in unemployment?

3. What are the economic costs associated with unemployment?

The textbook provides a discussion of these topics and the exercises that follow will help to advance your understanding.

# Important concepts and technical terms

## Match each lettered concept with the appropriate numbered phrase:

**a** Replacement ratio

**b** Supply-side economics

**c** Private cost of unemployment

**d** Structural unemployment

**e** Discouraged workers

**f** Demand-deficient unemployment

**g** Hysteresis

**h** Social cost of unemployment

**i** Frictional unemployment

**j** Long-term unemployed

**k** Natural rate of unemployment

**l** Classical unemployment

**1** Those members of the labour force who have remained in unemployment for a time span measured in months rather than weeks – in the UK in 2000, 40 per cent of the unemployed were so classified.

**2** People who have become depressed about the prospects of ever finding a job and decide to stop looking.

**3** The rate of unemployment when the labour market is in equilibrium.

**4** Unemployment which occurs when aggregate demand falls and wages and prices have not yet adjusted to restore full employment – sometimes known as 'Keynesian unemployment'.

**5** The ratio of unemployment or supplementary benefit that an unemployed worker gets from the government (transfer payments) relative to the average after-tax earnings of people in work.

**6** The unemployment created when the wage is deliberately maintained above the level at which the labour supply and labour demand schedules intersect.

**7** The irreducible minimum level of unemployment in a dynamic society, comprising people who are almost unemployable or are spending short spells in unemployment while between jobs.

**8** The cost to a worker of being out of work, the largest component being the wage forgone by not working.

**9** The use of microeconomic incentives to alter the level of full employment, the level of potential output and the natural rate of unemployment.

**10** A situation experienced by an economy when its long-run equilibrium depends upon the path it has followed in the short run.

**11** The cost to society of being below full employment, including lost output and human suffering.

**12** Unemployment arising from a mismatch of skills and job opportunities as the pattern of demand and production changes.

## Exercises

**1** Remember the economy of Hypothetica? It is now having unemployment problems. Below are presented some data on the flows in the labour market in a particular year. ('Real' data on some of these flows are hard to come by, so any resemblance between these numbers and those for any real economy you know about is purely fortuitous.) Data are in 000s.

At the beginning of the year the labour force is 26 900, of whom 2900 are unemployed. We also have:

| | | |
|---|---|---|
| (i) | Discouraged workers | 600 |
| (ii) | Job-losers/lay-offs | 1500 |
| (iii) | Retiring, temporarily leaving | 100 |
| (iv) | Quits | 700 |
| (v) | New hires, recalls | 2000 |
| (vi) | Re-entrants, new entrants | 500 |
| (vii) | Taking a job (not previously unemployed) | 100 |

(a) How many workers joined and left the unemployed during the year?
(b) How many people joined and left the labour force during the year?
(c) How did the size of the unemployed labour force change during the year?
(d) Calculate the size of the total labour force and unemployment at the end of the year.
(e) In the UK in 2004, unemployment began the year at 1.36 million. During the year, 3.16 million joined the register and 3.25 million left it. What would this suggest for the level of unemployment at the end of the year?

**2** State whether each of the following reasons for unemployment would be classified as frictional, structural, demand-deficient or classical, and which represent voluntary or involuntary unemployment.

(a) Unemployment resulting from the decline of the textile industry and the expansion of the micro-computer industry.
(b) Individuals who are between jobs.
(c) People whose physical or mental condition renders them unemployable.
(d) Unemployment resulting from the real wage being too high for labour market equilibrium.
(e) Unemployment arising from slow adjustment following a reduction in aggregate demand.

**3** Table 27–1 presents unemployment rates as a percentage of the national average for the standard regions in Great Britain for 1974, 1989, 1996 and 2004. *Health warning*: This question requires thought!

(a) The figures in Table 27–1 are ranked in ascending order of unemployment in 1974. Comment on the major differences and similarities revealed in the 1996 and 2004 rankings.

**Table 27–1** Regional unemployment rate as a percentage of the national (GB) average

| | 1974 (%) | 1989 (%) | 1996 (%) | 2004 (%) |
|---|---|---|---|---|
| South East | 60 | 65 | 96 | 83 |
| East Anglia | 80 | 60 | 77 | 72 |
| West Midlands | 84 | 105 | 101 | 117 |
| East Midlands | 88 | 90 | 95 | 100 |
| Yorkshire & Humberside | 104 | 123 | 109 | 100 |
| South West | 108 | 87 | 85 | 62 |
| North West | 136 | 137 | 108 | 98 |
| Wales | 148 | 124 | 105 | 96 |
| Scotland | 156 | 152 | 103 | 121 |
| North | 180 | 160 | 131 | 113 |
| Great Britain | 100 | 100 | 100 | 100 |

Source: ONS, Monthly Digest of Statistics.

(b) How does the analysis of types of unemployment help you to think about why these regional dispari-ties have arisen and persist through time?

**4** Table 27–2 shows how labour demand and supply vary with the real wage in a small economy. Suppose the real wage is fixed at $5 per hour.

(a) What is the level of employment?
(b) Calculate the level of unemployment.
(c) How much of the unemployment is involuntary and how much is voluntary?

Suppose now that workers base their decisions on take-home pay, that the real wage is flexible and that workers are paying $2 in income tax.

(d) What is the equilibrium wage as paid by firms and the net take-home pay of those employed?
(e) What are the levels of employment and unemploy-ment? Is there excess demand for labour?

**Table 27–2** Labour demand and supply (000)

| Real wage ($/hour) | Labour demand | Job acceptances | Labour force |
|---|---|---|---|
| 1 | 130 | 70 | 101 |
| 2 | 120 | 80 | 108 |
| 3 | 110 | 90 | 115 |
| 4 | 100 | 100 | 122 |
| 5 | 90 | 110 | 129 |
| 6 | 80 | 120 | 136 |

**(f)** How much of the unemployment is involuntary and how much is voluntary?

Finally, suppose that income tax is removed.

**(g)** What is the equilibrium real wage?

**(h)** What are the levels of employment and unemployment? By how much has unemployment changed?

**(i)** How much of the remaining unemployment is involuntary and how much is voluntary?

**5** Suppose that a labour market begins in equilibrium. We are to investigate the effects of a change in real oil prices such as happened in the 1970s, causing many energy-intensive firms to become economically obsolete. The effects of this on the labour market are shown in Fig. 27–1.

**Figure 27–1** The effects of a supply shock

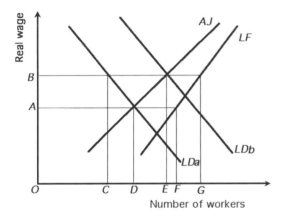

**(a)** If Fig. 27–1 is to illustrate the situation described, which of the labour demand schedules $LD_a$ and $LD_b$ represents the initial position? Explain your answer.

**(b)** Identify the equilibrium levels of employment and the real wage in this initial position.

**(c)** What is the natural rate of unemployment?

Now suppose that the oil price shock occurs.

**(d)** Assume that the real wage fails to adjust immediately – identify the levels of employment and unemployment.

**(e)** As real wages adjust, to what equilibrium values of employment and the real wage will the market tend?

**(f)** What will be the natural rate of unemployment?

**(g)** Has the natural rate increased, decreased or stayed the same? Why should that be?

**6** Which of the following factors may have contributed to the fall in the natural rate of unemployment in the UK during the 1990s?

**(a)** An increase in unemployment benefits.

**(b)** A decline in international competitiveness.

**(c)** A reduction in trade union power.

**(d)** An increase in world trade.

**(e)** The recession in British manufacturing industry.

**(f)** Technical progress.

**(g)** An increase in the participation rate of married women.

**(h)** Changes in employers' labour taxes.

**7** Below are listed a number of policies which could be used to reduce (or prevent a rise in) the long-run rate of unemployment. In each case, explain the disadvantages of the policy.

**(a)** Force firms to make high redundancy payments to discourage them from sacking workers too readily.

**(b)** The reduction or elimination of unemployment benefit.

**(c)** Wages cut by an incomes policy.

**(d)** An expansionary fiscal policy.

**(e)** Subsidize manufacturing industry.

**8** This exercise involves an application of indifference curves, which we first encountered in Chapter 5. You may wish to remind yourself of their application to labour supply (see Section 12–4 of the main text). Figure 27–2 is to be used to analyse the effects of a cut in the rate of income tax on the supply of labour by an individual (Jayne). $I_1$, $I_2$ and $I_3$ are indifference curves depicting Jayne's preferences for income and leisure. *ACD* and *BCD* are alternative

**Figure 27–2** Income tax and the supply of labour

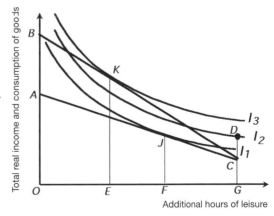

budget lines, which assume that Jayne receives some non-labour income, some of which must be given up if she chooses to work. The horizontal axis is labelled 'additional' hours of leisure as Jayne never chooses to have less than 12 hours of leisure daily.

(a)   How would you expect a cut in the income tax rate to affect the budget lines?

(b)   This being so, which must be the initial budget line in our story?

(c)   Identify Jayne's initial choice point.

(d)   At this point, what is Jayne's total income? How many hours does she work?

(e)   Identify Jayne's choice point after the income tax cut. How many hours does she now work?

**9**   Figure 27–3 shows the changing conditions in an economy's labour market. Suppose that this market has moved from an initial equilibrium in which employment was $L_1$ and the real wage was $W_1$, and has now settled at a new long-run equilibrium with employment $L_2$ and real wage $W_2$. $LD$ represents labour demand and $AJ$ is the job acceptances schedule. Notice that employment is lower in this final situation. Which of the following arguments could explain the situation?

**Figure 27–3**   The effects of hysteresis

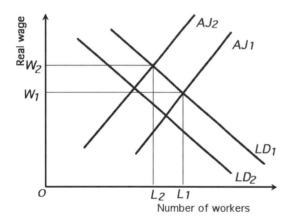

(a)   A temporary recession increases unemployment and discourages potential workers from looking for jobs. This carries on even when the recession is over.

(b)   Firms reduce capital stock during a recession, so that labour demand fails to readjust fully when the recession is over.

(c)   A recession makes workers less enthusiastic about job search and reduces firms' need to advertise for

workers. Previous levels of job search are not recaptured after the recession.

(d)   Wage-bargaining is carried out by employed workers (insiders). A recession reduces employment and this situation is exploited by the still-employed workers in negotiating higher real wages for themselves at the recession's end.

**10**   This exercise explores some of the differences between classical and demand-deficient unemployment within our labour market diagram (Fig. 27–4).

**Figure 27–4**   Classical and demand-deficient unemployment

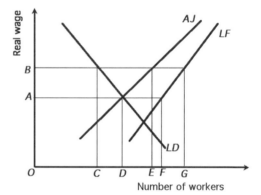

(a)   Identify the equilibrium real wage, employment and the natural rate of unemployment.

We now consider classical unemployment, which is readily shown in Fig. 27–4. Suppose that the real wage is stuck at $OB$.

(b)   Identify labour demand and the amounts of voluntary and involuntary unemployment.

This much we have seen already – but how may we show demand-deficient unemployment? We have seen that this unemployment results from sluggish adjustment. Suppose that prices and wages are rigid in the short run, with the price level at too high a level to clear the goods market.

(c)   Firms see stocks building up but cannot adjust price immediately – how do they react?

(d)   Suppose that the real wage is at $OA$, but firms reduce output to prevent the build-up of stocks, so employ only $OC$ workers. Identify the amounts of voluntary and involuntary unemployment.

(e)   How does this affect households' incomes?

## True/False

**1**   The ONS publishes accurate monthly figures of the number of people who are unemployed in the UK.

**2**   The unemployment rate is lower for women than for men.

**3**   Minimum wage legislation may result in classical unemployment.

**4**   The natural rate of unemployment is entirely composed of voluntary unemployment.

**5**   Shortening the working week and sharing out the work among more people is a long-run solution to unemployment.

**6**   The actual rate of unemployment is always close to the natural rate.

**7**   A major reason for the decrease in unemployment in the UK in recent years has been the changing composition of the labour force, with increasing numbers of young workers and women seeking employment.

**8**   In the long run, the performance of the economy can be changed only by affecting the level of full employment and the corresponding level of potential output.

**9**   Government expenditure on extra police officers will add less to employment than an equivalent increase in the value of spending on nuclear electricity.

**10**   When unemployment is involuntary, the case for active policy is stronger, as the private costs are higher.

**11**   Unemployment is always a bad thing.

**12**   Freedom of choice is important, so if people choose to be unemployed, society need not be concerned about voluntary unemployment.

## Economics in action

### Temps' rights

(Adapted from an article by Bill Saunders, *The Guardian*, 9 August 2004)

Britain's employers are looking nervously over their shoulders as the European Agency Workers Directive steams towards Westminster. The Directive, which grants temps rights equal to those enjoyed by their permanent colleagues, is now seen as unstoppable. All that remains is to settle how long a period temps must work to qualify for their rights. The TUC thinks a day, the CBI a year. The government is likely to aim for a compromise of six weeks.

Temping is often credited as the reason why unemployment is lower here than in France and Germany. Temps represent flexibility. Temps allow businesses to expand quickly in the event of a sudden upturn, and allow employers to increase the workforce without committing themselves for ever. Employers and the recruiting industry argue that if businesses do not have this flexibility, they might prefer not to expand at all.

## Questions

**1**   Why might the widespread use of temporary workers in the UK lead to a lower natural rate of unemployment?

**2**   Why might an increase in the rights of temporary workers increase the UK's natural rate of unemployment?

## Questions for thought

**1**   Why was unemployment in the UK higher in the 1980s than in the 1970s and early 2000s?

**2**   Suppose a society had developed in which there were generally accepted implicit agreements between firms and workers that male workers had lifetime jobs. How would you expect this to affect the nature of unemployment and the efficiency of the labour market?

**3**   Discuss why it is important that policy to combat unemployment is tailored to the underlying cause.

# chapter twenty-eight

# Exchange rates and the balance of payments

## Learning outcomes

**By the end of this chapter, you should understand:**

- The foreign exchange market
- Balance of payments accounts
- Determinants of current account flows
- Perfect capital mobility
- Speculative behaviour and capital flows
- Internal and external balance
- The long-run equilibrium real exchange rate

## Key learning blocks

In this chapter you will begin your understanding of *open economy macroeconomics*. We start with exchange rates and the balance of payments. You are required to understand the following core issues:

1. What types of exchange systems exist?
2. What is the balance of payments?
3. What are internal and external balances?

The textbook moves through each of these topics. The questions that follow will help to develop your understanding.

# Important concepts and technical terms

## Match each lettered concept with the appropriate numbered phrase:

**a** Balance of payments

**b** Purchasing power parity (PPP) path

**c** Appreciation

**d** Real exchange rate

**e** Perfect capital mobility

**f** Foreign exchange reserves

**g** Capital account

**h** Current account

**i** Speculation

**j** Exchange rate

**1** The price at which two currencies exchange.

**2** A systematic record of all transactions between residents of one country and the rest of the world.

**3** A record of international flows of goods and services and other net income from abroad.

**4** The stock of foreign currency held by the domestic central bank.

**5** A record of international transactions in capital assets.

**6** A rise in the international value of a currency.

**7** Exists when vast amounts of money flow between countries when there are asset price differentials.

**8** A measurement of the relative price of goods from different countries when measured in a common currency.

**9** The path of the nominal exchange rate that would keep the real exchange rate constant over a given period.

**10** Purchase of an asset for resale in the expectation that the price will rise in the near future.

## Exercises

**1** Table 28–1 contains items from the UK balance of payments accounts for 2004, in £ million. In this version of the accounts, three categories of transactions are distinguished – the *current account* (as described in the main text), the *capital account* (which identifies transactions involving the transfer of fixed assets, mainly by migrants) and the *financial account* (which covers transactions in financial assets).

Calculate:

(a) The visible balance.
(b) The invisible balance.
(c) The current account balance.
(d) The overall balance of payments.
(e) Comment on the size of the net errors and omissions.

**2** Figure 28–1 (overleaf) shows the position in the foreign exchange market: *DD* is the demand schedule for sterling and *SS* the supply schedule. Assume a two-country world (UK and USA).

**Table 28–1    The UK balance of payments, 2004 Q1**

| Item | £ million |
|------|-----------|
| Exports of goods | 44 715 |
| Exports of services | 23 505 |
| Net investment income | 6 783 |
| Net errors and omissions | 9 774 |
| Transfers (net) | –2 942 |
| Imports of goods | 58 662 |
| Imports of services | 18 722 |
| Net transactions in financial assets and liabilities | –5 141 |
| Capital account | 663 |

*Source: Balance of Payments First Release.*

(a) Explain briefly how the two schedules arise.
(b) Identify the exchange rate that would prevail under a 'clean float'. What would be the state of the overall balance of payments at this exchange rate?
(c) Suppose the exchange rate were set at *OA* under a fixed exchange rate regime. What intervention would be required by the central bank? What would

**Figure 28-1** The foreign exchange market

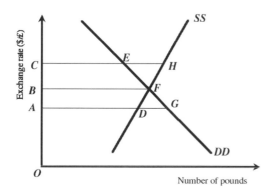

(e) If the authorities wished to maintain the exchange rate at *OC* in the long run, what sort of measures would be required?

**3** This exercise considers the effect of various shocks upon the internal and external balance of an economy. For each shock in Table 28–2, indicate the effects on the assumption that the economy is initially in both internal and external balance.

**4** Table 28–3 presents data relating to price movements in the UK and the USA and the nominal $/£ exchange rate for the years 1990–2003.

be the state of the balance of payments?

(d) Suppose the exchange rate were set at *OC*. Identify the situation of the balance of payments and the necessary central bank intervention.

(a) Using these data, calculate the real exchange rate for the years 1990–2003.

(b) Plot both real and nominal exchange rates against time.

## Table 28-2 Shocks and balances

| Nature of shock | Internal | | External current account balance | |
| | Boom | Slump | Deficit | Surplus |
|---|---|---|---|---|
| Reduction in autonomous consumption | | | | |
| Increase in real exchange rate | | | | |
| Tighter monetary and fiscal policy | | | | |
| Increase in world income | | | | |
| Increase in consumption with easier monetary and fiscal policy | | | | |

## Table 28-3 Prices and the exchange rate, 1990–2003

| Year | US$/£ exchange rate | UK price index | US price index | Real exchange rate | PPP exchange rate |
|---|---|---|---|---|---|
| 1990 | 1.93 | 74 | 76 | | |
| 1991 | 1.87 | 78 | 79 | | |
| 1992 | 1.52 | 81 | 81 | | |
| 1993 | 1.48 | 83 | 84 | | |
| 1994 | 1.56 | 85 | 86 | | |
| 1995 | 1.55 | 88 | 89 | | |
| 1996 | 1.71 | 90 | 91 | | |
| 1997 | 1.65 | 92 | 93 | | |
| 1998 | 1.66 | 96 | 95 | | |
| 1999 | 1.61 | 97 | 97 | | |
| 2000 | 1.50 | 100 | 100 | | |
| 2001 | 1.46 | 102 | 103 | | |
| 2002 | 1.61 | 103 | 104 | | |
| 2003 | 1.79 | 106 | 107 | | |

*Sources: UK Office for National Statistics; US Bureau of Labor Statistics.*

(c) Comment on the path of the real exchange rate during this period.

(d) Calculate the purchasing power parity (PPP) path for the exchange rate relative to 1990.

**5** Suppose that you have £100 idle which you wish to lend for a year. In Britain the current market rate of interest is 12 per cent, but if you choose you could lend your funds in the USA where the current interest rate is 9 per cent. The present nominal exchange rate is $1.70/£.

(a) What additional piece of information is required to enable you to take a decision on whether to lend in the UK or in the USA?

(b) Suppose that you expect the exchange rate at the end of the year to be $1.50/£: where will you invest?

(c) Where would you invest if you expected the exchange rate to fall only to $1.65/£?

(d) Given that you expect the exchange rate to fall to $1.65/£, where would you invest if the US interest rate were 8 per cent?

(e) Would you imagine expectations about future exchange rates to be stable or volatile? Does it matter?

**6** Within a two-country (UK and US) model, identify the effect on the UK exchange rate of each of the following:

(a) Americans want to buy more British assets.

(b) A fall in the American demand for Scotch whisky.

(c) An increase in the British demand for bourbon.

(d) An increase in the number of US tourists visiting the UK.

(e) A drop in the UK demand for shares in American companies.

(f) An increase in US interest rates.

**7** Which of the following (*ceteris paribus*) would move the UK's balance of payments towards a current account surplus?

(a) An increased number of tourists visiting the UK from the USA and Japan.

(b) An increase in dividends from UK investments in the USA.

(c) Increased export earnings from the sale of antique china to Japan.

(d) The hiring of fewer American films for showing in the UK.

(e) The sale of UK investments in American industry.

(f) A fall in the sales of Scotch whisky in the USA.

(g) An increase in official exchange reserves.

**8** Explain how increased domestic productivity may lead to reductions in international competitiveness.

**9** If a government incurs significant international debt, how will this influence the long-run exchange rate?

**10** Do you think fixed or floating exchange rates are preferable?

## True/False

**1** The $/£ exchange rate measures the international value of sterling.

**2** Under a fixed exchange rate regime the authorities undertake to maintain the exchange rate at its equilibrium level.

**3** Invisible trade is a component of the capital account.

**4** In the absence of government intervention in the foreign exchange market, the exchange rate adjusts to equate the supply of and demand for domestic currency.

**5** A fall in the international value of sterling makes British goods cheaper in foreign currency and foreign goods more expensive in sterling, and thus increases the quantity of British exports and reduces the quantity of goods imported to Britain.

**6** The economy is operating at its potential level of output when the external balance is zero.

**7** Official financing is a measure of the public sector deficit.

**8** A rise in the real exchange rate reduces the competitiveness of the domestic economy.

**9** Interest parity exists when interest rates across economies are equalized

**10** The Euro is a fixed exchange rate system.

**Economics in action**

### How to slay America's monster trade gap?

(Adapted from an article in *The Economist*, 22 June 2004)

America's trade gap is growing again. Worse, it may be extremely hard to close it without causing much economic pain – and not just for Americans.

America continues to import much more than it exports while investing more than it saves. According to figures released last Friday, its current account deficit, having narrowed to 4.6 per cent of GDP at the end of 2003, has widened again to 5.1 per cent of GDP. Were we expecting too much from a fall in the dollar?

A recent study illustrates the difficulty. To narrow the deficit by 2 percentage points by the end of 2004, the greenback would have to lose about a quarter of its current value by the end of this year. Since China, Malaysia and other Asian countries peg their currencies to the dollar, Japan and the Euro area would bear the brunt of the dollar's fall. They would not bear it easily.

**Questions**

**1** Why will China and Malaysia's policies of pegging their currencies to the dollar prevent a narrowing of the US trade deficit?

**2** Why will Japan and the Eurozone's policies of floating against the dollar have the result that these regions will bear the brunt of the dollar's fall?

**Questions for thought**

**1** During the mid-1980s, the government began to pay increasing attention to the exchange rate as a target for economy policy. Why was this? What implications did it have for the general conduct of policy? Does the UK currently target the exchange rate of the pound?

**2** This question offers you a different way of thinking about the balance of payments position for an economy.

We argue first that the current account position depends upon income: as domestic income rises, imports also rise and the current account becomes more negative. The capital account depends upon the domestic interest rate relative to the rest of the world. Thus if home interest rates are relatively high, there will tend to be a capital inflow. (We assume that capital is not perfectly mobile; if it were, home interest rates would always be the same as the world level.)

The balance of payments is zero when a current account deficit (surplus) is matched by a capital account surplus (deficit). At a higher level of income, a higher interest rate is required, so that the higher current account deficit can be matched by a larger capital account surplus. This maintains balance of payments 'equilibrium'. We can envisage this as the line *BP* in Fig. 28–2, showing all the combinations of *Y* and *R* in which the overall balance of payments is zero. Below the *BP* line, the balance of payments is in overall deficit, above it there is a surplus. The position of the *BP* line depends upon international competitiveness and net exports.

We can bring this analysis together with the *IS–LM* curves, as in Fig. 28–3. At the intersection of the three lines, we have general equilibrium – zero balance of payments – plus equilibrium in the goods and money markets. We will assume fixed prices for the moment.

**Figure 28–2**   The BP line

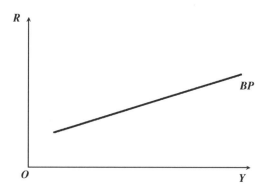

**Figure 28–3**   The BP line with IS–LM

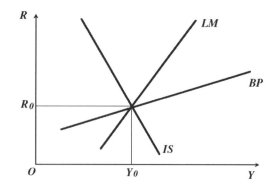

(a) Analyse the effects of an increase in money supply in this economy. Assume that the exchange rate is fixed and that, in the short run, goods and money markets remain in equilibrium – but that the balance of payments may be non-zero initially.

(b) Analyse the effects of an increase in government expenditure, again assuming that the authorities are operating under a fixed exchange rate regime.

# chapter twenty-nine

# Open economy macroeconomics

## Learning outcomes

**By the end of this chapter, you should understand:**

- Price and output adjustment under fixed exchange rates
- Monetary and fiscal policy under fixed exchange rates
- The effects of devaluation
- What determines floating exchange rates
- Monetary and fiscal policy under floating exchange rates

## Key learning blocks

In this chapter you will explore the relationships between domestic demand-side policies and exchange rate determination. By the end of the chapter you will need to be familiar with the following central issues:

1 Macroeconomic policy under fixed exchange rates.

2 Macroeconomic policy under floating exchange rates.

The textbook discusses each of these topics in turn. The exercises that follow will help to develop your understanding.

# Important concepts and technical terms

## Match each lettered concept with the appropriate numbered phrase:

**a** Open economy macroeconomics

**b** Sterilization

**c** Par value

**d** Monetary sovereignty

**e** Capital controls

**f** Fixed exchange rates

**g** Floating exchange rates

**h** Devaluation

**1** The study of economies in which international transactions play a significant role.

**2** An exchange rate system which is market-based.

**3** An exchange rate which the government agrees to defend.

**4** An ability to use monetary policy to control domestic economic activity.

**5** Regulations preventing private sector capital flows.

**6** An exchange rate system which is controlled by the government.

**7** An open market operation (OMO) between domestic money and bonds to offset changes in the money supply.

**8** Reduce the par value of a currency.

## Exercises

**1** This exercise explores the effects of a devaluation for an economy operating under a fixed-exchange rate regime. The economy to be considered adjusts sluggishly to shocks and is initially in a state of both internal and external balance. We consider the effects of devaluation in the short, medium and long run.

*The short run*:
**(a)** What is the immediate effect of the devaluation on international competitiveness?
**(b)** Mention some of the factors that may impede adjustment in the short run.
**(c)** What determines the initial impact on the current account balance?

*The medium term*:
**(d)** Recall that the economy began at full employment: what does this imply for output and prices in the medium term?
**(e)** Are there any policy measures that could evade this problem?

*The long run*:
**(f)** Can the lower real exchange rate be sustained in the long run? Explain your answer.
**(g)** Under what circumstances might a devaluation be an appropriate policy reaction?

**2** Comment briefly on the short-run effectiveness (or otherwise) of monetary and fiscal policy in each of the following economies:
**(a)** A closed economy.
**(b)** An open economy with fixed exchange rate and perfect capital mobility.
**(c)** An open economy with floating exchange rate and perfect capital mobility.
**(d)** An open economy with floating exchange rate and imperfect capital mobility.

**3** Consider an open economy which adjusts sluggishly to shocks. A floating-exchange rate regime is operating and the economy begins in long-run equilibrium. The authorities initiate a 20 per cent increase in nominal money supply.
**(a)** What will be the eventual increase in the domestic price level?
**(b)** What will be the eventual change in the real and nominal exchange rates?
**(c)** What will be the initial change in domestic interest rates?
**(d)** Sketch a diagram to show the adjustment path of the nominal exchange rate towards its long-run equilibrium, and comment briefly on the pattern.

**4** Consider an economy with a fixed-exchange rate system and capital controls.

**(a)** How would a deficit on the balance of payments effect the Bank of England's foreign currency reserves?

**(b)** Similarly, how would a balance of payments deficit effect the UK domestic money supply?

**(c)** How does sterilization offset the problems raised in *(b)*?

**(d)** For how long will sterilization work?

**5** Now consider an economy with a fixed exchange rate and perfect capital mobility.

**(a)** With a balance of payments deficit, how can the central bank prevent one-way capital flows out of the country?

**(b)** Why will sterilization not work?

**(c)** Will the Taylor rule work in such an economy?

**(d)** If monetary sovereignty is undermined, how will an economy return to its long-run equilibrium following a recession?

**6** Consider an economy with floating exchange rates.

**(a)** What will happen to foreign exchange reserves if the balance of payments is in surplus?

**(b)** Is it possible to target the inflation rate and exchange rate at the same time using interest rates?

**(c)** How will deviations in domestic and foreign monetary relate to changes in the nominal and real exchange rate?

**(d)** How does purchasing power parity (PPP) relate to the nominal exchange rate?

**7** If inflation is currently high, will entry into a fixed-exchange rate system be a sensible policy decision?

**8** Do you think fixed exchange rates are nothing more than opportunities to make profits?

**9** Why is it important that the UK government convinces the money markets of its commitment to prudence?

**10** How will expectations of the long-run exchange rate have changed following the decision to hand over monetary policy to the Bank of England?

## True/False

**1** Sterilization of the domestic money supply under fixed exchange rates can be effective only in the short run.

**2** Under fixed exchange rates, the ability of an economy to deal automatically with a shock depends on its source.

**3** Devaluation need not improve the current account.

**4** There is only one real exchange rate compatible with both internal and external balance.

**5** The nominal exchange rate always follows the purchasing power parity (PPP) path.

**6** The best policy for the government to adopt is to choose exchange rate and money supply to ensure internal and external balance.

**7** The exploitation of North Sea oil led to an increase in the real sterling exchange rate which deepened the recession in the UK in the early 1980s.

## Economics in action

### Time to hit the brakes

(Adapted from an article in *The Economist*, 13 May 2004)

China's sizzling economy needs to be slowed down. The undervalued yuan is one important cause of China's credit boom and rising inflation. China's capital controls are porous, and investors all over Asia are betting on a currency revaluation by buying property in Shanghai or Beijing or putting their money into yuan deposits to take advantage of interest rates higher than the paltry level available in America.

The yuan has been more or less pegged against the dollar since 1995. If, as a result of capital inflows, there is an excess supply of foreign currency, the central bank must buy it and sell yuan to keep the exchange rate stable. This injects new liquidity into the banking system, thereby feeding the credit boom. The central bank has been issuing bonds to mop up the liquidity, but this 'sterilization' is getting harder as the amounts swell. The bank has had trouble selling enough bonds in recent months, so the money supply continues to surge.

### Questions

**1** Why might tighter fiscal policy be a better way of slowing the Chinese economy?

**2** What is sterilization?

## Questions for thought

**1**    Why stop at the Euro: should we have one global currency?

**2**    Can central banks be tasked with managing the exchange rate?

# chapter thirty

# Economic growth

## Learning outcomes

By the end of this chapter, you should understand:

- Growth in potential output
- Malthus' forecast of eventual starvation
- How technical progress and capital accumulation made Malthus' forecast wrong
- The neoclassical model of economic growth
- The convergence hypothesis
- The growth performance of rich and poor countries
- Whether policy can affect growth
- Whether growth must stop to save the environment

## Key learning blocks

This chapter moves the focus of the analysis from looking at the current equilibrium level of GDP to *how will GDP develop in the future?* In order to address this question, you will need to understand the following issues:

1. What is economic growth?
2. What factors generate economic growth?
3. What is the distinction between exogenous and endogenous growth theories?

The textbook moves through each of these topics. The exercises that follow will help in developing your understanding.

# Important concepts and technical terms

## Match each lettered concept with the appropriate numbered phrase:

**a** Economic growth

**b** Growth accounting

**c** Neoclassical growth theory

**d** Human capital

**e** Embodied technical progress

**f** Renewable resource

**g** Depletable resource

**h** Capital widening

**i** Steady-state path

**j** Solow residual

**k** Capital deepening

**l** Convergence hypothesis

**m** Endogenous growth

**n** Catch-up

**1** The assertion that poor countries grow more quickly than average, but rich countries grow more slowly.

**2** The part of output growth not explained by the growth of measured inputs.

**3** Capital accumulation which extends the existing capital per worker to new extra workers.

**4** In neoclassical growth theory, the trend growth path along which output, capital and labour are all growing at the same rate.

**5** The annual percentage increase in the potential real output of an economy.

**6** The process by which poor countries may be able to close the gap between themselves and the rich countries as a result of the convergence hypothesis.

**7** A resource which need never be exhausted if harvested with care.

**8** Advances in knowledge incorporated in 'new' capital or labour inputs.

**9** The stock of expertise accumulated by a worker.

**10** The use of growth theory to decompose actual output behaviour into the parts explained by changes in various inputs and the part residually explained by technical progress.

**11** Economic growth determined within economic theory, rather than being simply dependent upon external factors such as population growth.

**12** A theory of economic growth devised by Bob Solow, which focuses on explaining the long-run growth of potential output, but is not concerned with how the actual rate reaches the potential rate.

**13** Capital accumulation which raises capital per worker for all workers.

**14** A resource of which only finite stocks are available.

## Exercises

**1** Which of the following items reflect genuine economic growth?

**(a)** A decrease in unemployment.

**(b)** An increase in the utilization of capital.

**(c)** An increase in the proportion of the population entering the labour force.

**(d)** An increase in the rate of change of potential output.

**(e)** A movement towards the production possibility frontier (PPF).

**(f)** Continuous movement of the production possibility frontier (PPF).

**2** We have seen that output may be increased either by an increase in inputs or by technical progress. (We neglect economies of scale for the moment.) This exercise explores how this may happen in a practical situation. Below are listed a number of ways by which the output of a word-processor operator might be increased. State whether each involves an increase in input or technical progress.

**(a)** Modification introduced to improve the quality of the existing computer.
**(b)** Purchase of a new improved computer.
**(c)** Making the operator work her lunch hour without pay.
**(d)** Sending the operator to night school to improve her technique.
**(e)** Our word-processor operator gaining experience and producing better-quality work.
**(f)** Introduction of CD rather than floppy disk storage media.

If technical progress is to be measured as a residual, which of the above items will be included?

**3** Identify each of the following as a depletable or renewable resource:

**(a)** Wheat.
**(b)** Oil.
**(c)** Whales.
**(d)** Copper.
**(e)** Trees.
**(f)** Rain.

**Figure 30–1** Growth in manufacturing output per worker per hour 2001–02

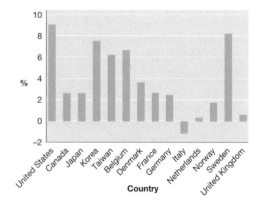

*Source: US Bureau of Labor Statistics, 2004.*

**4** Figure 30–1 provides the growth rate of manufacturing output per worker per hour for 14 leading countries.

**(a)** When measuring productivity growth, why use output per worker per hour, rather than just output per worker?
**(b)** Is it fair to say that productivity is growing faster in the USA?

**5** Which of the following items might be said to have contributed to accelerated productivity growth since 2000?

**(a)** Low inflation.
**(b)** Growing company profitability.
**(c)** Flexible labour markets.
**(d)** Technology boom.
**(e)** A higher number of graduates.
**(f)** End of the Cold War.

**6** Which of the following policy suggestions are appropriate for improving economic growth in an economy?

**(a)** The encouragement of R&D.
**(b)** A reduction in marginal tax rates to increase labour supply.
**(c)** Investment grants.
**(d)** The establishment of training and education schemes to improve human capital.
**(e)** An expansion of aggregate demand to increase the level of employment.
**(f)** The encouragement of dissemination of new knowledge and techniques.

**7** Consider an economy in which there is no technical progress, the labour force grows at a constant rate, $n$, and saving is proportional to income. The production function displays diminishing marginal product of capital.

**(a)** What is the steady-state rate of economic growth?
**(b)** If for some reason the economy is below its long-run growth path, what adjustments take place to enable return to equilibrium?
**(c)** What difference does it make to your analysis if labour-augmenting technical progress takes place at a rate $t$?
**(d)** What is implied for the long-run relative growth rate of countries if all have access to technical knowledge?
**(e)** What factors might impede the process you have described in (*d*)?

(f) Explain how externalities in human and physical capital may affect economic growth.

(g) What role might the government play in the economic growth process?

**8** Figure 30–2 illustrates neoclassical growth. The rays $n_1k$ and $n_2k$ show investment per person needed to maintain capital per person if labour grows at rates $n_1$ and $n_2$, respectively; $y$ shows how output per person varies with capital per person. Under the assumption that saving is proportional to income, $sy$ shows saving and investment per person.

**Figure 30–2** The neoclassical growth model

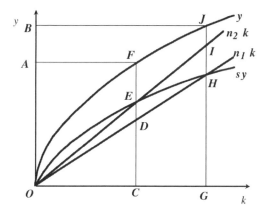

(a) Which ray represents the lower rate of growth of the labour force?

(b) What is the steady-state position for the economy?

(c) Identify the levels of capital per worker and output per worker in this steady state.

(d) What is the rate of growth?

(e) What difference would it make to the steady state if there were a higher rate of growth of labour?

(f) Would a higher rate of savings mean higher or lower output growth?

**9** Figure 30–3 shows the Solow diagram for an economy. When an economy is relatively undeveloped, we might argue that all available resources must be used to try to maintain minimum subsistence survival. In Fig. 30–2, $k_0$ represents a critical level of capital per person which is just sufficient to generate the critical income level above which people can begin to save. For an economy in each of the positions labelled $A–E$, identify whether capital per person is increasing or decreasing, and the long-run level of $k$ where the economy would settle.

**Figure 30–3** A low-level equilibrium trap

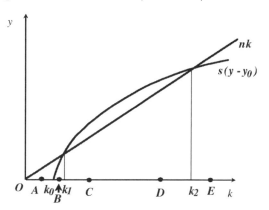

## True/False

**1** Per capita real GDP is a reasonable measure of the living standards of people in a country.

**2** An annual growth rate of 2 per cent p. a. leads to a sevenfold increase in real output in less than a century.

**3** The purpose of investment is to increase the capital stock.

**4** Invention is futile without innovation, which in turn requires investment.

**5** Sustained growth cannot occur if production relies on a factor whose supply is largely fixed.

**6** The potential rate of return on investment in people in the UK is probably quite high.

**7** In the neoclassical growth theory, output, capital and labour all grow at the same rate.

**8** Capital deepening is needed to extend the existing capital stock to accommodate immigrant workers.

**9** Higher savings enable a higher long-run rate of growth.

**10** Given the convergence hypothesis, we can expect all poor countries to catch up with the richer countries.

**11** Growth may be stimulated by capital externalities: that is, higher capital in one firm increases capital productivity in other firms.

**12** A crucial element in the rapid growth of the East Asian 'Tigers' was rapid growth in measured inputs.

## Economics in action

### US miracle is based on longer hours for less pay

(Adapted from an article by Doug Henwood, *The Guardian*, 2 February 2004)

In the late 1990s the USA was famous across the globe for its 'New Economy'. Computers had unleashed a productivity miracle. Or had they? Labour productivity measures real output per hour of labour. There are serious problems in estimating both the numerator and denominator of the productivity equation.

The labour inputs to the productivity calculations are not hours worked but hours paid. At Wal-Mart, many store managers work 60- or 70-hour weeks, but the productivity statistics assume far less. The same goes for the computer industry. The British Labour Survey (BLS) assumes that executives in the hi-tech sector work normal 35- or 40-hour weeks. To anyone in the industry, that assumption is hilarious.

There are plenty of problems with measuring output, too. Take, for example, the computer. If today's $1000 PC is twice as fast as last year's then, according to conventional economic logic, its 'real' value is twice that of the 2003 model. But if you are typing letters or email, does the speed increase make a difference?

## Questions

**1** Assess whether or not the productivity boom in the USA has boosted economic welfare.

**2** If increased computer processing power has aided productivity growth, why might it be better to examine the productivity development of a specific sector, such as banking?

## Questions for thought

**1** Explain how the price system can help to deal with the problem of depletion of a scarce resource, but may not always cope with the preservation of a renewable resource.

**2** Table 30–1 shows estimates of GNP per capita in 1997 and its average annual real growth rate in the period 1975–97, together with some other information which you may find helpful. To what extent do these data offer support for the convergence hypothesis?

**3** What are the major factors affecting the rate of economic growth? Comment on whether the government should introduce a policy to stimulate growth. At which factors should the policy be aimed?

| Table 30–1 | GNP per capita and other indicators | | | | | |
|---|---|---|---|---|---|---|
| Country | GNP per capita (US$, 1997) | Average annual % growth rate (1975–97) | GDP per capita (PPP$, 1997) | Gross domestic investment (% of GDP, 1997) | Adult literacy rate (%, 1997) | Life expectancy at birth (years, 1997) |
| Sierra Leone | 160 | −2.2 | 410 | 9 | 33.3 | 37.2 |
| Rwanda | 210 | −0.5 | 660 | 19 | 33.1 | 47.0 |
| Zambia | 370 | −1.7 | 960 | 15 | 75.1 | 40.1 |
| Cameroon | 620 | 0.1 | 1 890 | 10 | 71.7 | 54.7 |
| Sri Lanka | 800 | 3.2 | 2 490 | 27 | 90.7 | 73.1 |
| China | 860 | 7.8 | 3 130 | 35 | 82.9 | 69.8 |
| Peru | 2 610 | −0.3 | 4 680 | 25 | 88.7 | 68.3 |
| Thailand | 2 740 | 5.7 | 6 690 | 41 | 94.7 | 68.8 |
| Brazil | 4 790 | 1.1 | 6 480 | 20 | 84.0 | 68.8 |
| Korea (Rep.) | 10 550 | 6.8 | 13 590 | 35 | 97.2 | 72.4 |
| Italy | 20 170 | 2.2 | 20 290 | 18 | 98.3 | 78.2 |
| UK | 20 870 | 1.9 | 20 730 | 16 | 99.0 | 77.2 |
| France | 26 300 | 1.7 | 22 030 | 18 | 99.0 | 78.1 |
| USA | 29 080 | 1.6 | 29 010 | 18 | 99.0 | 76.7 |
| Singapore | 32 810 | 5.7 | 24 070 | 29 | 91.4 | 77.1 |
| Japan | 38 160 | 2.8 | 28 460 | 37 | 99.0 | 80.0 |

*Sources: Human Development Report 1999; World Development Report 1998/99.*

# chapter thirty-one

# Business cycles

## Learning outcomes

**By the end of this chapter, you should understand:**

- The differences between trend growth and economic cycles

- Why business cycles occur

- Why output gaps may fluctuate

- Whether potential output also fluctuates

- Whether national business cycles are now more correlated

- UK business cycles

## Key learning blocks

If you think that economics is a subject of controversies, then this chapter will certainly not change your mind! The theories surrounding *business cycles* are numerous and you are required to understand the following issues:

1. What is the business cycle?

2. How can business cycles be modelled as variations in actual output?

3. How can business cycles be modelled as variations in potential output?

The textbook moves through each of these topics and the exercises that follow will help to further your understanding.

# Important concepts and technical terms

## Match each lettered concept with the appropriate numbered phrase:

**a** Slump

**b** Accelerator model

**c** Recovery

**d** Boom

**e** Recession

**f** Trend path of output

**g** Political business cycle

**h** Persistence

**i** Ceilings and floors

**j** Real business cycle

**k** Real-wage puzzle

**l** International business cycle

**1** A period in which the economy is growing less quickly than trend output.

**2** The peak of the cycle.

**3** A theory that firms guess future output and profits by extrapolating past output growth, so that an increase in the desired level of investment requires an increase in output growth.

**4** The smooth path which output follows in the long run once the short-term fluctuations are averaged out.

**5** The trough of the cycle.

**6** A theory that short-term fluctuations of total output represent fluctuations of potential output.

**7** The phase of the cycle following a slump, in which output climbs above its trend path.

**8** Constraints which prevent cycles from exploding indefinitely.

**9** The idea that national economies follow similar cyclical paths through time.

**10** The notion that temporary shocks may have long-term effects, as households and firms take decisions that involve trade-offs between the present and the future.

**11** A suggestion that the business cycle is related to the election cycle.

**12** The observation that real wages do not follow the expected pattern over the business cycle.

## Exercises

**1** Figure 31–1 shows the path of a hypothetical economy fluctuating around a smooth trend. For each of the labelled points, identify the phase of the cycle. How would you interpret the horizontal distance from *A* to *F*?

**2** Which of the following factors might be expected to affect the level of investment?

**(a)** Past profitability.
**(b)** The present value of future operating profits.
**(c)** Real interest rates.
**(d)** Expectations about future sales.
**(e)** Past output growth.

**Figure 31–1** The business cycle

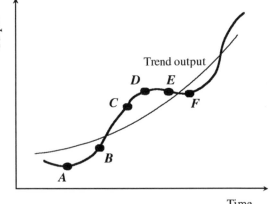

How might a combination of some of these factors give rise to a business cycle?

**3** This exercise concerns the multiplier–accelerator model and entails some simple calculations. Suppose we have a fixed-price closed economy with no government, such that:

$$Yt = Ct + It$$

where  $Yt$ = national income in time period $t$
$Ct$ = consumption in period $t$
$It$  = investment in period $t$

Further, suppose that consumption in the current period depends upon income in the previous period:

$$Ct = 0.5\,Yt - 1$$

(0.5 is the marginal propensity to consume)

Investment comprises two parts, an autonomous element *(A)* and a part which depends upon past changes in output:

$$It = A + v\,(Yt - 1 - Yt - 2)$$

where $v$ = the 'acceleration coefficient'

Initially, autonomous investment is 30 and the economy is in equilibrium with $Y = 60$, $C = 30$ and $I = 30$.

We now consider what happens if there is an increase in autonomous investment from 30 to 40. The new equilibrium is $Y = 80$, $C = 40$ and $I = 40$, but our model enables us to trace the adjustment path through time. This can be done as in Table 31–1, under alternative assumptions about $v$, the acceleration coefficient. For $v = 0.2$, we have provided some initial calculations with an explanation.

For $v = 0.2$, period 0 shows the original equilibrium. In period 1, investment increases to 40 but consumption has not yet changed. In period 2, consumption is 0.5 × 70 and investment is 40 + 0.2 × (70 − 60) = 42 and

$Y = 77$. Complete the remaining entries in Table 31–1, and repeat the exercise for $v = 0.8$: you will find that the adjustment path is very different. (If you have access to a computer, you may like to set up a spreadsheet to simulate adjustment paths for other values of $c$ and $v$.)

**4** Figure 31–2 shows a production possibility frontier (*PPF*) between present and future consumption: this idea first appeared back in Chapter 14, if you want to go back and check it out. $U_0$ and $U_1$ illustrate household preferences between consuming resources now as opposed to in the future.

**Figure 31–2** The trade-off between present and future consumption

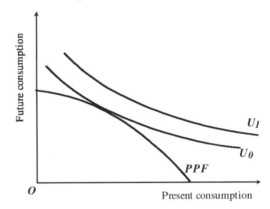

(a) Mark on your diagram the choice point for society.

Suppose now that there is some temporary technological 'shock' that enables this society to increase its production possibilities.

(b) What effect would this have on Fig. 31–2?
(c) What is the effect on present consumption?
(d) What is the effect on future consumption?
(e) What long-run consequences does this have for the society?
(f) Under what conditions would present consumption react differently?
(g) What does all this have to do with business cycles?

**5** Which of the following may give rise to persistence, and thus ensure that temporary shocks may have long-run effects?

(a) Diminishing marginal utility of income.
(b) Strong preference for present consumption.
(c) High availability of investment opportunities.
(d) Strong motivation to leave bequests.
(e) Ricardian equivalence.

| Table 31–1 | A multiplier-accelerator model | | | | | |
|---|---|---|---|---|---|---|
| | **v = 0.2** | | | **v = 0.8** | | |
| **Time period** | **C** | **I** | **Y** | **C** | **I** | **Y** |
| 0 | 30 | 30 | 60 | 30 | 30 | 60 |
| 1 | 30 | 40 | 70 | 30 | 40 | 70 |
| 2 | 35 | 42 | 77 | | | |
| 3 | | | | | | |
| 4 | | | | | | |
| 5 | | | | | | |
| 6 | | | | | | |

**6** For this exercise, you need to invoke your imagination a little. Imagine that you are living in a society which has just emerged from a deep recession. Unemployment is falling, real output is rising, prospects are good and you feel confident and ready for anything.

**(a)** Your bank writes to you offering to lend you money to spend on consumption at a special rate. Are you more likely to accept the offer than when the economy had been deep in recession and all was gloom and doom?

**(b)** So you borrow. You get yourself a Porsche and an electronic organizer. What has happened to your net indebtedness?

**(c)** The clock moves on, the economy does not keep booming for ever. Interest rates begin to rise. Now what has happened to your debt?

**(d)** When you had borrowed, you had used your flat in London as collateral. Property prices begin to fall. The shares that you had so eagerly added to your portfolio two years ago are heading for the floor. Do you still feel so confident? What do you do about it?

**(e)** What relevance does this have in analysing the events of the 1980s and early 1990s?

**7** Which of the following factors may increase the integration of the world economy and thus encourage the international transmission of the business cycle?

**(a)** The removal of protectionist policies.

**(b)** Improvements in transport and telecommunications.

**(c)** The Single European Market (SEM).

**(d)** The General Agreement on Tariffs and Trade (GATT) and the operations of the World Trade Organization (WTO).

**(e)** Financial deregulation.

**(f)** The integration of the global financial market.

**(g)** Policy coordination between countries.

**8** In Exercise 1 of Chapter 19, you calculated growth rates for the UK, the USA and Spain (see 'Answers', Fig. A19–2). To what extent do these results support the notion of a common international business cycle?

## True/False

**1** In the long run, fluctuations of output around potential output are unimportant.

**2** Short-run fluctuations in output can be explained by fluctuations in aggregate demand.

**3** Governments cause the business cycle by invoking popular policies in the run-up to elections and unpopular ones once safely elected.

**4** In the multiplier–accelerator model, the less firms' decisions respond to changes in past output, the more pronounced the cycle.

**5** Changes in stocks help to explain why the economy is likely to spend several years during the phase of recovery or recession.

**6** The business cycle cannot exist in theory, because the economy always tends very rapidly to equilibrium.

**7** Real wages rise in a slump because cutting back on workers raises the marginal product of labour.

**8** Real business cycle theories are usually theories of persistence rather than of cycles.

**9** According to real business cycle theory, it is very important for governments to intervene in order to stabilize the economy over the cycle.

**10** Increased global integration encourages the international transmission of the business cycle.

**11** Recovery from the recession of 1990–91 was slow and weak, because of the huge burden of household debt that had built up during the 1980s.

## Economics in action

### Oil prices surge to record highs

(Adapted from an article on BBC News Online, 9 August 2004)

The price of crude oil is hovering around record-breaking peaks after unrest in Iraq halted production. US light crude rose to $44.99 overnight, a 21-year record high.

Companies, including British Airways, are feeling the effect of higher fuel and raw material costs, while there are worries that consumers may spend less. The rise also resulted in a warning for UK motorists to expect price increases at the petrol pump.

The latest rise in crude prices was sparked by disruptions to Iraqi oil exports. On Monday, officials shut down oil fields in the south of the country after threats of sabotage from fighters loyal to the Shia cleric Moqtada Sadr. Fears are also growing of an attack on oil installations in Saudi Arabia.

## Questions

**1** Explain how the oil price crisis might cause a recession by creating a fluctuating output gap.

**2** Explain how the oil price crisis might cause a recession by creating a fluctuation in potential output.

## Questions for thought

**1** To what extent can the existence of business cycles be linked with the notion of hysteresis?

**2** This question considers the political business cycle and uses concepts developed earlier in the book, in particular notions about indifference curves and short- and long-run Phillips curves.

In Fig. 31–3, *LRPC* is the long-run Phillips curve; $SPC_0$ and $SPC_1$ are short-run Phillips curves reflecting different inflation expectations. The curves $I_1$–$I_4$ are indifference curves which represent how the government perceives the preferences of the electorate for different combinations of inflation and unemployment. The shape of these curves reflects the

fact that the two 'goods' are 'bads'! Utility increases from $I_1$ to $I_2$ to $I_3$ to $I_4$. The economy begins in long-run equilibrium with no inflation.

**(a)** What is the current unemployment level?
**(b)** What is the perceived utility level of the electorate?
**(c)** An election approaches; what measures can the government take to make the electorate feel better off? At what point would the economy be in the short run?
**(d)** What happens as the economy adjusts?
**(e)** What is the perceived utility level of the electorate?
**(f)** Supposing that the next election is five years away, where might the economy be taken next, and where might it eventually settle?
**(g)** Do you think that this model explains the actions of UK governments in the 1980s and 1990s?

**Figure 31–3** The political business cycle

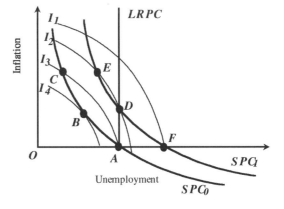

# chapter thirty-two

# Macroeconomics: taking stock

## Learning outcomes

**By the end of this chapter, you should understand:**

- How different views of how the macroeconomy works result from differences in key assumptions regarding prices and wages

- The effect of different assumptions about the speed of price and wage adjustment

- The effect of different assumptions about how expectations are formed

- The role of real wage flexibility

- The concept of hysteresis

- Different schools of macroeconomic thought

## Key learning blocks

This chapter brings together an analysis of the competing *macroeconomic theories*. You need to be familiar with the following issues:

1. How the competing theories differ in their assumptions about the economy.

2. How understanding about labour and product markets are essential to understanding the macroeconomy.

3. How the role of expectations is built into each model.

The textbook moves through each theory in turn and the exercises that follow will help to develop your understanding.

# Important concepts and technical terms

## Match each lettered concept with the appropriate numbered phrase:

**a** Exogenous expectations

**b** Moderate Keynesians

**c** Market clearing

**d** Rational expectations

**e** New Classical macroeconomics

**f** Real-wage hypothesis

**g** Extrapolative expectations

**h** Gradualist monetarists

**i** Potential output

**j** Extreme Keynesians

**k** Hysteresis

**l** New Keynesians

**1** The level of output that firms wish to supply when there is full employment.

**2** A group of economists who insist that markets not only fail to clear in the short run but also may not clear in the long run.

**3** The assumption that real wages are rigidly inflexible.

**4** A school of economists who believe that the restoration of full employment is not immediate but that adjustment will not be too lengthy.

**5** A theory of expectations formation which says that people make good use of the information that is available today and do not make forecasts that are already knowably incorrect.

**6** A school of economists whose ideas may be summarized as 'short-run Keynesian and long-run monetarist'.

**7** Expectations formed on the basis of past experience.

**8** Expectations formed independently of the rest of the analysis being undertaken.

**9** A situation in which the quantity that sellers wish to supply in a market equals the quantity that purchasers wish to demand.

**10** The view that temporary shocks affect the long-run equilibrium.

**11** A school of economists whose analysis is based on the twin principles of almost instantaneous market clearing and rational expectations.

**12** A school of economists who set out to provide microeconomic foundations for Keynesian macroeconomics.

## Exercises

**1** The old joke says that if you were to line up all the economists in the world, they would never reach a conclusion. Which of the following may help to explain why economists sometimes disagree?

**(a)** Judgements about the relative cost to society of ills such as unemployment and inflation involve normative issues on which economists may differ, even if they agree about positive economic theory.

**(b)** Economists cannot carry out laboratory experiments that enable theories to be proved true or false.

**(c)** We do not have enough data to allow more than tentative evidence to be presented.

**(d)** It is not clear whether and how quickly markets clear.

**(e)** We cannot precisely define the process of expectations formation in the real-world economy.

**2** Associate each of the following viewpoints with one of the 'schools' discussed in this chapter.

**(a)** Full employment will be reached in a reasonable period of time.

**(b)** Long-run demand-deficient unemployment is feasible.

**(c)** The short run and long run are indistinguishable because adjustment is rapid.

**(d)** Short-run stabilization could be important because adjustment may be sluggish.

**(e)** Policies should be concentrated on the short run.

**(f)** Expectations are formed rationally.

**3** **(a)** What do you expect to be the rate of inflation in the coming year?

**(b)** What information did you use in order to form that expectation?

**(c)** If you had responsibility for setting prices or negotiating wage settlements, would you form your expectations more carefully? What additional information would you seek?

**4** Figure 32–1 shows our usual labour market story: $LD_0$, $LD_1$ represent labour demand curves; $LF$ shows the number of people prepared to register in the labour force at each real wage; $AJ$ shows those prepared to accept jobs. The economy begins in equilibrium with labour demand $LD_0$. An exogenous shock affects labour productivity and reduces labour demand to $LD_1$.

**(a)** Identify the original real wage and unemployment level.

**Figure 32–1** The labour market

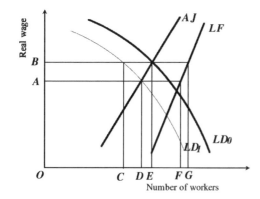

After the shock:

**(b)** How would an Extreme Keynesian view the long-run prospects for the labour market?

**(c)** How would a Gradualist monetarist and a Moderate Keynesian view the labour market in the medium and the long term? How would you distinguish the two?

**(d)** Identify the new short-run position of the market according to the New Classical school.

**(e)** How would the groups differ in their approach to policy?

**(f)** How would the analysis be affected by hysteresis?

**5** Which of the schools are most likely to adopt the following policy measures?

**(a)** Contractionary monetary policy to combat inflation, as the transitional cost of unemployment will be quite short-lived.

**(b)** Reduction of money supply to eliminate inflation; output and employment will not be affected.

**(c)** Import controls to protect domestic employment during an expansion of aggregate demand.

**(d)** Incomes policy to speed adjustment.

**(e)** Demand management to stimulate investment and thus raise potential output.

**6** Rank the following markets in order of their likely speed of adjustment (most rapid first):

**(a)** The market for goods.

**(b)** The money market.

**(c)** The labour market.

**(d)** The foreign exchange market.

Explain your answer.

**7** Consider an economy in deep recession which operates under an Extreme Keynesian perspective.

**(a)** Draw an *IS–LM* diagram to depict the equilibrium situation for this economy.

**(b)** On your diagram, show why it is that nominal wage and price adjustments will not be effective in stimulating the level of real output.

**(c)** Would a monetary expansion be any more effective?

**(d)** How could the economy escape from recession?

**(e)** How would your diagram have differed if you had been considering an economy operating under New Classical or Gradualist monetarist assumptions?

**8** Macroeconomics: where do you stand?

## True/False

**1** Economists agree about positive issues but disagree on normative matters.

**2** A rise in unemployment provides support for Keynesian analysis of the economy in which a deficiency of aggregate demand may move the economy away from full employment.

**3** According to New Classical macroeconomics, government policy can move the economy away from full employment only if agents are surprised by the policy.

**4** The New Classicals believe that the dramatic rise in UK unemployment in the early 1980s had almost nothing to do with a fall in aggregate demand.

**5** Gradualist monetarists subscribe to the view that an increase in money supply can increase output and employment in the long run, but that the adjustment process is gradual.

**6** According to the Gradualist monetarists, the government's chief responsibility is to increase potential output by supply-side policies and by bringing inflation under control.

**7** Moderate Keynesians argue that supply-side policies are irrelevant and that attention should be focused on demand management.

**8** According to some Moderate Keynesians, demand management may be a significant supply-side policy.

**9** Extreme Keynesians argue that supply-side policies are irrelevant and that attention should be focused on demand management.

**10** Macroeconomists never consider microeconomic issues.

## Economics in action

### The Keynesian temptation

(Adapted from an article in *The Economist*, 6 May 2004)

The German government considers spending its way out of trouble. The idea is certainly germinating. Chancellor Gerhard Schröder and Hans Eichel, his finance minister, met on 28 April to discuss saying 'farewell to budget tightening'.

In contemplating a Keynesian shift, Mr Schröder may be taking a lead from Peter Bofinger, an economist at Würzburg University. The government has focused too much on structural reform and not enough on sustaining demand, argues Mr Bofinger, who was recently appointed to the German Council of Economic Experts. Yet most other economists make a case that any shift would be harmful. The country's problem is not growth itself, but low growth potential, says Hans-Werner Sinn, president of IFO, an economic think-tank.

## Questions

**1** 'The government has focused too much on structural reform and not enough on sustaining demand.' What elements of this statement are Keynesian and what elements are classical?

**2** 'The country's problem is not growth itself, but low growth potential.' What are the implications for aggregate supply if there is low growth potential?

## Questions for thought

**1** Discuss the proposition that the best stabilization policy is one of non-intervention.

**2** Discuss whether government policy should be permitted to react to changing circumstances, or whether it should be guided by predetermined rules.

**3** Consider the economic policies of the current government and opposition. Can you trace these policies to particular areas of the macroeconomic spectrum?

# part five

# The world economy

# chapter thirty-three

# International trade

## Learning outcomes

**By the end of this chapter, you should understand:**

- Patterns of international trade
- Comparative advantage and the gains from trade
- Determinants of comparative advantage
- Why two-way trade occurs for the same product
- Trade policy
- The principle of targeting
- Motives for tariffs

## Key learning blocks

In this chapter you will examine *international trade*. The areas which you are required to understand in detail are:

1. What are the current patterns in world trade?
2. How does the theory of comparative advantage explain international trade?
3. How might a government restrict international trade?

The textbook covers each of these issues in detail and the exercises that follow will help to develop your understanding.

# Important concepts and technical terms

## Match each lettered concept with the appropriate numbered phrase:

(a) Non-tariff barriers (NTBs)

(b) Import tariff

(c) Absolute advantage

(d) Import quotas

(e) Export subsidy

(f) Commercial policy

(g) Optimal tariff

(h) Infant industry argument

(i) Law of comparative advantage

(j) GATT

(k) Factor endowments

(l) Deadweight loss of a tariff

**1** An import duty requiring the importer of a good to pay a specified fraction of the world price to the government.

**2** A commercial policy designed to increase exports by granting producers an additional sum above the domestic price per unit exported.

**3** The amounts of capital and labour available in an economy.

**4** Government policy that influences international trade through taxes or subsidies or through direct restrictions on imports and exports.

**5** Administrative regulations that discriminate against foreign goods and favour home goods.

**6** The waste arising from the domestic overproduction and domestic underconsumption of a good where imports are subject to a tariff.

**7** A principle which states that countries specialize in producing and exporting goods that they produce at a lower relative cost than other countries.

**8** Restrictions imposed on the maximum quantity of imports.

**9** The ability to produce goods with lower unit labour requirements than in other countries.

**10** Tariffs designed to restrict imports until the benefit of the last import equals its cost to society as a whole.

**11** A justification of a tariff on the grounds that a developing industry needs protection until established.

**12** A commitment by a large number of countries in the post-war period to reduce tariffs successively and to dismantle trade restrictions, now embodied in the World Trade Organization (WTO).

## Exercises

**1**    Table 33–1 shows how the exports of a number of countries were divided between five commodity groups in 2001.

**(a)** What do these figures suggest about the factor and resource endowments in these countries and the pattern of comparative advantage?

**(b)** Given recent changes in the composition of world exports (see Section 33–1 of the main text), how would you assess the future prospects for these countries?

**(c)** What additional information would you require to feel confident in your answers?

**2**    This exercise examines the gains from trade in a two-country, two-good model. To simplify matters for the time being, we assume that the two countries share a common currency; this allows us to ignore the exchange rate. The two countries are called Anywaria and Someland; the two goods are bicycles and boots.

**Table 33–1   Structure of merchandise exports, 2001**

| Country | Percentage share of merchandise exports | | | | |
| | Agricultural raw materials | Fuels | Ores and metals | Manufactured goods | Machinery and transport |
| --- | --- | --- | --- | --- | --- |
| Australia | 6 | 21 | 19 | 8 | 11 |
| Ethiopia | 23 | 0 | 3 | 13 | 0 |
| Germany | 1 | 2 | 2 | 22 | 51 |
| Japan | 1 | 0 | 1 | 18 | 67 |
| Pakistan | 2 | 2 | 0 | 83 | 1 |
| Saudi Arabia | 0 | 90 | 0 | 2 | 0 |
| Singapore | 0 | 8 | 1 | 12 | 64 |
| UK | 0 | 8 | 2 | 21 | 44 |

Source: www.UNCTAD.org

The unit labour requirements of the two goods in each country are shown in Table 33–2; we assume constant returns to scale.

**Table 33–2   Production techniques**

| | Unit labour requirements (hours per unit output) | |
| | Anywaria | Someland |
| --- | --- | --- |
| Bicycles | 60 | 120 |
| Boots | 30 | 40 |

(a) Which of the countries has an absolute advantage in the production of the two commodities?

(b) Calculate the opportunity cost of bicycles in terms of boots and of boots in terms of bicycles for each of the countries.

(c) Which country has a comparative advantage in the production of bicycles?

Suppose there is no trade. Each of the two economies has 300 workers who work 40 hours per week. Initially, each country devotes half of its resources to producing each of the two commodities.

(d) Complete Table 33–3.

**Table 33–3   Production of bicycles and boots, no-trade case**

| | Anywaria | Someland | 'World' output |
| --- | --- | --- | --- |
| Bicycles | | | |
| Boots | | | |

Trade now takes place under the following conditions: the country with a comparative advantage in boot production produces only boots. The other country produces sufficient bicycles to maintain the world 'no-trade' output, devoting the remaining resources to boot production.

(e) Complete Table 33–4 and comment on the gains from trade.

**Table 33–4   Production of bicycles and boots**

| | Anywaria | Someland | 'World' output |
| --- | --- | --- | --- |
| Bicycles | | | |
| Boots | | | |

(f) On a single diagram, plot the production possibility frontier (PPF) for each country. What aspect of your diagram is indicative of potential gains from trade?

**3** This exercise extends the analysis of Exercise 2 by recognizing that our two economies have different currencies and labour costs. Unit labour requirements are as set out before (in Table 33–2). The hourly wage rate in Anywaria is A$5; in Someland it is S$4.50.

(a) Calculate unit labour costs for the two goods in each country.

(b) Calculate unit labour costs in terms of Somelandish dollars if the exchange rate is A$1 = S$1.8.

(c) Calculate unit labour costs in terms of Somelandish dollars if the exchange rate is A$1 = S$1.2.

(d) Comment on the range of values for the exchange rate within which trade may take place. Explain your answer.

(e) Within this simple world, what factors will determine the equilibrium exchange rate?

**4**   Which of the following factors favour(s) intra-industry trade and which act(s) against it?

**(a)**   Product differentiation.
**(b)**   International integration.
**(c)**   Existence of tariff barriers.
**(d)**   Availability of economies of scale in the production of individual brands.
**(e)**   High transport costs.
**(f)**   Homogeneous commodity.

**5**   Below are listed a selection of arguments which have been advanced to support the existence of tariffs. Identify each as a 'first-best', 'second-best' or 'non'-argument.

**(a)**   The need to defend domestic producers against unfair competition based on cheap foreign labour.
**(b)**   The need to maintain a national defence industry in case of war.
**(c)**   A desire to restrict imports until the benefits of the last imported unit are equalized with its cost to society as a whole.
**(d)**   The need to nurture a newly developing domestic industry.
**(e)**   A wish to prevent dumping by foreign producers.
**(f)**   The government needs a cheap and easy way of obtaining revenue.

**6**   Which of the following factors may have adverse effects for a country attempting to protect employment by the imposition of tariffs?

**(a)**   Retaliation in export markets.
**(b)**   Loss of consumer surplus.
**(c)**   Generation of tariff revenue.
**(d)**   Reduced exploitation of comparative advantage.
**(e)**   Resource cost of production inefficiency.
**(f)**   Reduced import penetration.

**7**   Figure 33–1 shows the domestic demand (*DD*) and supply (*SS*) of a commodity with and without the imposition of a tariff, the world price being given by *OB*.

**(a)**   Identify the domestic price and the quantity imported in a situation of free trade.

Suppose now that a tariff is imposed on imports of this commodity.

**(b)**   Identify the domestic price in the new situation, and the quantity imported.
**(c)**   By how much does domestic production of this commodity change?
**(d)**   Identify the area which represents the extra consumer payments for the quantity purchased.

**Figure 33–1**   A tariff

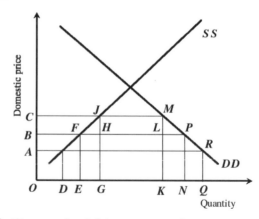

**(e)**   How much of this accrues to the government as tariff revenue and how much to domestic producers as additional rents?
**(f)**   Explain the remaining part of these extra consumer payments.
**(g)**   Identify the surplus of consumer benefits over social marginal cost which is sacrificed by society in reducing its consumption of this good.
**(h)**   What is the total welfare cost of this tariff?

**8**   Figure 33–2 shows the domestic demand (*DD*) and supply (*SS*) of a commodity, the export of which the government wishes to encourage. *OA* represents the world price.

**Figure 33–2**   An export subsidy

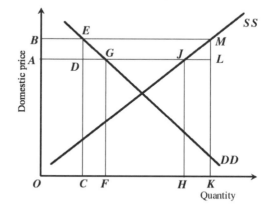

**(a)**   Identify the domestic price and the quantity exported in a situation of free trade.

The government now imposes an export subsidy.

**(b)**   Identify the new domestic price and quantity exported.
**(c)**   By how much does domestic production increase?
**(d)**   By how much does domestic consumption fall?
**(e)**   Identify the decrease in consumer surplus.

**(f)** What is the social cost of the extra production (i.e. the social cost of producing goods whose marginal cost exceeds the world price)?

**(g)** Why would the government wish to introduce this policy?

**(h)** How else could the same objective be achieved?

**9** Wodgets are available on the world market at a price of £3 each. We consider an economy in which the domestic supply of wodgets is given by:

$Qs = 1000\,p$ (where $p$ is the domestic price).

The demand for wodgets is:

$Qd = 10\,000 - 1000\,p$

Assuming there are no tariffs:

**(a)** What will be the quantity of wodgets imported?

**(b)** What quantity of wodgets will be produced in the domestic market?

If the government places a tariff of £2 on imported wodgets:

**(c)** Identify the new level of domestic production.

**(d)** How much revenue will the government receive from the tariff?

**(e)** Calculate the deadweight loss arising from the tariff.

**10** The Multi-Fibre Arrangement (MFA) restricts the increase of imports of many textiles and clothes from developing into developed countries including the UK. This exercise explores the effect of such quota agreements on the domestic market using Fig. 33–3, which shows the domestic demand curve (**DD**) and supply curve (**SS**) for a commodity. **OA** is the world price.

**Figure 33–3** Quota restrictions

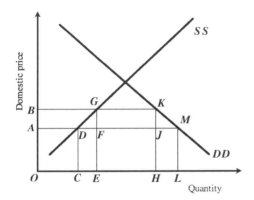

**(a)** What would be the level of imports in the absence of restriction?

A quota restriction is now imposed which limits imports to the amount **FJ**.

**(b)** What is the new domestic price?

**(c)** Identify the change in domestic production and consumption.

**(d)** Explain what is represented by the area **FGKJ**.

**(e)** Identify the total welfare cost.

**(f)** Who gains from this and who loses?

## True/False

**1** More than half of world trade is between the industrialized countries.

**2** Manufactured goods comprise more than 80 per cent of exports from Asia.

**3** International trade is worthwhile so long as one country has an absolute advantage in production.

**4** Comparative advantage reflects international differences in the opportunity costs of producing different goods.

**5** If a country has a relatively abundant endowment of a particular factor, it will tend to have a comparative advantage in the production of goods which use that factor intensively.

**6** The existence of comparative advantage tends to increase the amount of intra-industry trade.

**7** The law of comparative advantage ensures that there are gains from trade which make everyone better off.

**8** The imposition of a tariff stimulates domestic consumption.

**9** The case for free trade rests partly on the analysis of the deadweight burden arising from the existence of tariff barriers.

**10** The need to protect infant industries is a powerful argument in favour of tariff barriers.

**11** In the 1990s, tariff levels throughout the world economy were probably as low as they had ever been.

**12** Some countries attempt to restrict imports by imposing rigorous or complicated rules concerning the specification of imported goods.

## Economics in action

### Shrimp wars

(Adapted from an article in *The Economist*, 8 July 2004)

The Southern Shrimp Alliance, a group of shrimp fishermen and processors from eight US states, has long accused its rivals in Thailand, China, Vietnam, India, Ecuador and Brazil of dumping their produce on the American market. On July 6, the US Commerce Department, concluding that China and Vietnam were selling the little crustaceans below their fair value, imposed anti-dumping duties of up to 93.13 per cent on shrimp from Vietnam and up to 112.81 per cent on shrimp from China.

Kim Chauvin, an activist says: 'I don't understand how they expect Americans to compete with countries that have slave labour and pay people 33 cents an hour.'

Wally Stevens, a seafood distributor in Boston, argues that the damage is self-inflicted. The domestic industry has tried to compete on price alone – impossible, since trawlers and fuel are so expensive – instead of marketing to a niche: the sort of sophisticated consumers who seek out boutique pinot noirs from Oregon. The duties are likely to raise the price of shrimp to the American consumer by 44 per cent.

## Questions

**1** How would you go about calculating the fair value of shrimp?

**2** Would you have supported the US shrimp industry?

## Questions for thought

**1** Can a country create comparative advantage?

**2** This question extends some aspects of the analysis in this chapter of a two-country, two-good world. The two countries are *A* and *B*, the two goods *X* and *Y*. Figure 33–4 focuses on country *A*, illustrating

**Figure 33–4** Country A: production and preferences

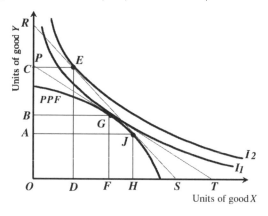

the production possibility frontier (*PPF*) and some indifference curves ($I_1$, $I_2$) depicting the community's preference for the two goods.

Suppose that initially there is no trade, and that the domestic price ratio is given by the line *PT*.

**(a)** At what point will the economy choose to produce?

**(b)** If the 'world' price ratio is also given by *PT*, what is implied for comparative advantage and the gains from trade?

Suppose now that the world price ratio is given by *RS*, but the domestic price ratio by *PT*.

**(c)** What are the implications for the comparative advantage of country *A*?

With international trade in this situation, country *A* can move to any point along *RS* by exporting and importing goods.

**(d)** At what points will country *A* choose to produce and consume?

**(e)** Identify exports and imports.

In (*d*) and (*e*), we have seen that the quantities offered for exchange internationally depend upon the terms of trade (the world price ratio) and upon the preferences of people in country *A*. Of course, a similar story could be told for country *B*, showing the offers made for exchange. By examining the offers made by the two countries at different relative world prices, we can gain some insight into the equilibrium terms of trade.

Consider Fig. 33–5. The curve *UV* is the 'offer' curve for country *A*: it shows the quantities of good *X* offered in exchange for good *Y* at different terms of trade. The curve *NQ* shows the offer curve for country *B*, constructed in similar fashion.

**(f)** Interpret the line *OM* and explain the sense in which the point *W* represents an equilibrium.

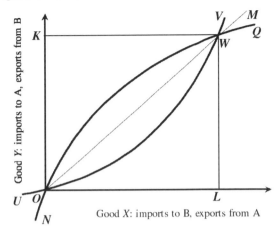

**Figure 33–5**   Offer curves

# Exchange rate regimes

## Learning outcomes

By the end of this chapter, you should understand:

- The contrast in different exchange rate regimes
- The gold standard
- An adjustable peg
- The 'impossible triad'
- Speculative attacks
- Floating exchange rates
- Motives for international policy coordination
- The European Monetary System (EMS)

## Key learning blocks

In this chapter you will explore additional issues associated with *exchange rates*. The issues that you are required to understand are:

1. What are the different exchange rate regimes?
2. How robustness, volatility and financial discipline are influenced by the choice of exchange rate regime.
3. The merits of international policy coordination.

The textbook covers each of these topics and the exercises that follow will aid your understanding.

# Important concepts and technical terms

## Match each lettered concept with the appropriate numbered phrase:

**a** PPP path

**b** Adjustable peg regime

**c** International competitiveness

**d** Capital controls

**e** Currency board

**f** Exchange rate speculation

**g** Gold standard

**h** Managed float

**i** European Monetary System (EMS)

**j** Financial discipline

**k** Speculative attack

**l** Dollar standard

**1** Measured by comparing the relative prices of the goods from different countries when using a common currency.

**2** The path for the nominal exchange rate that would maintain the level of international competitiveness constant over time.

**3** A situation that occurs when a country faces a sharp loss of reserves, a sharp depreciation, or both.

**4** An exchange rate system under which the government of each country fixes the price of gold in terms of its home currency, maintains convertibility of the domestic currency into gold and preserves 100 per cent cover.

**5** A regime in which the exchange rate floats but is influenced in the short run by government intervention.

**6** An exchange rate system which operated after the Second World War, in which countries agreed to fix their exchange rates against the dollar.

**7** A feature of fixed-exchange rate systems by which governments are forced to pursue policies which keep domestic inflation in line with world rates.

**8** The movement of investment funds between currencies in pursuit of the highest return in the light of expected exchange rate changes.

**9** Measures introduced by governments to defend pegged exchange rates by prohibiting, restricting or taxing the flow of private capital across countries.

**10** A tentative step towards fixed exchange rates involving members of the EU from 1979 onwards.

**11** A regime in which exchange rates are normally fixed but where countries are occasionally allowed to alter their exchange rate.

**12** A constitutional commitment to peg the exchange rate by giving up monetary independence.

## Exercises

**1** Below are listed a number of policy actions and situations. In each case, identify the sort of exchange rate regime in operation.

**(a)** The government carries out open market operations (OMOs) to prevent the exchange rate from falling so rapidly as to endanger the target inflation rate.

**(b)** The money supply decreases following a balance of payments deficit and a fall in the economy's gold reserves.

**(c)** A major crisis leads to a devaluation of the domestic currency.

**(d)** A contractionary fiscal policy is introduced after

successive years of balance of payments deficits and falls in the foreign exchange reserves.

(e) The foreign exchange markets are in continuous equilibrium with no government intervention via foreign exchange reserves.

(f) There is a fixed-exchange rate regime with automatic government reaction to disequilibrium.

(g) There is a flexible-exchange rate system in which the government has some discretion in exchange rate policy.

(h) A country experiencing high rates of inflation relative to other countries also experiences a depreciating nominal exchange rate which in the long run maintains a constant real exchange rate.

**2**    This exercise and the following one investigate the operation of the gold standard. Suppose the USA has fixed the par value of gold at $20.67 per ounce, while the UK par value is £4.25.

(a) What is the $/£ exchange rate?

Suppose that you begin with £85 and the exchange rate is $6/£.

(b) How much gold could you buy in the UK?
(c) Suppose instead that you exchange your pounds for dollars: how much gold could you then buy in the USA?
(d) If you then ship the gold back to Britain, what would it be worth in sterling?
(e) For how long would you expect the exchange rate to remain at $6/£?
(f) Describe the likely events should the exchange rate be $3/£.

Figure 34–1 shows the demand for *(D)* and supply of *(S)* pounds at different exchange rates under the gold standard.

**Figure 34–1**  The exchange rate and the gold standard

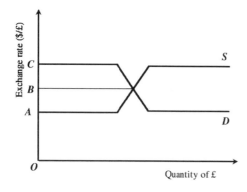

(g) Identify the gold parity exchange rate.
(h) Describe what happens at exchange rate *OC*.
(i) Describe what is happening between exchange rates *OA* and *OC*.

**3**    Two countries, say the UK and the USA, are operating under the gold standard, both countries beginning in both internal and external balance. There is then a fall in the American average propensity to import from the UK at each income level.

(a) What is the short-run impact on UK exports and the balance of payments?
(b) Describe the effect of this on aggregate demand, output and employment if UK wages and prices do not immediately respond.
(c) How does this affect the exchange rate and UK gold reserves?
(d) What does this in turn imply for money supply?
(e) Describe how the UK now manages to return to internal and external balance.
(f) Briefly outline the effects upon the US economy.

**4**    Three countries, *A*, *B* and *C*, are all experiencing relatively high rates of inflation. A floating-exchange rate regime is in operation.

Country *A* wants to reduce the rate of inflation, so introduces a restrictive monetary policy.

(a) What effect does this have on *A*'s exchange rate relative to the other two countries?
(b) How does this affect *A*'s competitiveness?
(c) Meanwhile, back in *B* and *C*, what is happening to the inflation rate?

Country *B* now gets worried about inflation and initiates a tight money policy.

(d) What effect does country *B*'s policy have on *C*'s exchange rate relative to the other two countries?
(e) Outline the effects of *B*'s policy on country *A*.

We could now, of course, consider what happens when country *C* decides to have a go at tight money – but instead:

(f) Comment briefly on the potential advantages of policy harmonization.

**5**    Which of the following were features of the dollar standard?

(a) The provision of an automatic mechanism for resolving imbalances in international payments.
(b) The removal of speculation problems, given the fixed nature of the exchange rate.

(c) At the fixed exchange rate, central banks were committed to buy or sell dollars from their stock of foreign exchange reserves or dollar holdings.

(d) A series of gradual exchange rate adjustments at frequent intervals.

(e) One hundred per cent backing of domestic currencies by dollar reserves.

(f) A relatively rapid increase in the world supply of dollars in the late 1960s, partly as a result of the Vietnam war.

**6**     Which of the following describes the response of an economy to a shock under a system of freely floating exchange rates? (*Note*: More than one response may be valid.)

(a) An autonomous increase in aggregate demand leads to an increase in imports, a balance of payments deficit (in the immediate run) and a depreciation of the domestic currency.

(b) A once-for-all reduction in domestic money supply leads to an appreciation of the exchange rate, which may overshoot in the short run.

(c) A decrease in aggregate demand leads to a balance of payments surplus and an increase in foreign exchange reserves.

(d) Domestic interest rates are increased by government action to slow down a depreciation of the exchange rate.

(e) A succession of balance of payments deficits enables the domestic government successfully to request a devaluation of the currency.

**7**     Which of the following is not a feature of a managed float?

(a) In the long run, the nominal exchange rate tends to follow the PPP path.

(b) Governments may sometimes intervene to smooth out short-run fluctuations in the exchange rate.

(c) The foreign exchange reserves remain constant.

(d) The net monetary inflow from abroad need not always be zero.

(e) Governments may operate in the foreign exchange market to influence the direction of movement of the exchange rate.

**8**     In the post-war period, both fixed- and floating-exchange rate systems have been tried, but there is still no consensus on which is the more effective. Critically evaluate the following statements concerning some of the relevant issues.

(a) Flexible exchange rates are better able to cope with major external shocks.

(b) Fixed exchange rates offer greater stability of trading conditions.

(c) Floating exchange rates enable individual countries to follow independent policies.

(d) Fixed-exchange rate systems may force governments to adopt other distortionary policy options, such as the imposition of tariffs or import quotas.

## True/False

**1**     Under the gold standard, 100 per cent backing for the money supply was always strictly adhered to.

**2**     Victorians were wrong to believe that Britain's trade deficits in the late nineteenth century were the result of laziness or decadence.

**3**     The crucial difference between the gold standard and the dollar standard was that under the latter there was no longer 100 per cent backing for the domestic currency.

**4**     The adjustable peg system effectively eliminated speculation by creating a state of certainty regarding future exchange rates.

**5**     The floating-exchange rate regime is flexible but not sufficiently so to cope with substantial differences in inflation rates between countries.

**6**     In practice, exchange rates have rarely been allowed to float absolutely freely during the period since 1973.

**7**     The volatility of the exchange rate under a floating system leads to great uncertainty and is likely to reduce the level of international trade and the amount of investment undertaken by firms competing in world markets.

**8**     Protectionism is more likely to occur under a fixed-exchange rate system.

**9**     Policy harmonization is important for economies with linked exchange rate mechanisms.

**10**     The EMS committed the central banks of member countries to intervene in foreign exchange markets whenever any of the currencies threatened to deviate from its par value against other member countries by more than an agreed amount.

**11** Countries that have pursued more stringent exchange rate regimes have typically had lower and more stable inflation rates than the rest of the world.

## Economics in action

### Convergence 'the enemy of growth'

(Adapted from an article by Derek Scott in *The Observer*, 21 March 2004)

Few people are against economic stability. But stability of what? Britain has had nearly 50 consecutive quarters of growth, averaging more than 2.5 per cent a year, with inflation hovering around 2.5 per cent. If that's not stability, it is difficult to know what is.

The Bank of England sets interest rates to meet the needs of the economy; it can do that only because the pound is free to float. Not perfect, not always comfortable for everyone but, overall, it works. EMU provides currency stability with other members, but at the cost of greater instability in the things that matter: output and jobs.

Interest rates can be too low as well as too high. If Britain had joined EMU at the start, interest rates would have been half the level judged appropriate by the Bank. Britain would have experienced another boom on the way to bust. Alternatively, fiscal policy would have tightened – taxes up or expenditure cut. Leaving aside the need to improve transport, schools and hospitals, this would have resulted in lost output and jobs. And that would be true if Britain joined today.

## Questions

**1** Do you think there is a simple trade-off between output stability and exchange rate stability?

**2** Explain why UK adoption of the Euro would lead to tighter fiscal policy.

## Questions for thought

**1** Discuss the proposition that governments will not behave responsibly unless forced to.

**2** Below are listed four criteria by which an exchange rate regime may be evaluated. Outline the merits and demerits of fixed and floating systems under each criterion.

**(a)** Robustness.

**(b)** Financial discipline.

**(c)** Volatility.

**(d)** Freedom from restrictions on trade and payment.

To what extent does the UK's post-war experience support the case for fixed or floating exchange rates?

# chapter thirty-five

# European integration

## Learning outcomes

By the end of this chapter, you should understand:

- The EU single market
- Why many EU countries formed a monetary union
- Macroeconomics in the Eurozone
- UK reluctance to join the EMS
- The progress of transition in Central and Eastern Europe (CEE)

## Key learning blocks

The European Union (EU) and European Monetary Union (EMU) are two of the most important issues facing the UK and you are now in a position to tackle the issues which arise from these topics. The areas which you need to understand are:

1. Why have an EU?
2. Why have monetary union?
3. How might the EU develop in the future?

The textbook covers these topics and the questions that follow will help to develop your understanding.

# Important concepts and technical terms

## Match each lettered concept with the appropriate numbered phrase:

**a** A monetary union

**b** EMU

**c** Common Agricultural Policy (CAP)

**d** SOE

**e** CEE

**f** Optimal currency area

**g** Maastricht Treaty

**h** Non-tariff barriers

**i** Exchange Rate Mechanism (ERM)

**j** Federal fiscal system

**k** European Central Bank (ECB)

**l** Cross-border takeovers

**1** Differences in national regulations or practices preventing free movement of goods, services and factors across countries.

**2** The largest programme administered by the EU, involving a system of administered high prices for agricultural commodities.

**3** A system by which each member country fixed a nominal exchange rate against each other participant, while jointly floating against the rest of the world.

**4** A system in which a group of states agrees to have permanently fixed exchange rates within the union, an integrated financial system and a single monetary authority responsible for setting the union's money supply.

**5** Central and Eastern Europe.

**6** The joining together of members of the EU in a monetary union.

**7** The authority with full responsibility for EU monetary policy.

**8** A system under which fiscal transfers between states help to cushion individual states from the effects of temporary local recession.

**9** A group of countries better off with a common currency than keeping separate national currencies.

**10** The treaty that set out the agreed route towards monetary union within Europe.

**11** A situation in which domestic firms buy into or sell out to firms based in other countries.

**12** A common feature of the former centrally planned economies (CPEs), in which enterprises were owned by the state.

## Exercises

**1** The creation of a Single European Market (SEM) by 1992 entailed a number of changes for EU members. For each of the following, state whether or not they were part of the 1992 reforms:

(a) The abolition of all remaining foreign exchange controls between EU members.

(b) The removal of frontier controls (delays), subject to retention of necessary safeguards for security, social and health reasons.

(c) The harmonization of all tax rates in EU member countries.

(d) The removal of all non-tariff barriers (NTBs) to trade within the EU.

(e) The creation of an economic area without frontiers in which the free movement of goods, persons, services and capital is ensured.

(f) Mutual recognition of regulations such that, for instance, a doctor who qualified in England could practise medicine in any other EU country.

**(g)** The adoption of a common currency within the EU.

**2** Which of the following constitute NTBs to trade?

**(a)** Differences in patent laws between countries.

**(b)** Safety standards which act to segment national markets.

**(c)** Voluntary export restraints (VERs) – bilateral agreements whereby an exporting country agrees to limit exports to a quota.

**(d)** Taxes imposed on imported goods.

**(e)** Sanitary requirements for imported meats and dairy products which are more stringent than for domestic goods.

**(f)** Quota limits imposed on the import of particular commodities.

**(g)** Packaging and labelling requirements.

**3** The entry of sterling into the Exchange Rate Mechanism (ERM) of the European Monetary System (EMS) was delayed until 1990. A number of reasons were put forward for this delay, some of which are listed below. In each case, consider the strength of the case made against entry.

**(a)** Sterling was a petrocurrency because of North Sea oil and is thus subject to volatility because of possible fluctuations in the price of oil.

**(b)** With London and Frankfurt being the only decontrolled financial centres in Europe, it would be inconvenient for the UK to join the ERM, because this would require the coordination of monetary policy.

**(c)** A significant proportion of UK trade is conducted with countries outside the EU.

**(d)** UK inflation was being controlled independently by the policies of the government in power, so the additional stability of the ERM was unnecessary.

**(e)** Independence of domestic monetary policy is important for the UK.

**(f)** The EMS was a result of muddled thinking, so it was better to bide one's time until things settled down.

You might like to discuss with your fellow students the extent to which these arguments continue to apply in the context of joining the single currency.

**4** Which of the following is/are characteristic of a monetary union?

**(a)** Fixed exchange rates within the union.

**(b)** A single currency.

**(c)** Freedom of capital movement.

**(d)** A single monetary authority for setting the union's money supply.

**(e)** A common interest rate policy.

**(f)** A federal government.

**(g)** A federal fiscal system.

**5** Consider a country that is part of a monetary union that has no federal system of fiscal transfers. Suppose that for some reason – perhaps trade union pressure – firms in the economy face an increase in costs which is passed on by producers in the form of higher prices. This exercise traces the path taken by the economy as it adjusts towards equilibrium.

**(a)** If the cost increase is restricted to firms in the domestic economy, what is the effect on competitiveness?

**(b)** Given that the exchange rate cannot adjust because of the rules of the monetary union, what is the effect on exports?

**(c)** What will be the consequences for output and employment?

**(d)** By what process will the economy now return to equilibrium?

**(e)** The Delors Report 1980 favoured the placing of ceilings on government budget deficits so that the return to equilibrium could not be encouraged by domestic fiscal policy. Would such expansionary fiscal action be effective, and why should it be outlawed?

**(f)** Explain how a system of federal fiscal transfers would alter the sequence of events.

**6** Identify each of the following as a cost or a benefit of '1992' or EMU:

**(a)** Greater efficiency in resource allocation.

**(b)** The removal of frontier controls.

**(c)** Loss of protection of domestic activity.

**(d)** Loss of sovereignty over interest rates.

**(e)** Intensified competition.

**(f)** Enhancement of labour mobility.

**(g)** A reduction of trade between Britain and the Commonwealth.

**(h)** Exchange rate certainty.

**(i)** Fuller exploitation of economies of scale.

**(j)** Establishment of a credible pre-commitment to controlling inflation.

**(k)** Inflexibility in adjusting to a loss of competitiveness.

**(l)** A reduction in transaction costs.

**(m)** A politically acceptable way for moving towards European integration.

**7** Figure 35–1 shows the situation facing a small country in Euroland. With the interest rate being set by the ECB, the country faces a fixed interest rate, $r_0$, so the LM curve is effectively horizontal. $Y_0$ represents potential output, but the country is in recession with the IS curve stuck at $IS_A$.

**Figure 35–1** A small country in Euroland

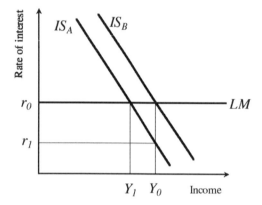

**(a)** How far would the interest rate need to fall for the economy to reach potential output?
**(b)** Is this a feasible solution?
**(c)** What steps could the government of the country take in order to reach $Y_0$?
**(d)** In the absence of intervention from the domestic government or the ECB, will the economy ever get to $Y_0$? If so, by what mechanism?

**8** For the UK, '1992' brought problems which had not been wholly anticipated. Instead of the smooth integration into the single market and progress towards even closer integration through monetary union, the UK was forced to suspend its membership of the ERM, bringing the temptation to retreat back to being a solitary island. Which of the following do you see as the best way forward, and why? Which is the most likely course?

**(a)** Give up the whole idea of joining the single currency, and go back to flexible exchange rates, thus retaining national sovereignty.
**(b)** Speed up the process of transition to EMU, and thus minimize vulnerability to speculative pressure.
**(c)** Return to the idea of sedate progression towards EMU, but introduce policies such as the 'Tobin tax' which would reduce the power and influence of the short-term speculators, and thus avoid the problems which led to the UK's exit from the ERM.

**9** Which of the following will promote an optimal currency zone in the EU?

**(a)** Increased trade among EU members.
**(b)** Increased trade by EU members with China.
**(c)** Increased rigidities in wage settlements across the EU.
**(d)** The rapid growth of e-commerce.

## True/False

**1** The swing in thinking against 'big government' and extensive regulation of the economy accelerated the moves towards European integration.

**2** A bank registered in Germany was, after 1992, permitted to operate in France or the UK.

**3** The '1992' reforms created a European Economic Area (EEA) almost as large as the USA or Japan.

**4** '1992' outlawed tariffs on trade between EU members.

**5** Cross-border takeovers and mergers of European firms will effectively preserve market power and prevent the gains from intensified competition that were intended to follow the 1992 reforms.

**6** English and Scottish banknotes both circulate in Scotland, proving that a monetary union need not have a single currency.

**7** The Maastricht Treaty was an agreement by all EU member nations to achieve monetary union by 1997.

**8** Countries gain most by keeping their monetary sovereignty when they are not integrated with potential partners, have a different structure and hence are likely to face different shocks, and cannot rely on domestic wage and price flexibility as a substitute for exchange rate controls.

**9** The EU Structural Funds provide a system of federal fiscal transfers which can help countries suffering from a temporary loss of competitiveness.

**10** The Bank of England's Monetary Policy Committee is more transparent in its operations than the ECB.

**11**  The high standards of education and health provision in the countries of Eastern Europe put them in a better position to be able to attain large productivity gains than many of today's less developed countries.

**12**  The substantial debts incurred by Eastern European countries to Western creditors are a substantial obstacle to further development.

## Economics in action

### Ever-expanding Union?

(Adapted from an article in *The Economist*, 29 April 2004)

Rather like the universe, it is possible to imagine an EU that goes on expanding, reaches a certain size and eventually implodes. So far, the EU continues in its expansionary phase. Already, there are worries that the current enlargement will prove a step too far. Getting agreement between 25 squabbling countries may prove near-impossible.

There are several small, prosperous, Western European states that the EU would welcome with open arms: Norway and Switzerland plus Iceland and micro-states such as Jersey, Liechtenstein and Monaco. These all have relationships with the EU offering them most of the benefits of membership while sparing them some of its obligations, so they are under no great pressure to join.

The countries that do want to join are mostly poor. What most attracts them are the big EU subsidies that helped lift earlier joiners, such as Spain and Ireland, from rags to riches.

### Questions

**1**  Using your understanding of game theory, assess whether 'Getting agreement between 25 squabbling countries may prove near-impossible'.

**2**  If the new members of the EU have joined for a 'hand out', why have the old members let them join?

## Questions for thought

**1**  Can the UK survive without adopting the Euro?

**2**  'The pressure for reform in Eastern Europe came more from discontent with past performance than from belief in the superiority of capitalist economies.' Do you think this overstates the situation?

**3**  Discuss the extent to which Euroland meets the conditions of an optimal currency area.

# chapter thirty-six

# Less developed countries

## Learning outcomes

**By the end of this chapter, you should understand:**

- Why poor countries are poor
- The role of exports of primary products
- The role of industrialization and the export of manufactures
- Whether foreign borrowing promotes development
- Other avenues for poverty reduction
- The importance of aid from rich countries

## Key learning blocks

In this chapter you will examine the economic situation of *less developed economies*. The issues which you need to understand are:

**1** Why might an economy be underdeveloped?

**2** How can a less developed economy be helped to grow?

**3** The different approaches to achieving economic development.

The textbook covers these issues in detail and the exercises that follow will help you to broaden your understanding.

# Important concepts and technical terms

## Match each lettered concept with the appropriate numbered phrase:

**a** Import substitution

**b** Less developed countries (LDCs)

**c** Primary commodities

**d** Buffer stock

**e** New protectionism

**f** Export-led growth

**g** Price volatility

**h** Newly industrialized countries (NICs)

**i** Aid

**j** Debt rescheduling

**k** International debt crisis

**l** Structural adjustment

**1** An organization aiming to stabilize a commodity market, buying when the price is low and selling when the price is high.

**2** Agricultural commodities, minerals and fuels: goods that may be inputs into a production process but are not outputs from such a process.

**3** Attempts by some industrial countries to protect domestic industries from competition from LDCs.

**4** Assistance from the rich North to the poor South in the form of subsidized loans, gifts of food, machinery or technical help, and the free provision of expert advisers.

**5** A situation in which LDCs have difficulty in meeting their debt repayments and interest payments, such that interest rates rise, aggravating the situation still further.

**6** The pursuit of supply-side policies aimed at increasing potential output by increasing efficiency.

**7** Production and income growth through exports rather than the displacement of imports.

**8** A group of countries that has successfully developed local industries and is growing rapidly and exporting manufactures.

**9** The low-income nations of the world, ranging from the very poor, such as Ethiopia and India, to the nearly rich, such as Argentina and Mexico.

**10** A policy of replacing imports by domestic production under the protection of high tariffs or import quotas.

**11** A situation in which prices are subject to extreme movements from year to year.

**12** A procedure whereby countries with difficulties in meeting their debts are either lent new money to meet existing loans or allowed to pay back the original loan over a longer time scale than originally negotiated.

## Exercises

**1**    Table 36–1 (overleaf) lists some data relating to various welfare measures for eight countries throughout the world. Why would we use these data as measures of economic welfare?

**2**    Demand for a primary product is stable, but the supply is subject to large fluctuations from year to year. The producers of the product decide to operate a buffer stock to stabilize revenue. Table 36–2 (overleaf) shows how demand varies with price.

Suppose the buffer stock is operated in such a way that price is stabilized at $70 per unit.

**Table 36–1** Welfare indicators, 2001

| Country | Average annual percentage growth rate of population | Percentage of GDP from agriculture | Life expectancy at birth (years) | Infant mortality rate (aged under 1) per 1000 live births | Population with access to safe water (%) | Adult literacy rate (%) |
|---|---|---|---|---|---|---|
| USA | 1.1 | 1.6 | 77.5 | 7.0 | 100.0 | 94.8 |
| UK | 0.1 | 1.0 | 77.4 | 6.0 | 100.0 | 95.4 |
| Argentina | 1.2 | 4.8 | 74.1 | 16.0 | 95.0 | 3.1 |
| Mexico | 1.5 | 4.4 | 73.4 | 24.0 | 88.0 | 8.6 |
| Thailand | 0.7 | 10.2 | 69.0 | 24.0 | 84.0 | 4.3 |
| Philippines | 2.1 | 15.2 | 69.5 | 29.0 | 86.0 | 4.9 |
| Nepal | 2.3 | 39.1 | 59.4 | 66.0 | 88.0 | 57.1 |
| Burundi | 1.9 | 50.0 | 41.8 | 114.0 | 78.0 | 50.8 |

*Source: World Development Report 2003.*

**Table 36–2** Demand for a primary product

| Price per unit ($) | Quantity demanded (000 units) |
|---|---|
| 100 | 300 |
| 90 | 325 |
| 80 | 350 |
| 70 | 375 |
| 60 | 400 |
| 50 | 425 |
| 40 | 450 |
| 30 | 475 |
| 20 | 500 |

**Figure 36–1** Commodity price stabilization

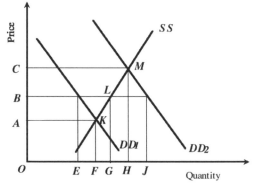

(a) In the first year of the buffer stock, supply turns out to be 450 (000) units. What would the equilibrium price have been without the buffer stock? How must the buffer stock act to stabilize price at $70?

(b) Supply is 350 in the second year. Identify what equilibrium price would have been, the quantity bought or sold by the buffer stock and the cumulative quantity of the commodity held by the buffer stock.

(c) In the following five years, supply turns out, successively, to be 375, 425, 400, 325 and 475. Trace the cumulative quantity held by the buffer stock.

(d) What price would on average have kept the buffer stock stable?

**3** Consider the market for a primary commodity in which supply is stable, but the position of the demand schedule varies with the business cycle

experienced by the industrial nations. The position is illustrated in Fig. 36–1.

*SS* represents the supply curve. When the industrial nations are in the trough of the cycle, demand is at $DD_1$; at the peak, demand for the commodity is $DD_2$.

(a) Identify equilibrium price and revenue at the trough of the cycle.

(b) Identify equilibrium price and revenue at the peak of the cycle.

Suppose now that a buffer stock is established with the aim of stabilizing price at *OB*.

(c) Identify quantity supplied and total revenue if demand were such as to make *OB* the equilibrium price.

(d) Describe the actions of the buffer stock and revenue accruing to producers in the trough of the cycle.

(e) Describe the actions of the buffer stock and revenue accruing to producers in the peak of the cycle.

**4** Consider two economies, representative of low-income and high-income nations. In the period 1965–85, the low-income country experiences an annual growth rate of 2.9 per cent p.a. compared with 1.6 per cent p.a. for the higher-income economy. Suppose the low-income country begins with GNP per capita of $380, compared with $8460 for the high-income economy. Calculate the absolute difference between GNP per capita in the two countries and investigate whether the differential widens or narrows over a five-year period given the above growth rates.

**5** Table 36–3 presents data on growth rates and the share of manufactures in exports for a selection of countries. Identify the newly industrialized countries (NICs).

**6** Which of the following would be regarded as typical features of the LDCs?

(a) Low productivity in agriculture.
(b) High dependence on primary commodities.
(c) Meagre provision of infrastructure.
(d) Low population growth.
(e) Low propensity to import.
(f) Rapidly expanding labour force.

Which of these features might be seen as the most damaging to prospects for economic development?

**7** This exercise explores issues of static and dynamic comparative advantage in the context of LDCs.

(a) Many LDCs have a relative scarcity of physical and human capital, as compared with natural resources or unskilled labour. Where is their comparative advantage likely to rest?
(b) Does the historical pattern of primary product prices have implications for the product specialization suggested by your answer to (a)?
(c) Might an import substitution policy serve to alter a country's comparative advantage? What are the disadvantages of this approach?
(d) Discuss whether export promotion is likely to be a superior strategy.

**8** The transfer of aid between countries involves both (rich) donors and (poor) recipients. In this exercise, we explore some of the motivations on each side. If you find the questions at all obscure, please tackle them in conjunction with the commentary provided in the main text.

(a) It might be argued that donors provide aid for humanitarian motives. Does your experience of the governments of industrial nations suggest this to be a sufficient explanation for aid flows?
(b) What political motivations might donors have for granting aid?
(c) Many aid transactions involve the movement of commodities between countries, either directly or as an indirect result of aid. How might donor countries advance their own economic self-interest through the granting of aid?
(d) From the recipients' perspective, why might there be political reasons for accepting aid?

| Table 36–3 Industry, growth and trade | | | |
|---|---|---|---|
| Country | Annual real per capita GNP growth 1975–95 | Share of manufacturers in exports (%) | |
| | | 1960 | 2003 |
| A | 1.5 | 3 | 53 |
| B | −1.8 | 1 | 17 |
| C | 3.2 | 0 | 73 |
| D | 5.8 | 26 | 84 |
| E | 0.7 | 29 | 37 |
| F | 5.7 | 80 | 93 |
| G | 0.3 | 5 | 26 |
| H | 7.0 | 14 | 87 |
| I | 3.8 | 4 | 14 |

*Sources: World Development Report 2003; Human Development Report 2003.*

**Table 36–4**    Debt indicators for developing countries, 1980–83

| Indicators | 1980 | 1981 | 1982 | 1983 |
|---|---|---|---|---|
| Ratio of debt to GDP | 19.2 | 21.9 | 24.9 | 26.7 |
| Ratio of debt to exports | 76.1 | 90.8 | 90.8 | 121.4 |
| Debt service ratio | 13.6 | 16.6 | 16.6 | 20.7 |
| Ratio of interest service to GNP | 1.5 | 1.9 | 1.9 | 2.2 |
| Total debt outstanding and disbursed ($ billion) | 424.8 | 482.6 | 538.0 | 595.8 |
| *of which* Official | 157.5 | 172.3 | 190.9 | 208.5 |
| Private | 267.3 | 310.3 | 347.1 | 387.3 |

Note: calculations are based on a sample of 90 developing countries.

Source: World Development Report 1984.

(e)  The economic motivation for accepting aid seems obvious . . . but might there be disadvantages for an independent country?

(f)  Why should free trade be superior to aid for encouraging development?

**9**    Consider Table 36–4, and then relate the figures to the statements that follow. Which of the statements are supported by the figures in Table 36–4?

(a)  The size of debt relative to GNP was increasing steadily during the period.

(b)  An increasing share of exports was being taken up by the servicing of existing debt.

(c)  Borrowing from commercial banks and other private sources grew in importance relative to borrowing from official sources.

(d)  During the period, the amount of debt grew such that, even if an entire year's exports were devoted to paying off the debt, it still would not suffice.

Since the early 1980s, the debt situation does not seem to have improved dramatically. Table 36–5 offers more recent data for a number of countries in Sub-Saharan Africa.

**10**    Examine Table 36–6. Which of these two countries would you expect to have the higher GNP per capita?

**Table 36–5**    Debt indicators for some Sub-Saharan African countries

| Country | Debt service ratio (debt service as percentage of exports of goods and services) | | | Total external debt | |
|---|---|---|---|---|---|
| | | | | As percentage of GNP | US$ bn |
| | 1980 | 1997 | 2002 | 1997 | 1997 |
| Ethiopia | 7 | 12 | 20.6 | 159 | 10.1 |
| Mozambique | – | 19 | 2.7 | 233 | 6.0 |
| Uganda | 17 | 22 | 10.8 | 57 | 3.7 |
| Côte d'Ivoire | 39 | 27 | 8.1 | 165 | 15.6 |
| Tanzania | 26 | 13 | 7.3 | 97 | 7.2 |
| Ghana | 13 | 30 | 8.9 | 89 | 6.0 |
| Kenya | 21 | 22 | 11.4 | 65 | 6.5 |

Source: Human Development Report 1999, 2004.

| Table 36–6 | Social indicators for two countries | |
|---|---|---|
| Indicator | Country X | Country Y |
| Life expectancy at birth (years) (1993) | 72 | 56.3 |
| Adult literacy (%) (1993) | 89.6 | 60.8 |
| Combined school enrolment ratio (%) (1993) | 66 | 48 |
| Infant mortality per 1000 live births (1993) | 17 | 62 |
| Population per doctor (1988–91) | 7143 | 12500 |
| Daily calorie supply per capita (1992) | 2275 | 1981 |
| Pupil:teacher ratio (primary) (1992) | 29 | 20 |

Source: Human Development Report 2004.

## True/False

**1** In 1997, 35 per cent of the world's people lived in low-income countries, with an average income for the year of about £220 per person.

**2** A major problem of the LDCs is the lack of both physical and financial capital.

**3** The tribal customs prevalent in some LDCs inhibit the development of enterprise and initiative.

**4** The law of comparative advantage proves that the best route to prosperity is for the LDCs to export primary commodities to the rest of the world.

**5** The reduction of price volatility by the use of a buffer stock is most necessary and most successful when demand and supply are relatively elastic.

**6** Import substitution is doomed to failure because it involves the concentration of resources into industries in which an economy has a comparative disadvantage.

**7** On average, the NICs grew twice as rapidly as the rich industrialized nations during the 1970s.

**8** Debt rescheduling has avoided default by a number of LDCs on external loan repayments; such defaults would have had major repercussions for financial institutions in the leading developed countries.

**9** Structural adjustment programmes (SAPs) are measures designed by rich countries to keep poor countries in their place.

**10** The quickest way to equalize world income distribution would probably be to permit free migration between countries.

**11** More aid is what is needed to solve the problems of the LDCs.

## Economics in action

### Doing the sums on Africa

(Adapted from an article in *The Economist*, 20 May 2004)

Small amounts spent on promoting Africa's economy can save billions. In every aspect of Africa's complex plight an ounce of prevention will be worth a ton of treatment. In recent years America gave a negligible $4 million a year to Ethiopia to boost agricultural productivity, but then responded with around $500 million in emergency food aid in 2003 when the crops failed. In the 1990s America gave less than $50 million a year for Africa to prevent AIDS, so now will spend $3 bn per year to treat the disease after it has spread to more than 50 million Africans.

Strip out sums for emergencies such as food aid and anti-retroviral medicines, military assistance, debt service, as well as sums paid to American consultants rather than to African countries, and total American development assistance for Africa will be less than $1 bn this year for more than 700 million Africans.

## Questions

**1** Why does such a needy place as Africa receive such little help from the developed world?

**2** How might globalization alleviate global poverty?

## Questions for thought

**1** Is it feasible for LDCs to achieve economic development without external assistance? What implications would arise if some LDCs defaulted on their international debt?

**2** In the late 1990s, an initiative was launched by which highly-indebted poor countries (HIPCs) could qualify for debt forgiveness if they could demonstrate their commitment to a programme of structural adjustment over a period of years. Discuss the economic reasoning underlying this idea.

**3** The performance of many LDCs (especially in Africa) in terms of economic growth has been disappointing since the 1970s, with a number of countries having lower real GNP per capita in the 1990s than they did in the mid-1960s. To what extent does this reflect market failure and to what extent does it result from policies adopted and events occurring in the industrial economies?

**4** Suppose that you are asked to make an assessment of the economic performance of a number of countries. Explain why such a task would be an exercise in normative economics.

# Answers and comments

# Chapter One Answers
## Economics and the economy

### Important concepts and technical terms

**1** f  **4** d  **7** i  **10** b

**2** k  **5** h  **8** c  **11** l

**3** j  **6** a  **9** g  **12** e

### Exercises

**1**  (a)  The straight line $PPF_a$ in Fig. Al–1 represents the production possibility frontier (PPF) for this society.

(b)  $PPF_b$ is the new PPF. The change in technology enables more coconuts to be 'produced' than before, without any reduction in output of turtle eggs.

**Figure A1–1**  The effect of technical change

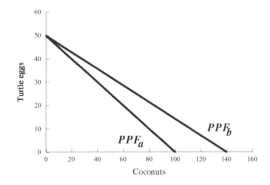

**2**  (a)  Combinations (i) and (iv) lie on the PPF and thus represent points of *efficient* production. Combinations (ii) and (v) lie outside the frontier and are thus *unattainable* with the resources available. Combination (iii) lies within the frontier and is a point of inefficient production. Not all the available resources are being fully or effectively used.

(b)  100 watches must be given up for the 20 cameras when the society begins at (300, 40).

(c)  200 watches must be given up for the 20 cameras when the society begins at (200, 60).

(d)  The difference in shape results from the *law of diminishing returns*. On the tropical island, the amounts produced by a worker did not vary according to whether other workers were engaged in the same activity. In the cameras and

watches case, this is not so: as more workers are used to produce cameras, the greater the number of watch cases has to be given up. This is explained in Section 1–2 of the main text.

**3**  (a) C.  (b) D.  (c) A.  (d) B.

**4**  (a), (d), (g) and (h) are positive statements, containing objective descriptions of economies and the way they work; (b), (e) and (i) are normative statements which rely upon value judgements for their validity. Statement (c) contains elements of both: it includes a (positive) statement of fact about the distribution of world population and income but also rests on a (normative) value judgement that this was 'too unjust'.

**5**  (a), (d), (g) and (h) deal with economy-wide issues and are thus the concern of macroeconomics; (b), (c), (e) and (f) are devoted to more detailed microeconomic issues.

**6**  (a) C.  (b) A.  (c) B.

**7**  (d).

**8**  Only (a) would be untrue for a command economy. Remember, though, that no pure command economy actually exists. Countries of the former Soviet bloc began to make the transition to being market economies in 1989–91, but even in their heyday they could not have been described as 'pure' command economies.

### True/False

**1**  False: the claim of economics to be a science rests not on its subject matter, but upon its methods of analysis.

**2**  1974 true, 2004 less so. In 1974 the UK economy was more reliant on oil than in 2004.

**3**  True.

**4**  True.

**5**  True.

**6**  False: while being closer to a command economy than many others, China increasingly tolerates and encourages the existence of some private markets as it moves towards a more market-based system.

**7**    Sorry: this was a trick question! This is another example of a normative statement which rests on a subjective value judgement. As a result, it can never be proven to be either true or false.

**8**    False: don't forget services! The production of services may be more difficult to measure than that of goods, but is important none the less.

**9**    True: many disagreements between economists reflect differences in beliefs and values (normative statements), rather than differences of opinion about objective analysis.

## Economics in action

**1**    Microeconomics is the study of individual economic units, such as the behaviour of consumers and firms. Macroeconomics is the study of economic activity at the level of the entire economy. Therefore, the level of mortgage borrowings is a microeconomic issue. As the interest rate changes, then the price of a mortgage changes and individuals are willing to borrow more as the loan becomes cheaper and less as it becomes more expensive. However, since mortgage borrowings are rising across the entire economy, this is also a macroeconomic issue. Especially as individuals may be increasing their borrowings in order to fund consumption. Moreover, if the Bank of England raises interest rates to stem the rise in mortgage activity, then this may have implications not only for borrowers, but also for firms and the government.

**2**    In terms of microeconomics, a rise in interest rates will increase the price of loans and may lead to a

reduction in the number of new mortgages. It will also increase the cost of existing borrowings, meaning that individuals have to transfer income from current consumption and saving to higher debt repayments. In terms of macroeconomics, the reduction in consumption among mortgage holders may lead to fewer purchases in shops, a falling consumption of new cars, holidays, etc. This will harm company profits and employment levels across the economy.

## Questions for thought

**1**    *Hint*: It is rare that an economic issue involves only one of the three basic questions.

**2**    *Hint*: So far, we have considered only an economy in a single time period. Here, the production of one of the goods directly affects what can be produced in the future.

**3**    Country **A** (which is Uganda) remains very heavily dependent upon agriculture; the share of industrial activity here rose very little between 1965 and 1997. In contrast, Country **B** (Indonesia) has seen a marked expansion of industry, but agriculture remains important, with a 16 per cent share in GDP. The trend towards industrialization and away from agriculture has been much more rapid in Country **C**; this is South Korea, one of the so-called newly industrialized countries (NICs) of East Asia. Country **D** (Japan) displays the more stable characteristics of an industrial economy, but with an expanding service sector. Box 1–1 in the main text discusses some of these issues. Problems of less developed countries (LDCs) are discussed again in Chapter 36.

# Chapter Two Answers

## Tools of economic analysis

### Important concepts and technical terms

| | | | |
|---|---|---|---|
| **1** g | **5** c | **9** k | **13** n |
| **2** m | **6** i | **10** e | **14** l |
| **3** f | **7** d | **11** b | |
| **4** j | **8** a | **12** h | |

### Exercises

**1**    *(a)*, *(c)* and *(d)* comprise information for the same variables at different points in time: they are thus time series. *(b)* and *(f)* are straightforward *cross-section* data series, observing different individuals or groups of individuals at an instant in time. *(e)* is a different sort of data set: it is a cross-section repeated at different points in time. It thus combines features of both cross-section and time series. Often known

**Table A2–1** Steel imports and consumption, 1976–2004

| Year | UK steel imports, million tonnes | UK steel consumption, million tonnes | UK steel imports (1976 = 100) | UK steel consumption (1976 = 100) | UK steel imports as a percentage of total steel consumption |
|------|------|------|------|------|------|
| 1976 | 103.6 | 498.7 | 100 | 100 | 21 |
| 1982 | 96.2 | 271.4 | 93 | 54 | 35 |
| 1988 | 114.4 | 364.8 | 110 | 73 | 31 |
| 1994 | 126.7 | 336.1 | 122 | 67 | 38 |
| 2000 | 162.6 | 298.0 | 157 | 60 | 55 |
| 2004 | 168.0 | 272.8 | 162 | 55 | 62 |

as *panel data*, such series are rare because of the expense of collecting the information and the difficulty in recontacting the same individuals in different periods.

**2** **(a)** Over the period 1976–2004, UK steel consumption fell, while the UK's imports of steel grew.

**(b)** See Table A2–1.

**(c)** UK steel imports between 1976 and 2004 grew by 62 per cent, while UK consumption of steel fell by 45 per cent. Overall, imports as a percentage of total consumption grew from 21 per cent to 62 per cent. These patterns can be explained by the reduction in UK manufacturing. The UK steel industry declined, and so did the manufacturing of cars and ships, which require steel. The UK is now a more service-based economy, which obviously requires less steel.

**3** **(a)** and **(b)** See Table A2–2.

**(c)** Inflation for the non-smoking teetotaller is calculated directly from the price index for 'other goods and services'. Our non-smoking teetotaller experiences similar (but slightly lower) inflation rates to the representative person, but the difference is relatively minor. This suggests that the rate of change of prices of alcohol and tobacco did differ greatly from other prices in this period, perhaps reflecting government taxation policy.

**(d)** The charts, shown in Figs A2–1 and A2–2, reinforce this analysis, with a higher inflation rate for alcohol and tobacco, especially throughout 1999–2002.

**Figure A2–1** Price indices, 1998–2003

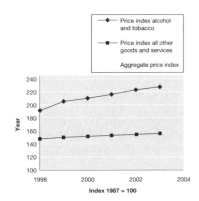

**Table A2–2** Price indices, 1998–2003 (1987 = 100)

| Year | 1998 | 1999 | 2000 | 2001 | 2002 | 2003 |
|------|------|------|------|------|------|------|
| Price index, alcohol and tobacco | 192.3 | 202.6 | 210.3 | 216.9 | 222.3 | 228.0 |
| Price index, all other goods and services | 147.6 | 148.1 | 149.7 | 160.0 | 151.7 | 154.4 |
| Aggregate price index | 152.6 | 154.1 | 156.3 | 158.2 | 159.5 | 162.5 |
| Inflation | | 1.0 | 1.5 | 1.2 | 0.8 | 1.9 |
| Inflation for non-smoking teetotaller | | 0.3 | 1.1 | 0.9 | 0.5 | 1.8 |

**Figure A2–2** Inflation, 1999–2003

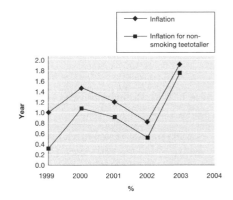

**4** **(a)** See Fig. A2–3.

**Figure A2–3** Imports and income

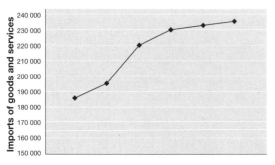

**(b)–(d)** There seems to be a positive association between real imports and household income. We might perhaps expect households to buy more imported goods at higher levels of real income, but this is not likely to be the only variable affecting imports. For instance, changes in the relative price of UK and foreign goods or changes in demand by UK firms for imported raw materials also influence the overall level of real imports. Indeed, we would expect that as real incomes increase, firms will need to import increased amounts of materials and machinery. You may have thought of other factors. When we focus upon this simple association, these elements are all covered by our assumption that 'other things are equal' and may explain why the scatter of points in Fig. A2–3 does not form a precise relationship.

**5** *(a)* ii. *(b)* iii. *(c)* iv. *(d)* i.

If we are considering just these simple relationships, the fitting of a straight line would not be appropriate for *(b)* or *(c)*.

**6** **(a)** An aggregate price index is required as a basis for comparison: we need the price of clothing relative to that of other goods.

**(b)** Real price index for clothing and footwear:

| 1998 | 1999 | 2000 | 2001 | 2002 | 2003 |
|------|------|------|------|------|------|
| 78.6 | 75.7 | 71.8 | 67.9 | 64.2 | 62.0 |

Method:

The 1998 figure is the price of clothing divided by the aggregate price index, all multiplied by 100.

**(c)** Prices for clothing have increased much less than other prices, so their real price has fallen since 1998 and continues to do so.

**7** **(a)** The model states that the quantity of chocolate bars demanded depends upon their price and upon the level of consumer incomes. You will find that this question is answered in Chapter 3 of the main text, where this example is used as an illustration.

**(b)** With income held constant, we would expect to see fewer chocolate bars demanded at a higher price – that is, we expect a *negative* association between these variables.

**(c)** With the price of chocolate bars held constant, an increase in income would probably lead to an increase in the quantity demanded – that is, we expect chocolate bars to be a normal good, and therefore we look for a *positive* association.

**(d)** A complete model would also incorporate the price of other goods, and consumer preferences, as we would expect these to affect the demand for chocolate bars.

**8** We calculate $3 \times 170 + 2 \times 186 + 5 \times 173 = 1747$. Then we must divide by the sum of the weights $(2 + 3 + 5 = 10)$, giving answer *(c)* 174.7.

**9** **(a)** 64 918

**(b)** 61 777

**(c)**

| 2003 Q1 | 2003 Q2 | 2003 Q3 | 2003 Q4 |
|---------|---------|---------|---------|
| 104.8 | 105.0 | 105.2 | 105.3 |

The results of this calculation look very much like an index of some kind – and that is exactly what they *do* represent. In fact, this calculation provides us with a price index based on 2001 = 100, known as the 'implicit deflator' of consumers' expenditure, or sometimes as the 'consumer price index'. It is always the case that:

$$\frac{\text{Variable at}}{\text{current prices}} = \frac{\text{Variable at}}{\text{constant prices}} \times \frac{\text{Price index}}{100}$$

**10** When asked to 'describe a trend', it is always tempting to go into great detail about all the ups and downs of the series. However, as economists it is more important for us to be able to filter the data and identify the salient features. It sometimes helps to lay a pencil on to the diagram so that it follows the overall trend of the line. For this graph, we see that the savings ratio rose steadily until 1980. The period after 1980 is less clear, with the 1980s showing a marked decline in the savings ratio, recovering only with the dawn of the 1990s, but then falling again towards the end of the period. The macroeconomic section of the textbook will shed more light on these patterns.

## True/False

**1**  False: admittedly economists cannot easily carry out laboratory experiments. This does not prevent us from applying scientific methods to economic problems and making the best we can of available information. There are other non-experimental sciences – astronomy, parts of biology, etc.

**2**  True: see Section 2–9 in the main text.

**3**  True: but we must be careful not to manipulate our charts to distort the picture so as to prove a point.

**4**  False: the association may be spurious – perhaps both variables depend upon a third one, or both happen to be growing over time.

**5**  True: but not invariably.

**6**  False: 'other things equal' is an assumption enabling us to simplify and to focus upon particular aspects of our model. However, we cannot ignore these other factors which affect the position of our curves and contribute to our explanation.

**7**  False: we may often assume a linear function for simplicity, but there are also many economic relationships which are non-linear.

**8**  False: facts cannot speak for themselves and can be interpreted only in the light of careful and informed reasoning.

**9**  True: of course, they also have other uses.

**10**  False: 'positive' refers to the direction of association between two variables.

**11**  False: inflation measures the *rate of change* of the price level.

**12**  True.

## Economics in action

**1**  Since the house price index is monthly, the data on house prices are more than likely to be collected on a monthly basis, indicating that the data are time series. However, there could be a cross-sectional element in that the Nationwide is saying that the data are also collected by region: North, South, East, etc. Therefore, the data may be better described as a *panel* (a combination of time series and cross-sectional data).

**2**  House price growth in April 2004 was 2.1 per cent (291–284.9)/284.9 × 100 = 2.1 per cent.

**3**  In 1993, the house price index was 100, therefore between 1993 and 2004 the house price index has increased by (291–100)/100 × 100 = 191 per cent. This is nominal growth; we would need to deflate by the rate of inflation over the same period in order to arrive at the real growth rate.

## Questions for thought

**1**  This question requires careful treatment. The preferred calculation uses the ratio of the weighted sum of the prices in year $Y$ to that in the base year; that is:

$$\frac{(2 \times 12) + (5 \times 80) + (3 \times 70)}{(2 \times 10) + (5 \times 100) + (3 \times 50)} \times 100 = 94.6.$$

Notice that if we first calculate the index for each commodity and then take a weighted average – as if calculating a retail price index (RPI) – we do *not* get the same answer. In this instance, we would get 106. This serves to illustrate that the RPI calculation is not an exact one.

**2**  Quantity of school lunches demanded = $f\{?\}$.

What items would you put in brackets? An obvious one is the price of school lunches – but what else would you include? Perhaps the price of competing 'goods', individual preferences, time of year, income, whatever.

**3**  The 'classic' method of visually depicting relative shares is by means of a pie-chart (see Fig. A2–4).

**Figure A2–4**  Weights for the UK retail price index (RPI)

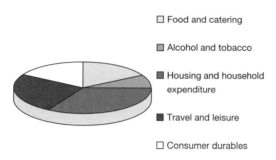

☐ Food and catering

▨ Alcohol and tobacco

▨ Housing and household
    expenditure

▧ Travel and leisure

☐ Consumer durables

**4**   One way of thinking about this issue is in terms of the demand for additional children. We might argue that a family taking a decision about whether to have another child may balance the marginal benefits they expect against the marginal costs. Remember that 'costs' in this context will include opportunity cost. So, if having an additional child means that one parent has to forgo earnings by remaining out of the labour market then this must be included in the calculation. We might argue on this basis that improved education and job opportunities for women in many less developed countries (LDCs) may increase the opportunity cost of having children, and thus lead to a slowing of the population growth rate.

# Chapter Three Answers

# Demand, supply and the market

## Important concepts and technical terms

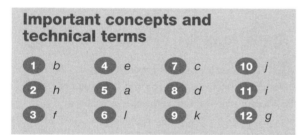

**1**  b     **4**  e     **7**  c     **10**  j

**2**  h     **5**  a     **8**  d     **11**  i

**3**  f     **6**  l     **9**  k     **12**  g

## Exercises

**1**   **(a)**  See Fig. A3–1.

**(b)**   Excess demand of 60 million tins/year.

**(c)**   Excess supply of 30 million tins/year.

**(d)**   50 million tins/year at a price of 24p.

**(e)**   60 million tins/year at a price of 28p.

**2**   See Table A3–1.

**Figure A3–1**  The market for baked beans

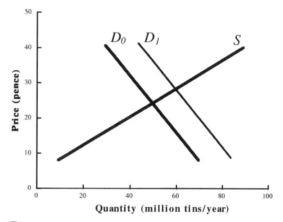

**3**   The movement could have been caused by *(b)*, *(a)* or *(d)*. Factors *(a)* and *(f)* would move the demand curve in the opposite direction; factors *(c)* and *(e)* would move the supply curve.

| Table A3–1   Movements of and along a curve | | | | |
|---|---|---|---|---|
| **Change in 'other things equal' category** | **Shift of demand curve** | **Movement along demand curve** | **Shift of supply curve** | **Movement along supply curve** |
| Change in price of competing good | ✓ | | | ✓ |
| Introduction of new technique of production | | ✓ | ✓ | |
| A craze for the good | ✓ | | | ✓ |
| A change in incomes | ✓ | | | ✓ |
| A change in the price of a material input | | ✓ | ✓ | |

**4**   The shift could have been caused by *(b)* or *(c)*; *(a)* may have been a response to a change in demand but will not initiate a shift in the demand curve. If the change in price results from a shift in supply, the result will be a movement *along* the demand curve.

**5**   The movement could have been caused by *(a)* or *(e)*. Factor *(c)* would move the supply curve in the opposite direction; factors *(b)* and *(d)* would move the demand curve.

**6**   *(a)*, *(b)* and *(d)* are likely to be 'normal' goods; *(c)* and *(e)* are likely to be 'inferior goods' – as incomes rise, we might expect the demand for these commodities to fall, as consumers find they can afford other alternatives.

**7**   The answer here depends very much upon individual preferences! Most would regard strawberries and fresh cream as being complements. Others may like raspberries and/or ice cream with their strawberries. However, in the final analysis, most goods will turn out to be substitutes – if you spend more on strawberries, you must spend less on other goods.

**8**   **(a)**  $P_2$, $Q_3$.

**(b)**  $P_1$.

**(c)**  $Q_1$.

**(d)**  $(Q_4 - Q_1)$.

**(e)**  $P_2$. A minimum price will be effective only if set above the equilibrium level.

**(f)**  $Q_3$.

**(g)**  None.

**9**   *(a)* or *(b)* could cause a rise in house prices. Factors *(a)* and *(d)* will lead to movements of the supply curve, whereas *(b)* and *(c)* affect the demand curve. Try drawing a diagram to see the effects of these movements.

**10**   **(a)**  See Fig. A3–2.

**(b)**  Price 18p, quantity 44 units. So far, so good. It's the next bit that's tricky: the key is to think through the supplier's decision process. Suppose the market price is 20p: 5p of this goes in tax to the government, and the supplier receives 15p – at which price we know he or she is pre-pared to supply 35 units per year. Using this sort of argu-ment, we can construct a new supply schedule showing how much will be supplied at each (gross of tax) price.

**(c)**  The new supply curve is given by $S^*S^*$ in Fig. A3–2; the vertical distance between $SS$ and $S^*S^*$ is 5p.

**(d)**  Price 21p, quantity 38 units. Notice that price does not rise by the full amount of the tax.

**Figure A3–2**   A tax on good *X*

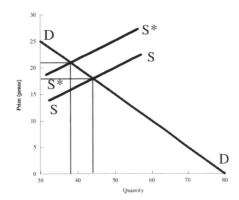

**True/False**

**1**   False: the demand curve itself shows how buyers respond to price changes.

**2**   False: some goods may be 'inferior'.

**3**   True.

**4**   False: there may be periods when markets adjust sluggishly towards equilibrium. Government intervention may prevent adjustment to equilibrium.

**5**   False: an 'inferior' good is one for which demand falls as incomes rise.

**6**   True: see Box 3–1 in the main text.

**7**   True.

**8**   False: if effective, such legislation may lead to a fall in employment (see Section 3–9 of the main text).

**9**   True: but a more precise economist's view of complementarity awaits in Chapter 6.

**10**   False: see Exercise 10.

**11**   True: see Section 3–8 of the main text.

## Economics in action

**1** With higher expected passenger numbers, the airlines' demand curve for take-off and landing slots shifts to the right, leading to an increase in the equilibrium price.

**2** The government's decision to block the building of a third runway effectively reduces future supply of take-off and landing slots. This leads to an increased equilibrium price for runway access. Some commentators suspect that the airlines were pleased with the decision to block the third runway as it raises the value of slots currently on their balance sheet.

## Questions for thought

**1** The market in this situation will be displaying a state of excess supply: producers are prepared to supply more of the commodity at the given price than consumers are prepared to demand. From the perspective of the producers, they are likely to find that their stocks of unsold goods begin to build up. In subsequent periods, producers are likely to react to this by reducing the price to induce higher sales and by reducing the amount of the commodity being produced. As producers do this and the price begins to fall, we would expect some consumers who previously curtailed their consumption because of the high price to increase their demand for the good. If the price is set below the equilibrium price, the reverse forces are likely to be seen: producers will find that their stocks of the commodity are run down, and they may find that some consumers are trying to jump the queue by offering a higher price for the good. In other words, there is excess demand and, perhaps, rationing as not all consumers can buy although they would like to. Thus price will tend to be bid up, and producers will tend to increase their supply of the good as the price rises. This is one way in which we can argue that if the market is left to its own devices, price will tend to move towards the equilibrium level: the level at which demand just matches supply. Much economic analysis relies on this sort of adjustment towards equilibrium, as we will see as we delve more deeply into economics. Further discussion in economics centres around why the adjustment may not always happen – but that is a story for later.

**2** The result depends crucially on the steepness of the demand curve: the coffee market is discussed in Chapter 5 of the main text.

**3** There are many such examples: in particular, we may consider whether a pair of goods are complements or substitutes.

**4** *Hint:* See Box 3–3 in the main text.

# Chapter Four Answers

## Elasticities of demand and supply

### Important concepts and technical terms

| | | | |
|---|---|---|---|
| **1** *i* | **5** *a* | **9** *m* | **13** *l* |
| **2** *b* | **6** *e* | **10** *j* | **14** *h* |
| **3** *d* | **7** *n* | **11** *g* | |
| **4** *k* | **8** *f* | **12** *c* | |

### Exercises

**1** **(a)** See Fig. A4–1.

**(b)** The demand curve being a straight line, the response to a 30p reduction in price will always be an increase of

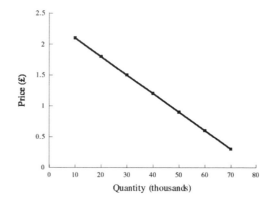

**Figure A4–1** The demand curve for rice popsicles

10 000 in the quantity demanded – at least within the range of prices shown.

**(c)–(d)** See Table A4–1.

**Table A4–1   The demand for rice popsicles**

| Price per packet (£p) | Quantity demanded (000) | Total spending (revenue) (£ 000) | Own-price elasticity of demand |
|---|---|---|---|
| 2.10 | 10 | 21 | –7.0 |
| 1.80 | 20 | 36 | –3.0 |
| 1.50 | 30 | 45 | –1.67 |
| 1.20 | 40 | 48 | –1.0 |
| 0.90 | 50 | 45 | –0.6 |
| 0.60 | 60 | 36 | –0.3 |
| 0.30 | 70 | 21 | |

Notice that we cannot calculate the elasticity for a reduction in price at a price of 30p, as we are not told what happens to demand if price falls below this level. We could, of course, calculate elasticities for price increases instead.

**(e)** See Fig. A4–2.

**Figure A4–2** Total spending on (revenue from) rice popsicles

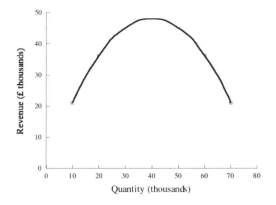

**(f)** At a price of £1.20.

**(g)** At a price of £1.20. Expenditure is always greatest at the point of unit elasticity.

**(h)** (i) At prices above £1.20.
     (ii) At prices below £1.20.

Notice in this exercise how the value of the elasticity varies at different points along the demand curve, although its slope does not change. This means that you should remember not to describe a linear demand curve as being either 'elastic' or 'inelastic': it is *both*, depending on where we measure it.

**2**  **(a)** For the own-price elasticities we need to use the top left–bottom right diagonal of Table 4–2. For instance, the response of the demand for food to a 1 per cent change in the price of food is –0.25. The demand for food is thus inelastic, as we might expect. The demand for beer is also inelastic, although the response is stronger than for food. The demand for wine is elastic (–1.20).

**(b)** Using the cross-price elasticities in the first column of Table 4.2, we see that an increase (say) in the price of food will lead to a fall in the quantity of wine demanded but an increase in the quantity of beer demanded. This implies that, in response to the change in the price of food, food and wine may well be complements, but food and beer seem more likely to be substitutes.

**(c)** An increase in the price of food causes a contraction in the demand for wine, shifting the demand curve to *DF* in Fig. A4–3 (food and wine are complements). The cross-price elasticity of demand for wine with respect to the price of beer is positive, indicating that these goods are substitutes. The demand curve moves to *DB*.

**Figure A4–3** The demand for wine in Mythuania

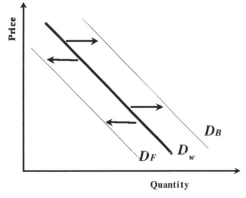

**Table A4–2   Using the income elasticity to categorize goods**

| Good | Income Year 1 £100 | Income Year 2 £200 | Budget share (year 1) | Budget share (year 2) | Income elasticity of demand | Normal (No) or or inferior (I) good | Luxury (L) or necessity (Ne) |
|---|---|---|---|---|---|---|---|
| A | £30 | £50 | 30% | 25% | 2/3 | No | Ne |
| B | £30 | £70 | 20% | 35% | 4/3 | No | L |
| C | £25 | £20 | 25% | 10% | –1/5 | I | Ne |
| D | £15 | £60 | 15% | 30% | 3 | No | L |

**3** See Table A4–2 on page 221.

**4** If the price of electricity increases, other things being equal, we would expect households to switch to alternative energy sources – perhaps installing gas central heating or using gas for cooking. However, such changes will not take place immediately, so in the short run the demand for electricity will be relatively inelastic *(DD)*. The long-run demand curve is thus represented by *dd*, the more elastic of the two.

**5** For goods *X* and *Y* see Fig. A4–4. The demand curve for good Z would remain static: with an income elasticity of demand of zero, a change in income has no effect upon demand.

**Figure A4–4** The effect of income on demand

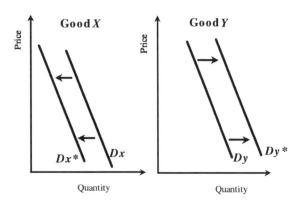

**6** The terminology 'inferior' and 'normal' goods used by economists habitually creates confusion among students. The terms are used to describe the way in which demand for a good varies with changes in *income*. Thus in tackling this question, it is the income elasticity that is important. We can see that good *(a)* is an inferior good: demand falls when income rises. Good *(d)* is a normal good, having a positive income elasticity. In the remaining cases *(b)*, *(c)* and *(e)*, we would say that an economist would not describe them either as 'inferior' or as 'normal' goods.

A positive own-price elasticity suggests a very unusual demand curve, with an increase in price leading to an increase in demand. This curiosum will be encountered in Chapter 6 of the main text.

**7** For Flora, tea and coffee are substitutes (cross-price elasticity positive), whereas sugar and coffee are complements (cross-price elasticity negative). Sugar and tea would probably display a cross-elasticity close to zero, or slightly negative.

**8** Increased by 25 per cent.

**9** Estimates of own-price elasticities for commodities close in definition to those in the table may be found in Section 4–1 of the main text.

**10** **(a)** See Fig. A4–5.

**(b)** A positive relationship.

**(c)** Bacon seems to be a 'normal' good, with consumption increasing with income. However, the rate at which consumption increases slackens off at higher incomes: this is very clear in the diagram.

**Figure A4–5** The relationship between consumption of bacon and income

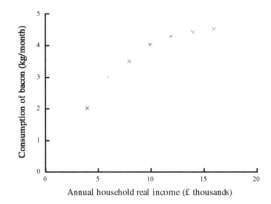

**(d)** See Fig. A4–6.

Such a curve showing the relationship between the consumption (quantity) of a good and income is sometimes known as an *Engel curve*.

**Figure A4–6** The relationship between consumption and income for an inferior good

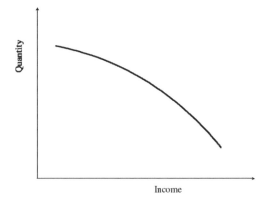

**11** So here we have an economy that is prospering: real incomes are expected to increase rapidly. The best prospects are seen for the Bechans (best chance) sector, with a strong

positive income elasticity of demand. Demand is likely to grow for the OK-ish sector, but at a slower rate than income itself grows. Zegroes will face zero growth, as the income elasticity is zero, whereas there is no hope for the Nohoes, with a strong negative income elasticity.

## True/False

**1**   True: see Section 4–1 of the main text.

**2**   False: if in doubt, see your answers to Exercise **1** of this chapter.

**3**   False.

**4**   True: see Section 4–2 of the main text and also Exercise **1** of this chapter.

**5**   False: the more narrowly defined the commodity, the more likely it is that there are readily available substitutes. Demand will thus tend to be highly sensitive to price.

**6**   False: only if the income elasticity is greater than 1 – see your answers to Exercise **3** of this chapter.

**7**   False.

**8**   False: if relative prices are unchanged, and incomes increase at the same rate as prices, the pattern of expenditure will not change.

**9**   False: see Section 4–3 of the main text.

**10**   True: again see Section 4–3 of the main text.

**11**   False: somebody somewhere must be producing 'inferior' goods.

**12**   True.

## Economics in action

**1**   The article provides only data on singles' sales and singles' pricing, it does not provide any information on total revenue. The basic idea behind elasticity-based pricing is to raise total revenue. Higher prices will lead to falling demand, but with inelastic demand higher prices will lead to higher total revenues. Before deciding whether the pricing policies have been a success or failure, we need to see the total revenue data.

**2**   Yes, demand for music singles does appear to be more elastic at higher prices. As prices have increased consumers of singles are suspected of switching to albums.

## Questions for thought

**1**   Price volatility will be discussed later on (Chapter 26).

*Hint*: Think about the main factors influencing elasticity and sketch some diagrams to assess the effect on price of a supply shift under alternative assumptions about the demand elasticity.

**2**   Factor *(d)* lies at the heart of this question. Consumers are likely to respond more strongly to a change in the price of a commodity if there are substitutes readily available. The other factors can be interpreted in the light of this. A 'necessity' can be seen as a commodity for which there are no close substitutes, so demand will be relatively inelastic. When a commodity is very narrowly defined (e.g. a particular brand of detergent), then there will tend to be more substitutes (other brands) available, so demand may be relatively elastic. For some commodities, consumers may be unable to adjust demand in the short run, whereas flexibility (elasticity) may be greater in the long run. If you have an oil-fired central heating system, there is no substitute for oil in the short run.

**3**   Volatility caused by weather conditions is of course an influence on the supply side, and is similar to the discussion of the market for peanuts that we saw in Chapter 3. However, it is also probable that demand-side factors will influence the market. For instance, changes in preferences over time, between coffee and tea, may have a big influence on demand. If demand falls to the extent that coffee producers cannot sell all their output, then they are likely to decrease acreage devoted to coffee, so that in the long run a new equilibrium will be reached. This shows you how prices can act as a signal to guide the allocation of resources so as to match the pattern of demand. In fact, the coffee market is even more complicated, as there is a so-called 'futures' market in coffee, whereby coffee can be bought and sold at an agreed price at some day in the future.

**4**   With an income elasticity of –0.4, bus travel is income inelastic and inferior. A rise in income would lead to a reduced demand for bus travel. Hence, the willingness to demand bus travel will be greater in areas where income is lower. With an own-price elasticity of −1.2 bus travel is price elastic. A reduction in fares, perhaps through a subsidy, will increase the demand for bus travel. Finally, a cross-price elasticity of +2.1 with trains suggests that bus travel is an

elastic substitute for trains. An increase in the price of train travel will lead to a proportionately larger increase in the demand for buses. So the bus company should price below trains and on routes where people on lower incomes travel.

# Chapter Five Answers

## Consumer choice and demand decisions

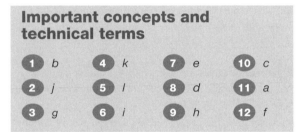

**Important concepts and technical terms**

| | | | | | | | |
|---|---|---|---|---|---|---|---|
| **1** | b | **4** | k | **7** | e | **10** | c |
| **2** | j | **5** | l | **8** | d | **11** | a |
| **3** | g | **6** | i | **9** | h | **12** | f |

### Exercises

**1**  If you are doubtful about how to draw a budget line, the simplest way to go about it is to calculate how much of each good Ashley could buy if he were to spend his entire allowance on it. Mark these two points on the graph (one on each axis) and join them. This exercise should reveal that a change in one price alters the *slope* of the budget line, leaving the other intercept unchanged. An equal proportional change in both prices (e.g. *(d)* compared with *(a)*) has the same effect as a change in income (e.g. *(e)* compared with *(a)*) – namely, the budget line changes in position but not in slope.

**2**  **(a)** See Fig. A5–1.

**(b)** $IC_3$.

**(c)** $IC_1$.

**Figure A5–1** Ashley's indifference curves

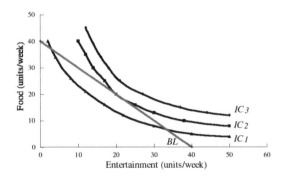

**(d)** Bundle C confers most utility, being on $1C_3$.
Bundles $A$ and $D$ are both on $1C_2$ and would be ranked equally.
Bundle $B$ confers less utility, being on $IC_1$.
Bundle E is below $1C_1$ and confers least utility.

**(e)** No, we need to know Ashley's budget constraint.

**(f)** $BL$ in Fig. A5–1 is the relevant budget line: it just touches indifference curve $IC_2$ at (2OE, 20F). This point represents the highest level of satisfaction that Ashley can reach given his budget constraint.

**3**  *(d)*.

**4**  (1) *d*    (4) *e*
(2) *c*    (5) *b*
(3) *a*    (6) *f*

**5**  **(a)** See Fig. A5–2.

**Figure A5–2** The income expansion path

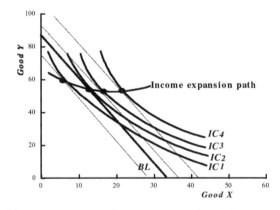

**(b)** As income expands, consumption of good X increases (X is a 'normal' good) but consumption of good Y decreases (Y is an 'inferior' good).

**(c)** Upward-sloping to the right.

**(d)** No. In a two-good world, it is not feasible for both goods to be 'inferior'. For instance, suppose income falls with prices constant – clearly, the consumer could not consume more of both goods, as would be the case if both were 'inferior'!

**6** **(a)** As the price of good *X* varies, the budget line changes its slope, while still cutting the *Y* axis at the same point: we can draw a series of budget lines, each tangent to an indifference curve on the diagram. This is done in Fig. A5–3.

**Figure A5–3** The effect on purchasing pattern of a change in the price of *X*

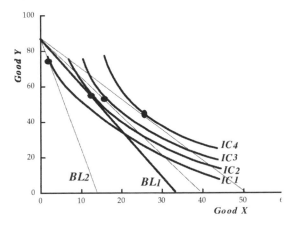

**(b)** Yes, if we know Christopher's money income, we can calculate the price of *X* corresponding to each budget line and we can read off the demand for *X* at each price. Indeed, we can get a rough idea of the demand curve by reference to the intercepts of the budget lines on the *X* axis. If we call the original price '1', then the relative price for budget line *BL₂* is approximately $33/14 = 2.36$ ($33$ is the *BL₁* intercept and $14$ the *BL₂* intercept). Reading off the *X* quantities, we get the following:

| Price | Quantity |
|-------|----------|
| 2.36 | 2 |
| 1.00 | 15 |
| 0.75 | 24 |
| 0.59 | 32 |

You might like to plot these on a diagram. This analysis provides the theoretical underpinning of the demand curve. We see that its position and slope will depend upon income and upon preferences.

**(c)** The demand for good *Y* increases as the price of *X* increases, indicating a strong substitution effect.

**7** If only tastes change, *Q* remains unattainable, so the answer cannot be *(a)*. Options *(c)* and *(d)* both move the budget line closer to the origin; *(e)* leaves the budget line unchanged. Hence, the answer is *(b)*. Try sketching in the budget lines.

**8** **(a)** See Fig. A5–4.

**Figure A5–4** The effect of a price fall

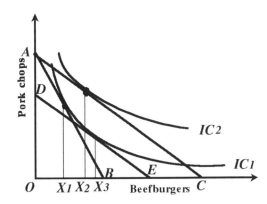

For a price *fall* we need to discover the resulting increase in real income. We do this by drawing in a new budget line *(DE)* which is parallel to the new budget line *AC* and tangent to the 'old' indifference curve *IC₁*. The substitution effect is from $X_1$ to $X_3$ and the real income effect from $X_3$ to $X_2$. This way of analysing the real income effect is sometimes known as the 'compensating income variation method'. It entails answering the question, 'What level of money income at the new relative prices would just allow Debbie to attain the original utility level?' If you have understood this, read on – otherwise, be warned that we are about to confuse you! We *could* have asked an alternative question – namely, 'What level of money income at the *old* relative prices would be equivalent to Debbie's *new* utility level?' We would analyse this by drawing another 'ghost' budget line parallel to *AB* at a tangent to $1C_2$ – try it on your diagram. This is sometimes known as the 'equivalent income variation method'.

**(b)** As drawn, beefburgers are a 'normal' good, although the income effect is relatively small.

**(c)** They work.

**(d)** If beefburgers were an 'inferior' good.

**9** **(a)** Yes, it is quite consistent for him to choose to be at point *F*: it merely requires that his indifference curves are sufficiently steep that *F* (previously unattainable) lies on a higher indifference curve than *E*.

**(b)** If Eliot is consistent in his preferences, there is no way he would choose to be at *G*. Both *E* and *G* were available options in the initial period; indeed, initially Eliot could have chosen a point to the north-east of *G*, with more of both goods – but yet he chose to be at *E*. If he now chooses *G*, it must be because of a change in tastes. You can confirm this by drawing indifference curves tangential to points *E* and *G*: you will find that they must intersect, indicating inconsistency.

**(c)** *CE*.

**(d)** They have changed: see comment on **9***(b)*.

**10** **(a)** Two cassettes give Frank 630 utils, and 10 magazines give him 371, a total of 1001 utils.

**(b)** See columns (2) and (5) of Table A5–1.

**(c)** See Fig. A5–5.

**Figure A5–5** Frank's MU schedule for cassettes

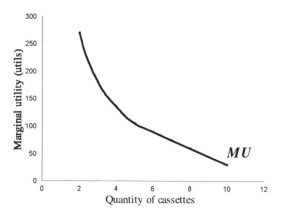

**(d)** No, because we have not taken into account the relative prices of the two goods.

**(e)** He could afford just four cassettes, which would give him 945 utils – less than his original choice.

**(f)** See columns (3) and (6) of Table A5–1.

**(g)** Frank maximizes utility by adjusting his expenditure such that $MUm/Pm$ is equal to $MUc/Pc$. You will see from Table A5–1 that this occurs when he buys three cassettes and five magazines. His total expenditure is unchanged, but he now receives 1042 utils.

## True/False

**1** True: see Section 5–1 of the main text.

**2** True.

**3** True.

**4** True: see Section 5–1 of the main text.

**5** False: the individual can always improve on such a point.

**6** False: the slope depends only on the prices.

**7** True.

**8** False: see Section 5–3 of the main text.

**9** True.

**10** True: see Section 5–3 of the main text.

**11** False: if the income effect is working against the substitution effect, then $X$ must be an 'inferior' good.

**12** False: in general, consumers potentially gain by freedom to choose (see Section 5–6 of the main text).

**Table A5–1** Frank's utility from magazines and cassettes

| Number consumed | Magazines | | | Cassettes | | |
|---|---|---|---|---|---|---|
| | (1) Utility (utils) | (2) Marginal utility | (3) MUm/Pm | (4) Utility (utils) | (5) Marginal utility | (6) MUc/Pc |
| 1 | 60 | | | 360 | | |
| 2 | 111 | 51 | 34.0 | 630 | 270 | 36 |
| 3 | 156 | 45 | 30.0 | 810 | 180 | 24 |
| 4 | 196 | 40 | 26.7 | 945 | 135 | 18 |
| 5 | 232 | 36 | 24.0 | 1050 | 105 | 14 |
| 6 | 265 | 33 | 22.0 | 1140 | 90 | 12 |
| 7 | 295 | 30 | 20.0 | 1215 | 75 | 10 |
| 8 | 322 | 27 | 18.0 | 1275 | 60 | 8 |
| 9 | 347 | 25 | 16.7 | 1320 | 45 | 6 |
| 10 | 371 | 24 | 16.0 | 1350 | 30 | 4 |

## Economics in action

**1** As products become more expensive then we would rationally expect consumers to substitute a cheaper product for an expensive one. That is, consumers will display the substitution effect in their consumption behaviour. Given that Spanish holidays are becoming more expensive in terms of both hotel prices and the rising value of the Euro, consumers will substitute away.

**2** There are three explanations for a rise in demand for long-haul holidays: (i) they have become cheaper – a substitution effect; (ii) rising incomes mean that they have become more affordable – a positive income effect; and (iii) there is perhaps a growing taste and preference for long-haul as opposed to short-haul travel.

## Questions for thought

**1** *Hint*: These effects are sometimes referred to as the 'bandwagon' and 'snob' effects. The slope of the market demand curve will be affected.

**2** *Some hints*:

(a) What happens as you move along an indifference curve? What happens to utility if the quantity of $Y_a$ stays constant but the quantity of 'good' $X_a$ increases? Possible example: medicine and sweets?

(b) Even if you like cream doughnuts, how would you feel about eating 50 of them – or more?

(c) What would be the substitution effect of a price change? (Possible example: right and left shoes?)

**3** Consider Fig. A5–6. The shape of the indifference curves reflects our individual's preferences between income and leisure. At the wage rate represented by $BL_1$ the choice is at *A*: 16 hours of leisure are chosen and hence eight hours of work. The dashed budget line shows a higher wage rate. As we have drawn it, our individual chooses less leisure, more work. This topic will be examined again later on, when we find that the reaction to an increase in the wage rate could be to work more or fewer hours (see Section 12–4 of the main text).

**4** The answer is *(d)*; this is explained in the Appendix to Chapter 5 in the main text.

**Figure A5–6** The choice between income and leisure

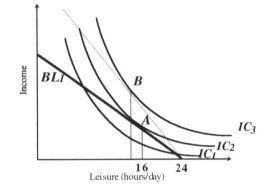

## Chapter Six Answers

# Introducing supply decisions

### Important concepts and technical terms

| | | | | | | | |
|---|---|---|---|---|---|---|---|
| **1** | *l* | **5** | *j* | **9** | *d* | **13** | *g* |
| **2** | *m* | **6** | *i* | **10** | *h* | **14** | *o* |
| **3** | *k* | **7** | *e* | **11** | *a* | **15** | *f* |
| **4** | *n* | **8** | *b* | **12** | *c* | | |

### Exercises

**1**    (a) Partnership      (c) Company
         (b) Partnership      (d) Sole trader

## Lex Pretend & Sons Limited

Income Statement for the year ended 31 December 2004

| | | |
|---|---:|---:|
| Revenue: 5000 units of good X sold at £40 each | £200 000 | |
| 4000 units of good Y sold at £75 each | 300 000 | |
| | | £500 000 |
| Deduct expenditures | | |
| Wages | 335 000 | |
| Rent | 25 000 | |
| Travel expenses | 19 000 | |
| Advertising | 28 000 | |
| Telephone | 8 000 | |
| Stationery and other office expenses | 15 000 | |
| | | 430 000 |
| Net income (profits) before tax | | 70 000 |
| Corporation tax at 30% | | 21 000 |
| Net income (profits) after tax | | £49 000 |

**3**   (a)   £27 000    (d)   £2500

     (b)   £28 000    (e)   £50 500

     (c)   £21 000    (f)   £4500

**4**

## GSC Limited

Balance Sheet

31 March 2004

| Assets | | Liabilities | |
|---|---:|---|---:|
| Cash in hand | £30 000 | Accounts payable | £40 000 |
| Accounts receivable | 55 000 | Wages payable | 25 000 |
| Inventories | 80 000 | Salaries payable | 30 000 |
| Buildings | | Mortgage | 180 000 |
| (Original value £300 000) | 240 000 | Bank loan | 50 000 |
| Other equipment | | | |
| (Original value £250 000) | 200 000 | Total | 325 000 |
| | | Net worth | 280 000 |
| Total assets | £605 000 | | £605 000 |

**5**   See Table A6–1.

**6**   (b).

**7**   (a)   See Fig. A6–1.

(b)   Marginal cost $(MC_0)$ intersects marginal revenue $(MR_0)$ at an output level of about 3 units per week.

(c)   Total revenue continues to increase while marginal revenue is positive. After an output level of about 5 units per week marginal revenue would become negative. Total revenue is thus maximized at 5 units per week.

(d)   $MC_1$ in Fig. A6–1 represents the new marginal cost schedule, $MC_1 = MR_0$ at an output level of about 2 units per week: a cost increase thus causes output to fall.

(e)   $MR_1$ in Fig. A6–1 represents the new marginal revenue schedule, $MC_0 = MR_1$ at an output level of about 4 units per week – i.e. output has increased.

**8**   All of these could provide motivation for decision-makers in firms, although some may be relevant mainly where there is a separation of ownership and control. In such a situation, there may be a conflict of interest between owners and managers (the principal–agent problem). The shareholders (owners/principals) may prefer the firm to maximize profits, but the managers (agents) may prefer to

| Table A6–1 | Profits, marginal revenue and marginal cost | | | | | |
|---|---|---|---|---|---|---|
| Total production (units/week) | Price received (£) | Total revenue (£) | Total costs (£) | Profit (£) | Marginal revenue (£) | Marginal cost (£) |
| 1 | 25 | 25 | 10 | 15 | | |
| | | | | | 21 | 13 |
| 2 | 23 | 46 | 23 | 23 | | |
| | | | | | 14 | 15 |
| 3 | 20 | 60 | 38 | 22 | | |
| | | | | | 12 | 17 |
| 4 | 18 | 72 | 55 | 17 | | |
| | | | | | 3 | 20 |
| 5 | 15 | 75 | 75 | 0 | | |
| | | | | | 0 | 23 |
| 6 | 12½ | 75 | 98 | −23 | | |

*Profits are maximized at an output level of 2 units per week.*

**Figure A6–1**  Marginal cost and marginal revenue

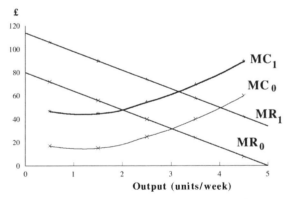

maximize sales, market share or growth. For more discussion of firms' motivations, see Section 6–3 of the main text. The separation problem is most important where it is difficult for the owners to monitor the actions of managers – for example, where there are many small shareholders.

Economists tend to focus on profit maximization *(a)* as being a reasonable approximation to reality – and convenient for analysis.

## True/False

**1**   True: see Section 6–1 of the main text.

**2**   False: the balance sheet sets out assets and liabilities of a firm at a particular date.

**3**   False: of course, nobody wants to end up with worthless shares, but shareholders are liable only for the amount they put into the firm and no more.

**4**   False: opportunity cost must also be considered.

**5**   True.

**6**   True: see Section 6–2 of the main text.

**7**   False.

**8**   True: see Section 6–5 of the main text.

**9**   False: unless you can convince your bank manager that all will be well, the long term may never come! Most new businesses (and many old ones) need to borrow to help them through periods of low cash flow.

**10**   True: see Section 6–4 of the main text.

**11**   True: remember Exercise 7?

**12**   False!

**13**   True: see Section 6–5 of the main text.

**14**   True: see Box 6–2 in the main text.

## Economics in action

**1** The shareholders in Sainsbury's own the company and they hire managers to run the company on their behalf. Therefore, the shareholders are the principals and the managers are the agents.

**2** Arguably, there was a separation of ownership from control problem as the chairman tried to extract a £2.4 million performance bonus when the company was underperforming. However, the shareholders were able to force the chairman out. This suggests that a small number of shareholders with reasonably large stakes in the company were able to discipline management, indicating that the agency costs associated with the separation of ownership from control were minimal. It should also be noted that in the case of Sainsbury's, the founding family are still a significant shareholder, leading to a less diffuse shareholding and a greater ability to control managers.

## Questions for thought

**1** Some hints may be found in Section 6–5 of the main text; it will also be discussed again in Chapter 8.

**2** If you are reading this, you have decided that the opportunity cost is not excessive – or you would have hurried on to Chapter 7! Opportunity cost is involved every time we make a choice between alternatives: spending money in one way precludes us from buying other items; taking time to do something prevents us from doing something else.

**3** **(a)** One possibility is that the managers' aims will be to ensure job security and to safeguard a good salary. These objectives *may* not coincide with profit maximization, especially if the managers' salaries are seen to be associated with sales or market share.

**(b)** The problem is that it may not be a straightforward matter for you to monitor the managers, or to assess whether output and price have been set so as to maximize profits.

**(c)** The managers may be aware that a hostile takeover could well be followed by changes in management. This may provide an incentive for profit maximization, which may reduce the likelihood of a takeover.

**(d)** The threat of a hostile takeover may lead to short-termism. It may be more difficult to undertake long-term investment if the firm becomes vulnerable to takeover in the transition. Box 7–2 in the main text argues that firms in the UK and USA suffer in this way relative to firms in Germany or Japan, where there is a different approach to corporate finance.

**(e)** You need to find some way of setting appropriate incentives for the managers, perhaps by seeing that they hold some shares in the company. If you are anxious about the long-term position of the company, then you might wish to take measures to reduce the probability of a takeover or to limit its effects on the existing management. Box 7–2 in the main text explores these and other issues in more depth.

# Chapter Seven Answers

# Costs and supply

## Important concepts and technical terms

| | | | |
|---|---|---|---|
| **1** a | **5** n | **9** e | **13** g |
| **2** l | **6** f | **10** j | **14** k |
| **3** h | **7** d | **11** b | |
| **4** m | **8** i | **12** c | |

## Exercises

**1** **(a)** and **(b)** The calculations for *(a)* are needed to tackle part *(b)*. Total costs for each technique are set out in Table A7–1; the preferred technique for each output level has been indicated by lines of enclosure. At low levels of output, technique A provides the least-cost method of production – notice that this technique is relatively labour-intensive, using more labour but less capital than the alternatives. However, as output levels increase, technique B becomes more efficient, and then technique C takes over when output reaches 6 units/week – this being the most capital-intensive technique.

**Table A7–1    Total cost and the choice of technique**

| Output (units/week) | Total cost technique A | Total cost technique B | Total cost technique C |
|---|---|---|---|
| 1 | 2 600 | 2 800 | 3 200 |
| 2 | 5 000 | 5 200 | 5 600 |
| 3 | 7 400 | 7 600 | 8 000 |
| 4 | 10 200 | 10 000 | 10 800 |
| 5 | 14 200 | 13 600 | 14 000 |
| 6 | 19 800 | 18 200 | 17 600 |
| 7 | 27 200 | 24 200 | 21 800 |

**Table A7–2    Total cost and the choice of technique after the change in labour cost**

| Output (units/week) | Total cost technique A | Total cost technique B | Total cost technique C |
|---|---|---|---|
| 1 | 3 500 | 3 400 | 3 600 |
| 2 | 6 900 | 6 200 | 6 400 |
| 3 | 10 300 | 9 000 | 9 200 |
| 4 | 14 300 | 11 800 | 12 400 |
| 5 | 20 100 | 16 000 | 16 000 |
| 6 | 28 300 | 21 500 | 20 000 |
| 7 | 39 200 | 28 700 | 24 700 |

(c) If labour becomes more expensive relative to capital, we expect the firm to move towards more capital-intensive techniques. In particular, we expect a move away from technique A in this exercise – and this is what happens, as you can see in Table A7–2.

(d) See Table A7–2.

**2**  (a) See Table A7–3.

(b) See Fig. A7–1.

(c) At 2 units/week.

(d) It is always the case that $LMC = LAC$ at the minimum point of $LAC$ – thus the intersection is at 2 units/week of output.

**3**  (a) Up to 2 units/week.

(b) In excess of 2 units/week.

(c) 2 units/week.

**Table A7–3    Output and long-run total cost**

| Output (units/week) | Total cost (£) | Long-run average cost | Long-run marginal cost |
|---|---|---|---|
| 0 | 0 | | |
| 1 | 32 | 32.0 | 32 |
| 2 | 48 | 24.0 | 16 |
| 3 | 82 | 27.3 | 34 |
| 4 | 140 | 35.0 | 58 |
| 5 | 228 | 45.6 | 88 |
| 6 | 352 | 58.7 | 124 |

**Figure A7–1**  Long-run average cost and long-run marginal cost

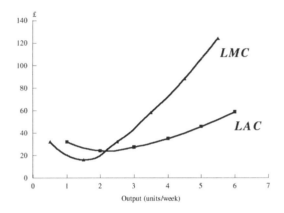

(d) This point represents the switch-over from falling $LAC$ to rising $LAC$ from increasing to decreasing returns to scale. *At that point*, the firm has constant returns to scale.

**4**  (a) is a tempting response, but incorrect. Diminishing returns to a factor do not require that the extra units used diminish in quality; nor need total product fall: it is marginal product that diminishes. Response (c) is an interesting observation (in jargon, this describes a 'pecuniary external diseconomy of scale'), but it is not pertinent to diminishing returns. If you think about it you will realize that (d) describes increasing returns to a factor; (e) is concerned with revenue rather than costs. This leaves us with (b) as the correct response: diminishing returns are indeed concerned with the returns to the variable factor.

**5**  All of them.

**6**  (a) See Table A7–4.

(b) See Fig. A7–2.

### Table A7–4 Short-run costs of production

| Output (units/week) | Short-run average variable cost (SAVC) | Short-run average fixed cost (SAFC) | Short-run average total cost (SATC) | Short-run total cost (STC) | Short-run marginal cost (SMC) |
|---|---|---|---|---|---|
| 1 | 17 | 45.0 | 62.0 | 62 | 17 |
| 2 | 15 | 22.5 | 37.5 | 75 | 13 |
| 3 | 14 | 15.0 | 29.0 | 87 | 12 |
| 4 | 15 | 11.25 | 26.25 | 105 | 18 |
| 5 | 19 | 9.0 | 28.0 | 140 | 35 |
| 6 | 29 | 7.5 | 36.5 | 219 | 79 |

SAFC = £45 divided by output; SATC = SAVC + SAFC; STC = SATC multiplied by output.

**Figure A7–2** Short-run average total cost, short-run average variable cost and short-run marginal cost

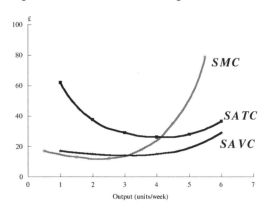

**Figure A7–3** Average and marginal product of labour

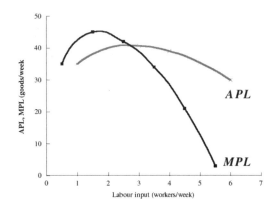

(c) In the short run, the firm cannot adjust its capital input. If it wishes to change the level of output, it must do so by altering labour input. However, with capital input fixed, diminishing returns to labour set in rapidly, such that the marginal product of labour falls. For this reason, the marginal cost of producing more output may be very high in the short run.

**7** (a) See Table A7–5.

(b) See Fig. A7–3.

### Table A7–5 Output and labour input

| Labour input (workers/week) | Output (goods/week) | Marginal product of labour | Average product of labour |
|---|---|---|---|
| 0 | 0 | | |
| 1 | 35 | 35 | 35.0 |
| 2 | 80 | 45 | 40.0 |
| 3 | 122 | 42 | 40.6 |
| 4 | 156 | 34 | 39.0 |
| 5 | 177 | 21 | 35.4 |
| 6 | 180 | 3 | 30.0 |

(c) *MPL* turns down close to 1 worker/week: this is the point at which diminishing returns set in.

(d) *MPL* must cut *APL* at its maximum point – i.e. just below 3 workers/week.

(e) A change in the level of capital input affects the position of *MPL* and *APL*. An increase in capital would move these curves upwards.

**8** (e), (f).

**9** (a) *OC* can be produced at minimum average cost.

(b) Decreasing returns to scale.

(c) That corresponding to $SATC_2$.

(d) The firm would have no choice in the short run but to produce using $SATC_2$. In the long run, it would pay to expand to $SATC_3$.

(e) See Fig. A7–4.

**10** See Table A7–6.

**Table A7–6    Short- and long-run decisions**

| Price (£) | Short-run decision | | | Long-run decision | | |
|---|---|---|---|---|---|---|
| | Produce at a profit | Produce at a loss | Close down | Produce at a profit | Produce at a loss | Close down |
| 18.0 | ✓ | | | ✓ | | |
| 5.0 | | | ✓ | | | ✓ |
| 7.0 | | | ✓ | | | ✓ |
| 13.0 | | ✓ | | ✓ | | |
| 11.50 | | ✓ | | | | ✓ |

*Notice that firms will never choose to produce at a loss in the long run.*

**Figure A7–4**   Short-run (and long-run) average cost

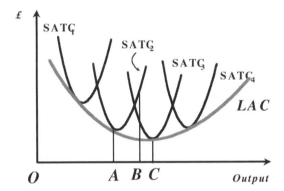

## True/False

**1**    False: it may seem like that sometimes, for economists often assume for simplicity that there are only these two factors. In reality, there may be others: managerial input, raw materials, energy – even bandages for the rest room! (See Section 7–1 of the main text.)

**2**    True: of course, the economies of scale may persist to quite high output levels (see Section 7–4 of the main text).

**3**    True: this was discussed in the writings of Adam Smith in the eighteenth century.

**4**    False: not all industries experience significant economies of scale.

**5**    False: remember Exercise 10?

**6**    False: price and average revenue are the same if all output is sold at the same price.

**7**    False: reference must also be made to the average condition, to see whether the firm should close down (see Section 7–6 of the main text).

**8**    True: see Section 7–7 of the main text.

**9**    True: see Section 7–5 of the main text.

**10**    True: see Section 7–4 of the main text.

**11**    True: sunk costs are sunk: what is important is the level of variable costs (see Box 7–2 in the main text).

**12**    False: the *LAC* curve touches each *SATC* curve but never cuts one.

## Economics in action

**1**    Toyota is gaining economies of scale in a number of interrelated ways. First, Toyota is simplifying its number of key components including engines and gearboxes. In this way, it can focus on manufacturing a large number of units across a limited number of ranges. Secondly, it is exploiting global demand levels as opposed to local country-level demand.

**2**    The potential drawbacks associated with this strategy are numerous. First, Toyota's engines and gearboxes will be standard across its range of vehicles. Customers may demand different engine and gearbox characteristics across the range. Second, shipping gearboxes and engines around the world will be expensive. Third, overseas assembly plants will need to hold high stocks of engines and gearboxes in case of delays in delivery from India. This will be costly. Finally, exports from India may be blocked with trade restrictions.

## Questions for thought

**1** In your discussion of this question, you will have to explore the issue of economies and diseconomies of scale. Average costs decline up to the 'minimum efficient scale' as a result of indivisibilities in the production process, specialization and (in some cases) benefits of large scale (see Section 8–4 of the main text). However, the level of output at which the minimum efficient scale (MES) is reached varies from industry to industry, with the type of activity and technology involved. These are some of the issues that you will need to consider. Try to think up some examples of industries in which there are likely to be significant economies of scale, and also industries where the MES is likely to be at a relatively low level of output. This process of relating theory to reality is an excellent way of confirming your understanding of the concepts.

**2** *Hint:* Remember the long-run/short-run distinction.

**3** There was some brief discussion of this at the end of Chapter 7 in the main text.

**4** The scope for economies of scale in many industries has been greatly affected by the IT revolution. Box 8–1 in the main text talks about this and we devote the whole of Chapter 11 to the information economy. The changing nature of capital and technology in many industries has affected the extent of economies of scale – not always in the same direction: notice how you can now buy spectacles almost anywhere without having to wait while lenses are ground in some remote central factory.

# Chapter Eight Answers

# Perfect competition and pure monopoly

## Important concepts and technical terms

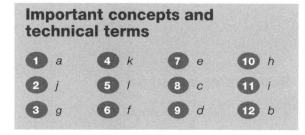

| | | | | | | | |
|---|---|---|---|---|---|---|---|
| **1** | a | **4** | k | **7** | e | **10** | h |
| **2** | j | **5** | l | **8** | c | **11** | i |
| **3** | g | **6** | f | **9** | d | **12** | b |

**Figure A8–1** A firm under perfect competition

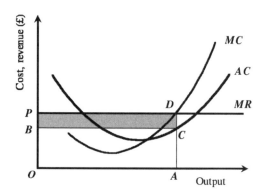

## Exercises

**1** **(a)** Profits would be maximized at output *OA* in Fig. A8–1 where *MC* = *MR*.

**(b)** Profits would be calculated by the excess of average revenue over average cost, multiplied by output – in Fig. A8–1, this is the area *PBCD*.

**(c)** This firm is making profits over and above 'normal profits', which are included in average cost. It is thus probable that Fig. A8–1 represents short-run equilibrium, as we would expect other firms to be encouraged to enter the industry by the lure of these supernormal profits. However, it could be a long-run equilibrium if this firm enjoys a cost advantage – perhaps a better geographical location. In this case, further entry would depend upon the marginal firm's performance.

**(d)** A decrease in demand would lead initially to a fall in the price of the good, and firms such as the one represented in Fig. A8–1 would experience a reduction in profits. In the long run, firms would be able to adjust their input structures to the new conditions, so that price would drift up again. (See Section 8–4 of the main text for a similar analysis of an increase in demand.)

**2** **(a)** *OB*: the price at which the firm just covers its variable costs.

**(b)** *CD*.

**(c)** *CDRP*: total cost less variable cost.

**(d)** Between *OB* and *OD*.

Chapter 8 Answers : Perfect competition and pure monopoly **235**

(e) The supply curve in the short run is the portion of the *SMC* curve above point *K*.

(f) Above *OD*.

**3** (a) Profit would be maximized at output *OQ* in Fig. A8–2 where *MR* = *MC*.

**Figure A8–2** A monopolist

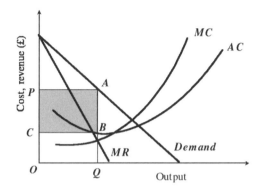

(b) The demand curve shows that the monopolist could sell *OQ* output at a price *OP*.

(c) Profits would be calculated, as before, as the excess of average revenue over average cost, multiplied by output – this is the area *PABC*.

(d) A decrease in demand would affect both 'Demand' and *MR* curves in Fig. A8–2, moving them to the left. *MC* and *MR* will now intersect at a lower level of output, so the monopolist will produce less.

**4** (a) *MR* = *LMC* at the output level *OD*.

(b) *OC*.

(c) *LAC* is just tangent to the demand curve at this point, so the monopolist makes only normal profits: supernormal profits are zero.

(d) If the monopolist were forced to charge a price equal to marginal cost, then an output of *OH* is indicated, with price *OB*. However, notice that in this situation *LAC* exceeds average revenue and the monopolist would close down, unless the authorities were prepared to offer a subsidy.

**5** (a) See Table A8–1.

(b) and (c) See Fig. A8–3.

(d) 4.

(e) 4.

(f) 4.

**6** (a) *OC*.

(b) *OE*.

(c) *OB*.

(d) *OF*.

**Table A8–1** A monopolist's revenue curves

| Demand (000/week) | Price (£) (average revenue) | Total revenue (£) | Marginal revenue (£) |
|---|---|---|---|
| 0 | 40 | 0 | |
| 1 | 35 | 35 | 35 |
| 2 | 30 | 60 | 25 |
| 3 | 25 | 75 | 15 |
| 4 | 20 | 80 | 5 |
| 5 | 15 | 75 | –5 |
| 6 | 10 | 60 | –15 |
| 7 | 5 | 35 | –25 |

**Figure A8–3** A monopolist's revenue curves

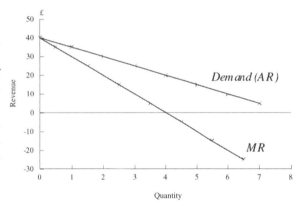

**7** (d).

**8** Option (a) relates only to a monopoly situation: the monopolist chooses output where *MC* = *MR*, at which point *AR* (hence the chosen price) exceeds *MR*. Thus (h) also applies only to the monopolist. In the case of situation (b), a firm under perfect competition has no influence over price, and thus faces a horizontal demand curve such that *AR* = *P* = *MR*. Situation (c) expresses the condition for firms to maximize profits, so applies to all market situations in which firms attempt to maximize profits, whether perfect competition, monopoly or other forms of market structure which we will encounter in Chapter 9. Option (d) is a feature of the long-run situation under perfect competition if firms are equally efficient: it could also relate to a monopolist, but this depends upon the position of the average cost curve relative to the demand curve. In many cases, we expect the monopolist to be able to make positive profits even in long-run equilibrium, depending on the strength of barriers to entry. Situations *(e)* and *(f)* relate to a monopoly situation. A monopoly will remain a monopoly only if new firms can be excluded from the market by some means. In the case of *(f)*, a firm under perfect competition can choose only output and must accept the price as given; the monopolist can choose a combination of price and output, but is still subject to the demand curve. Perfect competition assumes that there are no barriers to entry *(g)*; it is this characteristic that leads to the long-run equilibrium position for the industry which we will see later is highly desirable for society as a whole, where price is set equal to marginal cost (situation *(i)*). This is in contrast to monopoly, in which price can be set above marginal cost.

**9**   *(d)*.

**10**   **(a)**   Under perfect competition, industry equilibrium would be where demand *(D)* equals supply *(LRSS)* – that is, at price *OA* and output *OG*.

**(b)**   In the short run, the monopolist will set marginal revenue *(MRm)* equal to short-run marginal cost *(SMCm)*. Output is reduced to *OF* and price increased to *OB*.

**(c)**   In the long run, the monopolist will close down some plants and equate *MRm* with long-run marginal cost *(LMCm)*. Output is reduced further to *OE* and price raised to *OC*.

**(d)**   The monopolist will still operate each individual plant at its minimum *LAC*. *LAC* is thus given by *OA* – and profits by the area *ACHK*.

## True/False

**1**   True.

**2**   False: the increased flexibility in the long run makes the long-run supply curve flatter than in the short run.

**3**   False: the firm is said to be making just normal profits when economic profits are zero (see Section 8–2 of the main text).

**4**   False: such an industry is a natural monopoly (see Section 8–8 of the main text).

**5**   False: we must also consider the quantity that would be supplied by firms who are not currently operating in the market, but who would enter if market price were at a higher level.

**6**   False: a monopolist will never produce on the inelastic part of the demand curve (see Section 8–7 of the main text).

**7**   False: draw the diagram to check.

**8**   False: even where efficiency is the same, the monopolist has influence on price and can use this market power to make supernormal profits.

**9**   False.

**10**   True.

**11**   True.

**12**   True: see Section 8–10 of the main text.

## Economics in action

**1**   **(a)**   Many buyers and sellers. There are certainly many buyers with air travel increasing steadily. Many sellers is a little more difficult. The article suggests that 54 low-cost flyers are crowding into the European market, but they do not all compete on the same routes. If they all competed between London and Paris then, yes, there would be many sellers. While this is not true, the emergence of low-cost carriers has increased the number of competitors on particular routes.

**(b)**   Homogeneous product. To some extent this is true, but an important differentiation is the use of less popular airports by the low-cost carriers.

**(c)**   Perfect information. True, it is very easy to check prices across suppliers using the Internet.

**(d)**   No barriers to entry or exit. True and false. Entry is expensive, requiring landing slots and the purchase or leasing of aircraft. But once entered, it is easy to move aircraft between routes.

**2**   If capacity exits the market, then supply and competition are both reduced. Prices should rise and profits increase. However, this may attract entrants into the industry, thus reducing profits. Moreover, the ease of entry, by simply leasing an aircraft, means that the threat of entry is high. This threat of entry may keep prices and profits around the 'normal' level. This idea will be discussed further in Chapter 8 under contestable markets.

## Questions for thought

**1** *Hint:* What could threaten the monopolist's long-term position? A crucial factor determining whether a monopolist will decide to take full advantage of its market position is the strength of the barriers to entry. If the monopolist thinks there is a possibility that other firms may be able to enter the industry, then there may be a reluctance to make large profits, for fear of attracting attention. It is also possible that the monopolist may not want to attract the attention of the government: this will be discussed further in Chapter 18.

**2** In approaching this question, think in particular about the situation for the firm when the industry is in long-run equilibrium. This may be contrasted with the monopoly position, where the firm always produces below the minimum efficient scale.

**3** (a) *OcM*: the output at which $LMC = MR$ in the combined market.

(b) *OcN* (= $O_1E$), this being the price to clear the combined market.

(c) At the price of $O_1E$, demand in market 1 would be $O_1H$ and demand in market 2 would be $O_2K$. Notice, of course, that the scales of the three diagrams are common, and that $O_1H + O_2K = OcM$.

(d) Marginal revenue is $O_1B$ in market 1 and $O_2I$ in market 2. This large difference has important implications for profits.

(e) In *(d)*, it was clear that marginal revenue in market 2 was much higher than in market 1. If the monopolist can increase sales in market 2 and reduce sales in market 1, the additional revenue from the former will more than offset the lost revenue of the latter, and profits will increase. It will pay to continue this switching until marginal revenue is equal in the two markets.

(f) To equalize marginal revenue in the two submarkets, the monopolist would sell in market 1 at a price of $O_1F$ and in market 2 at a price of $O_2J$; sales would be $O_1G$ and $O_2L$, respectively. Again, $O_1G + O_2L = OcM$.

Notice that this analysis depends upon the nature of the commodity (cannot be resold), the separation of the market and the differing elasticities of demand in the two markets.

It is also worth noticing that if *LMC* cut *MR* much further to the left in Fig. 8–7(c), it could be that without discrimination no sales at all are made in market 2.

**4** (a) *AML*.

(b) *CMH*.

(c) Part has gone to the monopolist as profits *(ACHK)*; the remainder (triangle *KHL*) is a 'deadweight loss' to society. We may argue that this is the irrecoverable loss to society that results from the presence of monopoly in this market.

# Chapter Nine Answers

## Market structure and imperfect competition

### Important concepts and technical terms

| | | | | | | | |
|---|---|---|---|---|---|---|---|
| **1** | b | **6** | k | **11** | g | **16** | n |
| **2** | a | **7** | h | **12** | l | **17** | c |
| **3** | i | **8** | n | **13** | o | | |
| **4** | q | **9** | f | **14** | m | | |
| **5** | j | **10** | e | **15** | d | | |

### Exercises

**1** (a) D.

(b) B.

(c) A.

(d) C.

(e) E: we haven't talked about monopsony yet, but it is defined in Chapter 9 of the main text.

(f) B/C: although a monopolist in the supply of rail transport, the supplier would doubtless be aware of potential competition from other forms of transport, and would thus perhaps behave more like an oligopolist than a monopolist. We discussed the example of Eurostar in 'Economics in action' in Chapter 9.

**2** **(a)** A: because of the existence of substantial economies of scale relative to market size.

**(b)** B, E: in both industries, the biggest three firms supply a small proportion of the market. In addition, it is clear that no great scale economies exist, in that the minimum efficient size is very small relative to market size.

**(c)** C, D seem capable of supporting just a handful of firms.

**(d)** Oligopoly is unlikely to arise in either B or E, with the large number of firms likely to be present in these industries. Could A be an oligopoly? It is perhaps not impossible: we cannot know for sure, as we only have the three-firm concentration ratio; nor do we know whether the firm(s) is (are) actually operating at minimum efficient scale. The monopolist may be prevented by law from exploiting its position – or may have other 'industries' with which to compete (see example (f) in Exercise 1). The steepness of the average cost curve below minimum efficient scale is also important. For more details, see Section 9–1 in the main text.

**3** (b), (c), (d), (e), (f) and (h) are all typical characteristics of such an industry – see Section 9–2 of the main text. As for the other factors: first, in long-run equilibrium, firms find themselves in tangency equilibrium with average revenue just covering average costs – so no monopoly profits (a) are to be reaped in the long run. If this were not so, then there would be an incentive for more firms to enter the market. Second, monopolistic competition is typified by a large number of firms, so the opportunities for collusion (g) are limited.

**4** **(a)** $MR = MC$ at output $OG$.

**(b)** $OF$.

**(c)** Yes: the area $EFLK$.

**(d)** This must be a short-run equilibrium. The presence of supernormal profits will attract new entrants into the industry, causing our firm's demand curve to become more elastic at any price and to shift to the left. This is because of the increased availability of substitutes and because the firm loses some customers to the new entrants. The process continues until the typical firm is in tangency equilibrium, with its demand curve just touching the long-run average cost curve, making only normal profits.

**5**

| Influence | Encourages collusion | Favours non-cooperation |
|---|---|---|
| | (Tick one column) | |
| Barriers to entry | ✓ | |
| Product is non-standard | | ✓ |
| Demand and costs are stable | ✓ | |
| Collusion is legal | ✓ | |
| Secrecy about price and output | | ✓ |
| Collusion is illegal | | ✓ |
| Easy communication of price and output | ✓ | |
| Standard product | ✓ | |

**6** Figure 9–2 shows the typical shape of the famous 'kinked demand curve'. A feature of this model is the stability of prices, so we can accept statement (a). The price discrimination model can also produce a demand curve with a kink in it – but in that case, the kink faces the other way (see Fig. 9–2). We thus reject (b). As this is an oligopoly model, and the 'kink' occurs because the firm is aware of its rivals' actions, statement (c) is likely to be acceptable. Statement (d) has no foundation.

**7** **(a)** Given that Y produces 'low', you (X) can make profits of 15 by also producing 'low' or 20 by producing 'high'. For this period, you maximize profits by producing 'high' – but notice that, in so doing, you reduce the profit made by Y.

**(b)** With you producing 'high', firm Y must also produce 'high' to maximize profits.

**(c)** Given the answer to (b), it seems probable that Y will indeed produce 'high', in which case your only option is also to produce 'high'. In actual fact, your dominant strategy is to produce 'high' – it pays you to do this whatever Y does if we are concerned only with the single time period.

**(d)** If we start thinking in terms of a sequence of time periods, it should be clear that both firms could be better off if they agree to produce 'low'. If you can be sure that firm Y will produce 'low' and will continue to do so, then it will pay you to decide to produce 'low' also.

**(e)** One possibility is to announce a punishment strategy. You threaten to produce 'high' in all future periods if Y cheats on the agreement. The threat is credible only if Y believes that you would actually find it in your best interests to carry it out.

**(f)** One possibility is that you enter into a pre-commitment to produce 'low', restricting your own future options.

**(g)** The arguments here are similar, but the penalties if both firms produce high are much more severe. If firm **X** announces its intention of producing 'high', firm **Y** knows that it can survive only by producing 'low'. However, **X** would also go under if **Y** produces 'high', so **Y** could also announce its intention of producing 'high', and the question then is whether one firm (or both) will give way. This is sometimes known as the 'chicken' game, because of its similarity to the game of chicken in which two cars rush headlong towards each other, testing each other's nerves. We could still end up with the firms destroying each other if neither gives way.

**8** (*a*) is an innocent barrier: if the minimum efficient scale (MES) is high relative to market demand, then we are heading towards a natural monopoly situation. Option (*b*) may well be strategic: potential entrants will perceive that staying in this market will require R&D expenditure and may thus be deterred. Also, R&D expenditure may lead to the generating of patents (*c*) for the future, further preventing entry. Firms have been known to take out a whole range of patents on items that may or may not prove profitable, thus being ready to exploit any ideas that turn out well. Having said that, it may be in society's best interests for firms to undertake R&D expenditure, and the patent system is in place to ensure that there is some incentive for innovation and invention. Items (*d*), (*e*) and (*f*) are other ways in which the incumbent firm(s) may deter potential entrants; you will find more detailed discussion in Section 9–6 of the main text. The final item (*g*) could be either innocent or strategic. Existing firms may have 'innocent' advantages in locations or experience which make it difficult for new entrants to compete. On the other hand, the advantage may be another offspring of past R&D effort, and thus partly strategic. Indeed, the closer we look at these barriers, the more difficult it becomes to distinguish between the innocent and the strategic. Take barrier (*f*), for example. A firm may hold excess capacity in order to add credibility to an announced threat of predatory pricing. This is a strategic move. However, a firm may install additional capacity in the expectation of a future increase in demand for its product. This is simply good business practice.

**9** With the protection of the patent, the monopolist may have enjoyed a period making profits above the opportunity cost of capital, as we examined in Chapter 9. The patent barrier will have prevented entry of other firms who might have been attracted by the lure of profits. When

the patent expires, the market becomes contestable and these other potential competitors are likely to attempt entry. As entry takes place, the former monopolist's demand curve is likely to shift to the left and to become more elastic, as some customers switch to the new firms. Do you recognize this story? We are back in the world of monopolistic competition and heading for long-run tangency equilibrium.

**10** We cannot offer comments on this, as we do not know what firms operate in your neighbourhood.

**11** **(a)** There is a negative relationship between the output of firm **A** and firm **B**. As **B** increases its output, **A** will cut back.

**(b)** If **B** cuts back production by one unit, **A** will not increase production by one unit. The reason is that **A** can gain more benefit from the price rise resulting from lower supply. What does this mean about the elasticity of demand?

**(c)** Point **E** depicts the Nash equilibrium. This is where the reaction functions intersect and at this point each firm is making an optimal response given the actions of its rivals.

**(d)** If firm **A** gained access to more productive technology then it might be expected that the marginal cost curve of firm **A** would reduce. Hence, firm **A** would be more willing to produce output for any given level of output produced by **B**. Therefore, firm **A**'s reaction function would move out to the right.

**(e)** Firms in perfect competition are price-takers. They do not take into account the output decisions of their rivals. Therefore each firm would have a reaction function which was independent of its rival's decisions. In the case of firm **A**, this would be a horizontal line, indicating that the output of **A** is constant irrespective of the output chosen by **B** (and all the other firms).

**12** I do not think your parents or the bank manager will appreciate the advice that we are about to provide, especially if they have paid for this book. By moving first you can gain an advantage, because then your rival has to react to your move. Therefore the key point when moving first is to take a position which will limit the ability of the rival to react. In the Stackelberg example in the book firm **A** was able to restrict the output reaction of firm **B** by moving first. So when you need to ask your parents for some money (as all students do) then you need to think strategically. The most worrying reaction which is available to your parents is to refuse your requests. Therefore how can you make a move which blocks the refusal option?

## True/False

**1**   True.

**2**   True.

**3**   False: in these conditions a monopoly would be unlikely (see Section 9–1 of the main text).

**4**   True: see Section 9–2 of the main text.

**5**   True: a firm's behaviour is determined by its perceptions about the actions of other firms. Thus firms will be prepared to raise price if it is known that all firms face an increase in costs.

**6**   False: the kinked demand curve may be the most famous of oligopoly models but, as this chapter has shown, it is by no means the only way in which economists have tried to analyse such markets.

**7**   False: 'dominant' has nothing to do with winning; the question is whether the strategy dominates other possible strategies the firm can adopt, given what other firms may do. (See Section 9–4 of the main text.)

**8**   True: this is also discussed in Section 9–4 of the main text.

**9**   Not necessarily true: for this tactic to be successful, it must be apparent that the threat of a punishment strategy is a credible one.

**10**   This may be 'true' in the short run, but it could be 'false' in the long run. If there is a threat of new entry into the industry, it may pay to use limit pricing to deter potential entrants.

**11**   True: see Section 9–5 of the main text.

**12**   True: see Section 9–6 of the main text.

**13**   True: see Section 9–5 of the main text.

**14**   False: see Section 9–5 of the main text and the Stackelberg model.

**15**   False: see Section 9–5 of the main text.

## Economics in action

**1**   There are a number of features which will foster a cartel in the memory chip market. First, a small number of dominant players, in this case Micron, Samsung and Infineon. Second, a homogeneous product such as memory chips, which enhances price competition. Thirdly, falling demand in an environment of excess capacity, which without collusion will force down prices.

**2**   One solution to combating the cartel is to lodge a protest with the competition authorities. An alternative is to support a weaker player in the market. Either shift orders to the weaker player in return for a discount; and/or flood the market with excess stock bought from the weaker player, thereby undercutting the cartel. Sometimes, threatening such behaviour is enough to dissuade collusion.

## Questions for thought

**1**   No hints are offered for this question: think about it!

**2**   **(a)** In the market as a whole (panel (c)), profits are maximized where $MCc—MRc$ at output $Oce$.

**(b)**   Price will be set at $OcW$ ($= OaE = ObL$).

**(c)**   Accepting the cartel level of marginal revenue (at $OcX = OaF = ObN$), firm $A$ produces $OaK$ and firm $B$, $ObS$. Notice that $OaK + ObS = Oce$ (although it may not look like that in Fig. 9–4, where the horizontal scale of panel (c) has been compressed to squeeze it on to the page).

**(d)**   Firm $A$ makes profits of $EFGJ$ and firm $B$ makes $LMQP$. Firm $A$'s cost advantage is reflected in a much higher level of profit and a higher market share.

**(e)**   If firm $B$ were to act as if it were a price-taker at $ObL$, it would attempt to maximize profits by increasing output to $ObV$, where $MCb$ = perceived $MR$. This again illustrates the tension inherent in a cartel situation.

**(f)**   Of course, firm $B$ is not really a price-taker in this market, and if firm $B$ increases output from $ObS$ to $ObV$, market price will fall (in panel (c)), and overall cartel profits will fall. Indeed, price could fall to such an extent that firm $B$ (with its high average cost) makes losses. This is especially likely if firm $A$ also begins to increase output.

**3**   Perhaps the key question to ask in this context is what information the tobacco manufacturers are really conveying by advertising. It cannot be that they want to tell us that their products will kill us, so what else could it be?

Psychologically, perhaps they are merely looking to transmit a subliminal message to existing consumers to encourage them to continue smoking their particular brand. Another way of thinking about this is that one piece of information that we do learn from tobacco advertising is simply that the tobacco firms are prepared to spend lots of money on advertising . . . i.e. we might interpret this as a sign of commitment to the market, and to maintaining the quality of the product.

**④** From the economist's point of view, there is no doubting the value of the model of perfect competition. It provides a key benchmark against which we can compare the resource implications of alternative market structures. By seeing how real-life markets diverge from the perfectly competitive ideal, we may be able to analyse whether society is suffering a loss of overall welfare. We may even be able to do something about it by framing an appropriate policy to encourage competition and improved resource allocation.

# Chapter Ten Answers

## The labour market

### Important concepts and technical terms

| | | | |
|---|---|---|---|
| **①** d | **④** k | **⑦** l | **⑩** g |
| **②** a | **⑤** f | **⑧** h | **⑪** b |
| **③** i | **⑥** j | **⑨** c | **⑫** e |

### Exercises

**①**   **(a)** and **(b)** See Table A10–1 (overleaf).

**(c)**  See Fig. A10–1.

**Figure A10–1**  MVPL, MRPL

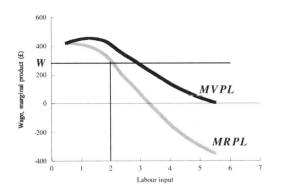

**(d)**  Adding the wage cost line to Fig. A10–1 shows that profit will be maximized at 2 units of labour input – the firm will continue to hire labour as long as the **MRPL** exceeds the wage.

**(e)**  With 2 units of labour input, total revenue is $80 \times 10 = 800$.

Capital cost is 200; wage cost is $280 \times 2 = 560$. Profits are $800 - 200 - 560 = £40$.

**②**   **(a)** *OD*.

**(b)**  *OC*.

**(c)**  *OA*.

**(d)**  *OB*.

**(e)**  Both tend to reduce labour demand.

**③**   See Fig. A10–2.

**Figure A10–2**  An individual's supply of labour

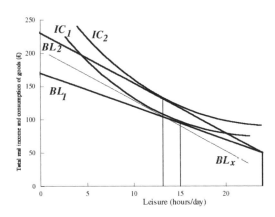

**(a)**  With the wage rate at £2.50, and with £20 unearned income, the maximum earnings for 24 hours would be $20 + 24 \times 2.5 = £80$ (but wouldn't George be tired!). The budget line is thus $BL_1$.

**(b)**  $BL_1$ is at a tangent to $IC_1$ at about 15 hours' leisure – so George works nine hours.

**(c)**  The budget line moves to $BL_2$.

**(d)**  George now chooses to work more hours and take only about 13 hours' leisure.

| Labour input (workers/week) | Output (goods/week) | Marginal physical product of labour (MPL) | Price (£) | Total revenue | Marginal revenue per unit output | Marginal value product of labour (MVPL) | Marginal revenue product of labour (MRPL) |
|---|---|---|---|---|---|---|---|
| 0 | 0 | | | 0 | | | |
| 1 | 35 | 35 | 12 | 420 | 12.00 | 420 | 420.00 |
| 2 | 80 | 45 | 10 | 800 | 8.44 | 450 | 378.00 |
| 3 | 122 | 42 | 8 | 976 | 4.19 | 336 | 176.00 |
| 4 | 156 | 34 | 6 | 936 | −1.18 | 204 | −40.12 |
| 5 | 177 | 21 | 4 | 708 | −10.86 | 84 | −228.00 |
| 6 | 180 | 3 | 2 | 360 | −116.00 | 6 | −348.00 |

**Table 10–1** Output and labour supply of labour

(e) The 'income' effect can be seen by adding a new budget line parallel to $BL_2$, tangent to $IC_1$. This is $BL_x$ in Fig. A10–2. It shows leisure to be a normal good for George.

**4** (a) Wage would be $OB$ and employment $OJ$.

(b) As demand for its product declines, the industry must reduce prices: this will affect the marginal revenue product of labour and reduce labour demand. In the diagram, this could be represented by a move to $D'_L$ with a new equilibrium at wage $OA$ and employment $OI$. The supply curve is not affected.

(c) As wages increase elsewhere, clerical workers will prefer to leave in quest of better pay, so the supply of labour to our industry falls to $S'_L$. In the new equilibrium, wage is $OE$ and employment $OH$. The demand curve is not affected.

(d) With demand $D'L$, supply $SL$ and wage $OB$ there is excess supply of labour – i.e. unemployment. There are $GJ$ workers who would like to obtain work in the industry, but cannot at that wage rate.

**5** (a) $OP$.

(b) $OPYZ$.

(c) $PRWY$.

(d) $OQ$.

**6** (a) $OAED$.

(b) $ABE$.

(c) Economic rent would be higher, transfer earnings correspondingly lower.

**7** (b).

**8** See Fig. A10–3.

**Figure A10–3** Cost minimization for a firm

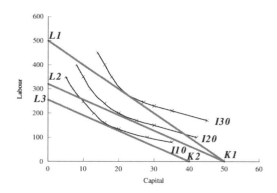

(a) The isoquants are labelled $I_{10}$, $I_{20}$ and $I_{30}$ on the diagram. (If you are unfamiliar with these concepts, you should consult the Appendix to Chapter 10 in the main text.)

(b) The isocost line is given by the line $L_1 K_1$.

(c) The isocost line is tangent to the $I_{30}$ isoquant, so the maximum possible output is 30 units, for which the firm uses 290 units of labour and 21 units of capital.

(d) The new isocost is $L_2 K_1$.

(e) 20 units of output, using 200 units of labour and 20 units of capital.

(f) Labour use is reduced by 31 per cent and capital use by only 4.8 per cent. This is as we would expect – the 'output effect' leads to a reduction in both inputs, but the change in relative factor prices leads to a substitution effect towards capital.

(g) The isocost line $L_3 K_2$ shows that the firm produces 10 units of output, with 160 labour and 16 capital.

**9** All of them: these are discussed in Section 10–7 of the main text.

**10** See the discussion in Section 10–7 of the main text.

## True/False

**1** False: non-monetary differences in working conditions will give rise to an equalizing wage differential (see the introduction to Chapter 10 in the main text).

**2** False: the firm will tend to employ relatively more capital, but will probably employ less of both (see Exercise **8** of this chapter).

**3** True.

**4** True: statements 3 and 4 are equivalent (see Section 10–2 of the main text).

**5** True.

**6** False: $MRPL < MVPL$.

**7** False: this ignores the effect of changing industry supply upon output price (see Section 10–3 of the main text).

**8** False: an individual may choose to enjoy more leisure and work fewer hours (see Section 10–4 of the main text).

**9** True.

**10** True: see Section 10–5 of the main text.

**11** True: see Section 10–6 of the main text.

**12** True: see Section 10–7 of the main text.

## Economics in action

**1** Given that Janine was willing to work for £10 000 less than she is now, it might be argued that her economic rent is the extra £10 000 she is now being paid. But if she is now aware that the market rate for a risk analyst is £10 000 higher, then maybe she has raised her reservation wage by £10 000. If so, then her economic rent is 0.

**2** The problem with the marginal revenue product theory of labour demand is that it assumes a free and open market in labour, where the labour is fairly homogeneous and is traded regularly. In practice, many jobs are differentiated even within the same office or work environment. Moreover, labour is traded infrequently and therefore market conditions are always changing. In one month 50 workers may apply for a job, the month after only one may apply. This will have an impact on wage negotiations between employer and potential employee.

## Questions for thought

**1** The methods are equivalent: think about the nature of short-run marginal cost.

**2** **(a)** Point $A$.

**(b)** The budget line is given by the line $BC$ in Fig. A10–4.

**(c)** If Helen were to work, then she would choose to be at point $X$, where the budget line is at a tangent to $IC_1$. Here she would be working six hours per day. However, she will not in fact do this, as she obtains more utility by not working and being at point $A$ on indifference curve $IC_2$.

**(d)** The effect of overtime, paid at a premium rate, is to kink the budget line after eight hours' work, shown by the line $CDE$ in Fig. A10–4.

**(e)** Helen can now reach a tangency point with $IC_3$ and will work $(12 - L_0)$ hours.

**3** **(a)** The isocost which has a tangency point with the $3X$ isoquant is $C_2$ (tangency at point $C$ in Fig. 10–8).

**(b)** The distance from $G$ to $C$ is much smaller than from $C$ to $F$: more labour is needed to increase output from $3X$ to $4X$ than from $2X$ to $3X$. We are observing diminishing returns to a variable factor, in this case, labour.

**(c)** Notice the relative distances between the points $ABCDE$. At first, the isoquants move closer together, but then they get further apart as output increases. At first, there are economies of scale, but then diseconomies set in: the long-run average cost curve is U-shaped.

**Figure A10–4** Labour supply with overtime

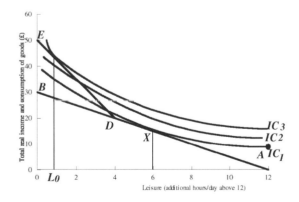

# Chapter Eleven Answers
## Different types of labour

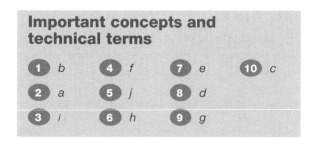

### Important concepts and technical terms

**1** b    **4** f    **7** e    **10** c

**2** a    **5** j    **8** d

**3** i    **6** h    **9** g

### Exercises

**1**   (a) Total benefits amount to 2500 + 9000 = 11 500. Total costs amount to 3000 + 7000 = 10 000 (both in 'present value' (PV) terms). Ian would thus choose further education, as the benefits outweigh the costs.

(b) If Ian were to fail to obtain the qualification, then the additional future income would not be forthcoming. In the calculations, Ian would reduce his valuation of this item.

(c) Joanne would place a lower valuation on the non-monetary benefits of student life. Whether or not she decides to continue in education depends upon how little she expects to enjoy herself.

(d) Keith is likely to use a different discount rate when assessing the present value of future costs and benefits. On the other hand, he could place a high valuation on 'student life', so again his decision could go either way.

**2**   (a) See Fig. A11–1.

**Figure A11–1** Age–earnings profiles for three groups of workers

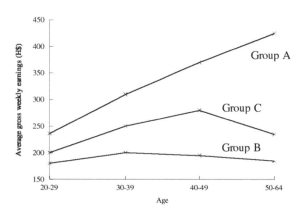

(b) (i) Group **C**.

(ii) Group **B**.

(iii) Group **A**.

Profiles based upon authentic UK information may be seen in Section 11–1 of the main text.

**3**   (a) and (c) could be explained in terms of differences in occupational structure, and by themselves do not provide evidence of discrimination. It is possible that differences in occupational choice may reflect earlier discrimination in educational opportunities, but that is a separate issue. Observation (b) avoids the occupational explanation, but differences in pay here may reflect employers' different evaluation of the future productivity of men and women rather than overt discrimination. Observation (d) offers the strongest evidence of discrimination, as here we have a closely defined skill level and presumably similar marginal products of black and white workers, and yet we observe differences in earnings. For more discussion, see Section 11–2 of the main text.

**4**   (a) Wage *OA*, employment *OH*.

(b) *OC*.

(c) *DBDB*: the demand curve becomes more elastic.

(d) Wage *OC*, employment *OD*.

(e) *OB*.

**5**   These are all arguments that have been advanced to explain the differential in pay between men and women. Factor (a) is true, but we can adjust for it by considering pay of full-time workers only – and we find that the differential is still substantial. Men do tend to work in different occupations and industries (b), partly because of biological differences (f), which make men more suited to heavy physical labour. In the past, there has also been a tendency for manufacturing activity to be male-dominated and for services to be more female-based. As the structure of the economy has changed, this has been one factor which has led to an ever-increasing proportion of females in total employment. Firms may often perceive that women are more likely to have their working-life interrupted by the demands of child-bearing and child-rearing. This may lead them to offer less training to women (c), and perhaps to promote them less rapidly, as they see that the returns on their training expenditure may be lessened by these career interruptions. Educational choices made by females tend to be different from those of males (d) and (e):

there is still a tendency for fewer females to take mathematical or scientific subjects, and for fewer women to proceed to higher education. This may mean that they end up in lower-paid occupations. Some of these factors can be taken into account in calculations of the wage differential between the genders, but it seems that some differential remains, so that there is still some discrimination *(g)* in levels of pay offered by employers to males and females, but it is probably less widespread than in earlier years.

**6**    **(a)**  The earnings forgone by not accepting employment in another occupation, perhaps in manufacturing industry.

**(b)**  The high future expected returns will attract some people into the professions; others may prefer to earn now; others may not feel themselves well-suited to life in a white-collar or professional occupation.

**(c)**  The manufacturing sector in the UK has been in decline for a number of years now, and unemployment is especially high among young people. This may lower the opportunity cost of undertaking professional training, as alternative earnings opportunities may be limited. This is thus likely to lead to an increase in the demand for training, and ultimately entry to the profession. Of course, there will still be some individuals who realize that their talents and abilities are not likely to lead them to receive high returns in the professions.

**(d)**  In the long run, the results are unclear. The changing structure of the economy may continue to move against manufacturing activity, such that the demand for members of the professions continues to expand. On the other hand, the increased numbers of qualified entrants to the profession will have an effect on the supply curve. If you sketch a demand and supply diagram, you will be able to check out the possible effects of these movements for yourself.

**7**    Trade unions will be in a relatively strong situation when *(a)* there is excess demand for labour, or when *(b)* there is a closed shop. However, if *(c)* the *MRPL* is below the wage rate, then their position in arguing for even higher wages is considerably weakened. Similarly, when *(d)* unemployment is at a relatively high level, employers will have less need to bid for labour by offering higher wages. If *(e)* the demand for labour is highly inelastic, the trade union's position is relatively strong, for it may be able to negotiate higher wages with very little fall in employment levels. However, if the union *(f)* faces a monopsony buyer of labour, it will find that its own market power is partly matched by that of the employer.

**8**    **(a)**  These rates of return compare very favourably with the rates of return typically expected on investment projects involving physical assets, especially in Africa and Latin America. This emphasizes the importance of human capital, especially in less developed countries (LDCs).

**(b)**  Education levels in many LDCs are much lower than in the industrial countries, whether we measure them in terms of literacy rates or mean years of schooling received. Thus the returns to investing in education are high, because there is so much potential. None the less, in many cases investment in human capital remains low, either because physical capital is more tangible and therefore seems more important, or simply because of lack of resources.

**(c)**  Private returns are maximized at 'higher' levels in Africa and Asia, and are equal in Latin America and the industrial countries.

**(d)**  Social returns, however, are higher at secondary level in all the country groups.

**(e)**  Unfortunately, in many LDCs the political influence of those who are likely to benefit from higher education has distorted resource allocation away from the secondary (and primary) sector in favour of higher education. Higher education tends to be heavily subsidized, but open only to a minority, in spite of the fact that higher social returns are available in the secondary stage.

**(f)**  A further problem is that different groups in society will perceive the returns from education in different ways. A poor rural family may expect to gain much less from education and to face higher costs than a rich urban family. This may be especially the case in terms of the opportunity cost of education; for example, it may be that a poor family sees a child in school as a child not working in the fields. This may be especially significant at secondary school level. This may help explain the political pressures mentioned in *(e)*.

## True/False

**1**    True.

**2**    False: workers with general training are highly mobile between firms, so it pays the firm to offer low pay during training but relatively high pay to the qualified worker (see Section 11–1 of the main text).

**3**    False: degree training may act as a signalling device.

**4**   False: this statement ignores the opportunity cost of further schooling and the different marginal utilities of income of rich and poor families.

**5**   True: and notice it is the perception that is important, not the actuality (see Section 11–2 of the main text).

**6**   False: the difference in pay may reflect other factors, such as occupational choice, educational training and so on. This is not to say that there may not be discrimination in some covert or overt form in some parts of the economy.

**7**   True: see discussion in Section 11–2 of the main text.

**8**   False: the true figure is just over one-half (see Section 11–3 of the main text).

**9**   False: we should not compare these low-paid workers with other groups of workers, but rather should ask what rates of pay they would have received in the absence of the union.

**10**   True.

**11**   No longer true.

## Economics in action

**1**   Informational asymmetry occurs when one individual knows more about themselves than another individual. This clearly occurs in the case of the recruitment and selection of workers. The potential employee, having an informational advantage, can select those aspects of their individual characteristics and employment history which they wish to share with the potential employer. The employer knows this risk exists and will ordinarily seek to avoid making an adverse selection, that is hiring an individual who is not as good as they appear on their CV.

**2**   Women in their 30s may be more likely to fib or hide information on their CV if they fear a greater degree of labour market discrimination. A source of discrimination for such women may be career breaks to have children or employment breaks to follow husbands/partners when they change job and location.

## Questions for thought

**1**   This issue is tackled towards the end of Section 11–1 in the main text. It is one example where there may be a divergence between the interests of the individual and those of society at large. This sort of situation is reconsidered in Chapters 16 and 17.

**2**   This issue is discussed towards the end of Section 11–3 in the main text.

**3**   We would normally expect that a trade union will bargain for higher wages, and that this would be at the cost of accepting a lower employment level. There is one exception to this, however. Consider Fig. A11–2.

**Figure A11–2**   Do trade unions always reduce employment?

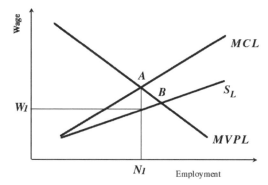

Suppose a firm operating with perfect competition in the product market is a monopsonist in the labour market. $S_L$ represents the supply curve of labour and $MC_L$ the marginal cost of labour as faced by the firm: *MVPL* constitutes the demand curve for labour. Before the trade union appears on the scene, the firm employs $N_1$ at a wage of $W_1$. When the firm is unionized, it is possible to negotiate with the firm to be at any position along the *MVPL*. At any point along the section *AB* it is possible for the union to negotiate both an increase in wages and an increase in employment. This is a very special case, which is why this question appears in the 'Questions for thought' section of the chapter.

**4**   If we regard the trade union as a monopoly seller of labour, then we can think of $D_L$ as being the equivalent of the 'AR' curve faced by the monopolist. Associated with this AR curve there is of course also an 'MR' curve, which we can think of as the 'marginal returns' from selling labour. This will have the form shown in Fig. A11–3, with a slope twice as steep as $D_L$. If we then think of $S_L$ as being the equivalent of the marginal cost curve of the monopolist, then the returns to selling labour ('profits') are maximized where $MR = S_L$, at employment level $N_T$ and wage $W_T$.

**5**   A shift from manufacturing to services will create structural unemployment. Women will be attracted into the labour force by the new service sector jobs in say retailing. Meanwhile men with manufacturing skills will find it difficult to move into the service sector. Overall unemployment will rise.

**Figure A11–3**   A trade union in a labour market

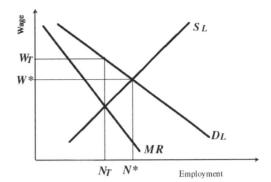

# Chapter Twelve Answers

## Factor markets and income distribution

### Important concepts and technical terms

**1**  c       **5**  m       **9**  b       **13**  j

**2**  a       **6**  n       **10**  d       **14**  g

**3**  l       **7**  k       **11**  e

**4**  i       **8**  f       **12**  h

### Exercises

**1**   (a)  Stock.

(b)   Stock.

(c)   Flow.

(d)   Stock

(e)   Flow.

(f)   Flow.

**2**   (a)  The rate of interest may be calculated as the constant annual coupon payment (£10) divided by the bond price (£62.50), i.e. 10/62.5 = 0.16, or 16 per cent.

(b)   13⅓ per cent.

(c)   Price of bond = present value = coupon value/interest rate, i.e. price = 10/0.08 = £125.

**3**   (a)  12 per cent.

(b)   12 – 14 = 2 per cent (approximately).

(c)   With a negative real rate of interest, Lucy would do better to spend the money now, as the return on money saved is not sufficient to compensate for changing goods prices.

(d)   The real rate of interest would then be +2 per cent, and Lucy might be encouraged to save the money and spend later – unless she is impatient for the goods!

**4**   To calculate the break-even price for the machine, we simply sum the present value rows of Table A12–1, with the following results.

**Table A12–1   Present value calculations**

| Data | Year 1 | Year 2 | Year 3 |
|---|---|---|---|
| Stream of earnings | 2000 | 2000 | 2000 |
| Scrap value | | | 6000 |
| Present value | | | |
| (a) $r$ = 8% | 1851.85* | 1714.68* | 6350.66 |
| Present value | | | |
| (b) $r$ = 10% | 1818.18 | 1652.89 | 6010.52 |
| Present value | | | |
| (c) $r$ = 8%; | 1980.20 | 1960.59 | 7764.72 |
| inflation = 7% | | | |

Notes: * The present value (PV) of £2000 in Year 1 when the rate of interest is 8 per cent is calculated as:

$$2000/(1.08) = 1851.85$$

After Year 2, the calculation is 2000/(1.08)2

The PV calculations for (c) are based on a real interest rate of 1 per cent – i.e. after 1 year:

$$2000/1.01 = 1980.20$$

(See the Appendix to Chapter 12 in the main text for details.)

(a) £1851.85 + £1714.68 + £6350.66 = £9917.19.

(b) £9841.59.

(c) £11 705.51.

**5** (a) Equilibrium will occur when the rental rate is the same as the two sectors, and when their joint demand exhausts the supply of land. This happens when the rental is *OA*, at which level, *OD* land is used for agriculture and *OH* for industry. (Note that *OD = HJ*.)

(b) In the short run, land use cannot change, so *OD* is used for agriculture and *OH* for industry.

(c) The rental rate in agriculture increases to *OC*, but the rental in industry remains at *OA*.

(d) In the long run, the high rental rate in agriculture relative to that on industrial land encourages the transfer of land from industry to agriculture. This continues until the rental is the same for both sectors. This occurs at rental *OB*, with *OE* land in agricultural use and *OG* in industry. *OE + OG = OJ*.

**6** (a) Annual cost of the machine is calculated as the real interest cost plus the cost of maintenance and depreciation, i.e.:

25 000 × (0.10 − 0.08 + 0.12) = £3500.

This is the required rental – the proceeds necessary for the firm to cover the opportunity cost of buying the equipment.

(b) An increase in the inflation rate reduces the real interest cost of the loan, so the required rental falls to £3000.

**7** (a) In order to identify the initial position, we need first to understand what change is to take place. A reduction in the wage, which makes capital relatively more expensive, will shift the demand curve for capital to the right. Thus *DB* in Fig. 12–2 must be the initial position: quantity is *OD* and the rental on capital is *OB*.

(b) The rental rate on capital when the market is in long-run equilibrium represents the opportunity cost of capital.

(c) After the wage cut, we find that capital is fixed in the short run at *SSC*, and the rental rate will thus increase to *OC*, with quantity remaining at *OD*.

(d) This position cannot be sustained: the rental *OC* is now above the opportunity cost of capital, *OB*, so capital will be attracted into this industry.

(e) The industry will settle in the long run when the rental on capital has returned to the original (long-run equilibrium) rate of *OB*; the quantity of capital is now *OH*.

(f) We normally think of these additions to capital in an industry as being investment.

**8** All statements are valid: see Section 12–11 of the main text.

**9** The straight line *OA* in Fig. A12–1 would represent a perfectly equal distribution of income. *LC₁* represents the distribution of original income in the UK and *LC₂* the distribution of post-tax income – noticeably nearer to the straight line. *LC₃* shows that the distribution of after-tax income in Brazil in 1995 was very skewed.

**Figure A12–1** Lorenz curves

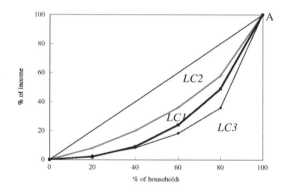

**10** (a) *D* is the equilibrium, where the price line, PPF, and indifference curve all touch.

(b) *OE* represents maximum current consumption, *OC* is actual consumption, so the difference *CE* is savings.

(c) *OA*: but starvation may set in before the 'future' is reached if no resources are currently consumed.

(d) By the slope of the PPF.

(e) The rate of interest.

**11** Suppose the interest rate increases. The consumer's trade-off between current and future consumption changes, as more future consumption can be obtained for a given sacrifice in the present. The substitution effect thus suggests that savings will increase with the interest rate. The real income effect is likely to operate in the reverse direction: at higher interest rates less saving is required to generate a given future income level. We cannot be certain of the net effect, but it is probable that the substitution effect will win – that is, higher interest rates will tend to encourage savings.

**12** (b) and (*f*) would cause the PPF to steepen; (*a*) affects the shape of the society's indifference curves. (*c*) and (*d*) affect the slope of the price line; (*e*) refers to a movement along the PPF.

## True/False

**1**    False: not government bonds (see the introduction to Chapter 12 in the the main text).

**2**    True.

**3**    False: the rental payments must be discounted to give the present value (PV).

**4**    False: it is the real interest rate that matters.

**5**    True.

**6**    False: even in the short run, capital services can be varied to some extent by overtime working, shift adjustment, etc. (see Section 12–5 of the main text).

**7**    True.

**8**    True to an extent: but, as with labour, all land is not the same and some land may, in practice, command relatively high rentals because of its characteristics.

**9**    True.

**10**    True: see Section 12–10 of the main text.

**11**    False: declined from 64.3 per cent to 63.4 per cent (see Section 12–11 of the main text).

**12**    True: see Section 12–11 of the main text.

## Economics in action

**1**    Chelsea and Kensington is the UK wealth 'hotspot' with the highest number of individuals earning more than £60 000 a year. High Peak has shown the fastest growth rate in the number of individuals earning more than £60 000.

**2**    A simple explanation for why the rich keep getting richer is that high labour income enables the purchase of additional income-generating assets. So the accumulation of wealth supports the accumulation of income-generating assets. Therefore, the rich, when compared with the poor, are less reliant on labour income. The rich have diversified sources of wealth which enable better long-term growth in wealth (it might be argued).

## Questions for thought

**1**    The distinction between economic rent and transfer earnings is discussed in Section 12–6 of the main text.

**2**    Clearly, energy is a crucial input to almost every production process, and there is an extent to which we can think of energy as being a potential substitute for other factors. For instance, we may think of choices of technology which allow alternative combinations of labour, capital and energy. This became important especially after the oil price shocks, where the sudden change in the real price of energy caused a search for more energy-efficient techniques of production.

# Chapter Thirteen Answers

## Risk and information

## Important concepts and technical terms

| | | | | | | | |
|---|---|---|---|---|---|---|---|
| **1** | c | **5** | n | **9** | b | **13** | i |
| **2** | a | **6** | k | **10** | d | **14** | h |
| **3** | l | **7** | f | **11** | e | | |
| **4** | m | **8** | j | **12** | g | | |

## Exercises

**1**    **(a)** Maureen is risk-averse.

Nora is a risk-lover.

Olga is risk-neutral.

**(d)** You may well have been risk-averse like Maureen in choosing not to buy in *(b)*. However, Maureen tells us that if she had lots of money, she might accept the deal. This, of course, reflects the diminishing marginal utility of wealth (see Section 13–1 of the main text).

**2** Risk-pooling occurs in situations *(b)*, *(c)* and *(e)*, where relatively large numbers of people face the risk, each with a relatively small likelihood of needing to claim.

**3** Moral hazard is present in cases *(a)*, *(b)* and *(d)*. In case *(d)*, the probability of rain is unaffected by the insurance, but the size of the bills is not. *(c)* and *(e)* are concerned with adverse selection.

**4** **(a)** £24.

**(b)** £12.

**(c)** £18.

**(d)** 50 per cent.

**(e)** Still £18.

**(f)** The chance that both industries hit bad times together is now only 25 per cent, so you have reduced the risk by diversifying.

**5** **(a)** 3.

**(b)** 4.

**(c)** 5. See Box 13–2 in the main text.

**(d)** 2.

**(e)** 1.

**6** If the Efficient Markets theory of the stock market is correct, then any method relying on past information is doomed to failure, as current share prices already incorporate the effects of past information. The best hope is to be the first trader to respond to new relevant information – i.e. option *(e)*. If the market were a casino, then option *(b)* might be as effective as anything else (see Section 13–5 of the main text).

**7** *(c)* and *(e)* are correct: a share with negative beta tends to move against the market, and thus reduces the risk of a portfolio. Most shares move with the market, and thus have a beta close to 1.

**8** *(a)*.

## True/False

**1** False: on the contrary, the risk-lover gains utility from risk (see Section 13–1 of the main text).

**2** True.

**3** True: see Section 13–2 of the main text.

**4** True.

**5** False: see Section 13–3 of the main text.

**6** True: see Section 13–4 of the main text.

**7** True: this was James Tobin's characterization.

**8** False: it is precisely when share returns are negatively correlated that diversification is most successful.

**9** False: low beta shares will be highly valued (see Section 13–4 of the main text).

**10** True: see Section 13–5 of the main text.

**11** False: whether or not prices would be stabilized is irrelevant; the point is that a forward market in cars is not a viable proposition (see Section 13–6 of the main text).

**12** False: they would be speculating.

## Economics in action

**1** Stocks that seem to have little in common can be described as having 'independent returns'. The word 'independent' is important, signifying that the financial returns from one stock are unrelated to the level of financial returns from another stock.

**2** Consider two portfolios. The first has two stocks which have independent returns. The second has two stocks that are highly dependent upon each other. The returns from the first portfolio will be less risky as the returns from each stock are likely to balance each other, when one is high and the other may be low. In the second portfolio, risk is greater with returns across the two stocks moving together, resulting in less smoothing of the returns over time.

**3** You can reduce the risk of a portfolio only by adding stocks with independent returns. It is therefore difficult to keep finding and adding stocks that have returns which are independent of stocks already in the portfolio. For example, adding another bank to a portfolio which already contains a bank is unlikely to reduce risk, as the banks' returns will be correlated.

## Questions for thought

**1** See Section 13–3 of the main text.

**2** and **3** See Section 13–5 of the main text.

**4** Moral hazard may be thought to be a potential problem in the case of unemployment insurance. In the case of health insurance, adverse selection is a possibility.

# Chapter Fourteen Answers

## The information economy

### Important concepts and technical terms

| | | | | | | | |
|---|---|---|---|---|---|---|---|
| **1** | b | **4** | e | **7** | d | **10** | k |
| **2** | f | **5** | a | **8** | c | **11** | i |
| **3** | h | **6** | l | **9** | j | **12** | g |

### Exercises

**1** Section 14–1 of the main text discusses the characteristics of information, or E-products. The key feature is that they can be digitally encoded, which means that they can be transmitted rapidly, accurately and cheaply. This clearly excludes tangible goods such as the pencil, refrigerator and computer. Of course, in their own way, each is critical to the transmission of information. Indeed, the computer is a key part of the infrastructure that has enabled the information economy to take off as it has. Why did we include the refrigerator in this list, when it seems such an odd one out? As this book was being prepared, the TV programme *Tomorrow's World* highlighted a refrigerator connected to the Internet which enabled the consumer to keep a shopping list up to date by monitoring what was removed from storage. The other items on the list may be information products, although attendance at live music concerts and football matches is not yet a thing of the past.

**2** **(a)** We doubt that you would subscribe sight unseen, as this is an example of an 'experience product' – one that you need to sample in order to evaluate its worth.

**(b)** All these things may be an inducement. Reputation of the provider (i) may reassure you as to the quality of the product, especially if you have personal experience on which to draw (iii), or if you can sample the product in person in order to evaluate it (ii, iv). Firms providing services over the Internet often use such offers to try to attract customers. As for (v), we all do strange things at times of panic!

**3** **(a)** Production costs (A) in this context are the fixed costs of producing an information product, whereas reproduction and distribution are variable costs.

**(b)** The fixed costs entailed in producing an information product are often substantial. The compilation of an electronic dictionary, or the recording of a soundtrack, may be large. However, it is a characteristic of information products that the variable costs, of reproduction and distribution (for example, via the Internet), may be negligible.

**(c)** With large fixed costs and negligible marginal costs, there are likely to be large economies of scale in the production of these goods and services.

**4** **(a)** *C*.

**(b)** *D*.

**(c)** The more people that use the network, the more attractive it becomes to others. For example, the more people with email accounts, the more useful email becomes. So, the demand curve shifts to the right.

**(d)** *DB* would be the demand curve, and *F* the equilibrium quantity demanded.

**(e)** See the demand curve *DL* in Fig. A14–1 (overleaf).

**5** There is a sense in which each of these goods is subject to some versioning. Books are discussed in Section 14–3 of the main text. Price discrimination is achieved by issuing a book first in hardback only, then subsequently in paperback – and in some cases at remaindered prices at an even later date. This picks up different groups of buyers. Railways and air travel are 'versioned' through the provision of First Class or Business Class travel arrangements.

**Figure A14–1** Demand with a network externally

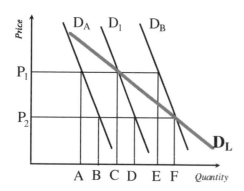

Computer software also comes in different versions – sometimes a basic version is issued free, with consumers having the option to purchase a 'professional' edition once they become tied in to the product. As for sausages, look in your local Tesco or other supermarket. You will find basic sausages on sale, but also 'finest' designer sausages in a variety of flavours.

**6** **(a)** This describes the attribute of an 'experience product' – until you have tried it you cannot judge it.

**(b)** However, once you have bought a piece of information, you don't need to buy it again. This complicates things for the producer, who cannot give you the product to sample without destroying its value to you. However, a number of ways of getting around this have been devised.

**(c)** One of the big problems with information is that there is so much of it about! It is easy to get into a situation of 'information overload', where there is so much information that it is useless to you because you cannot find your way around it. This is where search engines become invaluable.

**(d)** This relates to the issue of switching costs. Once you become committed to a product, you may find that the costs of switching become substantial. The cost of reformatting all your files so that you can use a new word processor or graphics package may be more hassle than you are prepared to face.

**(e)** Finally, this relates to the existence of network externalities. Fax machines caught on only when lots of people had them, more than a century after the technology was invented.

**7** **(a)** £95: your costs of £30, and the client's hassle costs of £65.

**(b)** It does not seem likely to be worthwhile, as the switching costs exceed the expected profit stream.

**(c)** Now perhaps it is viable.

**(d)** You could afford to offer the client a couple of month's free access that would compensate her for the hassle of switching, or you could devote some funds to advertising the product to convince her that there were benefits in switching.

**(e)** It would make sense for Comp.or to find a way of exaggerating the switching costs to make it more difficult for her to change to your product.

**8** **(a)** At these prices, Anna would buy pizza and Bob would buy treacle tart, so revenue would be £6.

**(b)** Now, Anna would still buy pizza, Bob would still buy treacle tart and Caroline would buy both. Revenue would be £8.

**(c)** Now the supermarket gets the best possible deal. By bundling the goods in this way, Anna buys pizza (at £3), Bob buys treacle tart (also at £3) and Caroline buys both (for £4). Revenue is £10.

**(d)** The reward card schemes run by supermarkets enable them to keep a close watch on who buys what and at what prices. They can use this information to devise tailored deals for individual customers.
(This exercise is based on an example used by Robin Mason in 'Reward cards: who profits?', *Economic Review*, 17(1), September 1999.)

**9** Given that most information products display substantial economies of scale, it is virtually impossible for perfectly competitive markets to develop, as the largest firm is always in a position of cost leadership relative to smaller firms. The market is thus likely to develop into a monopoly (Windows runs on an estimated 90 per cent of PCs around the world), or possibly a sequence of monopolistically competitive markets, in which there is much product differentiation serving niche consumer groups.

## True/False

**1** False: the expected increase is much larger. In early 2000, it was predicted that e-commerce would rise from £13 bn to £150 bn in Western Europe between 1999 and 2005.

**2** False: it took even less time than this – see Fig. 14–1 in the main text.

**3** True: at least to some extent. Suppliers of information products need to adopt a strategy that allows you to sample the product without giving you all of it – see Section 14–2 of the main text.

**4**  True: see Section 14–2 of the main text.

**5**  True: see the discussion of switching costs in Section 14–2 of the main text. Of course, there may be a price at which a user may be prepared to switch, if the benefits of the new package are sufficiently attractive.

**6**  True: see the discussion of network externalities in Section 14–2 of the main text.

**7**  False: the existence of strong economies of scale makes perfect competition an extremely unlikely result – see Section 14–3 of the main text.

**8**  True: see Section 14–3 of the main text.

**9**  True: bundling is discussed in Section 14–3 of the main text.

**10**  It depends . . . strategic alliances may facilitate cost reductions and enable firms to deliver an improved product to consumers. However, we also know that collusion between firms in an oligopoly market may lead to a deadweight loss for society by impairing resource allocation.

**11**  False: the Europeans resolved this issue in the early 1990s, enabling rapid expansion and access to economies of scale that were denied to US firms. See Section 14–4 of the main text.

**12**  False: this chapter has shown how economics provides insights into the effects of the information revolution – see Section 14–5 of the main text.

## Economics in action

**1**  E-products are generally thought to have very high fixed costs and very low marginal costs. The setting up of Internet servers, developing websites and promoting websites is an expensive set-up cost. But the provision of ticketing services to an individual customer is very cheap. There is no need for a ticket salesperson, or an office/shop to locate them in. Therefore, if two similar companies can merge, they can exploit economies of scale and reduce costs.

**2**  If fixed costs are high, then selling more tickets will reduce average fixed costs. Therefore, moving from 10 per cent to 20 per cent of the market will help to cover the very high fixed costs of operating an Internet-based business.

## Questions for thought

**1**  Economics has a simple story to tell about Internet pricing – if you price a good at zero, too much of the good will be demanded, and there is likely to be a congestion problem. Even if marginal costs of providing the service are zero, some fixed charge needs to be levied to cover the fixed costs. (This issue is discussed more fully by Martin Chalkley in 'Internet economics', *Economic Review*, 16(4), April 1999.)

**2**  Firms are often reluctant to lose their individual identities by merging into a single firm, and sometimes the management culture of different companies makes a merger difficult to manage. Strategic alliances offer much more flexibility. If market conditions change, then it is not too difficult to disentangle the two partners, whereas the demerging of companies is far more costly. At the end of the day, it comes down to transactions costs. There are costs involved with both mergers and alliances. Mergers impose inflexibility and other costs. In an alliance, each firm must monitor how the other partner is working. The question is which set of costs is the greater. Presumably Microsoft and Intel decided that the costs of a merger were excessive as compared to the potential benefits.

**3**  We are not going to pronounce on this topic one way or the other. The discussion in the main text of the economic principles surrounding this case should give you plenty of material to enable discussion of the topic with your fellow students. Indeed, by the time you read this the matter may have progressed further than the interim judgment of the US Justice Department against Microsoft.

# Chapter Fifteen Answers

## Welfare economics

### Important concepts and technical terms

| | | | | | | | |
|---|---|---|---|---|---|---|---|
| **1** | d | **4** | g | **7** | f | **10** | i |
| **2** | a | **5** | k | **8** | e | **11** | j |
| **3** | b | **6** | l | **9** | h | **12** | c |

### Exercises

**1** (a) *D*, *F* and *H* each make at least one of our two subjects better off without making the other worse off. For instance, at *D* Ursula is better off and Vince no worse off. Both are better off at *F*.

(b) *C* and *E*.

(c) *B* and *G* cannot be judged either superior or inferior to *A*: in each case one individual is better off, but at the expense of the other. This does not mean that 'society' is indifferent between *A*, *B* and *G*. The three points represent distributions of goods between which the Pareto criterion cannot judge.

(d) *C*, *E*.

(e) *A*, *B*, *G*.

(f) *D*, *F*, *H*.

**2** (a) £10, this being the purchase price of books.

(b) 2, reflecting the ratio of prices (marginal utility) of the two goods.

(c) Marginal cost of the last book was £10, last unit of food, £20. Under perfect competition, equilibrium price = marginal cost (this was discussed in Chapter 9).

(d) As 'job satisfaction' is equal in the two sectors, so too will be the wage rate in equilibrium – otherwise there would be movement of labour.

(e) 2:1.

(f) 2, reflecting the difference in the marginal physical product of labour.

(g) The allocation is Pareto-efficient – there is no feasible reallocation of resources which will make society better off.

If you have had difficulty following the chain of arguments in this exercise, you should re-read Section 15–2 in the main text, where a similar exercise is discussed in more detail.

**3** (a) Price *OC*, quantity *OG*.

(b) The new supply curve is *SA*. Equilibrium price would be *OD*, quantity *OF*. Tax is *AD*.

(c) Marginal social cost is *OA*. Marginal consumer benefit is *OD*. This allocation is socially inefficient, as too few books are being produced.

(d) Price *OK*, quantity *OP*.

(e) It is not a satisfactory allocation because marginal social cost *(OM)* is greater than marginal private benefit *(OK)* at this price: 'too much' food is being produced.

(f) The books tax causes a distortion, such that *MSC* represents the true marginal social cost in terms of the utility forgone by using resources in food rather than books.

(g) The preferred output would be *ON* at price *OL*, where the marginal social cost equals the marginal social benefit of food production. This could be achieved by a tax of size *JL*. This topic is discussed in Section 15–3 of the main text.

**4** (b), (c) and (e) all indicate that distortions exist which lead to market failure. (a) – traffic congestion – is not ' evidence of market failure. Just as the optimal level of pollution may not be zero, so there may be some 'optimal' level of congestion. As far as (d) is concerned, it is not the divergence of marginal social and private benefit which matters: the issue is whether marginal social cost is equated to marginal benefit.

**5** Pavement-fouling imposes a cost on society in that it reduces the utility of other people or forces someone to bear the cost of clearing it. The absence of a charge for dog ownership would tend to lead to there being more dogs than is socially efficient. Many economists would argue that a price control (increasing the fee) is preferable to a quantity control.

**6** (a) *E*.

(b) *MSCY*: the marginal social cost lies below the marginal private cost to the individual firm when production externalities are beneficial (see Section 15–5 of the main text).

(c) *J*: this is the point where the marginal social cost equals the marginal social benefit.

(d) The area *EHJ*.

**7** (a): firm initially produces 7 units of output, where *MPC* = *MR*, and then restricts output to 3 units, where (*MPC* + *MSC* of pollution) = *MR*.

**8**  (*b*) and (*e*): these options relate directly to the Pareto criterion.

**9**  Here, all the options are correct. If the local authority wants to increase revenue, it is vital that demand be inelastic (as we saw in Chapter 5). If the authority wishes to relieve congestion, as the wording implies, then this is tantamount to saying that option (*b*) holds. Option (*c*) is closely allied to (*a*), in that demand would not be likely to be inelastic if there were alternative car parking facilities in the town centre.

**10**  In approaching any issue involving externalities, the aim for society is to reach a position in which marginal social cost is equal to marginal social benefit. As far as pollution is concerned, we must balance the benefits of pollution reduction against the costs entailed in achieving it. This analysis suggests that the total elimination of pollution would not necessarily take society to its most preferred position. This is explained more fully in Section 15–5 of the main text.

Figure A15–1 may help to explain what is going on here. Suppose we have an industry in which private firms face costs given by *MPC*, but in which production causes pollution, such that society faces higher marginal costs given by *MSC*. If firms are free to produce as much as they like, equilibrium is attained at *Q*, although you can see in Fig. A15–1 that *Q\** would be preferred. The shaded area represents the deadweight loss imposed on society by being at *Q* instead of at *Q\**. This is the excess of *MSC* over *MSB* between *Q\** and *Q*. However, the question was about the optimal level of pollution, and whether this would be zero. Clearly in Fig. A15–1 it is not zero – *MSC* > *MPC* even at *Q\**.

**Figure A15–1**  Pollution

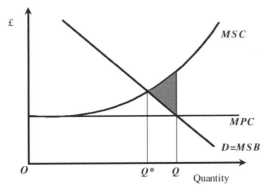

**True/False**

**1**  True.

**2**  True: see Section 15–1 of the main text.

**3**  False: one non-competitive market is sufficient distortion to prevent Pareto-efficiency.

**4**  False: the second-best theory says it is better to spread the distortion across all sectors (see Section 15–3 of the main text).

**5**  True: given our definition of market failure (see Section 15–4 of the main text).

**6**  True.

**7**  False: the reverse is so (see Section 15–6 of the main text).

**8**  False.

**9**  False: the optimal level of pollution need not be zero.

**10**  True: see Section 15–7 of the main text.

**11**  False: no economy could afford such priority. (See an article by Anil Markandya and Pamela Mason, 'Air pollution and health', *Economic Review*, 17(2), November 1999.)

**12**  True.

**Economics in action**

**1**  Horizontal equity exists when equal people are treated equally. For example, individuals of the same gender, race or educational attainment will not be discriminated against by employers and therefore they will receive the same wage rate. Vertical equity calls for people of different circumstances to be treated differently. For example, high-income earners could be taxed at higher rates and people of limited means could be provided with tax benefits and social security payments by the government.

Therefore, the social security system provides assistance to the unemployed, low-income earners and the incapacitated by raising taxes on the well-off, a system which tries to tackle vertical inequity.

**2**  In part, the social security system seeks to solve the inequitable consequences of markets. The low-earnings characteristics of some occupations such as cleaning, restaurant work or security are derived from the market wage for these occupations. While this market wage might be efficient, many would not describe it as equitable. Many people generate not only an income, but also a sense of self-worth from employment and living in their own home. But when wage rates are not sufficiently high to achieve this then some individuals are not motivated to work.

Social security payments may help to solve these problems by subsidizing workers' earnings and their housing costs. But unfortunately such a system may also motivate individuals to be reliant upon the state rather than themselves. Therefore there may only be a limited desire to engage with the labour market by low-income earners. As a consequence, if the incentives are wrong, people in need of the welfare state may overconsume its services. This could be viewed as a negative externality and would therefore represent a market failure.

Whether this is problematic clearly depends upon your own viewpoint. Some individuals might find the situation unacceptable, while others might see it as an undesirable and/or unavoidable aspect of the welfare system.

## Questions for thought

**1**  The topic of nuclear energy remains a contentious one: there are many private and social costs and benefits which need to be considered before an objective evaluation can be reached. One aim of this chapter has been to offer you a framework for thinking about issues such as this.

**2**  The granting of property rights would entitle these suffering people to compensation – perhaps from the football club for damage and disruption, or from noisy neighbours (re-read Section 15–5 of the main text).

# Chapter Sixteen Answers

## Government spending and revenue

### Important concepts and technical terms

| | | | | | | | |
|---|---|---|---|---|---|---|---|
| **1** b | **5** n | **9** j | **13** f |
| **2** l | **6** k | **10** a | **14** e |
| **3** g | **7** i | **11** c | |
| **4** m | **8** d | **12** h | |

### Exercises

**1**  **(a)**  See Fig. A16–1.

**(b)**  We would expect to find a closer link between the overall size of the revenue and expenditure pies, with the government seeking to achieve a closer balance of the two. Moreover, the amount of debt interest should reduce as the government seeks to repay the national debt in good years, and reduce borrowings to a minimum during lean years.

**Figure A16–1**  Patterns of government expenditure and revenue, 2003

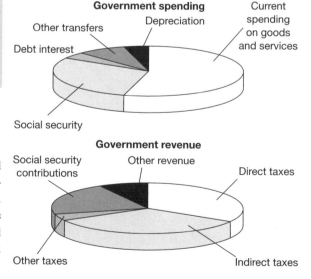

(c)  A global economic slowdown should result in higher expenditure on transfer payments and social security for the unemployed. At the same time, with lower profits and less employment, taxes, social security contributions and even VAT receipts should all fall.

**2**  See Table A16–1.

**3**  (a)  As this is a pure public good, one individual's consumption of the good does not prevent others from also consuming it; thus the marginal social benefit **DD** should be the vertical summation of $D_1$ and $D_2$ – and we have of course drawn it that way.

(b)  **OA**.

(c)  If individual 1 actually pays **OA** for this good, then individual 2 need not pay at all in order to consume it. One of the characteristics of a public good is that individuals cannot be excluded from consuming it. This is at the heart of the 'free-rider' problem entailed with public goods.

(d)  The marginal social benefit is given by the **DD** schedule – i.e. the amount **OE**.

(e)  At this point, marginal cost is at **OB**, which is well below marginal social benefit, suggesting that too little of the good is being produced.

(f)  At **OG**, where marginal social benefit is equal to marginal cost.

**4**  (a)  In a free market, equilibrium in the market is where marginal social benefit (demand) is equal to marginal private cost (supply) at quantity **OE** (and price **OA**).

(b)  The socially efficient quantity is where **MSB** equals marginal social cost: the quantity **OD**.

(c)  The triangle **GHI**.

(d)  The tax required is that which would induce producers to take decisions on the basis of **MSC** rather than **MPC**. A tax of the amount **GJ** would accomplish this.

(e)  There are a number of possible examples. An obvious one might be pollution, or traffic congestion.

**5**  In a situation where social costs are less than private costs, there will be a tendency for too little of the good to be produced, so a subsidy to firms might be appropriate. Option *(a)* would have the opposite effect. Conversely, if social costs are above private costs (as they were in Exercise **4**), then too much of the good will be produced in a free market, and a tax is the appropriate response. This eliminates option *(b)* and leads us to option *(c)* as being the correct answer.

**6**  (a)  **SSa** is labour supply without the tax; **SSb** is the post-tax supply curve.

(b)  Wage **OB**; hours **OI**.

(c)  Reduced from **OI** to **OE**.

(d)  **OC**.

(e)  **OA**: **AC** is the amount of the tax.

(f)  Tax revenue is **ACHF**.

(g)  **FHJ**.

(h)  Workers **ABGF**; firms **BCHG**. (Compare this with Exercise **2** in Chapter 4.)

(i)  **OC**.

(j)  **OA**.

(k)  **ACHF**.

(l)  There is no distortion.

(m)  The tax falls entirely on the workers.

**7**  To an extent, statements *(f)* and *(g)* encapsulate the central arguments. The Tiebout model emphasizes the importance of choice to individuals, which may be more readily facilitated by having small jurisdictions *(g)*. We may see statements *(a)*, *(d)* and *(e)* as being in support of this view. However, public goods by their very nature are non-exclusive *(b)*, so when jurisdiction areas are relatively small, non-residents are able to avail themselves of the facilities provided: a beneficial externality, which may be difficult to accommodate within the market price system. Statement *(e)* ceases to be valid. Expanding the area of jurisdiction reduces this effect *(f)*.

| Table A16–1 | Marginal and average tax rates (all figures expressed in percentage terms) | | | | |
|---|---|---|---|---|---|
| | Scheme A (30% tax on income over £5000) | | Scheme B (30% tax on income over £5000) (50% tax on income over £10 000) | | |
| Income level (£) | Marginal rate (%) | Average rate (%) | Marginal rate (%) | Average rate (%) | |
| 3 000 | 0 | 0.0 | 0 | 0.0 | |
| 9 000 | 30 | 13.3 | 30 | 13.3 | |
| 12 000 | 30 | 17.5 | 50 | 20.8 | |
| 20 000 | 30 | 22.5 | 50 | 32.5 | |

*Both schemes are progressive, with average tax rates rising with income: Scheme B is more progressive, as intuition suggests, with average rates rising more rapidly.*

**8** The diversity in pattern of tax revenues is substantial. Some of these differences may be easier to explain than others. For example, social security systems are still largely absent in many developing countries, so it may not be a great surprise to see the zero entries for Cameroon, India and Zambia. In some societies, governments do not find it politically easy to levy direct taxes on income. From the data, it seems that Bolivia is a prime example of such a society. Countries that are open to international trade, and that rely heavily on exports, tend to avoid taxes on international trade. With the successive tariff reduction rounds of the post-war period, such taxes are little used by the industrial countries anyway, as you can see in the case of the UK. Countries such as Cameroon and India continue to remain heavily dependent on taxes on international trade and transactions. We will discuss this issue more carefully later in the book. The UK's VAT forms part of the taxes on domestic goods and services. For some countries, such as Bolivia and Zambia in Table 16–1, indirect taxes on goods offer a relatively straightforward method of raising revenue.

## True/False

**1** False: the decline in unemployment in the late 1980s brought with it a fall in the ratio of transfer payments to national income.

**2** True.

**3** True: see Section 16–1 of the main text.

**4** False: in the case of a football match, there is the possibility of exclusion (see Section 16–2 of the main text).

**5** False: this is an example of a transfer payment, which serves to redistribute income between groups in society (see Section 16–2 of the main text).

**6** True: see Section 16–3 of the main text.

**7** False: this is not necessarily so. The key feature of public goods is that the government should determine how much is produced, but this need not entail direct production.

**8** False: see Section 16–3 of the main text.

**9** True: this results from the typical consumption patterns of 'rich' and 'poor'.

**10** False: the statement is too strong. It may be that this effect would be evident in some countries, but it has by no means been proved and many economists remain sceptical (see Section 16–4 of the main text).

**11** True: see Section 16–2 of the main text.

**12** True: see Section 16–6 of the main text. Whether we mind this happening may be a different matter.

## Economics in action

**1** Good or bad, Gordon Brown has been fairly consistently committed to fiscal prudence and his 'Golden Rules', enough to repeat his views to a collection of businessmen at the Confederation of British Industry (CBI), many of whom have little commercial interest in spending plans for health, education, the environment or defence. What is important is Gordon Brown's continued commitment and then credibility in delivery of managed public finances.

**2** The subtlety in message is that the primary objective is to manage government spending and revenue. Arguably, if the government wished to prioritize spending on education and health, then it would have to engage in massive borrowing and hence reduce fiscal prudence to a secondary objective.

## Questions for thought

**1** *Hint*: Is income tax a progressive or a regressive tax? How about expenditure taxes?

**2** (a) Where $D$ (marginal social benefit) = $MSCa$; price $OE$, quantity $OF$.

(b) Where $D$ ($MSB$) = $MSCg$; price $OC$, quantity $OI$.

(c) Setting price at $OC$, quantity will be $OI$. At this point, marginal social cost exceeds marginal social benefit, and the deadweight loss is given by the area $HJK$.

(d) Setting quantity at $OI$, price will be $OC$; the deadweight loss is again $HJK$.

(e) No: the loss is the same in both cases.

(f) Where $Da$ = $MSC$; price $OP$, quantity $OU$.

(g) Where $Dg$ = $MSC$; price $ON$, quantity $OR$.

(h) Setting price at $ON$, quantity will be $OW$, at which point $MSC$ exceeds $MSB$ ($Da$). The deadweight loss is area $VXY$.

(i) Setting quantity at $OR$, price will be $OQ$. Now marginal social benefit exceeds $MSC$: too little of this commodity is being produced. The deadweight loss is now $TSV$.

(j) The price- and quantity-setting policies no longer produce the same outcome. In Fig. 16–5, the deadweight loss is smaller under a price-setting regime than a quantity-based policy. Notice that this may not always be the case; the outcome will depend upon the steepness of both the demand curve and the *MSC* curve. You could see this by sketching a version of Fig. 16–5 in which *MSC* was steeper and *D* was flatter.

# Chapter Seventeen Answers

## Industrial policy and competition policy

### Important concepts and technical terms

| | | | | | | | |
|---|---|---|---|---|---|---|---|
| **1** | a | **5** | k | **9** | c | **13** | f |
| **2** | i | **6** | e | **10** | n | **14** | o |
| **3** | g | **7** | d | **11** | h | **15** | l |
| **4** | j | **8** | m | **12** | b | | |

### Exercises

**1** (*a*) and (*b*) are examples of vertical mergers. If in (*a*) the vehicle manufacturer took over the tyre producer, this could be described as 'backward vertical integration' – the vehicle firm is expanding activity back down the production process. A vehicle firm expanding by buying car distributors would be indulging in 'forward vertical integration'. (*c*) represents a conglomerate merger – there is no direct production link between tobacco and cosmetics. (*d*) is an example of a horizontal merger where the firms presumably hope to benefit from economies of scale.

**2** (a) Price *OB*, output *OS*.
(b) Price *OC*, output *OR*.
(c) The area *KLN*.
(d) *ABKJ*.
(e) *ACLJ*.
(f) The most likely explanation is that the monopolist is able to exploit economies of scale.

**3** (a) Output *OC*, price *OE*.
(b) *BCG*.
(c) *AGBF*. Notice that this area also represents monopoly profits.
(d) This is the sum of consumer and producer surpluses – that is, the area *ACGF*.
(e) Output *OH*, price *OA*.

(f) *ACI*.
(g) There is no producer surplus in this position: firms are making only normal profits.
(h) *ACI*. Notice that this is appreciably larger than *ACGF*, which was the social surplus under monopoly. Another way of looking at this is that the difference between the surplus in the two situations (i.e. *FGI*) represents the social cost of monopoly.
(i) The same as (*e*).

**4** (*c*): this was the only merger blocked by the EC Commission (see Box 17–5 in the main text).

**5** Option (*d*). As to why conglomerate mergers became important in the late 1980s, this may partly have been a result of the opportunities offered by financial deregulation, partly the idea that diversification offered security, and partly other factors. Notice that the trend towards conglomerate mergers was to some extent reversed in the early 1990s. (See Section 17–5 of the main text.)

**6** (*a*) and (*b*).

**7** (*f*): this is the only factor mentioned which leads to a reduction in competition. If you sketch a diagram, you will see that, if cross-elasticity falls and thus the demand curve becomes steeper, the deadweight loss to society increases.

**8** (a) *LMCA*.
(b) Output *OG*, price *OE*.
(c) The triangle *EFI*.
(d) As the market opens up, it is possible that there will be a reduction in X-inefficiency, causing costs to fall to *LMCB*.
(e) Output *OR*, price *OA*.
(f) *AFS*.
(g) Most obviously, consumer surplus has increased greatly, although the monopolist (who is also a member of society!) is no longer making large profits. The other gain

is in productive efficiency, in the sense that resources are being more effectively used in the production of this good.

**9** All of them.

**10** Policies *(a)*, *(f)* and *(h)* are elements of competition policy. Item *(i)* can also be viewed in this way, being one way of tackling the 'natural monopoly' problem. The other policies would be regarded as belonging to industrial policy.

## True/False

**1** True: see Section 17–3 of the main text.

**2** False: few estimates have been set so high, although Cowling and Mueller set it as high as 7 per cent.

**3** True: see Section 17–4 of the main text.

**4** True: but society may wish to take steps to ensure a just distribution of the monopoly profits.

**5** This could be regarded as true or false: it depends upon your point of view. Most economists would tend to be sceptical.

**6** True enough, but the extent to which this directly affects merger activity is not clear. There may be several reason for such abandonments. (Search the *Journal of Industrial Economics* for evidence on the performance effects of mergers.)

**7** False: this ignores locational externalities, which may be significant (see Section 17–2 of the main text).

**8** False: see Section 17–3 of the main text for a discussion of this important concept.

**9** True.

**10** False: more than one-half of such expenditure in the UK is related to military defence.

**11** Not necessarily true: it is important to approach this question carefully – see Section 17–1 of the main text.

**12** Often false: if structural change must take place, then it may be unwise to try to resist it; better to manage the adjustment. However, unless new industries can be developed to replace old ones, it may sometimes be desirable to ease the transition by temporarily subsidizing 'lame ducks'.

## Economics in action

**1** The findings could add weight to the argument that any deadweight loss from monopoly will be short-lived and minimal. Research and innovation that leads to new products and processes, does not appear to result in any significant competitive advantage, with only 2.2 per cent of all social gains going to firms. Innovation is a facilitator of competition rather than a barrier to competition. High innovation rates should therefore reduce the need for competition policies.

**2** Promoting innovation and enterprise, from the evidence of Nordhaus, appears a very attractive policy for consumers. But with such low payback rates for companies, innovation does not present much of an incentive for enterprise and entrepreneurship.

## Questions for thought

**1** Concentration is not bad for society in itself. A market may be dominated by very few firms, but if those firms are competing vigorously with each other, there is no reason to suppose that society will suffer. However, where firms collude to avoid competition then society may incur the deadweight loss from the abuse of market power. Nonetheless, legislation in the USA has been more preoccupied with the evils of concentration than with collusion. In the UK, a more pragmatic attitude has seen individual cases judged on their own merits.

**2** This section of the chapter is headed 'Questions for thought', so you cannot expect answers too easily. This is not a straightforward example of a cartel. Ask yourself who suffers from the alleged collusion, and who gains. Consider, shareholders, footballers, fans in the stand and fans at home.

**3** In many towns around in the world, you will find that real estate agents are concentrated in one particular part of town, but you can buy a newspaper almost anywhere.

**4** You might at first think that the best location for our mobile ice-cream seller would be at *C*, as far away from the competition as possible. But if you think more carefully about it, you will realize that the best she could do then is to sell to half of the sunbathers – the half who will be nearer to her than to the kiosk. However, if she located at *B*, she would sell to all the sunbathers between *B* and *C*, and to half of the rest. However, even better is to locate at *A*, close to the kiosk, and then sweep up the whole market. Similar arguments apply if there are two mobile sellers, although they are not both operating strategically, anticipating each other's actions. They will end up next to each other in the middle of the beach. This result was noted many years ago by a US economist called Hotelling.

# Chapter Eighteen Answers

## Natural monopoly: public or private?

### Important concepts and technical terms

| | | | |
|---|---|---|---|
| **1** h | **4** j | **7** f | **10** k |
| **2** b | **5** a | **8** d | **11** g |
| **3** l | **6** i | **9** e | **12** c |

### Exercises

**1**　All have been advanced at one time or another: see Section 18–1 of the main text. The validity of these arguments has been questioned, partly because managers of nationalized industries have been seen to face poor incentives for efficiency – hence the great privatization debate.

**2**　In recent privatization debates, many claims have been made, covering most of those mentioned, with the probable exception of *(e)*. Some of the effects may be of limited significance in practice or of only short-run relevance. For instance, effect *(d)* is important only in the short run, when the proceeds from the sale of an industry can be used to help fund expenditure. Time alone will reveal the importance of these effects. (Discussion of rail privatization may be found in an article by Antony Dnes, *Economic Review*, September 1997.)

**3**　(a) *LMC* = *MR* at output *OG*, price *OF*.

(b) The area *HJQ*.

(c) *EFJI*.

(d) *P* = *LMC* at output *OP*, price *OA*.

(e) At this point, long-run average costs *(OB)* exceed average revenue *(OA)*, and a private monopolist would be forced out of business.

**4**　Thoughts *(a)*, *(c)*, *(e)* and *(g)* might incline you towards privatization, but the remainder represent the opposite point of view. Unless you have strong prior views taking you in one direction or the other, we expect you found it quite difficult to weigh up the arguments and come to a firm decision. As you learn more about economics, you will find that there are many areas like this where there are no clear-cut or definitive answers.

**5**　All of these industries, more commonly known as 'utilities', were once nationalized: it was only in the 1980s that they were privatized. It is now interesting to note that assessing whether they should be nationalized is such an alien thought. Perhaps the fact that most utilities have performed reasonably well as privatized companies and that competition has increased limits any case for renationalization.

**6**　Tabulating the net private and social gains from each of the projects, we find the following:

| Project | Financial profit (loss) | Net overall gain (loss) |
|---|---|---|
| A | 20 | (40) |
| B | (30) | 70 |
| C | 50 | 40 |

The net overall gain (loss) column takes account of both private and social costs and benefits.

(a) Profits are maximized by choosing project C – but notice that the net overall gain, while positive, is smaller than the private gain accruing to the firm.

(b) Revenue is maximized by project A, but this is clearly bad news for the community at large, as this project shows a net overall loss.

(c) The project that maximizes economic welfare generally is project B, although this entails a financial loss for the enterprise.

**7**　(a) The necessary subsidy would be represented by the area *ABRQ*.

(b) The fixed charge is needed to cover the withdrawn subsidy *(ABRQ)*; the per unit charge would be *AB*.

(c) The variable charge would need to cover marginal cost: *OA*.

**(d)** Where $AC = AR$, at output $OK$, price $OC$.

**(e)** The area $NLQ$.

**(f)** The managers would have incentive to produce efficiently; and average costs will increase.

**8** **(a)** Rent will be $OB$ and the quantity of housing $OF$.

**(b)** By offering rent vouchers to the needy, the demand for housing will be increased, from $DD$ to $DDX$; rents will rise to $OE$, and the quantity to $OG$.

**(c)** In this situation, the supply of housing will increase from $SS$ to $SSX$; in equilibrium, rents fall to $OA$ (demand is still at $DD$, of course), and the quantity of housing rises to $OH$.

**(d)** As Fig. 18–2 was drawn, there is little difference in the effect of the quantity of housing, although there is a dramatic difference in rent levels. In practice, the result will depend upon the elasticities of demand and supply in the market.

**(e)** Clearly the major difference between the two schemes is the effect upon rent. This in turn will have an effect on income distribution, with landlords gaining perhaps substantially from the voucher scheme.

**9** **(a)** A belief in the efficacy of free market forces had been growing for some time when Mrs Thatcher became Prime Minister in 1979. During the period of her administrations, great efforts were made to disengage the government – to withdraw from sectors of the economy where it was believed that market forces could be effective. The Private Finance Initiative (PFI) was one such initiative, launched in November 1992 after the main wave of privatization was seen to be complete.

**(b)** It had long been argued that the public sector needed to take a lead in the provision of social infrastructure such as roads and hospitals, where it was not obvious as to how it was possible for there to be competition in provision. The PFI handled this by putting such projects out to competitive tendering, undertaking to buy back the services to flow from the projects after completion.

**(c)** A key reason for doing this is to provide improved incentives for efficiency. When the public sector is solely responsible for social infrastructure, it is argued that there is little true accountability. As a result, a certain amount of X-inefficiency creeps in. It was hoped that this would be squeezed out through the operations of the PFI.

**(d)** This is indeed how the scheme is intended to work. Instead of owning a hospital or a road, the public sector purchased the flow of services provided by these assets from the private sector.

**(e)** While some PFIs have led to improved infrastructure delivery times, there are a number of problem cases. New school buildings are behind schedule, the maintenance of rail track has been problematic and the development of IT systems for the NHS and the Inland Revenue has suffered teething troubles. In many cases the private sector suppliers blame the public sector bureaucracy.

**(f)** This is certainly an issue to be taken into account, as we expect the private sector to be concerned with a rather shorter time horizon than the government. We would also expect a private firm to use a very different discount rate, partly reflecting risk-averseness but also acknowledging that the government may take social returns as well as private returns into account.

## True/False

**1** False: the deadweight burden would be reduced but not eliminated.

**2** False: the initial effects were encouraging to those who believe in free markets, but subsequently the establishment of strategic barriers to entry eroded these benefits (see Box 18–1 in the main text).

**3** False: nationalized industries should use a lower discount rate and undertake some projects that the private sector would consider unprofitable.

**4** True: peak-time users pay higher prices to reflect the higher marginal cost of supplying them.

**5** True: see Section 18–1 of the main text.

**6** False: in practice, individual shareholders have little influence and face a free-rider problem (see Section 18–3 of the main text).

**7** Not always true: for instance, private oil companies operating in the North Sea have been faced with petroleum revenue tax, often at very high rates.

**8** There is no simple true/false response to this one: in part, it depends upon how the proceeds are disposed.

**9** False: most were underpriced, in the sense that the opening free market price was higher than the offer price. However, Enterprise Oil opened at the offer price and Britoil opened below it. (See Section 18–4 of the main text.)

**10** True.

## Economics in action

**1** Competition has bred confusion in consumers' minds. Too many product offerings have made it difficult for consumers to see who offers a directory enquiries service, who charges what price for the service and who can actually provide an accurate service. However, such confusion may be only short-lived; in the longer term, more successful providers of such services should become established with consumers.

**2** Making the market completely open is only one strategy for increasing competition. It may have been possible to manage an increase in competition by creating an auction with a small number of licences to operate directory enquiries. Offering around four slots may have led to a cartel, but a larger number of slots, such as 10, may have helped to reduce such problems.

## Questions for thought

**1** This issue is discussed at some length in Section 18–3 of the main text.

**2** We know this is a big question, covering much of the material of this chapter. However, it will do you no harm to try to marshal your thoughts and to focus on the salient points. This is part of the economist's skill.

# Chapter Nineteen Answers

## Introduction to macroeconomics

### Important concepts and technical terms

**1** n  **5** m  **9** c  **13** h
**2** i  **6** f  **10** k  **14** a
**3** o  **7** e  **11** d  **15** g
**4** p  **8** b  **12** j  **16** l

### Exercises

**1** See Table A19–1.

(a) The annual inflation rate is calculated from the consumer price index (CPI) using the method described in Section 2–4 of the main text. Thus for the UK, the inflation rate for 1992–93 is calculated as:

$$100 \times ((94.4 - 92.9)/92.9 = 1.61$$

(b) See Fig. A19–1.

**Table A19–1**   Inflation, 1992–2002

| Year | UK Consumer price index (CPI) | Inflation rate (%) | USA Consume pricer index (CPI) | Inflation rate (%) | Spain Consumer price index (CPI) | Inflation rate (%) |
|---|---|---|---|---|---|---|
| 1992 | 92.9 | | 92.1 | | 87.2 | |
| 1993 | 94.4 | 1.61 | 94.8 | 2.93 | 91.2 | 4.59 |
| 1994 | 96.7 | 2.44 | 97.3 | 2.64 | 95.5 | 4.71 |
| 1995 | 100.0 | 3.41 | 100.0 | 2.77 | 100.0 | 4.71 |
| 1996 | 102.4 | 2.40 | 102.9 | 2.90 | 103.6 | 3.60 |
| 1997 | 105.7 | 3.22 | 105.3 | 2.33 | 105.6 | 1.93 |
| 1998 | 109.3 | 3.41 | 107.0 | 1.61 | 107.5 | 1.80 |
| 1999 | 112.1 | 2.56 | 108.2 | 1.12 | 115.4 | 7.35 |
| 2000 | 114.6 | 2.23 | 109.0 | 0.74 | 120.3 | 4.25 |
| 2001 | 117.2 | 2.27 | 111.5 | 2.29 | 123.5 | 2.66 |
| 2002 | 121.0 | 3.24 | 112.8 | 1.17 | 126.0 | 2.02 |

**Figure A19–1**   Inflation in the UK, USA and Spain, 1992–2002

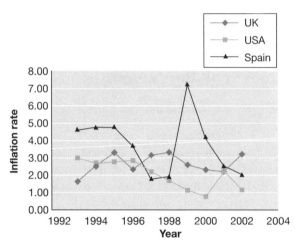

**Figure A19–2**   GDP growth in the UK, USA and Spain, 1992–2002

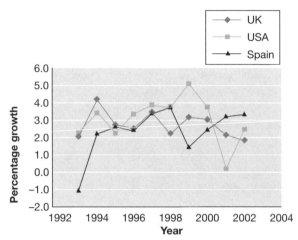

(c)   UK, 32 per cent; USA, 22 per cent; Spain, 44 per cent.

(d)   USA.

(e)   Inflation fell substantially in all three countries, but the USA experienced the greatest deceleration.

(f)   The growth rates are calculated in the same way as the inflation rates: see Table A19–2.

(g)   See Fig. A19–2.

(h)   UK, 31 per cent; USA, 35 per cent; Spain, 30 per cent.

**2**   (a)  Planned consumption plus planned investment is 150 + 50 = 200.

(b)   Production less expenditure is 210 – 200 = 10. This quantity represents an unplanned addition to inventories.

(c)   Income less consumption is 210 – 150 = 60.

(d)   Planned investment plus stock changes is 50 + 10 = 60.

Thus actual investment = actual savings.

(e)   Producers have not sold as much output as they expected and witness an increase in stock levels. Two responses are possible: to reduce output or reduce price. As we begin to build our model of an economy in Chapter 20, we will initially assume that prices are fixed – so the response to an unplanned increase in stocks will be to reduce output.

| **Table A19–2**   National production and economic growth, 1992–2002 | | | | | |
| --- | --- | --- | --- | --- | --- |
| | **UK** | | **USA** | | **Spain** |
| | GDP index | Growth rate (%) | GDP index | Growth rate (%) | GDP index | Growth rate (%) |
| 1992 | 91.4 | | 92.3 | | 96.3 | |
| 1993 | 93.3 | 2.1 | 94.5 | 2.4 | 95.2 | –1.1 |
| 1994 | 97.3 | 4.3 | 97.8 | 3.5 | 97.4 | 2.3 |
| 1995 | 100.0 | 2.8 | 100.0 | 2.2 | 100.0 | 2.7 |
| 1996 | 102.6 | 2.6 | 103.4 | 3.4 | 102.4 | 2.4 |
| 1997 | 106.2 | 3.5 | 107.5 | 4.0 | 106.0 | 3.5 |
| 1998 | 108.5 | 2.2 | 111.7 | 3.9 | 110.1 | 3.9 |
| 1999 | 111.9 | 3.1 | 117.4 | 5.1 | 111.8 | 1.5 |
| 2000 | 115.3 | 3.0 | 121.8 | 3.7 | 115.7 | 3.5 |
| 2001 | 117.8 | 2.2 | 122.1 | 0.2 | 120.6 | 4.2 |
| 2002 | 119.9 | 1.8 | 125.1 | 2.5 | 125.8 | 4.3 |

**Table A19–3  Value added in each transaction**

| Good (1) | Seller (2) | Buyer (3) | Transaction value (£) (4) | Value added (£) (5) |
|---|---|---|---|---|
| Steel | Steel producer | Machine tool-maker | 1000 | 1000 |
| Steel | Steel producer | Bicycle manufacturer | 2500 | 2500 |
| Rubber | Rubber producer | Tyre producer | 600 | 600 |
| Machine | Machine tool-maker | Bicycle manufacturer | 1800 | 800 |
| Tyres | Tyre producer | Bicycle manufacturer | 1000 | 400 |
| Bicycles | Bicycle manufacturer | Final consumers | 8000 | 4500 |

**3**  It may be helpful to begin by translating these terms into the notation of the main text.

| Item | Notation in main text |
|---|---|
| Final consumption expenditure | $C$ |
| Fixed investment *plus* stock changes | $I$ |
| Government final consumption | $G$ |
| Exports | $X$ |
| Imports | $Z$ |
| Taxes on products *less* subsidies | $T_e$ |

The remaining terms should be familiar, although you may not have encountered the item 'other indirect taxes'. These taxes are on expenditure by firms and do not register in the expenditure-side calculation.

(a)  GDP at market prices is $C + I + G + X - Z = 842\ 162$.
(b)  GNP at market prices is $GDPmp$ + net income from abroad $= 853\ 736$.
(c)  GDP at basic prices is $GDPmp - T_e = 745\ 818$.
(d)  NNP at market prices is $GNPmp$ – capital consumption = $764\ 965$.
(e)  Net national income at basic prices is $NNPmp - T_e = 668\ 784$.
(f)  From the income side, $GDPbp$ = profits/rent + employment income + mixed income + $T_e$ + other indirect taxes $= 843\ 789$.
(g)  In an ideal world, the two methods should give the same results. However, in practice the problems of accurate measurement are too great. If you look in the ONS *Blue Book* you will see that there is a 'statistical discrepancy' item, which is used in the accounts to create consistency between the estimates.

**4**  The simplest way to clarify this question is to tabulate the transactions as in Table A19–3, and then calculate the value added entailed in each transaction. This was done in Section 19–4 of the main text.

Check that you understand how column (5) is obtained. For instance, value added by the bicycle manufacturer is the transaction value (£8000) *less* the value of goods used up in the production process – namely, tyres (£1000) and steel (£2500) – but not the machine, which is not 'used up' but kept for future use also.

(a)  The contribution is the sum of the value added in column (5) = £9800.
(b)  Total final expenditure is composed of two elements – consumers' expenditure on bicycles (£8000) and the bicycle manufacturer's purchase of machine tools (£1800), totalling £9800.

**5**  (a)  At a very simple level the savings rate has declined because the level of consumption has increased. A key driver of consumption in the latter part of the period has been low interest rates and the increased willingness to take on debt to fuel consumption. Low rates of return on savings accounts and stock markets have also dented individuals' enthusiasm for saving.

(b)  Lower savings rates mean fewer leakages from the circular flow of income, leading to the higher flows of expenditure and income within the economy (circular flow of income).

**6**

| Year | Nominal GDP | GDP deflator | Real GDP |
|---|---|---|---|
| 2001 | 994 309 | 100.0 | |
| 2003 | 1 099 896 | 106.3 | |
| Growth | 10.62 | 6.30 | 4.32 |

The growth rate in nominal GDP is 10.62 per cent, the growth rate in the GDP deflator was 6.3 per cent, therefore real GDP growth must have been $10.62 - 6.3 = 4.32$ per cent.

**7**  The key to tackling this question is in the expenditure-side national income accounting, which states that:

$$Y = C + I + G + NX$$

The question provides information about national income *(Y)*, private expenditure *(C)*, investment *(I)* and government expenditure *(G)*, so we can calculate net exports *(NX)* as:

$$NX = Y - (C + I + G)$$

For year 1,

$$NX = 500 - (200 + 250 + 50) = 0$$

Thus in year 1, we infer that exports and imports exactly balanced each other. The balance of trade was thus zero – neither in surplus nor in deficit.

In year 2, the expenditure items (especially investment) rose by more than national income, so the net exports were –150, a balance of trade deficit.

In year 3, government and private expenditures fell while national income continued to rise. The balance of trade moved into surplus (+50).

**8** **(a)** In order to calculate real GNP, we need to deflate the GNP index by the price index. This process reveals an increase in the real GNP index from 102.9 to 103.8, an increase of 0.9 per cent.

**(b)** We can see that the population of the country increased by about 1 per cent from year 1 to year 2: a slightly more rapid rise than in real GNP. Statement *(b)* is thus false: real GNP per capita fell.

**(c)** The fact that real GNP per capita fell does not imply that all people were worse off in year 2. We do not know about the distribution of income in the country.

**(d)** The total population increased between year 1 and year 2, but without knowing about the age distribution and about people's decisions about labour force participation, we can say nothing about changes in the working population.

**9** The general rule to adopt is that, if an item can be valued and is reported, then, so long as it is notionally part of GNP, it will be included. This includes *(a)*, *(b)*, *(d)*, *(f)* and *(h)*, although we cannot always guarantee the full reporting of all these items. Item *(c)* relates to a transfer payment and is not notionally part of GNP. *(e)* is immeasurable, and *(g)* cannot easily be valued, although GNP will include wages paid to those responsible for providing leisure services. Hedgerow fruit *(i)* are neither valued nor reported, unless you choose to visit a pick-your-own fruit farm!

## True/False

**1** True: see Section 19–1 of the main text.

**2** False: Japan's economy has struggled for many years. Only recently has it showed signs of good economic growth.

**3** False: many other countries, especially in Latin America, have experienced much more rapid inflation than the UK – for instance, the average annual rate of inflation in Brazil between 1990 and 1997 was 475.2 per cent! (See *World Development Report* 1998/99.)

**4** False: although unemployment did decrease substantially at this time, it was by no means as high as tenfold.

**5** True: see Section 19–3 of the main text.

**6** False, and silly: whether an economy is 'closed' or 'open' depends upon whether it is open to international trade – not upon the rate of closure of firms (see Section 19–4 of the main text).

**7** True.

**8** It is true that actual savings will always equal actual investment in such an economy: this results from the way we choose to define these variables. There is no necessity, however, for planned savings and investment to be always equal.

**9** False: indirect taxes must be *deducted* from *GDPmp* to give *GDPbp*.

**10** True.

**11** False: if measured at current prices, GNP incorporates price changes – this is nominal GNP, not real GNP.

**12** False: real GNP may not be an ideal measure of welfare, but it is the best measure we have which is available on a regular basis.

## Economics in action

**1** With rising consumption then savings leakages are expected to increase. A rising exchange rate will reduce export leakages, while a rise in tax rates will increase leakages, but nothing is said of UK investment rates.

**2** A rising interest rate will impact on the circular flow. It should dampen consumption and investments funded by borrowings. It may also lead to an appreciation of the pound, leading to a reduction in exports and an increase in imports. So, rising interest rates should dampen the level of expenditure throughout the circular flow of income.

## Questions for thought

**1** Some discussion of more comprehensive measures is included in Section 19–5 of the main text. In particular, notice the multidimensional approach introduced by Tony Blair in 1999. (This is discussed in *Economic Review Data Supplement*, September 1999.)

**2** The existence of unrecorded economic activity will bias downwards the measurements of GNP in whatever country. In making international comparisons, we may also face problems with income distribution and currency conversions.

**3** You might like to illustrate your discussion by using your answers to Exercise **6**.

# Chapter Twenty Answers

## Output and aggregate demand

### Important concepts and technical terms

| | | | |
|---|---|---|---|
| **1** b | **4** g | **7** l | **10** i |
| **2** a | **5** h | **8** j | **11** d |
| **3** k | **6** c | **9** e | **12** f |

### Exercises

**1** **(a)** See Table A20–1 (overleaf).

**(b)** See Fig. A20–1 (overleaf).

**(c)** We drew our line using a statistical procedure called 'regression': its slope is 0.662.

**(d)** In focusing upon this simple relationship between consumption and income, we have made a number of assumptions, especially concerning autonomous consumption. We have also assumed that the relationship can be viewed as a straight line. Only if all these assumptions are valid can we regard our estimate of the marginal propensity as 'reasonable'. This must be interpreted in the light of economics (what we are trying to measure) as well as of statistics (how we try to measure it).

**(e)** See Fig. A20–2 (overleaf).

**(f)** Given $Y = C + S$, there must be a close correspondence between the two lines. If we write $C = a + bY$, then it is easily seen that $S = -a + (1 - b) Y$. It should thus be no surprise that the slope of the savings line is $1 - 0.662 = 0.338$.

**(g)** $1/0.338 = 2.959$.

Again, we should interpret this figure with caution.

**2** **(a)** and **(b)** Answers are contained in Table A20–2 (overleaf).

**(c)** With income at 100, aggregate demand is 130, so that stocks will be rapidly run down. Producers are likely to react by producing more output in the next period.

**(d)** With income at 350, aggregate demand is only 305 and producers will find that they cannot sell their output, so stocks begin to build up. They are thus likely to reduce the output in the next period.

**(e)** Only at income of 200 do we find that aggregate demand equals aggregate supply – or, equivalently, that planned investment equals planned savings. This, then, is the equilibrium level of income.

**(f)** As income increases by 50, consumption increases by 35, so the marginal propensity to consume is $35/50 = 0.7$.

**(g)** An increase in investment of H$15 bn to H$75 bn would carry equilibrium income to 250 – an increase of $15/0.3 = 50$.

## Table A20–1 Consumption, income and saving, 1992–2002

| Year | Households' final consumption expenditure | Real households' disposable income | Real savings | Savings rate |
|------|-----|-----|-----|-----|
| 1992 | 476 834 | 522 915 | 46 081 | 8.81 |
| 1993 | 490 594 | 537 310 | 46 716 | 8.69 |
| 1994 | 505 711 | 545 269 | 39 558 | 7.25 |
| 1995 | 514 042 | 557 940 | 43 898 | 7.87 |
| 1996 | 532 735 | 571 440 | 38 705 | 6.77 |
| 1997 | 552 138 | 595 043 | 42 905 | 7.21 |
| 1998 | 573 873 | 596 745 | 22 872 | 3.83 |
| 1999 | 599 185 | 616 235 | 17 050 | 2.77 |
| 2000 | 626 537 | 654 649 | 28 112 | 4.29 |
| 2001 | 645 981 | 685 263 | 39 282 | 5.73 |
| 2002 | 668 994 | 695 183 | 26 189 | 3.77 |

**Figure A20–1** Consumption and income

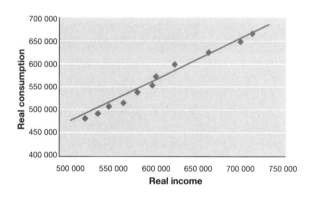

**Figure A20–2** Savings and income

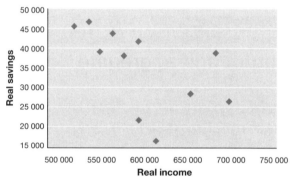

## Table A20–2 Income and consumption in Hypothetica (all in Hypothetical $ bn)

| Income (output) | Planned consumption | Planned investment | Savings | Aggregate demand | Unplanned inventory change | Actual investment |
|------|-----|-----|-----|-----|-----|-----|
| 50 | 35 | 60 | 15 | 95 | –45 | 15 |
| 100 | 70 | 60 | 30 | 130 | –30 | 30 |
| 150 | 105 | 60 | 45 | 165 | –15 | 45 |
| 200 | 140 | 60 | 60 | 200 | 0 | 60 |
| 250 | 175 | 60 | 75 | 235 | 15 | 75 |
| 300 | 210 | 60 | 90 | 270 | 30 | 90 |
| 350 | 245 | 60 | 105 | 305 | 45 | 105 |
| 400 | 280 | 60 | 120 | 340 | 60 | 120 |

**3** **(a)** See Fig. A20–3.

**Figure A20–3** The income–expenditure diagram

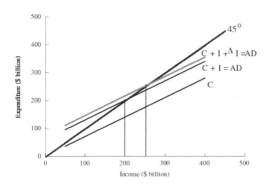

**(b)** Figure A20–3 confirms that equilibrium occurs at income of 200 – where the aggregate demand schedule meets the 45° line.

**(c)** The increase in investment shifts the aggregate demand schedule, giving a new equilibrium at income of 250.

**4** **(a)** See Fig. A20–4.

**Figure A20–4** Savings and investment

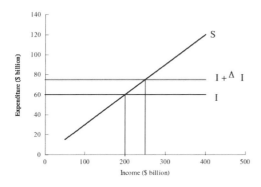

**(b)** Equilibrium is again seen to be at income of 200.

**(c)** Equilibrium at the new level of investment is at income of 250.

**(d)** The increase in investment initially affects income, inducing higher savings; the process continues until planned savings equal planned investment.

**5** **(a)** Aggregate demand is *OB:* there is excess demand at this point.

**(b)** Inventories will be run down to the extent of the excess demand, measured by *AB*.

**(c)** We expect firms to increase output in the next period.

**(d)** Income *OH* = planned expenditure *OD*.

**(e)** Aggregate planned expenditure is *OE:* there is excess supply at this point.

**(f)** Inventories will increase to the extent of the excess supply – namely, *EF*. Firms are likely to respond by reducing output.

**6** **(a)** Income *OF*, savings *OIB*.

**(b)** *OIC*.

**(c)** *OG*.

**(d)** *LM/NM*.

**(e)** *OIA*.

**(f)** *OE*.

**7** **(a)** *c*.

**(b)** Given $S = Y - C$,
$S = Y - A - cY$,
or $S = -A + (1 - c)Y$

**(c)** With $S = -400 + 0.25\ Y$,
if $S = 0$, $Y = 1600$.

**(d)** We now have $C = 400 + 0.75\ Y$, and equilibrium occurs when aggregate supply equals aggregate demand, i.e. when $Y = C + I$; that is, when $Y = 400 + 0.25\ Y + 500$.

Solving for $Y$, we find that equilibrium is at $Y = 3600$.

**8** **(a)** *XY/UX* is the slope of the consumption schedule: the marginal propensity to consume.

**(b)** At equilibrium *W*, *WY/OW* represents the ratio of consumption to income: the average propensity to consume.

**9** **(a)** *OG*.

**(b)** *AJ*.

**(c)** *OF*.

**(d)** *AL*.

**(e)** *OH*.

**10** **(a)** The column in Table A20–3 (overleaf) headed 'Aggregate demand 1' shows that equilibrium income = 300 (because consumption is then $0.7 \times 300 = 210$; so $C + I$ is $210 + 90 = 300$). Given the multiplier relationship, we could also calculate equilibrium as $Y = 1/(1 - MPC) = 90/0.3 = 300$.

**(b)** Using the column 'Aggregate demand 2' or $Y = 105/0.3$, we see that equilibrium output is now 350.

**(c)** The multiplier can be calculated as the ratio of the change in equilibrium income to the initiating change in investment (i.e. $50/15 = 3.33´$, or we simply calculate $1/(1 - MPC) = 1/0.3 = 3.33´$.

**(d)** With the higher propensity to consume, we get the column 'Aggregate demand 3' and an equilibrium of 450: $1/(1 - MPC) = 90/0.2 = 450$.

**(e)** Using the column 'Aggregate demand 4', equilibrium income is now 500.

**(f)** $50/10 = 5$.

| Table A20–3 Hypothetica revisited | | | | | | |
|---|---|---|---|---|---|---|
| Income (output) | Planned consumption (*MPC* = 0.7) | Aggregate demand 1 | Aggregate demand 2 | Planned consumption (*MPC* = 0.8) | Aggregate demand 3 | Aggregate demand 4 |
| 250 | 175 | 265 | 280 | 200 | 290 | 300 |
| 300 | 210 | 300 | 315 | 240 | 330 | 340 |
| 350 | 245 | 335 | 350 | 280 | 370 | 380 |
| 400 | 280 | 370 | 385 | 320 | 410 | 420 |
| 450 | 315 | 405 | 420 | 360 | 450 | 460 |
| 500 | 350 | 440 | 455 | 400 | 490 | 500 |
| 550 | 385 | 475 | 490 | 440 | 530 | 540 |
| 600 | 420 | 510 | 525 | 480 | 570 | 580 |

## True/False

**1** True: see the introduction to Chapter 20 in the main text.

**2** True.

**3** False: we make this simplifying assumption very often – but it is no more than an assumption and may not always be accurate (see Section 20–2 of the main text).

**4** True: we have set up the model such that income is either spent or saved.

**5** False: we have assumed investment to be autonomous to keep the model simple for the time being; later we will treat it more realistically and consider its determinants.

**6** True: see Box 20–1 in the main text.

**7** True: see Section 20–4 of the main text.

**8** True again.

**9** False: this statement is true only in equilibrium. We note that savings and investment plans are formulated independently by different agents and need not always be equal (see Section 20–5 of the main text).

**10** False: the slope depends upon the marginal propensity to consume; the position depends partly on the level of autonomous consumption (see Section 20–6 of the main text).

**11** True: see Section 20–7 of the main text.

**12** False: this is an expression of the paradox of thrift (see Section 20–8 of the main text).

## Economics in action

**1** The measurement problems associated with GDP become critical when assessing actual and potential GDP. First, what is the size of actual and potential GDP? Secondly, the difference between actual and potential GDP is the core issue for policy-makers. But with a lack of accuracy is measuring both, the difference between actual and potential GDP is also uncertain.

**2** It is difficult to know the answer to the question for any economy, never mind just Japan. However, in practice economists examine a number of independent estimates of GDP growth for an economy. These might be produced by the domestic government, investment banks, the International Monetary Fund (IMF) or the Organization for Economic Cooperation and Development (OECD).

## Questions for thought

**1** Remember the distinction between planned and actual (see Section 20–5 of the main text).

**2** We will consider consumption theory again in Chapter 25.

**3** This question looks ahead to Chapter 22.

# Chapter Twenty-one Answers

## Fiscal policy and foreign trade

### Important concepts and technical terms

| | | | |
|---|---|---|---|
| **1** k | **4** l | **7** f | **10** i |
| **2** a | **5** h | **8** c | **11** j |
| **3** d | **6** g | **9** b | **12** e |

### Exercises

**1**    (a) and (b) See Table A21–1.

(c)   At income H$350 bn, aggregate demand amounts to only H$306 bn; producers will see stocks building up and reduce output in the next period.

(d)   Equilibrium is where aggregate demand equals aggregate supply, at income H$250 bn. Equivalently, equilibrium occurs where $I + G = S + NT$ – again, of course, at income H$250 bn.

(e)   Government spending is H$50 bn; net taxes are $0.2 \times$ H$250 bn = H$50 bn. The budget is in balance.

(f)   With government spending at H$72 bn, equilibrium income increases to H$300 bn.

(g)   Government spending is now H$72 bn and net taxes are $0.2 \times$ H$300 bn = H$60 bn; the government is running a deficit of H$12 bn.

(h)   The multiplier is 50/22 = 2.27. Equivalently, it is $1/\{1 - c(1 - t)\} = 1/(1 - 0.56) = 2.27$.

**2**    (a)  Notice in Fig. A21–1 that the aggregate demand schedule is now less steep – this is the result of the taxation.

(b)   The diagram confirms that equilibrium occurs at income H$250 bn – where the aggregate demand schedule cuts the 45° line.

(c)   The increase in government spending moves the aggregate demand schedule to $AD'$, giving a new equilibrium income of H$300 bn.

**3**    (a)  See Table A21–2 (overleaf).

(b)   2250.

(c)   2500.

(d)   250/50 = 5.

(e)   See Table A21–2.

(f)   2500.

(g)   Zero.

(h)   With the introduction of government, equilibrium income has increased from 2250 to 2500, even though the government is spending no more than is collected through taxation (see Section 21–2 of the main text).

**Figure A21–1**   The income–expenditure diagram with government

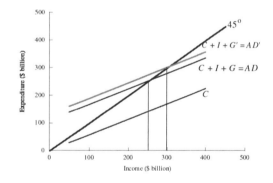

| Table A21–1 | Government comes to Hypothetica | | | | | | |
|---|---|---|---|---|---|---|---|
| Income/ output | Disposable income | Planned consumption | Planned investment | Government spending | Savings | Net taxes | Aggregate demand |
| 50 | 40 | 28 | 60 | 50 | 12 | 10 | 138 |
| 100 | 80 | 56 | 60 | 50 | 24 | 20 | 166 |
| 150 | 120 | 84 | 60 | 50 | 36 | 30 | 194 |
| 200 | 160 | 112 | 60 | 50 | 48 | 40 | 222 |
| 250 | 200 | 140 | 60 | 50 | 60 | 50 | 250 |
| 300 | 240 | 168 | 60 | 50 | 72 | 60 | 278 |
| 350 | 280 | 196 | 60 | 50 | 84 | 70 | 306 |
| 400 | 320 | 224 | 60 | 50 | 96 | 80 | 334 |

**Table A21–2    Government comes to Hypothetica**

| Income/ output | Consumption 1 | Investment | Aggregate demand 1 | Disposable income | Consumption 2 | Government spending | Aggregate demand 2 |
|---|---|---|---|---|---|---|---|
| 2000 | 1600 | 450 | 2050 | 1800 | 1440 | 250 | 2140 |
| 2250 | 1800 | 450 | 2250 | 2025 | 1620 | 250 | 2320 |
| 2500 | 2000 | 450 | 2450 | 2250 | 1800 | 250 | 2500 |
| 2750 | 2200 | 450 | 2650 | 2475 | 1980 | 250 | 2680 |
| 3000 | 2400 | 450 | 2850 | 2700 | 2160 | 250 | 2860 |

(i)    2750.

(j)    250/70=3.57.

**4**    (a)  See Fig. A21–2.

(b)    £500 million.

(c)    Up to £500 million.

(d)    At income above £500 million.

(e)    Net taxes at this point would be £80 million, so with government expenditure at £100 million, the government budget deficit is £20 million.

(f)    A surplus of £50 million.

**Figure A21–2**  The government budget

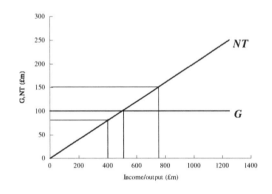

**5**    (a)  £100 bn × 0.08 = £8 bn.

(b)    We can approximate the real interest rate as the difference between the nominal rate and the rate of inflation (see Section 14–2 of the main text). In this context, the real interest rate is 8 − 6 = 2 per cent.

(c)    £100 bn × 0.02 = £2 bn.

(d)    It's not really cheating: although the government must pay out the £8 bn in nominal interest payments, tax revenues will increase with inflation, clawing back part of this amount. If national income is also increasing in real terms, this will add further to tax revenues. It is valid to take these effects into account.

**6**    (a)  See Fig. A21–3.

**Figure A21–3**  Imports and exports

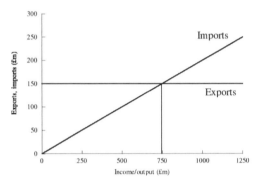

(b)    At this income level, imports are £200 million, while exports are £150 million – so there is a trade deficit of £50 million.

(c)    Imports £100 million, exports £150 million; trade surplus is £50 million.

(d)    At income £750 million.

(e)    In part (b), we saw that this level of income entails a trade deficit of £50 million. Such a deficit cannot be sustained in the long run, so fiscal policy to take the economy to full employment cannot be successful in the long run. Some commentators have regarded this constraint as the reason for Britain's slow rate of economic growth during the early post-war period.

**7**    (a)    $Y = \dfrac{1 + G}{\{1 - c(1 - t\}} = \dfrac{700}{0.28} = 2500$

(b)    $C = 0.8 \times 2500 \times 0.9 = 1800$

tax revenue = $0.1 \times 2500 = 250$

government budget surplus = $tY - G = 0$.

(c)    Disposable income was $2500 \times 0.9 = 2250$, is now $2500 \times 0.75 = 1830$, and has been reduced by 420.

(d)    Consumption falls by $0.8 \times 420 = 336$, but aggregate demand increases by $500 - 336 = 164$.

(e)    $Y = 1200/0.4 = 3000$.

**(f)** Government budget surplus = $tY - G = 750 - 750 = 0$.

**(g)** Multiplier = (change in $Y$)/(change in $G$) = $500/500$. In this case, the multiplier is unity.

**8** **(a)** *AB* is the aggregate demand schedule without foreign trade. Adding autonomous exports together with imports proportional to income moves the schedule to *CD*.

**(b)** *OG*.

**(c)** *OF*.

**(d)** *OE*: this corresponds to the point at which exports = imports. At this point, aggregate demand is the same on both *AB* and *CD*, as net exports are equal to zero.

**(e)** The multiplier is reduced by foreign trade through the effect of the marginal propensity to import (see Section 21–7 of the main text).

**9** **(a)** The national debt is the net accumulation of UK government deficits.

**(b)** The debt:GDP ratio fell throughout the period 1975–1990. A more marked decline can be seen in the late 1980s when the government was running a budget surplus. In the early 1990s a recession led to a drop in taxes and an expansion of fiscal policy through increased social security payments. Following Labour's election in 1997 a policy of fiscal prudence has been followed, with a targeted reduction in the debt:GDP ratio. However, to some extent the decline in the ratio has arguably been achieved with the help of a benign economic environment.

**(c)** It is sometimes argued that PSNCR must be kept low in order to keep the national debt under control. However, it is clear that the debt:GDP ratio was at a relatively low level in the early 1990s, not only relative to the UK situation since the 1970s, but also relative to other industrial economies (see Table 21–4 in the main text). An additional reason for monitoring the national debt carefully in the 1990s was that the debt:GDP ratio is a key element in the Maastricht criteria for entry into European monetary union (EMU).

**10** **(a)** It takes time to collect information about the economy and to realize that policy action is required.

**(b)** Having decided to take action, further time is needed to put changes in spending into practice: capital expenditure is inflexible, individual government departments will resist cuts in their own budgets.

**(c)** The multiplier is not an instantaneous process, but takes some time to work through the system – remember, the policy relies upon influencing the behaviour of agents such as households.

**(d)** There is likely to be uncertainty about how strong, reliable and rapid the effects of the policy will be.

**(e)** By the time the policy has taken effect, the other elements of aggregate demand may be at different levels, affecting the equilibrium level of income.

**(f)** Our model is still rudimentary: there are many routes by which fiscal policy may have indirect effects upon other components of demand – especially investment.

**(g)** There may be other policy objectives, such as the control of monetary growth or inflation, which could be endangered by the effects of fiscal policy.

**(h)** Before we are induced to take action to combat unemployment, we need to be sure that there really is a problem – that the economy is not already at full employment.

These issues are discussed in Box 21–2 in the main text.

## True/False

**1** False: more like one-fifth (see the introduction to Chapter 21 in the main text).

**2** False: the reverse is true (see Section 21–2 of the main text).

**3** True: although the proximity to full employment may be a relevant consideration.

**4** True.

**5** True.

**6** False: it may be misleading (see Section 21–4 of the main text).

**7** True.

**8** True.

**9** True: see Section 21–5 of the main text.

**10** True: France and Germany have been pursuing an expansionary fiscal policy, leading to a growing level of national debt.

**11** False: exports are about 25 per cent of GDP, but net exports (the difference between exports and imports) were much smaller (see Section 21–7 of the main text).

**12** False: there is the possibility of retaliation from competitors to consider.

## Economics in action

**1** An increase in taxation and a reduction in government spending would cut aggregate expenditure and therefore lead to a worsening of the German recession.

**2** The sale of the telecommunications and rail industries would raise additional revenues for the German government, which could be used to fund short-term government expenditure, thereby reducing the level of the budget deficit.

**3** The structural deficit is the level of deficit if the economy was at potential output, or long-run equilibrium. If the structural budget is in deficit, then the sale of national assets such as telecommunications and rail will reduce only the current budget deficit; in the long run the budget will fall to the equilibrium deficit level.

## Questions for thought

**1** The introduction of government and foreign trade has the effect of reducing the multiplier. By comparing two alternative equilibrium positions, we neglect the process by which the new equilibrium is attained. This process may be spread over many time periods (see Section 21–6 of the main text). For *hints* on the inadequacy of the model so far, see the *hints* on Question **3**.

**2** See Section 21–5 in the main text.

**3** At this stage, the model is clearly much abstracted from reality. In particular, we have not considered the financial side of the economy; nor have we thought about what happens if prices are free to vary, or how the interest rate is determined. Neither have we explored how investment expenditure is decided. In addition, even a cursory look at the 'real' world suggests that the economy changes through time. All these issues are tackled in the following chapters.

# Chapter Twenty-two Answers

## Money and banking

### Important concepts and technical terms

**1** c    **5** m    **9** d    **13** i

**2** a    **6** n    **10** e    **14** j

**3** l    **7** k    **11** f

**4** h    **8** b    **12** g

### Exercises

**1** **(a)** This exercise is intended to illustrate the inefficiency of the barter economy. It is possible in this case to arrange a sequence of transactions. For instance, Alice swaps with Henry; Daniel exchanges with Evelyn and then with Carol; Barry swaps with Gloria; Carol exchanges with Felix and then with Barry. The success of the sequence depends upon the ability of these people to agree fair quantities for exchange, as well as being able to sort out with whom to exchange – notice that poor Carol in our sequence

holds in turn doughnuts, figs and blackcurrant jam before she finally gets coconuts in the last round!

**(b)** Even in this simple world of only eight people with simple desires, the gains from there being a medium of exchange should be apparent – and notice that, by virtue of prices, the 'quantity' problem is also solved.

**2** **(a)** Gold is an example of commodity money – it is a substance with industrial uses which has at times been acceptable as a medium of exchange.

**(b)** A £1 coin is legal tender and token money – the value of the metal and cost of production is less than £1.

**(c)** Cigarettes have been used as commodity money – for example, in prisoner-of-war camps during the Second World War (see Section 22–1 of the main text), but normally would be considered not-money.

**(d)** A cheque is an example of IOU money – and also token money.

**(e)** Petrol is normally not-money – but *The Times* (11 December 1981) reported that parking fines in some towns in Argentina could be paid only in petrol, as inflation was

**Table A22–1   Commercial bank balance sheet (£ million)**

| Liabilities | | Assets | | Cash ratio | Public cash holdings | Money stock |
|---|---|---|---|---|---|---|
| Deposits | 200 | Cash | 20 | | | |
| | | Loans | 180 | | | |
| | 200 | | 200 | 10% | 10 | 210 |

eroding the value of money at such a rapid rate.

**(f)** The camera in part-exchange is not-money. It does not meet the requirement of being 'generally acceptable' and has value only in that particular transaction.

**(g)** A building society deposit is near money: it is readily converted into cash but cannot be used directly in payment.

**(h)** In general, these are considered not-money – but see the story of the singer Mademoiselle Zelie in Box 22–1 in the main text.

**3** **(a)** Joe Public is now holding £20 million instead of the desired £10 million and will presumably deposit the extra £10 million with the commercial bank.

**(b)** The bank is now holding £20 million cash with £90 million loans – and the cash ratio has increased to 20/110 = 18.2 per cent.

**(c)** The commercial bank will seek to make further loans to restore the desired 10 per cent cash ratio.

**(d)** Joe Public has now borrowed an extra £9 million, so cash holdings have increased to £19 million.

**(e)** The extra £9 million eventually finds its way back into the bank.

**(f)** And the bank's cash ratio is back up to 20/119 = 16.8 per cent, so the bank again will try to make further loans.

**(g)** Equilibrium is restored in the condition shown in Table A22–1.

**(h)** Each time the bank makes further loans to Joe Public, money stock increases by the amount of the loans. The original increase of £10 million leads to a £100 million increase of money stock by the time the system settles down.

**4** *(a)* is not a necessary characteristic. Once goldsmiths began to make loans to their customers, the 100 per cent backing of 'money' by gold deposits was weakened. When Britain left the Gold Standard, even legal tender ceased to be wholly backed by gold reserves. Characteristic *(b)* is also unnecessary: cheques are an accepted form of payment, but are not legal tender. Characteristics *(c)* and *(d)*, however, are crucial. The 'medium of exchange' function is central to what we mean by 'money'. Unless an asset has value in

future transactions, it will not be acceptable as a medium of exchange.

**5**  **(a)** The money multiplier is:

$$(cp + 1)/(cp + cb)$$

where $cp$ = the proportion of deposits held by the public as cash;

$cb$ = the proportion of deposits held by the banks as cash.

This is set out in Box 22–4 in the main text.

Here, we have $(0.25 + 1)/(0.25 + 0.05)\} = \{1.25/0.3\} = 4.17$.

**(b)** $M1 = \{(cp + 1)/(cp + cb)\} \times H = 4.17 \times 12 = 50.04$.

**(c)** $1.25/0.29 = 4.31$.

**(d)** $4.31 \times 12 = 51.72$.

**(e)** $1.30/0.35 = 3.71$.

**(f)** $3.71 \times 12 = 44.52$.

**(g)** It is clear that both $cp$ and $cb$ influence the size of the money stock. The question is whether either of these ratios can be influenced by policy action. The alternative is to operate on the stock of high-powered money itself. The question of money stock policy is raised in Chapter 24.

**6** **(a)** £7000.

**(b)** £9000.

**(c)** In Chapter 24, we will see that the cash ratio is one possible tool that the monetary authorities could use to influence banks' behaviour, although it was not used in the UK in the early 1990s. In periods when regulations have been in force, banks have been observed to hold 'excess reserves'. This may be to avoid being forced to borrow at a penal rate if the cash ratio comes under pressure, or may perhaps be because the opportunity cost of holding excess reserves is low – for instance, where interest-bearing assets may be held as part of required liquid asset reserves.

**7** The wide monetary base (M0) is defined as being notes and coin in circulation outside the Bank of England (40 596) plus bankers' operational deposits with the Banking Department of the Bank of England (72):

M0 = 29 192 + 186 = £40 668 million.

M4 is equal to M0 plus: banks' retail deposits (612 877), plus building society retail shares and deposits (146 951); plus wholesale deposits (289 769) = 1 090 121.

**8** **(a)** Cash is ultimately the most liquid asset, but offers no return.

**(b)** Equities offer a return in the form of dividends but are not very liquid and are highly risky – if the firm goes bankrupt, equities of that firm become worthless.

**(c)** Bonds are long-term financial assets offering a return (the coupon value) and the possibility of capital gains (or losses) if bond prices change. They are potentially liquid, but are affected by the uncertainty of future bond prices. Bonds are to be redeemed at a specific future date.

**(d)** Bills are short-term financial assets with less than one year to redemption. They are highly liquid and offer a reasonable return.

**(e)** See equities under (b).

**(f)** Perpetuities are bonds which are never repurchased by the original issuer. They are not very liquid.

For further discussion of these financial assets, see Box 22–3 in the main text.

**9** **(a)** An increase in real income leads to an increase in the demand for real money balances through both transactions and precautionary motives.

**(b)** If this is interpreted as a decrease in uncertainty, then money demand will fall through the operation of the precautionary motive.

**(c)** Reduces real money demand, mainly through the asset motive.

**(d)** This is the reverse of (c): nominal interest rates represent the opportunity cost of holding money.

**(e)** This will affect nominal money demand, but the demand for real money balances will be unaffected.

**(f)** If we consider broad money, this differential again represents the opportunity cost of holding money – so we expect a fall in real money demand.

**(g)** Increases real money demand through the precautionary motive.

**(h)** The effect depends upon how people react: if they do not change their spending patterns, then they may increase real money demand. However, they may choose to switch funds between money and bonds to earn a return on cash otherwise idle for part of the period, or they may choose to alter spending patterns by visiting the freezer food centre once a month.

**(i)** This item affects the supply of money: there may be an induced movement along the demand curve as interest rates change, but not a movement of the demand function. (This distinction between movements of and along a curve was first seen in Chapter 3.)

## True/False

**1** True: see the introduction to Chapter 22 in the main text.

**2** True: see Section 22–1 of the main text.

**3** False: only notes and coins are legal tender – bank deposits are customary or IOU money. Shopkeepers are not legally obliged to accept a cheque.

**4** True: see Section 22–2 of the main text.

**5** True: the goldsmiths could create money only by holding reserves of less than 100 per cent.

**6** False: insurance companies, pension funds and building societies are other examples of institutions which take in money in order to relend it (see Section 22–3 of the main text).

**7** True.

**8** False: in general, a higher return must be offered to compensate for loss of liquidity.

**9** True: see Section 22–4 of the main text.

**10** False: the monetary base also includes cash held by the banks (see Section 22–5 of the main text).

**11** False: examination of the money multiplier relationship suggests that the reverse is true.

**12** 'Trueish': it depends partly on why you want your money definition. If it is narrow money that you are trying to measure, you might not want to include building society deposits which are no more liquid than time deposits. Notice that building society deposits are included in the M2 and M4 definitions of money (see Section 22–6 of the main text).

**13** False: as income rises, the number of transactions should also increase, driving a higher demand for money.

**14** True: individuals hold money, a liquid asset, in order to faciliate unforeseen payments.

**15** True: as the interest rate on a bond falls, the opportunity cost of holding money falls and so the demand for money increases.

## Economics in action

**1** When the interest rate increases then the price of bonds falls in the market. A bond with a face value of £100, but paying an interest rate of 5 per cent, will trade for £95. But if interest rates rise to 6 per cent then the bond will trade for £94. The rise in interest rates leads to a capital depreciation of £1.

**2** The capital depreciation is suffered by the bond holder. But any holder of money will suffer an increased opportunity cost stemming from the increase in interest rates on the bond. Therefore, the demand for bonds is expected to increase. (See the speculative motive for holding money in Section 22–7 of the main text.)

## Questions for thought

**1** So far, we have talked mainly about the supply of money. This question is asking you to think about the demand for money. This is an important issue which will be considered in Chapter 23.

**2** How does the existence of credit cards affect the public's need to use cash? Suppose a significant number of motorists always buy petrol by credit card: what effect does this have on their need to hold cash? How does this affect the money multiplier – and hence money supply? There is some brief discussion of this topic in Section 22–5 of the main text.

# Chapter Twenty-three Answers

## Interest rates and monetary transmission

### Important concepts and technical terms

**1** b    **4** g    **7** d    **10** j

**2** i    **5** c    **8** f

**3** e    **6** a    **9** h

### Exercises

**1** See Table A23–1 (overleaf).

**2** (a) Recall that:

$M = \{ (cp + 1)/(cp + cb) \} \times H = 3.11 \times 12 = £37.32$ million.

(b) This has the effect of reducing the money multiplier from 3.11 to 2.8, so money supply falls to £33.6 million.

(c) This has the same effect as (b) – money supply falls to £33.6 million.

(d) This also has the same effect as (b) – money supply falls to £33.6 million.

(e) Reducing $H$ by £1 million reduces $M$ by the size of the money multiplier – i.e. by £3.11 million, to £34.21 million.

**3** (a) In assessing the growth of M4 we must first distinguish between real and nominal growth. Since inflation in the UK has averaged below 2.5 per cent throughout the period 2002–04, then we might estimate real M4 growth as rising from (6 – 2.5 = 3.5 per cent) in 2002 to (8 – 2.5 = 5.5 per cent) in 2004. The rise in M4 is clearly being driven by growth in M4 lending and M4 holdings of retail deposits.

(b) The volatility in M4 wholesale deposits probably reflects the speculative motive for holding money and the different interest rate sensitivity between retail and wholesale money holders. Retail investors, ordinary individuals, are probably less likely to switch from money to bonds as interest rates change. However, wholesale holders of money, such as banks, are more likely to substitute money holdings for bonds when interest rates change.

(c) The housing market boom has led to an increase in new mortgage advances which will increase M4 lending. With house prices rising, home owners' equity has also increased. Some individuals have remortgaged their homes in order to release the equity. This again leads to an increase in M4 lending.

For real £M3: $178.0 \times 100/139.7 = 127.4$.

These results are consistent with our observations, especially reflecting the changes in nominal interest rates – notice that, as predicted, holdings of real £M3 increased by more than those of real M1.

| Table A23–1 | Balance sheets of the Bank of England, May 2004 | | | |
|---|---|---|---|---|
| **Department** | **Assets** | **£ bn** | **Liabilities** | **£ bn** |
| **Issue** | Government securities | 13.5 | Notes in circulation | 34.5 |
| | Other securities | 11.4 | | |
| | Issue Department assets | 24.8 | Issue Department liabilities | 20.9 |
| **Banking** | Government securities | 1.8 | Public deposits | 0.7 |
| | Advances | 7.3 | Bankers' deposits | 1.9 |
| | Other assets | 13.7 | Reserves and other accounts | 14.5 |
| | Banking Department assets | 72.5 | Banking Department liabilities | 72.5 |

**4** (a) With money demand at $LL_0$ and money supply $MS_0$, equilibrium is achieved with real money balances $OF$ and interest rate $OA$.

(b) The position of the $LL$ schedule depends primarily upon real income, an increase in which could explain a move from $LL_0$ to $LL_1$.

(c) With money demand at $LL_1$, but money supply at $MS_0$ and interest rate still at $OA$, there is clearly an excess demand for money of an amount $FG$.

(d) This is mirrored by an equal excess supply of bonds, in response to which the price of bonds will fall, in turn causing the rate of interest to rise. This process continues until equilibrium is reached.

(e) The new equilibrium is at interest rate $OC$, at which point real money demand is equal to money supply $OF$.

(f) The authorities can operate either upon the stock of high-powered money or upon the money multiplier, as we have seen. The former could be achieved by open market operations (OMOs) to sell bills or bonds to the public. The money multiplier may be operated on by influencing the proportion of deposits held by the banks as cash.

(g) Equilibrium at interest rate $OD$, real money balances $OE$.

**5** The transactions demand for money (in nominal terms) is argued to depend upon nominal income – i.e. upon the price level and real income. Situations (a)–(d) would thus be expected to lead to an increase in transactions demand. Notice in (b) that the expectation of a price rise is sufficient to cause economic agents to alter their behaviour in anticipation. An increase in the rate of income tax (e) would reduce transactions demand. A fall in interest rates (f) would be expected to have a greater effect on the asset demand (and perhaps the precautionary demand) than on the transactions demand.

**6** All of them.

**7** Suppose that the money demand schedule is known

to be given by $LL$ in Fig. A23–1 and that the authorities set $L_0$ as the target level for money stock. By fixing the rate of interest at $R_0$, money supply can be allowed to self-adjust to the target level. This technique relies on the stability of the $LL$ curve – and upon the authorities having knowledge of it. If $LL$ is neither known nor stable, the possibility of achieving targets by this route is remote. The method also requires that equilibrium is readily and quickly achieved.

**8** In Exercise **8**, we saw how the authorities might set the interest rate at $R_0$ (in Fig. A23–1), and allow money demand to be at $L_0$. We might see the problem here as being the reverse: the authorities may set money supply at $L_0$ so that $R_0$ results from market equilibrium. However, two sorts of problem may arise. Firstly, there is the problem of achieving $L_0$ when the authorities do not have precise control of money supply. Secondly, there are still the problems of the stability of $LL$, as discussed in the answer to Exercise **8**.

**Figure A23–1** Monetary control through the interest rate

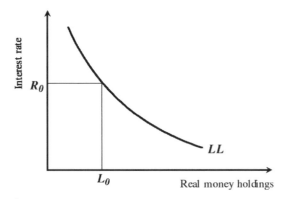

**9** (a) $OB$.

(b) The area $ABC$ reflects the fact that our individual must borrow in early life to maintain consumption above current income.

(c) By borrowing at the market rate of interest.

(d) This 'saving' is for two reasons – first, the individual must pay back the money borrowed in early life, together with the interest payments. Second, money must be set aside in order to maintain consumption after retirement.

(e) *EFGH* represents dissaving.

(f) By saving in middle age (see *(d)*).

(g) An increase in initial wealth shifts up the permanent income line and increases consumption.

(h) An increase in the interest rate reduces the present value of future income. The cost of borrowing in early life is increased. The permanent income level falls – and so will consumption. For more detailed discussion, see Section 23–1 of the main text.

**10** **(a)** A fall in the rate of interest implies an increase in the price of bonds. If the price of bonds increases, people will choose to hold less bonds and more money, so there is an increase in money supply.

(b) As the rate of interest falls, private consumption and investment tend to rise. (Fig. A23–2).

**Figure A23–2** The investment demand schedule

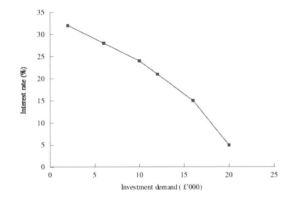

(c) Aggregate demand rises.

(d) This brings about an increase in equilibrium output. This shows the initial phase of the transmission mechanism of monetary policy.

(e) As equilibrium output rises, the transactions and precautionary demands for money increase.

(f) The increase in the demand for money leads to an increase in equilibrium interest rates (through the influence of the bond market); this will moderate the original increase in aggregate demand through the effects of the rate of interest on consumption and investment.

(g) The net effect is likely to be an increase in equilibrium output, unless neither consumption nor investment is sensitive to the rate of interest.

## True/False

**1** True: see Section 23–1 of the main text.

**2** False: in order to reduce money supply, the Bank must induce the banks to hold larger cash reserves (see Section 23–2 of the main text).

**3** True.

**4** False, of course: a reverse repo is a form of short-term borrowing. For instance, you might sell gilts to a bank, agreeing to repurchase at a specified price and date. See Box 23–1 in the main text.

**5** True: see Box 23–1 in the main text.

**6** False: for discussion of the Bank's role as lender of last resort, see Section 23–3 of the main text.

**7** True: see Section 23–4 of the main text.

**8** False: uncertainty provides the motivation for the precautionary demand for money.

**9** False: the nominal interest rate better reflects the interest differential between holding money and bonds.

**10** False: prices may vary in ways beyond the control of the Bank, so nominal money supply is more amenable to control (see Section 23–5 of the main text).

**11** True.

**12** True.

## Economics in action

**1** The transmission mechanism refers to how changes in monetary policy impact GDP. An increase in interest rates should reduce private consumption. Credit-fuelled consumption becomes more expensive and the net present value (NPV) of life-time income also falls. In terms of firms, an increase in interest rates reduces the demand for credit-financed investment. Since investment and consumption are two key components of aggregate expenditure, demand within the economy should fall, leading to a moderating effect on the growth in GDP and inflation.

**2** There is a short-term and a long-term view. Manufacturing firms may feel happy that the cost of borrowing has remained at 4.5 per cent; this will help consumers who buy manufacturers' goods and it will also help manufacturers who have credit facilities. But if the Bank of England fails to control the macroeconomy quickly enough, then a future lack of economic stability may be very damaging for manufacturers.

## Questions for thought

**1** **(a)** If you expect the rate of interest to rise, then you expect the price of bonds to fall – so you will hold all your wealth as money to avoid capital losses.

**(b)** If the rate of interest is high, and bond prices are correspondingly low, then you would probably choose to put all your wealth into bonds to reap capital gains when bond prices rise. When the interest rate reaches $Rc$ (the 'critical rate'), you no longer expect bond prices to change and will be indifferent between money and bonds.

**(c)** This analysis appeared in Keynes' General Theory, which referred to it as the 'speculative demand for money'. The

**Figure A23–3** The speculative demand for money

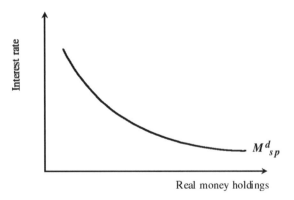

Real money holdings

aggregate relationship is shown in Fig. A23–3. The downward slope results from the assumption that different individuals have different expectations about $Rc$, but at some point the rate of interest becomes so low that everyone agrees that it can fall no further.

**2** The fallacy in the question as it stands is that it assumes that monetary policy can be conducted only through the control of money supply. This chapter has been arguing that the way to deal with this is to target interest rates rather than money supply. This is a viable option, and money supply can be affected indirectly by this route.

**3** **(a)** Under the permanent income hypothesis, we would not expect consumers to change their behaviour in response to a transitory change. Thus, if faced with a temporary fall in income, we would expect them to try to maintain existing patterns of consumption. Of course, this may not always be possible. For example, they may find themselves to be liquidity-constrained: that is, they may be unable to borrow in order to finance the level of consumption to which they are accustomed. Perhaps the bank does not accept their view that the reduction in income is only transitory.

In these circumstances, we find that consumption varies rather more with current income than would be predicted by the theory. Some empirical studies have found exactly this result.

**(b)** This is the Ricardian equivalence argument again. If consumers perceive the tax cuts to be transitory (in the sense that taxes will have to increase again at some time in the future so that the government can pay back the debt), then they will not respond to tax cuts by changing their consumption plans. Alternatively, they may perceive that it is only future generations that will have to pay back, or it may be that they were liquidity-constrained before the tax cuts. In these sorts of circumstances, consumption may react to tax cuts.

**4** You may wish to look back at Chapter 12 and 13 of the main text as well as Section 23–7.

# Chapter Twenty-four Answers

## Monetary and fiscal policy

### Important concepts and technical terms

| | | | |
|---|---|---|---|
| **1** b | **4** g | **7** k | **10** h |
| **2** a | **5** f | **8** i | **11** j |
| **3** e | **6** d | **9** c | |

### Exercises

**1** (a) The Bank of England is forecasting inflation over a period of two to three years. It is very easy to be confident about the inflation forecast for next month, it will be similar to this month. But the forecast two years ahead is much more difficult to predict and so the fan of forecasts must be wider.

(b) In 2004, the Bank of England forecast that inflation would rise above its target level of 2 per cent by 2006. It is therefore expected to increase interest rates in 2004 and 2005 in order to combat the expected rise in inflation. Is this what we observed?

**2** (a) Reducing direct tax rates has an immediate effect in increasing disposable income, which leads to an increase in consumption expenditure and hence aggregate demand.

(b) This leads to an increase in equilibrium output.

(c) As income rises, there is an increase in transactions and precautionary demand for money.

(d) Given fixed money supply, this leads to a fall in bond prices and an increase in interest rates.

(e) In turn, this leads to a fall in both investment and consumption.

(f) There is then a reduction in equilibrium output, owing to this 'crowding-out' of private expenditure.

(g) Complete crowding-out occurs when the demand for money is perfectly inelastic with respect to the interest rate: in this case, the interest rate continues to rise until consumption and investment fall sufficiently to return aggregate demand to its initial level.

**3** (a) *AB* is the (downward-sloping) *IS* curve; *CD* is the (upward-sloping) *LM* curve.

| Point | Money market | Goods market |
|---|---|---|
| E | Excess supply | Equilibrium |
| F | Equilibrium | Excess supply |
| G | Excess demand | Equilibrium |
| H | Equilibrium | Equilibrium |
| J | Equilibrium | Excess demand |

(b) Only at point *H* is there equilibrium in both markets.

(c) At *J* the money market is in equilibrium but there is excess demand for goods, tending to lead to an increase in output (and interest rates). A similar story could be told for each disequilibrium point – and under reasonable assumptions the economy can be seen to move towards equilibrium.

(d) (i) Shifts *IS* to the right.

(ii) Shifts *LM* to the right.

(iii) Shifts *IS* to the left.

(iv) This reduces real money supply – and so shifts *LM* to the left.

(v) This may be expected to increase autonomous consumption, as the poor tend to have a higher average propensity to consume: *IS* shifts to the right.

(vi) A messy one – an increase in wealth may lead to higher consumption (*IS* shifts to the right), but also to an increase in the asset demand for money (*LM* shifts to the left).

**4** (a) Income $Y_1$, interest rate $R_1$.

(b) An increase in government expenditure (or cuts in taxation).

(c) Income increases from $Y_1$ to $Y_4$.

(d) Income $Y_3$, interest rate $R_2$ using $LM_b$.

(e) Income $Y_2$, interest rate $R_3$ using $LM_a$.

(f) With $LM_b$ (relatively elastic), crowding-out is $Y_4 - Y_3$. With $LM_a$ (relatively inelastic), crowding-out is $Y_4 - Y_2$.

(g) The sensitivity of money demand to the interest rate and to income.

(h) By financing spending through an expansion of money supply, shifting *LM* to intersect $IS_1$ at income $Y_4$, interest rate $R_1$; this works satisfactorily in this fixed-price world, but may have side-effects if prices are free to vary – as we shall see.

**5** (a) Income $Y_3$; interest rate $R_1$.

(b) A reduction in real money supply. The methods by which this may be achieved were discussed in Chapter 23.

(c) Income $Y_2$; interest rate $R_3$ using $IS_b$.

(d) Income $Y_1$; interest rate $R_2$ using $IS_a$.

(e) The degree to which private expenditure (investment and consumption) is sensitive to the rate of interest. The flatter $IS$, the greater effect monetary policy has on the level of income.

**6** These arguments are fully explained in Box 24–1 in the main text.

**7** (a) We might convert the relationship into algebraic terms as:

$Ct = \beta \, Y^p_t = 0.93 \, Y^p_t$

where $\beta$ = marginal propensity to consume out of permanent income and $Y^p_t$ = current estimate of permanent income, which we could write as: $Y^p_t = Y^p_{t-1} + j\,(Y_t - Y^p_{t-1})$, where $j$ = the proportion of the change in disposable income expected to be permanent (here, 0.8)

$C_t$ = current consumption.

(b) $Y^p_t = 15\,000 + 0.8\,(25\,000 - 15\,000) = £23\,000$.

(c) The marginal propensity to consume out of current income ($Y_t$) is $\beta$ multiplied by $j$ – i.e. $0.93 \times 0.8 = 0.74$.

(d) The 'multiplier' is $1/(1 -$ the marginal propensity to spend on domestic output out of income).

Based on the marginal propensity to consume out of current income, we calculate the short-run multiplier as $1/(1 - 0.74) = 3.85$. However, in the long run (based on permanent income), we have $1/(1 - 0.93) = 14.28$.

This seems to suggest that fiscal policy should be more effective in the long, rather than the short, run. This runs against our normal expectation, but you should remember that we are still operating with a partial model. Once we have taken prices and exchange rates into account, the result will turn out to be very different. Notice that the multiplier here is telling us how far the $IS$ curve shifts following a change in government expenditure. Under the assumptions of this question, full adjustment to changing income takes a number of periods to work through – hence the result.

## True/False

**1** True: it is easy to set a target for money supply growth, but it is much more difficult to measure money supply growth and so the policy becomes difficult to implement and monitor.

**2** True: since the 1990s many economies have moved to inflation targeting.

**3** False: inflation and GDP are interlinked, stability in inflation can lead to stability in GDP. So targeting of inflation can aid targeting of GDP, although some economists may disagree.

**4** True: a central bank could be concerned with both current and future inflation, but perhaps it places a greater emphasis on future expected inflation.

**5** False: an increase in the target rate of inflation means that long-run interest rates can be lower, not higher.

**6** True: see Section 24–2 of the main text.

**7** False: the multiplier is reduced, perhaps substantially (see Section 24–4 of the main text).

**8** True: see Section 24–5 of the main text.

**9** True: the price level affects real money supply.

**10** False: monetary and fiscal policy have very different effects, especially in their influence on the composition of aggregate demand (see Section 24–6 of the main text).

**11** True: consideration of flexible prices, aggregate supply and full employment are our next topics.

## Economics in action

**1** The real interest rate is the nominal rate less the rate of inflation. Therefore, if the nominal rate of interest is 5 per cent and inflation is 2.5 per cent, then the real rate is $5 - 2.5 = 2.5$ per cent. However, if the nominal rate of interest is 1.5 per cent and inflation is 2.5 per cent, then the real rate of interest is $-1$ per cent. This will create an incentive to borrow money, because in real terms if you borrow £1000 then at the end of the year you will owe only £990. It is therefore of no surprise that household borrowing in the US has grown.

**2** The problems between fiscal and monetary policy are fairly similar. Uncertainty: how far is the economy from its full potential? Timing: over what period will a policy work? How strong will the policy response be? How might income, exports, savings and invesment rates change? However, while uncertainity and timing seem to be common to fiscal and monetary policy, offsetting problems such as crowding-out and Ricardian equivalence relate only to fiscal policy.

## Question for thought

**1** **(a)** The *IS* curve is derived by substituting for *T* in the consumption equation and then for *C* and *I* in the equilibrium condition – i.e. we impose equilibrium.

$$Y = A + c(Y - tY) - dR + B - iR + G.$$

We can then collect terms in *Y* and *R* and rearrange the equation:

$$Y = \frac{A + B + G}{\{1 - c(1 - t)\}} - \frac{(d + i)}{\{1 - c(1 - t)\}} \times R.$$

The first term represents the autonomous element.

**(b)** Similar steps are taken for the money market equation:

$$R = \frac{N - M}{m} - \frac{kP}{m} \times Y.$$

**(c)** Plugging in the values of the parameters:

*IS*: $Y = 4860 - 55.556\,R$.

*LM*: $R = -100 + 0.025\,Y$.

These are plotted in Fig. A24–1.

Equilibrium occurs with the rate of interest at 9 per cent, income at 4360.

**Figure A24–1**  *LM* equilibrium

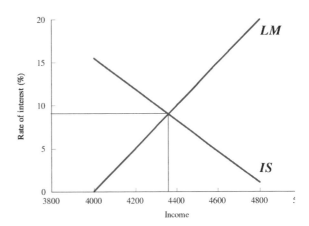

**(d)** $C = 700 + 0.8 \times (1 - 0.2) \times 4360 - 5 \times 9 = 3445.4$
$I = 400 - 15 \times 9 = 265$
$C + I + G = 3445.4 + 265 + 649.6 = 4360.$

**(e)** $Md = 0.25 \times 1 \times 4360 + 200 - 10 \times 9 = 1200.$

**(f)** $T = 0.2 \times 4360 = 872$
$G - T = 649.6 - 872 = -222.4$
A surplus of 222.4.

# Chapter Twenty-five Answers

## Aggregate supply, prices and adjustment to shocks

### Important concepts and technical terms

**1** *m*   **5** *i*   **9** *d*   **13** *e*

**2** *k*   **6** *a*   **10** *j*   **14** *g*

**3** *l*   **7** *f*   **11** *c*

**4** *h*   **8** *n*   **12** *b*

### Exercises

**1** **(a)** Income *OK*; interest rate *OD*; aggregate demand *OK*.

**(b)** *LM*ᵦ.

**(c)** Income *OJ*; interest rate *OF*; aggregate demand *OJ*.

**(d)** As price rises, the real value of money balances and other assets held by households is reduced. This has an effect on consumption and reduces aggregate demand, shifting *IS* to *IS*ᵦ, and equilibrium income, interest rate and aggregate demand respectively to *OH*, *OE* and *OH*.

**(e)** A fall in price moves *LM* from $LM_0$ to $LM_a$. In the absence of the real balance effect, equilibrium income and aggregate demand move to *OP* and the rate of interest to *OB*. The real balance effect moves *IS* from $IS_0$ to $IS_a$, so equilibrium income and aggregate demand are *OQ* with interest rate *OC*.

**(f)** The position of the *LM* schedule is partly determined by the size of real money supply. A change in price given fixed nominal money supply affects real money supply and thus moves the *LM* schedule.

**(g)** In Fig. A25–1 (overleaf) $MDS_1$ shows the macroeconomic demand schedule without taking account of the real balance effect, which affects the slope, resulting in $MDS_2$. The intersection of the two represents our original equilibrium point.

**Figure A25–1**  The macroeconomic demand schedule and the real balance effect

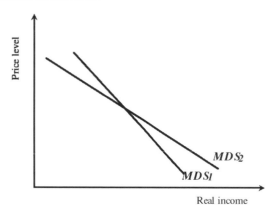

**2**    All the characteristics listed are features of the macroeconomic demand schedule – that's how we constructed it!

**3**    **(a)**  *OB*: where labour demand = job acceptances.

**(b)**  Employment *OF*; registered unemployment *FJ*.

**(c)**  The natural rate of unemployment is *FJ* – there is no involuntary unemployment.

**(d)**  Employment *OD*: this represents the number of people prepared to accept jobs at this real wage. Registered unemployment is *DH*. All those wishing to work at this real wage can obtain work – there is excess demand for labour – so there is no involuntary unemployment.

**(e)**  With excess demand for labour, firms will be prepared to offer high wages to attract labour, so the market moves towards equilibrium.

**(f)**  Employment *OE*: this represents labour demand at this real wage. Registered unemployment is *EK*, of which *EG* is voluntary, representing people who are willing to work but cannot find employment.

**(g)**  Eventually – or instantly, in the classical model – wages will drift downwards, and the market moves towards equilibrium.

**(h)**  In our static model, labour is the only variable input, so fixing employment implies the level of output/aggregate supply.

**(i)**  If the labour market is always in equilibrium, the level of employment – and hence aggregate supply – will be stable.

**4**    **(a)**  An increase in nominal money supply increases aggregate demand at each price, so the move must be from *MDS*_a to *MDS*_b.

**(b)**  Output *OD*; price *OA*.

**(c)**  Output *OD*; price *OB*; prices adjust instantaneously leav-

ing output unaffected; money feeds only prices.

**(d)**  A reduction in government spending is represented by a move from *MDS*_b to *MDS*_a.

**(e)**  Price *OB*; output *OD*.

**(f)**  Price *OA*; output *OD*.

**(g)**  Price still at *OB*; output reduced to *OC*.

**(h)**  *MDS* represents points at which planned spending equals actual output – to this extent, the goods market is in equilibrium. However, this may not represent equilibrium from the producers' perspective: there is no implication that planned output is equal to actual output.

**5**    **(a)**  This factor affects the workers' willingness to become unemployed and discourages adjustment.

**(b)**  In the absence of a redundancy agreement, firms may be more willing to make adjustments to the size of the workforce.

**(c)**  This may encourage adjustment, as firms have less need to 'hoard' unskilled labour.

**(d)**  This may discourage firms from adjusting employment and wage rates, as there is flexibility in labour input without needing to negotiate a new wage deal or indulge in hiring and firing. However, in the long run such adjustments may have to be made.

**(e)**  This also discourages firms from making adjustments to employment and wages.

**(f)**  If labour is scarce, firms may not be able to increase employment, and may be reluctant to lose workers. Workers may be more prepared to change jobs as they will perceive that it will not be difficult to find new jobs.

**(g)**  Firms may wish to hold on to trained labour if demand falls temporarily. Workers may recognize that their skills may not be readily transferred to other firms.

**6**    **(a)**  Demand shock.

**(b)**  Supply shock.

**(c)**  Supply.

**(d)**  Demand.

**(e)**  Demand.

**(f)**  Demand.

**(g)**  Supply.

**(h)**  Supply.

**7**    **(a)**  An increase in supply, increasing potential output.

**(b)**  A decrease in supply (see the discussion of an oil price increase in Section 25–8 of the main text).

**(c)**  This increases autonomous investment demand, so represents an increase in demand.

**(d)**  A (short-run) decrease in supply.

**(e)**  A decrease in demand.

**(f)** Given the differing propensities to consume of the 'rich' and the 'poor', this leads to an increase in autonomous consumption and in aggregate demand.

**(g)** This represents a fall in labour supply at any given real wage, and so there is a reduction in supply and potential output.

**8** The only effect of the increase in aggregate demand would be on the price level, which affects only *(c)* and *(e)*.

**9** All of them.

**10** **(a)** If the economy is in equilibrium, then it must be on the (long-run) aggregate supply curve *AS*; if we are to illustrate an increase in nominal money, *MDS* is to move to the right – so initially must be on *MDS*ₐ. The initial position is thus at output *OG*, price *OA*.

**(b)** Given full wage and price flexibility the economy moves straight to output *OG*, price *OD*.

**(c)** The increase in nominal money supply moves the macro-economic demand schedule from *MDS*ₐ to *MDS*ᵦ; with sluggish adjustment, the economy moves to a position on the short-run aggregate supply curve *SAS*𝒸 with output *OJ*, price *OB*. In the short run, this increase in output will be brought about through overtime working, etc., as firms cannot instantly adjust wages and employment.

**(d)** Firms find that there has been an increase in demand for their output and prices rise. In time, firms take on new workers, as adjusting employment is a more sensible long-run strategy than varying hours worked by the existing workforce. The *SAS* schedule begins to move – from *SAS*𝒸 to *SAS*ᵦ in the medium term, by which stage price has reached *OC* and output has fallen back to *OH*.

**(e)** Output *OG*, price *OD*.

**(f)** See Fig. A25–2.

**Figure A25–2** Labour market adjustment

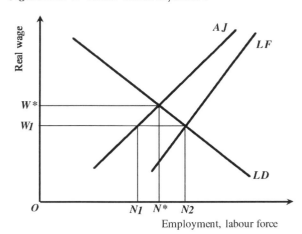

Employment, labour force

The market starts in equilibrium with real wage *W\** and employment *N\**. As the price level rises, the real wage falls – say, to *W*₁ – at which point we have to think rather carefully about what is happening. Labour demand has increased to *N*₂ but job acceptances have fallen to *N*₁. There is excess demand for labour, and if agents are always on the *AJ* function, employment falls at a time when output is rising. How do we explain this situation? It could be that in the short run workers prefer to hold on to their jobs rather than immediately incurring the costs of job search, perhaps because they realize that the real wage reduction is temporary and are prepared to be 'off' the *AJ* schedule. In addition, firms may be prepared to offer lots of overtime, increasing output by this means rather than by increasing employment. As firms seek to adjust employment levels, wages will be bid up, carrying the economy back towards equilibrium – back at *W\*N\**.

**(g)** When wages need to fall, we may expect resistance from workers and unions. When the adjustment is upwards, we may expect firms to be keen to adjust wages (there is excess demand for labour) and workers are unlikely to protest. We may thus imagine that the adjustment in this case may be more rapid.

**(h)** 10 per cent (see Section 25–7 of the main text).

## True/False

**1** True: see Section 25–1 of the main text.

**2** True.

**3** False: there will always be some unemployment, even at full employment (see Section 25–2 of the main text). Unemployment is more closely examined in Chapter 27.

**4** Silly: money illusion is the confusion of real and nominal variables.

**5** True: see Section 25–2 of the main text.

**6** True: see Section 25–4 of the main text.

**7** False: output is unaffected and only prices change.

**8** True: see Section 25–5 of the main text.

**9** False: firms are more likely to vary hours worked in the short run (see Section 25–6 of the main text).

**10** True: see Section 25–7 of the main text.

**11** False: a favourable supply shock leads to higher output, but lower price level (see Section 25–8 of the main text).

**12** True(ish): technology such as the Internet has increased productivity, leading to growth in aggregate supply and GDP.

## Economics in action

**1** Given the reasonably long data periods, it is arguable that the technology boom has led to a permanent increase in the long-run (steady-state) growth rate of the US economy. That is, the evidence over many years points to a permanent, rather than a temporary, shift in productivity and therefore aggregate supply.

**2** If aggregate supply has undergone a permanent and positive shock, then within our AD and AS diagrammatic framework, AS is shifting to the right faster than before. Without a change in interest rates, inflation will fall. If, however, the central bank is tasked with an inflation target, then long-run interest rates will have to fall in order to enable aggregate demand to grow and accommodate the increase in aggregate supply; and keep inflation at the target level.

## Questions for thought

**1** **(a)** The story should be familiar by now: briefly, a reduction in money wages leads to a falling price level, an increase in real money supply, a fall in interest rates and an expansion of consumption and investment – hence aggregate demand and output.

**(b)** The LM schedule of Fig. 25–5 has a horizontal section. This results from the (Keynesian) speculative demand for money discussed in the 'Questions for thought' in Chapter 23. $R_0$ represents an interest rate at which all agents expect a fall in bond prices and thus hold no bonds. It breaks the chain of part (a) because the interest rate cannot fall below $R_0$ and equilibrium income cannot increase beyond $Y_0$. The economy is stuck in what is often known as the 'liquidity trap'.

**(c)** If the real balance effect is strong enough, then falling prices have the effect of increasing autonomous consumption, thus shifting the IS schedule. Examination of Fig. 25–5 shows that, if IS moves to the right, the economy is able to escape from the liquidity trap.

**(d)** Fiscal policy would shift the IS schedule to the right and would be much more effective than monetary policy in this context.

**2** (c).

**3** Between 2001 and 2004, interest rates in the USA were reduced to historically low levels. At the same time, a massive fiscal stimulus was injected into the US economy, resulting in a very large fiscal deficit. Some may argue that the liquidity trap does not explain this particular chain of events. But with such low interest rates it is possible that the US government was concerned that a liquidity trap would need to be avoided by the additional injection of a fiscal stimulus.

# Chapter Twenty-six Answers

## Inflation, expectations and credibility

## Important concepts and technical terms

| | | | |
|---|---|---|---|
| **1** l | **5** k | **9** h | **13** n |
| **2** f | **6** c | **10** b | **14** e |
| **3** i | **7** m | **11** g | |
| **4** a | **8** d | **12** j | |

## Exercises

**1** **(a)** 10 per cent: the same percentage as nominal money stock. This follows from the assumption of the Quantity Theory that the velocity of circulation is constant.

**(b)** In the short run, producers react to the increase in demand by increasing output. The price level may also begin to rise – but the main effect is on output. (Recall Section 26–7 of the main text.) The nominal interest rate falls to induce people to hold a larger quantity of real money balances.

**(c)** As adjustment takes place, the level of real output falls back to its original equilibrium level and prices rise. In the eventual equilibrium, the price level will have risen by the full extent of the original increase in money stock, but real output will be unchanged and interest rates will have gradually climbed back to their original level.

**(d)** Using the analysis of Chapter 26, we may argue that the cost increase is passed on as a price increase, reducing real money supply, raising interest rates and reducing aggregate demand. Sluggish wages lead to unemployment.

**(e)** A government worried about unemployment may be tempted to accommodate the price rise by permitting an increase in nominal money.

**(f)** If the supply shock reduces long-run potential output, then the economy will eventually settle at this lower output level, which may entail higher unemployment. The more the authorities have tried to maintain output and employment by printing money, the higher the eventual price level – but output will still tend to its equilibrium level.

**(g)** A government concerned about inflation may refuse to accommodate the price rise, preferring to see unemployment rise in the short run.

**(h)** In the eventual equilibrium, real output will be at its potential level, but prices will be less high than in *(f)*.

**2** **(a)** 10 per cent.

**(b)** Given $MV = PY$, we calculate that in year 1, $P = MV/Y = 8000/4000 = 2$. In year 2, $P = 2.16$(ish). So the inflation rate was about 8 per cent.

**(c)** The real interest rate is approximately the difference between the nominal interest rate and the inflation rate. Here, $9 - 8 = 1$ per cent.

**(d)** Given that the money market is in equilibrium, then from $MV = PY$, $M/P = Y/V$.
Year 1: $4000/4 = 1000$
Year 2: $4065/4 = 1016.25$.

**3** This exercise closely follows the example pursued in Section 26–5 of the main text.

**(a)** Gross earnings are 3 per cent of £5000 = £150.

**(b)** 30 per cent of £150 = £45.

**(c)** Net savings are £105; the rate of return is $(105/5000) \times 100 = 2.1$ per cent. In the absence of inflation, nominal and real rates of return are the same.

**(d)** Gross earnings are 13 per cent of £5000 = £650. Tax is 30 per cent of £650 = £195.

**(e)** Net earnings are £455. Nominal rate of return is $(455/5000) \times 100 = 9.1$ per cent. Real rate of return is $9.1 - 10 = -0.9$ per cent.

**4** **(a)** See Fig. A26–1.

**Figure A26–1** Inflation and unemployment in the UK, 1990–2003

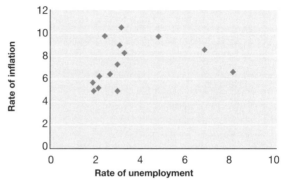

**(b)** There is little evidence of a stable relationship between inflation and unemployment, as suggested by Phillips. There is some suggestion of an expectations augmented Phillips curve relationship with a vertical pattern of observations, implying that unemployment remains constant as expectations regarding inflation change. The three observations to the left of the line might be indicative of some short-term deviation. But it is difficult to prove this using a simple scatter plot. Apart from the three outliers which lie to the left.

**5** **(a)** $SRPC_0$ is the zero-inflation Phillips curve, so the natural rate of unemployment is $OC$ where $SRPC_0$ cuts the horizontal axis.

**(b)** $OC$ is the natural rate, and the rate of inflation which will be stable at $OC$ with $SRPC_1$ is $OA$.

**(c)** Initially unemployment falls to $OB$, inflation rises to $OA$.

**(d)** This position is untenable because $SRPC_0$ is valid for zero expected inflation. Once workers realize that prices are rising at the rate $OA$, they will adjust expectations and $SRPC$ will move.

**(e)** Given answer *(b)*, the economy ends up back at unemployment $OC$ but with inflation $OA$.

**(f)** A determined government would carry the economy to $D$ in the short run.

**(g)** As expectations adjust, the short-run Phillips curve moves back down and unemployment falls back to the natural rate $OC$ with zero inflation.

**(h)** The attainment of equilibrium requires that expectations adjust before the government loses its nerve at the sight of all that unemployment.

(i)  It is possible that incomes policy may speed up the adjustment process by affecting expectations, and that unemployment need not rise so high or for so long.

**6**  Factors *(a)*, *(d)* and *(f)* stem from the demand side, whereas factors *(b)*, *(c)* and *(e)* affect the supply side. Item *(d)* may be debatable, in the sense that whereas aggregate demand may be increased, future wage negotiations may be at lower levels if take home pay has been improved. Some economists have argued that item *(e)* is an unlikely initial cause of inflation, as unions react to past events but do not initiate autonomous wage increases.

**7**  *(c)* and *(d)*.

**8**  *(d)*.

**9**  *(a)* is a real cost of inflation, but if inflation is anticipated it can be offset by the adjustment of tax thresholds; (b) is also a real cost, which can be minimized by indexation or by building in anticipated inflation. Cost *(c)* is mere illusion, as it ignores changes in money income, while (d) are real costs which are present whether or not inflation is anticipated. (e) is a real cost of inflation at an unpredictable rate; it is the effects of inflation on uncertainty and business confidence which have made inflation public enemy number one. (f) is an illusion: the cost is not a cost of inflation but the inevitable response to the adverse supply shock.

**10**  **(a)** Incomes policy can stem inflation only temporarily if other policy instruments are not used consistently and responsibly. At times in the past, incomes policy has been used against a backdrop of monetary expansion and thus had no chance of success. However, there could be a role for it if used in harness with other policies.

**(b)**  A problem in the past has been that governments have tried to achieve too much through a single policy.
**(c)**  Layard has argued that a permanent policy is needed; others have suggested that a policy known to be both temporary and consistent with other policies has a better chance of success.
**(d)**  If applied too rigorously, incomes policy could prevent desirable relative price changes.
**(e)**  Another Layard suggestion is that policies should be sure to offer proper incentives to both sides in the wage bargaining process.

## True/False

**1**  True: see the introduction to Chapter 26 in the main text.

**2**  True: in the sense that sustained inflation must always be accompanied by monetary expansion in excess of output growth. The direction of causality is not always clear (see Section 26–1 of the main text).

**3**  False: this is correct only when real money demand is constant.

**4**  True: see Section 26–2 of the main text.

**5**  True.

**6**  False: printing money is not the only way of financing a budget deficit (see Section 26–3 of the main text).

**7**  True: see Box 26–1 in the main text.

**8**  False: recent experience suggests that the Phillips curve cannot be exploited for policy purposes (see Section 26–4 of the main text).

**9**  True: see Section 26–5 of the main text.

**10**  False: the shoe-leather and menu costs remain; other costs result if institutions do not fully adapt.

**11**  True: see Section 26–6 of the main text.

**12**  False: in the long run, a tolerant attitude may lead to high rates of inflation with the consequent high menu and shoe-leather costs.

## Economics in action

**1**  Increased indebtedness of £1 trillion is representative of significant credit creation within the UK economy and therefore an increase in money supply. The Quantity Theory of money therefore predicts (under monetarist assumptions) that inflation will rise. Higher inflation will lead to higher interest rates, slower economic growth and perhaps a recession and increased unemployment.

**2** Debt is demanded by individuals and supplied by lenders based on current and future expected income flows. In a stable economy with low prices, as in the UK, then higher unsecured lending is likely to be offered to individuals with high and developing income profiles. Moreover, in a low-interest rate environment, the discounted value of future income flows are higher, leading to a increased willingness to take on debt.

## Questions for thought

**1** There is no definitive answer to this question, which takes us into the realm of normative economics. We may regard both unemployment and inflation as being economic 'bads'. To a certain degree, it is a question of judgement as to which inflicts most harm on society. Recent governments have argued that the control of inflation is an essential prerequisite to tackling unemployment via economic growth. Other commentators have argued that the rise in unemployment since the late 1970s was too high a price to pay for lower inflation. The debate continues.

**2** In the long run, velocity is likely to be determined by factors affecting the efficiency with which transactions may be carried out and will reflect real money demand. (What happens to velocity in a hyperinflation?) In the short run, velocity may at times reflect disequilibrium in the money market. For instance, in the mid-1970s velocity fell dramatically at a time when the authorities pursued an 'easy' money policy and there was perhaps excess supply of money. This was followed in the late 1970s by a period of higher-than-normal velocity. This was at a time when output was growing but Chancellor Healey was beginning to restrict money growth. From 1979, as inflation fell more rapidly than the rate of monetary growth, velocity fell again. Velocity may thus be a signal of conditions in the money market in the short run. Velocity is discussed in Box 26–1 in the main text.

**3** See Section 26–5 of the main text.

**4** (a) *OF*.

(b) The real rate *(OA)* plus the inflation rate *(AB)*: *OB*.

(c) *OC*.

(d) The real revenue from the inflation tax is given by the product of real money demand and the inflation rate, as explained in Box 26–2 in the main text. It is thus represented in Fig. 26–3 by the area *ABED*.

(e) In moving from *G* to *E*, there is a deadweight loss given by the triangle *DEG*. This reflects the fact that at a higher rate of inflation, agents are forgoing some of the benefits from using real money balances: the convenience of having cash available, etc.

(f) As the economy approaches hyperinflation, people economize more and more in their holdings of real money and the revenue from the inflation tax diminishes. This analysis does not seem to have deterred some countries (especially in Latin America) from attempting to finance their deficits in this way.

# Chapter Twenty-seven Answers

# Unemployment

## Important concepts and technical terms

| | | | |
|---|---|---|---|
| **1** j | **4** f | **7** i | **10** g |
| **2** e | **5** a | **8** c | **11** h |
| **3** k | **6** l | **9** b | **12** d |

## Exercises

**1** (a) Categories *(ii)*, *(iv)* and *(vi)* joined the unemployed, a total of 2700.
Categories *(i)* and *(v)* left = 2600.

(b) Categories *(vi)* and *(vii)* joined = 600.
Categories *(i)* and *(iii)* left = 700.

(c) Categories *(ii)*, *(iii)* and *(iv)* = 2300 left jobs; *(v)* and *(vii)* became employed = 2100; so the employed labour force fell by 200.

(d) Labour force 26 800, unemployed 3000. Although the employed labour force fell by 200, unemployment has risen by only 100.

(e) $1.36 + 3.16 − 3.25 = 1.27$ million.

The way the figures are compiled leaves a discrepancy between this and the actual figure of 1.29 million.

**2** (a) This is structural unemployment. If textile workers are refusing jobs which do not match their acquired skills, then we regard them as voluntarily unemployed.

(b) Frictional unemployment is also voluntary unemployment. Of course, there is a sense in which all unemployed (except school-leavers) are 'between jobs'. But here we refer to those in the process of changing jobs, perhaps having left one job in the knowledge that they have a new job starting in the near future.

(c) Usually regarded as part of frictional unemployment. This is a situation in which we may wish to remember that economists use words in a particular way. Some people in this group may want to work, but are incapable of work. As people, we may recognize these desires, but as economists we include them as part of voluntary unemployment.

(d) Classical unemployment. As individuals, those suffering unemployment for this reason may see themselves as being involuntarily unemployed. However, we remember that they may be unemployed through the choices of their ex-colleagues – for instance, if real wages are sustained at a high level through union market power. In this sense, this unemployment is voluntary.

(e) This is demand-deficient unemployment. Involuntary.

**3** The regional variation in unemployment has not been discussed explicitly in this chapter, which is why this question carries a health warning. However, you should by now have had sufficient practice to be able to think through some of the main issues, using the techniques presented.

(a) Comparing the columns, it is first apparent that some regions have maintained their relative positions. The South East, East Anglia and East Midlands continue to enjoy lower unemployment rates than the national average, although the South East suffered a relative deterioration in 1996. On the other hand, the North, Yorkshire and Humberside, the North West, Wales and Scotland continue to suffer more than most. The West Midlands fell dramatically down the rankings, starting below the national average and finishing above, in spite of some recovery after 1989. This in large measure may be attributed to the decline of manufacturing industry (especially motor vehicles) after 1974. The South West, on the other hand, improved its relative position.

(b) A fundamental issue is whether unemployment rates reflect the characteristics of the regions themselves or of the people who live there. If an area has a high proportion of young people, then we might expect high frictional unemployment, as such workers tend to switch between jobs more frequently. However, we are not presented with such information.

*Structural unemployment* may well contribute to our explanation, in the sense that different regions have differing employment structures. The immobility of labour between regions may create a mismatch between labour demand and supply. The decline of manufacturing in the West Midlands provides one instance of such unemployment. It has been noted that the recession of the early 1990s affected service sectors, and thus affected the differential between the South East and other regions.

*Classical unemployment* is less likely to vary between regions, but it is possible that national industry wage agreements may create wage scales which are locally inappropriate.

*Demand-deficient unemployment* may affect regions differently because of local product structure. In addition, regional disparities may be perpetuated by this route – if unemployment is high in a region, local demand will be low. No doubt you have thought of many other factors.

**4** (a) Employment is 90 (000).

(b) At a real wage of $5, 129 register as being part of the labour force, so total unemployment is $129 − 90 = 39$.

(c) From Table 27–2 we see that 110 would be prepared to accept jobs at this real wage, so involuntary unemployment is $110 − 90 = 20$; the remainder is voluntary.

(d) Firms pay $5 per hour and workers receive $3.

(e) Employment is 90, given by labour demand at $5 per hour. As for unemployment, net real wages are $3, so the registered labour force is 115 and unemployment is $115 − 90 = 25$. The labour market is in equilibrium, so there is no excess demand for labour – remember that the real wage paid by firms exceeds that received by workers. The workers receive $3 per hour, at which rate job acceptances amount to 90.

(f) All unemployment here is voluntary.

(g) Without tax, the equilibrium real wage is $4.

(h) Employment is 100, unemployment is $122 − 100 = 22$. Unemployment has fallen by 3.

(i) With the labour market in equilibrium, all unemployment is voluntary.

If you found this difficult, you might find that it helps to draw a diagram using the figures of Table 27–2. There is a similar figure in Section 27–4 of the main text.

**5** **(a)** $LD_b$ must be the original labour demand schedule. The effect of the adverse supply shock will be to reduce the marginal product of labour and hence labour demand.

**(b)** Real wage *OB*, employment *OE*.

**(c)** *EG*.

**(d)** Employment falls to *OC*, unemployment rises to *CG*.

**(e)** Real wages *OA*, employment *OD*.

**(f)** *DF*.

**(g)** The natural rate has risen. As the real wage falls, the replacement ratio rises and affects the natural rate.

**6** **(a)** An increase in unemployment benefits – a reduction in unemployment benefits is more likely to reduce the natural rate of unemployment.

**(b)** A decline in international competitiveness – unlikely to be true: an increase in international competitiveness may reduce the natural rate of unemployment.

**(c)** A reduction in trade union power – possibly true: a freer flexible labour market and less industrial disputes is likely to raise labour productivity and reduce the natural rate of unemployment.

**(d)** An increase in world trade – again, probably true: world trade has increased and is likely to increase demand for UK workers in the long term, leading to a reduction in the natural rate of unemployment.

**(e)** The recession in British manufacturing industry – not true, as a recession would lead to an increase in unemployment.

**(f)** Technical progress – potentially true, as improved information technology and other innovations may have improved labour productivity and led to a reduction in the natural rate of unemployment.

**(g)** An increase in the participation rate of married women – true: participation rates for women have increased, but will this impact on the natural rate? Previously, women may have been acting as housewives – they would not have declared themselves unemployed. So, increased participation may not impact on the natural rate of unemployment.

**(h)** Changes in employers' labour taxes – in recent years these taxes have increased in the UK, especially with a 1 per cent increase in National Insurance contributions. But this will increase the natural rate of unemployment.

**7** Policy (*a*) may cause immobility of labour and lead to distortions in resource allocation; (*b*) may cause high levels of personal suffering but not have substantial effects. It would appear that in some countries where no unemployment benefits are paid, high unemployment is associated with

poverty and high rates of criminal activity. Policy (*c*) may be politically difficult to enforce, and the effectiveness of incomes policy is in doubt. Incomes policy is discussed in Chapter 26. (*d*) may affect demand-deficient unemployment but will affect the natural rate only if it has an effect on expectations of firms and thus encourages investment, or if marginal tax cuts have an effect on labour supply by improving the incentive to work. (*e*) is potentially distortionary. It may prevent structural unemployment in the short run, but eventually the adjustment of employment structure will be necessary.

**8** **(a)** A cut in the income tax rate would steepen the budget line.

**(b)** *ACD*.

**(c)** *D*: $I_2$ is the highest indifference curve that Jayne can choose. If she works, the best she can do is at *J* on $I_1$.

**(d)** Income is *GD*; she does not work.

**(e)** *K* on $I_3$; she works *EG* hours.

**9** This exercise is based on the discussion of hysteresis in Box 27–3 in the main text. All of the arguments may be found there.

**(a)** This is the discouraged-worker effect emphasized by Professor Richard Layard.

**(b)** This argument has been studied by Professor Charlie Bean, but notice that it does not correspond directly to Fig. 27–3: in this story, it is labour demand which remains to the left of its original position after the recession, and labour supply is not affected.

**(c)** This explanation of hysteresis has been explored by Professor Chris Pissarides.

**(d)** This explanation has been emphasized by writers in both Europe and the USA.

Notice that if hysteresis does occur, it has important implications for policy strategy on the demand side as well as on the supply side. Read Box 27–3 in the main text for more details.

**10** **(a)** Real wage *OA*, employment *OD*, natural rate *DF*.

**(b)** Labour demand *OC*, voluntary unemployment *EG*, involuntary *CE*.

**(c)** With prices rigid, firms may well choose to reduce output – and hence employment – so that for a time they may be 'off' their *LD* schedule.

**(d)** Voluntary unemployment *DF*, involuntary *CD*. In this situation, we have involuntary unemployment even though the real wage is at its equilibrium level!

**(e)** The fall in employment reduces wage income and leads to a fall in demand for goods, confirming firms' beliefs that they cannot sell as much output as they would like!

Another way of viewing this story is that firms' pessimistic expectations actually shift the *LD* curve to the left, implying a new lower-wage equilibrium. Involuntary unemployment will arise because *OA* is now 'too high'.

## True/False

**1**    False: the monthly published series for claimant unemployment relate to those registered as unemployed, but this is almost certainly an underestimate of those who are actually unemployed.

**2**    True.

**3**    True: see Section 27–2 of the main text.

**4**    True.

**5**    False: this is the lump-of-labour fallacy, as explained in Box 27–1 in the main text.

**6**    False: although some economists would judge it to be closer than would others (see Section 27–3 of the main text).

**7**    True.

**8**    True: see Section 27–4 of the main text.

**9**    False: the reverse is true (see Section 27–5 of the main text).

**10**    True: see Section 27–6 of the main text.

**11**    False: for instance, some frictional unemployment may be necessary to allow reallocation of resources.

**12**    False: society may wish to take the social costs of unemployment into account.

## Economics in action

**1**    Temporary workers provide firms with employment flexibility: workers can be hired and fired with ease. Therefore, firms are more willing to hire, leading to a reduction in the natural rate of unemployment. Also hiring is easier: agencies providing temporary workers make searching and matching of workers with jobs easier. Finally, with reduced employment rights workers cost less to employ and so lead to an increase in demand for workers. Temporary employment is often also appealing to workers who are seeking permanent employment, as it can provide an income while searching.

**2**    UK firms have become accustomed to using flexible employment relationships. Setting the timeline at six weeks is only likely to increase the frequency with which temporary workers change employers, with firms seeking to use workers for fewer than six weeks at any one time.

## Questions for thought

**1**    Supply-side factors are vital in deciding whether there are grounds for believing that the natural rate has increased in the UK in recent years, and it is to these that your thoughts should turn (see also Section 27–3 in the main text).

**2**    One of the reasons that unemployment has tended to be relatively low in Japan, as compared with other industrialized economies, is the existence of this type of implicit agreement between firms. From the point of view of economic theory, we would expect such agreements to work against the efficiency of the labour market, as potentially this could restrict the ability of firms to make desirable adjustments to their workforce. For instance, it might be difficult for a firm in a declining sector to move to a more appropriate scale of activity. It might also make workers less likely to search for new jobs and occupations. Notice that the agreements do not apply to women.

**3**    You might like to discuss this with your fellow students. If you look back to the analysis that you went through in Exercise **10**, you may get some hints.

# Chapter Twenty-eight Answers

## Exchange rates and the balance of payments

### Important concepts and technical terms

**1** *j*   **4** *f*   **7** *e*   **10** *i*

**2** *a*   **5** *g*   **8** *d*

**3** *h*   **6** *c*   **9** *b*

### Exercises

**1**   (a) Exports – imports = 44 715 – 58 662 = –13 947.

(b) The invisible items here comprise services, net investment income and transfers. (You might like to know that the most important items in services were sea transport, civil aviation, travel and financial/other services. The item 'net investment income' includes interest, profits and dividends.) The invisible balance is 23 505 – 18 722 + 6783 – 2942 = 8624.

(c) The visible and invisible balances combine to form the current account balance: i.e. – 13 974 + 18 624 = –5296.

(d) The overall balance of payments must always be zero (given that official transactions are incorporated into the capital account); this is the sum of the current, capital and financial account balances and net errors and omissions: –5296 – 5141 + 663 + 9774 = 0.

(e) The net errors and omissions are high when compared with the size of the capital and current accounts. However, this level of error should be expected. The data is taken from the 'First Release', i.e. the first estimate of the UK Balance of Payments by the Office for National Statistics. Over time the estimate will be revised and hopefully the errors and omissions will fall.

**2**   (a) The *DD* schedule shows the demand for pounds by US residents wishing to buy British goods and assets. The *SS* schedule shows the supply of pounds from UK residents buying US goods and assets.

(b) *OB* is the equilibrium exchange rate with no government intervention. The balance of payments is zero at this point.

(c) At *OA* there is an excess demand for pounds (the distance *DG*) which must be supplied by the Bank of England in exchange for additions to its foreign exchange reserves. The balance of payments is in surplus here.

(d) At *OC* there is a balance of payments deficit of an amount *EH*: the Bank of England must purchase the excess supply of pounds, depleting its foreign exchange reserves in the process.

(e) In the long run, the balance of payments deficit cannot be sustained, as foreign exchange reserves are finite. To maintain *OC* as the exchange rate, the authorities must influence *DD* and *SS* such that *OC* is the equilibrium. Experience suggests that promotion of British goods in the USA is unlikely to do much for *DD*, so perhaps it is more likely that the authorities will discourage imports, perhaps by a contractionary policy. Direct import controls may be tempting but may provoke retaliation from trading partners. We saw similar arguments in Chapter 22 (see Exercise 6(e) of that chapter).

**3**   See Table A28–1 (overleaf). For more detail, see Section 28–4 of the main text.

**4**   (a) See Table A28–2 (overleaf).

(b) See Fig. A28–1.

**Figure A28–1** Nominal and real exchange rates, 1985–2005

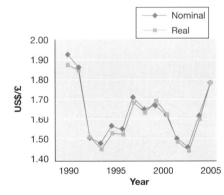

(c) The nominal and real exchange rate between the US dollar and the UK pound have followed each other closely since 1990. This is simply because the inflation rates between the two economies have been broadly similar (see Table A28–2). This perhaps reflects a common low inflation policy objective in the UK and the USA.

(d) See Table A28–2.

**Table A28–1    Shocks and balances**

| Nature of shock | Internal | | External current account balance | |
|---|---|---|---|---|
| | Boom | Slump | Deficit | Surplus |
| Reduction in autonomous consumption | | ✓ | | ✓ |
| Increase in real exchange rate | | ✓ | ✓ | |
| Tighter monetary and fiscal policy | | ✓ | | ✓ |
| Increase in world income | ✓ | | | ✓ |
| Increase in consumption with easier monetary and fiscal policy | ✓ | | ✓ | |

**Table A28–2    Prices and the exchange rate, 1990–2003**

| Year | US$/£ exchange rate | UK price index | US price index | Real exchange rate | PPP exchange rate |
|---|---|---|---|---|---|
| 1990 | 1.93 | 74 | 76 | 1.88 | 1.93 |
| 1991 | 1.87 | 78 | 79 | 1.85 | 1.90 |
| 1992 | 1.52 | 81 | 81 | 1.51 | 1.88 |
| 1993 | 1.48 | 83 | 84 | 1.46 | 1.91 |
| 1994 | 1.56 | 85 | 86 | 1.54 | 1.91 |
| 1995 | 1.55 | 88 | 89 | 1.53 | 1.90 |
| 1996 | 1.71 | 90 | 91 | 1.68 | 1.91 |
| 1997 | 1.65 | 92 | 93 | 1.63 | 1.89 |
| 1998 | 1.66 | 96 | 95 | 1.68 | 1.86 |
| 1999 | 1.61 | 97 | 97 | 1.62 | 1.87 |
| 2000 | 1.50 | 100 | 100 | 1.50 | 1.88 |
| 2001 | 1.46 | 102 | 103 | 1.44 | 1.90 |
| 2002 | 1.61 | 103 | 104 | 1.59 | 1.90 |
| 2003 | 1.79 | 106 | 107 | 1.78 | 1.89 |

**5**    In all the cases, if the funds are invested in Britain £112 is the end-year result. If funds are invested in the USA there is $170 to be loaned at the current exchange rate. Now read on.

(a)  The key missing element is the end-of-year exchange rate which we need to convert our dollars back into sterling.

(b)  Return in $ is 170 × 1.09 = 185.3. Converting to £ at the expected exchange rate yields 185.3/1.5 = £123.5. The depreciation more than compensates for the interest rate differential: you lend in the USA.

(c)  185.3/1.65 is approximately £112. You will be indifferent as to where you lend.

(d)  170 × 1.08 = 183.6; 183.6/1.65 = £111: you invest in Britain.

(e)  The expected exchange rate depends upon how you view the current rate as compared with the long-run equilib-rium rate. Such expectations could be very volatile, varying with your perception of factors affecting the economy. It matters because there are enormous quantities of internationally footloose funds in search of the best return.

**6**    If you have any difficulty with these, work out the effect on demand/supply of pounds and thus on the equilibrium exchange rate, perhaps with the help of a diagram.

(a)  Sterling appreciates.

(b)  Sterling depreciates.

(c)  Sterling depreciates.

(d)  Sterling appreciates.

(e)  Sterling appreciates.

(f)   An increase in US interest rates induces capital flows from the UK to the USA, so there is a depreciation of sterling.

**7** All but *(e)* and *(g)*.

**8** If a country becomes more productive because of access to new resources then it is likely to export some of the additional output which results from the greater productivity. This will create a current account imbalance. However, because in the long run internal and external balances must be zero, the long-run real exchange rate must appreciate in order to bring the current account back to zero. Thus productivity improvements can reduce international competitiveness. See Section 28–8 of the main text.

**9** When a country incurs significant levels of external debt then the country needs to earn foreign currency in order to pay back the debt. As a consequence, it needs to become more internationally competitive and this is achieved by lowering the long-run real exchange rate. See Section 28–8 of the main text.

**10** So far, you have been given little information about the benefits and costs associated with each exchange rate mechanism. This will be remedied in Chapter 29, when we show how the power of fiscal and monetary policy is altered by the use of fixed and floating exchange rates. However, at a very simple level you should be able to see that floating exchange rates tend to be volatile, while fixed exchange rates provide relative certainty. For this reason, many businesses and holidaymakers might prefer a fixed exchange rate. But, as suggested above, the arguments surrounding the use of fixed or floating exchange rates are much more complicated.

## True/False

**1** False: the dollar rate is important but is not the only relevant rate (see Section 28–1 of the main text).

**2** False: there is no guarantee that the chosen rate will turn out to be the equilibrium rate.

**3** False: sale and purchase of services and other invisibles belong to the current account (see Section 28–2 of the main text).

**4** True.

**5** False: we cannot assume *ceteris paribus* here – competitiveness also depends on relative inflation rates (see Section 28–3 of the main text).

**6** False: the internal balance is zero if the economy is operating at its potential output (see Section 28–7 of the main text).

**7** False: official financing is government intervention in the foreign exchange market (see Section 28–2 of the main text).

**8** True: as the real exchange rate increases then foreign consumers find it more expensive to buy UK products (see Section 28–4 of the main text).

**9** False: interest parity exists when interest rate differentials offset exchange rate differentials (see Section 28–6 of the main text).

**10** True and false: the Euro floats against other major currencies such as the dollar and the pound, but it has effectively fixed the exchange rate between the member states.

## Economics in action

**1** Since the Chinese and Malaysian currencies are pegged (fixed) to the dollar, then a fall in the value of the dollar will not lead to an improvement in the trade imbalance between the USA and China and Malaysia. Importantly, the USA cannot gain a competitive advantage against China by devaluing its own currency. Given that the USA imports a significant number of goods from China, the trade imbalance is likely to persist.

**2** Since Japanese yen and the Euro float against the dollar, then a fall in the value of the dollar will make the yen and the Euro more expensive for US consumers. This will lead to a reduction in demand for Japanese and Eurozone goods by US consumers, resulting in Japan and the Eurozone bearing the brunt of the dollar's fall.

## Questions for thought

**1** It must be remembered that any rapid depreciation of sterling tends to put upward pressure on prices in the short run. Import prices rise, increasing the demand for domestic substitutes for imported goods. We also expect the demand for exports to increase as competitiveness improves. This, of course, sounds like good news, but if domestic supply is relatively inelastic in the short run, there will inevitably be upward pressure on prices. In other words, if the government is intent on curbing inflation, it may be reluctant to allow the exchange rate to fall rapidly. Of course, once the exchange rate becomes the object of policy action, the government relinquishes independent control of the money supply. In terms of current UK policy, the exchange rate is not a central economic policy objective, unlike inflation and economic stability. But clearly the level of the pound, acting through the price of imports and exports, plays a role in the level of inflation and economic output. Therefore, the Bank of England is mindful of the exchange rate when setting interest rates.

**2** **(a)** An increase in the money supply will lead to the *LM* schedule shifting to the right. This will result in a new

goods and money market equilibrium, but a balance of payments deficit. The increase in money supply leads to a reduction in the interest rate. A lower relative interest rate to the rest of the world (without a compensating change in the exchange rate) will lead to an outflow of funds. Any current account deficit will now not be offset by the capital account.

**(b)** An increase in government expenditure will lead to the *IS* schedule shifting to the right. This will result in a new money and goods market equilibrium, but a balance of payments surplus. The equilibrium interest rate will rise, leading to an inflow of funds. The capital account will now be greater than the current account deficit, leading to a surplus on the balance of payments.

# Chapter Twenty-nine Answers

## Open economy macroeconomics

### Important concepts and technical terms

**1** *a*   **4** *d*   **7** *b*

**2** *g*   **5** *e*   **8** *h*

**3** *c*   **6** *f*

### Exercises

**1** **(a)** Competitiveness is improved: domestically produced goods become relatively cheap in both internal and external markets.

**(b)** Purchasers take time to adjust to new prices and may have existing contractual commitments; suppliers need time to adjust production levels.

**(c)** The elasticities of demand for imports and exports (the Marshall–Lerner condition), which determine the revenue response to the price changes.

**(d)** Eventually output will return to the full-employment level: competitiveness is eroded by increases in domestic prices and wages.

**(e)** A fiscal contraction could alleviate the pressure on aggregate demand.

**(f)** No: in the long run the supply side of the economy adjusts

to the increase in import prices.

**(g)** The most obvious circumstance is if initially the exchange rate were being held above its equilibrium level, resulting in balance of payments deficits.

**2** **(a)** In a closed economy, both monetary and fiscal policy may have short-run effects. In the long run, real output returns to its 'natural' level, but its composition may be affected by crowding-out following fiscal action.

**(b)** Monetary policy is totally ineffective domestically in this situation, with the authorities committed to maintaining the exchange rate. Fiscal policy has a relatively powerful effect in the short run.

**(c)** The effectiveness of fiscal policy is much reduced here by the rapid adjustment of interest rates, but monetary policy is rendered more effective.

**(d)** If capital is not perfectly mobile, interest rates will be slower to adjust, so the crowding-out effect of fiscal policy is retarded: fiscal policy may have short-run effects. Monetary policy is somewhat diluted by the same argument.

**3** **(a)** 20 per cent.

**(b)** The real exchange rate will be unchanged in the long run, but the nominal rate will need to fall by 20 per cent to maintain the real rate, given the price change.

**(c)** A fall.

**(d)** In Fig. A29–1, *e1* shows the original equilibrium nominal exchange rate. At time *t* the shock occurs, domestic interest rates fall and the nominal exchange rate must fall to prevent capital outflows and to maintain equilibrium in the exchange market. The nominal exchange rate overshoots its new equilibrium value $(e_2)$, falling initially to $e_3$ and then gradually adjusting as domestic prices adjust. The path thus involves a jump from *A* to *B* at the time of the shock and then adjustment to *C*.

**Figure A29–1**  Exchange rate overshooting

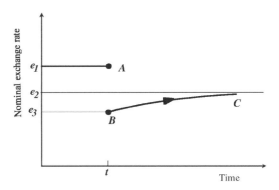

**4**  **(a)** The foreign exchange reserves will fall as the central bank buys pounds in exchange for dollars, Euros, etc. (see Section 29–1 of the main text).

**(b)** As the central bank is buying up pounds then the domestic money supply is falling (see Section 29–1 of the main text).

**(c)** The central bank can offset the reduction in the money supply by buying bonds, by either printing more money or using the money it has gained in the foreign exchange markets. This is simply an open market operation (see Sections 29–1, 23–2 and 23–5 of the main text).

**(d)** Sterilization deals with the foreign exchange problem, it does not deal with the causes of the problem (an undervalued pound). Hence sterilization must continue. But this can be only a short-term measure as the central bank will eventually run out of foreign currency reserves (see Section 29–1 of the main text).

**5**  **(a)** The central bank needs to provide an incentive to keep money inside the economy. The most obvious way to achieve this is to increase the domestic interest rate relative to that offered in other economies (see Section 29–1 of the main text).

**(b)** Any change in the money supply resulting from sterilization will generate a change in the interest rate. Which as we saw in *(a)* will lead to capital flight (see Section 29–1 of the main text).

**(c)** The Taylor rule links interest rates to inflation rates. But

under a fixed exchange rate, interest rates are used to target the exchange rate. So the Taylor rule cannot work (see Section 29–1 of the main text).

**(d)** While the nominal exchange rate is fixed, the real exchange rate can change. Hence the route to long-run equilibrium is through a fall in domestic prices relative to foreign prices (see Section 29–1 of the main text)

**6**  **(a)** If the currency is floating then there is no intervention in the currency markets, therefore the currency reserves remain constant (see Section 29–4 of the main text).

**(b)** No, the exchange rate is determined by the foreign currency markets. The inflation rate is targeted by the use of interest rates (see Section 29–4 of the main text).

**(c)** If there are differences in the inflation rates between two countries, then the nominal exchange rate will have to adjust in order to keep the real exchange rate constant (see Section 29–4 of the main text).

**(d)** Purchasing power parity (PPP) is achieved through arbitrage opportunities. As people buy and sell goods across borders to take advantage of the difference in domestic prices then the nominal exchange rate will adjust to a situation where the markets are arbitrage free (see Section 29–4 of the main text).

**7**  This is exactly what the UK government tried when it entered the European Exchange Rate Mechanism (ERM) in the early 1990s. With a fixed exchange rate and high inflation, the government is required to correct its inflationary problems or devalue its currency. The latter tends to be politically unpopular, but so does a recession (see Section 29–6 of the main text).

**8**  With fixed exchange rates, you run the risk of pricing the currency away from the true equilibrium price of the currency, or the price that would exist under a floating system. If the currency is overvalued then devaluation may occur. Assume the exchange rate between the US dollar and UK pound is $1.5 per pound. Borrow £1 million and you can convert this into $1.5 million. Wait and if the currency is devalued to £1 = $1 then you can take $1 million and pay off the loan. You are then left with $0.5 million to spend as you like. This is called 'leveraged speculation' and George Soros made (and lost) a fortune exploiting it.

**9**  Prudence has been a central concern for a variety of reasons. But it means that if fiscal policy is kept tight then inflationary pressures will be kept under control. If not, then real interest rates will have to rise and this will force up the value of the pound, thus reducing export opportunities (see Section 29–6 of the main text).

**10** If the Bank of England is responsible for inflation then inflationary expectations will be lower than when the government was responsible for managing interest rates and inflation. In essence, as a non-political organization the Bank of England is seen as a more credible manager of inflation than the government. As a result the Bank of England will not have to raise interest rates by as much to control inflation as the government. Therefore, with a rational expectation of lower long-term interest rates in the UK, the long run exchange rate will also be expected to fall.

## True/False

**1** True: see Section 29–1 of the main text.

**2** True: external shocks are more easily accommodated than domestic ones.

**3** True: see Section 29–3 of the main text.

**4** True: see Section 29–3 of the main text.

**5** False: it may deviate in the short run.

**6** False: this seems to imply that the government can independently choose both the exchange rate and money supply, which is not the case.

**7** True: see Section 29–6 of the main text.

## Economics in action

**1** The theory developed within the textbook is very clear: use fiscal policy under a fixed exchange rate and monetary policy under a floating exchange rate. The

Chinese yuan has been fixed against the US dollar since 1995, therefore fiscal policy would appear to be a more sensible means of controlling the overheating Chinese economy. As highlighted within the discussion, the use of monetary policies such as higher interest rates is only exacerbating the problems faced by the Chinese authorities, with higher inflows of foreign currency.

**2** Sterilization is the swapping of cash for bonds. In the case of China, there is too much money supply, so the Chinese authorities are trying to sell government bonds in return for cash, which can then be taken out of circulation. However, the demand for bonds is not infinite.

## Questions for thought

**1** One global currency? You have to ask yourself why is it optimal for a number of European countries to have a single currency. Robert Mundell would argue that the Eurozone is an optimal currency zone. This concept is discussed more fully in Chapter 35, but find the three major barriers to an optimal currency zone as described in this chapter and think about whether they would apply to the entire world.

**2** It is easy to set macroeconomic policy targets. Unfortunately, it is difficult to hit them. A significant problem is the trade-offs that are required. You could task the central bank with controlling inflation, but controlling inflation using interest rates might cause the exchange rate to rise above its target level. And, of course, if the exchange rate is fixed there is little point in tasking the monetary authorities with inflation targets, as monetary policy is weak.

# Chapter Thirty Answers

# Economic growth

## Important concepts and technical terms

| | | | | | | | |
|---|---|---|---|---|---|---|---|
| **1** | l | **5** | a | **9** | d | **13** | k |
| **2** | j | **6** | n | **10** | b | **14** | g |
| **3** | h | **7** | f | **11** | m | | |
| **4** | i | **8** | e | **12** | c | | |

## Exercises

**1** Items (d) and (f) describe an increase in potential output, and this is what we intend by talking about 'economic growth'. The other items all represent once-for-all changes in output, but not sustained growth.

**2** (a) Technical progress: but possibly measured in practice as an increase in capital input, the cost of improvement being registered as investment.

**(b)** Technical progress and/or an increase in capital.

**(c)** An increase in the utilization of labour – but will not be measured as such.

**(d)** An increase in human capital – an improvement in the quality of the labour input.

**(e)** Human capital again – but unmeasured.

**(f)** As with *(b)*, this is a combination of technical progress and an increase in capital input.

Much of the genuine technical progress is embodied either in capital input *((a), (b), (f))* or in labour *((d), (e))*. The extent to which technical progress is properly measured depends to a great extent on how carefully inputs are measured, and clearly the 'residual method' of calculation will be at best imprecise. Notice that item *(c)*, which has nothing to do with technical progress, may well be measured as such.

**3**  **(a)** Renewable.

**(b)** Depletable.

**(c)** Renewable.

**(d)** Depletable.

**(e)** Renewable – but with long gestation lags.

**(f)** We don't usually think of rain as a resource, but the terrible drought in Ethiopia in the mid-1980s and the associated famine reminds us of the fragility of the ecological balance. It is said that overenthusiastic tree-felling had dire effects upon rainfall.

**4**  **(a)** The simple reason for using output per worker per hour is that working hours can vary across economies. For example, in France workers are not, normally, allowed to work more than 35 hours per week. Most other EU members have now also adopted this law. But this is not the case in the USA. So, in comparing growth in output, it is important to control for the size of the workforce (per worker) and the working intensity of the workforce (per hour).

**(b)** No, it is not fair to say that productivity growth is higher in the USA. First, the growth rate figures are for one year only. By definition, productivity growth and economic growth are long-run transitions, therefore a longer data run is required before it is possible to say that the USA is growing fastest. Second, our data does not take account of the economic cycle. Growth in output per worker per hour could be higher in the USA because between 2001 and 2002 the US economy moved from a recession. Therefore, we are not observing productivity growth, we are instead seeing a higher utilization of labour under conditions of rising aggregate demand.

**5**  All the items mentioned have been invoked as potential contributors to the growth in productivity. Lower inflation helps firms to plan ahead with greater certainty,

leading to higher levels of investment and R&D. Increased profits during a period of economic stability help to finance investment in more productive assets, while positive externalities are exploited from the development of new productive technologies. A higher number of graduates increases the quality and productiveness of human capital, while perhaps the end of the Cold War enabled government to allocate resources away from defence and towards education, health and other economic and social infrastructure.

**6**  A policy for growth is one which enables sustained long-run growth of potential output, not mere once-for-all increases. Items *(a)*, *(c)*, *(d)* and *(f)* would thus be appropriate, but not *(b)* or *(e)*.

**7**  **(a)** $n$.

**(b)** If capital per worker is low, and the growth rate below the steady-state level, it will also be the case that savings per worker (and hence investment) will be seen to be higher than is needed to maintain that level of capital per worker. Capital deepening will therefore take place in the short run until the economy returns to the steady state.

**(c)** Not a lot: it just means that the steady-state growth rate is now $n + t$.

**(d)** The convergence hypothesis suggests that poorer countries will be able to take advantage of developments in technology from richer countries, and thus begin to catch up in terms of growth rates.

**(e)** Lack of necessary human capital or other complementary inputs may impede the progress of poor countries, as may an inappropriate political, social or economic environment.

**(f)** If a firm benefits from capital accumulation in other firms, or from the existence of human capital, then the overall growth rate should increase.

**(g)** The nature of beneficial externalities is such that free market forces will result in less production than is socially beneficial. Thus, for example, there may be inadequate human capital formation unless the government intervenes to correct the market failure.

**8**  **(a)** $n_1 k$.

**(b)** $H$, where $sy = n_1 k$.

**(c)** Capital per worker is $OG$ and output per worker is $OB$.

**(d)** The rate of growth of labour, $n_1$.

**(e)** With a growth rate of labour $n_2$, the steady state is at $E$. Growth of output is more rapid ($n_2 > n_1$), but more capital accumulation is needed for capital widening, and output per worker is lower in the new steady state.

(f) Higher savings may allow higher capital and output per worker, but the long-run growth path is still constrained by labour force growth in the neoclassical growth model.

**9** From points *C*, *D*, *E*, the economy will converge on $k_2$. At *E*, savings and investment are insufficient to maintain the capital:labour ratio, and the economy shrinks. From any point between $k_1$ and $k_2$, capital deepening takes place, and the economy moves towards $k_2$ – however close to $k_1$ we start. Below $k_1$, savings and investment are again insufficient to maintain the capital:labour ratio, and the economy shrinks. Countries in this region are stuck in a low-level equilibrium trap from which they cannot escape because they cannot generate a surplus for savings and investment. Notice that if an economy happens to start at $k_1$, it could in principle remain there. However, this is a highly unstable position, as any move away from this point in either direction will cause the economy to start to converge. The problem for a number of less developed countries (LDCs) is in getting to the right of $k_1$. For more details, see Box 30–2 in the main text.

## True/False

**1** False: in some countries (e.g. Brazil) there may be great inequality of income distribution (see Section 30–1 of the main text).

**2** True.

**3** False: part of investment is for replacement of existing capital (see Section 30–2 of the main text).

**4** True: see Section 30–3 of the main text.

**5** False: this rather Malthusian argument ignores the potential for productivity changes (see Section 30–4 of the main text).

**6** True: see Section 30–7 of the main text.

**7** True: see Section 30–4 of the main text.

**8** False: capital deepening increases capital per worker; it is capital widening that is needed to extend the capital stock as the labour force grows.

**9** False: in neoclassical growth theory, higher savings may yield a once-for-all increase in real output, but will not affect long-run growth (see Section 30–4 of the main text).

**10** False: unfortunately in reality we cannot rely on convergence taking place. Some countries are more able than others to take advantage of capital accumulation and technical progress (see Section 30–6 of the main text).

**11** True: this is at the heart of the theory of endogenous growth (see Section 30–7 of the main text).

**12** True: see Box 30–3 in the main text.

## Economics in action

**1** A central reason for pursuing economic growth is that ultimately higher GDP improves welfare across the economy (admittedly the overexploitation of non-renewable resources might not be welfare-enhancing). But if higher economic growth stems from more leisure being substituted for more (and perhaps even unpaid) work, then the welfare enhancement of economic growth is questionable.

**2** Given the difficulties associated with measuring productivity growth, it might be better to measure output growth in an industry where computers are a significant factor input. Banking is one such sector – where all accounts, client details and financial transactions are stored and carried out by computers. If computers have boosted productivity, then it should be very apparent in sectors which are heavily reliant on them.

## Questions for thought

**1** *Some hints*: What happens to price as a resource becomes more scarce? How does this affect incentives? On the matter of a renewable resource, think about short-run/long-run and private/social costs aspects.

**2** The convergence hypothesis argues that poor countries are likely to be able to grow at a rate above the average, whereas rich countries will grow more slowly. Thus in the long run growth rates will converge. The data in Table 30–1 do not seem to lend a great deal of support to this argument. During the 1980s, many of the world's low-income countries suffered negative growth rates, rather than showing any signs of catch-up. There are, of course, exceptions to this: in Table 30–1 Singapore, Korea, Thailand and China all grew at more than satisfactory rates. The final columns of the table hint at the importance of physical and human capital in the growth process. It could be argued that the 'slipstreaming effect' (whereby poor countries may be able to benefit from technology developed in the richer countries) is not accessible to very low-income countries, which have low levels of human capital, or perhaps inappropriate economic, social, cultural or political environments (see Box 30–3 in the main text for some further data). Note that the measurement of *GDP per capita* in PPP$ attempts to correct the GNP measure for distortions in official exchange rates.

**3**    The role of the government in promoting economic growth must flow from the theoretical arguments. If the steady-state growth path depends only on labour force growth, then the government's role may be extremely limited. However, if there are significant capital externalities, or other forms of market failure, then intervention may be justified, perhaps in subsidization of human capital formation, physical capital accumulation or research and development (R&D).

# Chapter Thirty-one Answers

## Business cycles

### Important concepts and technical terms

**1**  e       **4**  f       **7**  c       **10**  h

**2**  d       **5**  a       **8**  i       **11**  g

**3**  b       **6**  j       **9**  l       **12**  k

### Exercises

**1**    *A* is the slump phase, being the trough of the cycle.

*B* is the recovery.

*C* is the boom.

*D* is the boom – the peak of the cycle.

*E* is the recession.

*F* is the slump – the trough again.

The horizontal distance from *A* to *F* represents the (trough to trough) length of the cycle.

**2**    All of them, to some degree, although *(b)* is of course crucial in the investment decision. Indeed, we might argue that the other factors listed all have some influence on the way in which firms will perceive *(b)*. Some also affect the cost of borrowing: for instance, it may be less costly to finance investment from past profits than by borrowing in the market. However, ultimately, it is firms' expectations about the future which will be most important. The multiplier–accelerator model shows that if firms form expectations with reference to past output growth (factor *(e)*), then cycles in activity may be generated (see Section 31–2 in the main text for more detailed discussion).

**3**    See Table A31–1. With $v = 0.2$, the economy converges quite rapidly on the new equilibrium, but with $v = 0.8$ the adjustment path is cyclical and takes a lot longer. Other values of $v$ and $c$ can induce explosive cycles which never allow the economy to reach the new equilibrium.

| Table A31–1 | A multiplier–accelerator model | | | | | |
|---|---|---|---|---|---|---|
| | **$v = 0.2$** | | | **$v = 0.8$** | | |
| **Time period** | **C** | **I** | **Y** | **C** | **I** | **Y** |
| 0 | 30.00 | 30.00 | 60.00 | 30.00 | 30.00 | 60.00 |
| 1 | 30.00 | 40.00 | 70.00 | 30.00 | 40.00 | 70.00 |
| 2 | 35.00 | 42.00 | 77.00 | 35.00 | 48.00 | 83.00 |
| 3 | 38.50 | 41.40 | 79.90 | 41.50 | 50.40 | 91.90 |
| 4 | 39.95 | 40.58 | 80.53 | 45.95 | 47.12 | 93.07 |
| 5 | 40.26 | 40.13 | 80.39 | 46.54 | 40.94 | 87.48 |
| 6 | 40.20 | 39.97 | 80.17 | 43.74 | 35.52 | 79.26 |

**4** **(a)** The choice point would be at the tangency of $U_0$ and the production possibility frontier (PPF) at point *A* in Fig. A31–1. Notice that we are assuming here that the 'price line' would have the appropriate slope to encourage this choice.

**Figure A31–1** A temporary shock

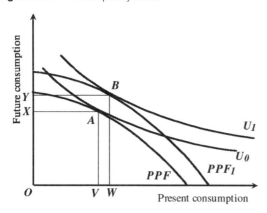

**(b)** The effect would be to move out the PPF, as shown in Fig. A31–1.

**(c)** Present consumption moves from *OV* to *OW*, as the choice point moves from *A* to *B*: in other words, given these curves the increase in production possibilities has very little effect on present consumption.

**(d)** However, future consumption increases substantially from *OX* to *OY*. Essentially, what is happening is that the society is devoting more resources to investment in the present, in order to consume more in the future.

**(e)** In the long run, this increase in investment is likely to shift the PPF even further, by expanding the production possibilities of the society.

**(f)** This reaction by society to the change in production possibilities occurs because the indifference curves between present and future consumption are relatively 'flat', reflecting a preference for future rather than present consumption. Had these curves been relatively much more steep, such that the tangency point came further to the right, then preferences would have been much more biased towards present consumption. In these circumstances, the reaction to the change in the PPF would have been much more rapid, in the sense that more resources would have been devoted to present consumption; the long-run effects would then be less marked.

**(g)** The analysis above suggests that temporary shocks may have persistent effects through time. If successive shocks move the PPF in different directions, then cycles may result from this persistence.

**5** (*a*) may help to explain persistence, in the sense that if people are subject to diminishing marginal utility of income, they may not feel the need to increase present consumption. However, if people show a strong preference for consumption in the present (*b*), then the case for persistence is much weakened. Factor (*c*) affects the shape of the PPF between present and future consumption. If there are many opportunities which allow present resources to be translated into future consumption opportunities, then this will tend to add to persistence. If the motivation to leave bequests is strong (*d*), then again there is a sense in which this implies a preference for future rather than present consumption – so persistence may occur. Ricardian equivalence (*e*; encountered in Chapter 25) seems at first to be out of place in the present discussion. However, if the 'shock' that jolts the economy is the result of a government intervention that people believe to be temporary, then they will act accordingly. Tax cuts intended to affect present consumption may not have that effect, but lead to an increase in savings.

**6** This exercise is like a parable of the 1980s. In the boom of the mid-1980s, consumers borrowed heavily and savings fell. This was noticeable not only in the UK, but also in other industrial economies such as the USA and Japan. Household indebtedness rose and asset prices fell. It is argued that recovery from the recession was delayed as consumers tried to remedy their debt positions (see Section 31–5 of the main text).

**7** All of them.

**8** The detailed year-to-year variations in growth rates do not suggest that all three economies follow precisely the same pattern throughout the period. The UK and the USA both hit recession in 1991, but Spain was later (1993). The dip in the UK growth rate in 1998 was not mirrored in the other two countries. A longer time span is needed to search for commonalities between countries. See also Fig. 31–3 in the main text, which shows common cycles in the EU, the USA and Japan using quarterly data, which demonstrate rather more variation than the annual averages. Figure 31–4 in the main text focuses on business cycles in countries within the EU.

## True/False

**1** Trueish: so long as we can afford to take a long-run view. Very often, the short-run problems are more obvious.

**2** False: there may be an association between the two, but for an explanation we need to understand why demand may fluctuate (see Section 31–1 of the main text).

**3** False: it is always tempting to want to blame the politicians for everything, but the 'political business cycle' does not provide a full explanation of cyclical fluctuations in economic behaviour.

**4** False: see Section 31–2 of the main text.

**5** True.

**6** False: the hypothesis that the economy always moves rapidly to equilibrium does not prevent us from having a theory which says that potential output itself may be subject to fluctuations.

**7** False: this is not what is observed in practice. See the discussion of the 'real wage puzzle' in Box 31–1 of the main text.

**8** True: see Section 31–3 of the main text.

**9** False: the opposite is the case (see Section 31–3 of the main text).

**10** True: see Section 31–4 of the main text.

**11** Trueish: this was a factor (see Section 31–5 of the main text), but probably not the only one. It is worth noting that parallel arguments have been advanced to explain the problems faced by low-income countries following heavy borrowing in international markets in the late 1970s. We will get to this in Chapter 36.

## Economics in action

**1** Business cycles associated with fluctuations in the output gap reflect equilibrium output and inflation away from potential output of the economy. High oil prices can reduce supply by increasing production costs; and similarly they can reduce demand by raising the general price level. So, higher oil prices might generate a recession.

**2** A successful attack on an oil installation in Iraq or Saudi Arabia would destroy the ability to supply oil and would represent a considerable reduction in the potential output of not only Iraq and Saudi Arabia, but also global economic output.

## Questions for thought

**1** Hysteresis (introduced in Chapter 27) is another story about the way in which temporary shocks may have persistent effects.

**2** **(a)** $OA$ – the natural rate.
**(b)** $I_3$.
**(c)** An expansion of aggregate demand could exploit the short-run Phillips trade-off and take the economy to point $B$ on $I_4$.
**(d)** Back to the natural rate at $D$.
**(e)** $I_2$: worse than originally because inflation is higher.
**(f)** Sliding 'up' $SPC_1$ does not produce much gain and cannot be sustained anyway – better to contract aggregate demand and move to point $F$ (making people worse off), recognizing that as expectations adjust, the economy returns to $A$ – hopefully in time to slide back up to $B$ as the next election comes round!
**(g)** The Thatcher and Major administrations' unswerving commitment to the long run could not have countenanced such a procedure – indeed, the very existence of the short-run trade-off has been questioned.

# Chapter Thirty-two Answers

## Macroeconomics: taking stock

### Important concepts and technical terms

| | | | |
|---|---|---|---|
| **1** i | **4** h | **7** g | **10** k |
| **2** j | **5** d | **8** a | **11** e |
| **3** f | **6** b | **9** c | **12** l |

### Exercises

**1**   All of them: see Section 32–1 in the main text.

**2**   **(a)** Gradualist monetarist.

**(b)**   Extreme Keynesian.

**(c)**   New Classical.

**(d)**   Moderate Keynesian.

**(e)**   Extreme Keynesian.

**(f)**   Rational expectations are not uniquely identified with a single school. It is an essential assumption of the New Classical macroeconomics, but there are also devotees in the Gradualist monetarist and Moderate Keynesian groups.

**3**   **(a)** We cannot of course supply you with an answer to this: apart from anything else, we don't know when you are reading it!

**(b)**   Most people asked for a casual guess about inflation will think back to what inflation has been in the last year – perhaps with an adjustment for current conditions or recent TV reports. The dominance of past experience in this process suggests extrapolative expectations.

**(c)**   We always take more care when it matters! Whether people research sufficiently thoroughly to justify the rational expectations hypothesis is, however, more contentious.

**4**   **(a)** Real wage *OB*, unemployment *EG* – the natural rate.

**(b)**   Given real wage inflexibility, the real wage could remain at *OB* and unemployment would rise to *CG*.

**(c)**   In the 'medium' term, the market could still be at real wage *OB*, unemployment *CG*; but in the long run, adjustment would take the real wage to *OA* and unemployment to *DF*. The two groups would differ in their definitions of

'medium' and 'long' term, with the Gradualist expecting the long run to be closer.

**(d)**   The New Classicals would expect rapid adjustment to the new equilibrium with real wage *OA* and unemployment at the new natural rate *DF*.

**(e)**   The Extreme Keynesians would want demand management to combat unemployment, which they view as being due to deficient demand. The Moderate Keynesians would perhaps want to allow some demand management to alleviate the short-run problem, or incomes policy to speed the adjustment – together with some long-run supply-side policies. The Gradualists would probably want to ride out the short-run crisis and concentrate on long-run supply-side policies. The New Classicals would not recognize the short-run problem, but *might* wish to try to reduce the natural rate of unemployment.

**(f)**   Under hysteresis, the temporary fall in *LD* could lead to a permanent shift in *AJ*, and a new long-run equilibrium with a lower employment level. See Exercise 9 in Chapter 27.

**5**   **(a)** Gradualist.

**(b)**   New Classical.

**(c)**   Extreme Keynesian.

**(d)**   Moderate Keynesian.

**(e)**   Moderate Keynesian.

**6**   (*d*), (*b*), (*a*), (*c*).

The foreign exchange market clears very rapidly indeed – at least, under floating exchange rates. The money market is hardly less quick. The goods market is more sluggish for a number of reasons – remember the oligopoly models of Chapter 10? There are also the menu costs of changing prices. The labour market is likely to be the slowest. For more detail, see Box 32–1 in the main text.

**7**   **(a)** Equilibrium would be at the intersection of $LM_0$ and *IS* in Fig. A32–1, with rate of interest *OB* and real output *OC*. The important thing to notice about this diagram is the relative slope of the *IS* and *LM* curves. In particular, the *IS* curve has been drawn to be almost vertical. This reflects the assumption of the Extreme Keynesians that investment will be highly insensitive to the rate of interest when the economy is in deep recession.

**(b)**   If prices were to be flexible downwards, then we would look for a rightward shift of the *LM* curve, because a fall

**Figure A32–1**  *IS–LM* in recession: an Extreme Keynesian view

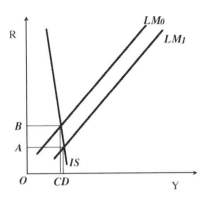

in the price level would imply an increase in real money supply. Thus *LM* might be seen to move from *LM*$_0$ to *LM*$_1$. However, given the steepness of the *IS* curve, this shift has little effect on output, which increases only slightly from *OC* to *OD*. Meanwhile, a substantial fall in the rate of interest (from *OB* to *OA*) is needed in order to restore equilibrium.

(c) A monetary expansion would have just the same effect as in (*b*), and is ineffectual in this situation.

(d) A fiscal expansion that shifted the *IS* curve to the right would have a far greater impact, and help to pull the economy out of recession: if you are prepared to accept the Extreme Keynesian argument on which this diagram is based.

(e) A major difference would be in the relative slopes of *IS* and *LM* in Fig. A32–1. Under New Classical or Gradualist monetarist views, the *LM* curve would be much steeper – if not vertical – and the *IS* curve would be much flatter, reflecting the view that investment (and consumption) would be much more sensitive to changes in the rate of interest. Sketch such a diagram for yourself and see the effect of these alternative assumptions.

**8**  You may find that your views do not place you firmly in any one school. This is not surprising, as there are considerable grey areas between our snapshots – which is why we refer to it as a 'spectrum'.

## True/False

**1**  False: there are some positive issues which would command general agreement, but there are others where a variety of opinion exists (see Section 32–1 of the main text).

**2**  False: the statement presumes that demand deficiency is the only cause of unemployment. Some

economists would attribute much of the rise to an increase in the natural rate.

**3**  True: see Section 32–2 of the main text.

**4**  True.

**5**  False: they would argue that output and employment may change in the short run but will gradually readjust to full employment. It is prices that are affected in the long run (see Section 32–3 of the main text).

**6**  True.

**7**  False: they would recognize the potential importance of supply-side policies in the long-run while wishing to carry out stabilization in the short run (see Section 32–4 of the main text).

**8**  True.

**9**  True: see Section 32–5 of the main text.

**10**  False: see Section 32–6 of the main text.

## Economics in action

**1**  Structural reform would be more generally associated with classical economists, seeking to free up the workings of the market-based economy. Sustaining demand is a Keynesian concern, seeking to ensure that there is sufficient demand in the economy to meet the potential supply.

**2**  Keynesians assume that aggregate supply is relatively elastic, enabling the economy to grow rapidly in the face of increased aggregate demand. But if there is little potential for the economy to grow, then by inference aggregate supply must be relatively inelastic (vertical).

## Questions for thought

**1**  This proposition rests on the belief that the economy will stabilize itself within a reasonable time span if left alone. In addition, it may be argued that misguided or mistimed policy action may have a destabilizing effect.

**2**  The debate about 'rules versus discretion' has been a long-lasting one. The discussion of the problems of fine-tuning (Chapter 22) is worth reviewing, as it highlights some of the problems of discretionary policy. Friedman and other Gradualists are heavily committed to the idea of pre-set rules.

**3**    No comment.

# Chapter Thirty-three Answers

## International trade

### Important concepts and technical terms

| 1 | b | 4 | f | 7 | i | 10 | g |
| 2 | e | 5 | a | 8 | d | 11 | h |
| 3 | k | 6 | l | 9 | c | 12 | j |

### Exercises

**1**    (a) It is fairly easy to see that factor endowment is a driver of trade. Saudi Arabia, with its vast oil resources, has very little else to export. The UK, Germany and Singapore are all fully developed economies with advanced education systems; well-functioning capital markets are able to support the development of capital-intensive industries which make manufactures and transport equipment. Less well-developed economies, such as Ethiopia, specialize in more labour-intensive products such as agricultural raw materials.

(b)    Recently, world trade has grown markedly, but in the main this growth has occurred between developed economies. The prospects for Ethiopia and Pakistan may be somewhat limited.

(c)    It is dangerous to read too much into these figures. In particular, the commodity groups are broad in coverage. No doubt there are some goods within 'other manufacturing' or 'other primary commodities' whose prospects are markedly different from the norm. We would thus need more detailed information about the commodities exported by each country. In addition, the import figures for these countries tend to indicate that countries import what they also export, which is at odds with the theory of comparative advantage; see the UNCTAD data set for yourself at www.unctad.org.

**2**    (a) Anywaria has the absolute advantage, having lower unit labour requirements for each good.

(b)    The opportunity cost of a unit of bicycle output is 2 units of boots in Anywaria and 3 units in Someland. The opportunity cost of a unit of boots output is 0.5 a unit of bicycles in Anywaria and 0.33 of a unit in Someland.

(c)    Anywaria has the comparative advantage in bicycles, having the lower opportunity cost.

(d)    See Table A33–1.

| Table A33–1 | Production of bicycles and boots, no-trade case | | |
| --- | --- | --- | --- |
| | Anywaria | Someland | 'World' output |
| Bicycles | 100 | 50 | 150 |
| Boots | 200 | 150 | 350 |

(e)    See Table A33–2.

| Table A33–2 | Production of bicycles and boots | | |
| --- | --- | --- | --- |
| | Anywaria | Someland | 'World' output |
| Bicycles | 150 | – | 150 |
| Boots | 100 | 300 | 400 |

World output of bicycles has been maintained at the no-trade level, but it has proved possible to increase the output of boots from 350 to 400 units. How these gains are distributed between the two economies is, of course, a separate issue. Indeed, the very feasibility of trade may depend on the exchange rate if the two countries do not share a common currency (see Exercise **3**).

(f)    In Fig. A33–1, $PPF_A$ and $PPF_S$ represent the production possibility frontiers for Anywaria and Someland, respectively. The key element which reveals the potential gains from trade is the difference in the slope of the two curves, reflecting the difference in opportunity costs.

**3**    (a) Unit labour costs:

Bicycles: A\$300 in Anywaria, S\$540 in Someland.
Boots: A\$150 in Anywaria, S\$180 in Someland.

(b)    See Table A33–3.

| Table A33–3 | Production of bicycles and boots | |
| --- | --- | --- |
| | Anywaria | Someland |
| Bicycles | 540 | 540 |
| Boots | 270 | 180 |

**Figure A33–1** Production possibilities for Anywaria and Someland

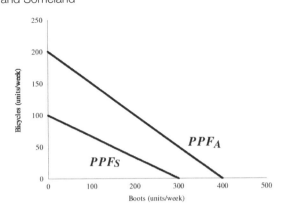

(c)   See Table A33–4.

| Table A33–4 | Production of bicycles and boots | |
|---|---|---|
| | **Anywaria** | **Someland** |
| Bicycles | 360 | 540 |
| Boots | 180 | 180 |

(d)   Trade will take place only at exchange rates between the values analysed in *(b)* and *(c)*, as one-way trade is not viable. With an exchange rate above A$1.8 = S$1, there would be no demand for Anywaria produce; below A$1.2, there is no demand for Somelandish output.

(e)   The equilibrium exchange rate will depend upon the size of demand for the goods in the two economies (see Section 33–2 of the main text).

**4**   *(a)*, *(b)* and *(d)* encourage intra-industry trade, but *(c)*, *(e)* and *(f)* work against it.

**5**   *(c)* is a first-best argument; *(b)*, *(d)* and *(f)* are second-best arguments – in each case, there are preferable and more direct methods of achieving the desired object; *(e)* is at best a second-best argument and may join *(a)* as a non-argument.

**6**   All of the factors mentioned are likely to ensue as a result of the imposition of tariffs. The question that remains is whether the effects will be adverse or not. In some cases, the answer is clear: tariffs impose resource and other costs on society and there is a deadweight loss arising from items *(b)* and *(e)*. Factor *(d)* is also part of this: society will be worse off because it is not making the best of its existing pattern of comparative advantage. If there is retaliation in export markets *(a)*, then this exacerbates the situation, in particular wiping out any gains that might have accrued from reducing import penetration *(f)*, which in any case is obtained at the cost of domestic inefficiency in production. The fact that imposing a tariff generates revenue for the authorities *(c)* is a

rather different argument. The proportion of government revenue that comes from taxes on international trade in the advanced industrial economies is very small. However, for a number of less developed countries (LDCs) who find raising tax revenue to be a problem, tariffs are an attractive proposition, as they are easier to administer than some other forms of tax. Certainly, the potential loss of tariff revenue is a considerable stumbling-block for some countries when they begin to consider trade liberalization.

**7**   (a)   Price *OB* (= world price), imports *FP* (the excess of domestic demand over domestic supply at this price).

(b)   Price *OC*, imports *JM*.

(c)   *EG*.

(d)   *BCML*.

(e)   Tariff revenue *HJML*, rents *BCJF*.

(f)   *FHJ* remains: this is the extra that society spends by producing cars domestically rather than importing them at the world price.

(g)   *LMP*.

(h)   *FHJ* + *LMP*.

**8**   (a)   Price *OA*, exports *GJ*.

(b)   Price *OB*, exports *EM*.

(c)   *HK*.

(d)   *CF*.

(e)   *DEG*.

(f)   *JLM*.

(g)   It is sometimes argued that economic growth can take place only if accompanied by an expansion of aggregate demand. If the authorities perceive the domestic market to be too limited, they may wish to encourage exports – but notice that part of the increase achieved is at the expense of domestic consumption.

(h)   A production subsidy would keep the domestic price at *OA*; the social cost would then be *JLM* rather than *JLM* + *DEG* (see Section 33–8 of the main text).

**9**   (a)   With wodgets being priced at the world price of £3, domestic producers supply 1000 × *p* = 3000 wodgets. However, demand is 10 000 – (1000 × 3) = 7000. Imports will thus be 7000 – 3000 = 4000.

(b)   We already calculated domestic supply at 3000 wodgets.

(c)   With a £2 tariff, the domestic price is £5, at which producers will supply 5000 wodgets.

(d)   At the higher domestic price, demand falls to 5000 wodgets. Domestic producers now supply the entire domestic market, imports are zero . . . and the government thus gets no revenue at all.

(e)   The loss of consumer surplus is the area of the triangle with 'height' £2 and 'base' 2000 units of wodgets – i.e.

the loss is £2000. As it happens, in this particular instance the production inefficiency triangle is the same size. This need not be the case – it depends on the elasticities of demand and supply. If you find all this difficult to envisage, try sketching the diagram.

**10** (a) *DM*.

(b) *OB*.

(c) Domestic production increases from *OC* to *OE*, but consumption falls from *OL* to *OH*.

(d) If this diagram had been describing a tariff, this area would have represented tariff revenue. With a quota, this revenue accrues either to foreign suppliers or to domestic importers.

(e) *DFG* + *JKM* + the proportion of *FGJK* accruing to foreign suppliers.

(f) The principal gainers from this sort of policy are the producers: the domestic producers who expand output in response to the higher price they receive, earning extra rents. Foreign producers also gain in the form of rents. You might be interested to know that export licences in Hong Kong in connection with this sort of 'Voluntary Export Restraint' (VER) policy have been tradable, and it has been estimated by the World Bank that rents from VERs on clothing alone comprised 1.4 per cent of Hong Kong's GDP in 1982–83! The losers? Society as a whole in the importing country, especially consumers, who must pay a higher price and lose consumer surplus.

## True/False

**1** True: see Section 33–1 of the main text.

**2** True: see Table 33–5 in the main text – but this would not be typical of less developed countries in other parts of the world.

**3** False: it is necessary for one country to have an absolute advantage in the production of at least one commodity, but it is not sufficient – comparative advantage is also important (see Section 33–2 of the main text).

**4** True.

**5** True.

**6** False: see Section 33–3 of the main text.

**7** False: comparative advantage ensures that potentially everyone may be better off but cannot guarantee that they will actually be so (see Section 33–4 of the main text).

**8** False: see Section 33–5 of the main text.

**9** True.

**10** False: it is a common argument but not a powerful one, and has often been misused (see Section 33–6 of the main text).

**11** True: see Section 33–7 of the main text.

**12** True: this is very common (see Section 33–8 of the main text).

## Economics in action

**1** It is difficult to calculate the fair value of any product. But if we return to our micro theory and the consideration of firms' costs, we argued that a firm would not be willing to supply goods and services at a price which was below average variable cost, as the firm would be unable to make a contribution to fixed costs. Therefore, a fair value for shrimp must be some price above the average variable cost of farming and then shipping shrimp into the USA.

**2** There are a number of reasons for supporting an industry with trade restrictions, but none really seems applicable to the shrimp industry. It is not in the national interest, it is not an infant industry, but perhaps it does represent a way of life. However, why has the industry not helped itself by differentiating itself from the low-cost Asian producers? The imposition of tariffs will reduce the incentive for the domestic industry to innovate. Most worrying is the projected 44 per cent rise in shrimp prices, to be paid by . . . the US consumer.

## Questions for thought

**1** The simple answer is 'it can try'. Perhaps more important than gaining access to, or discovering new sources of, factor endowments such as oil deposits is the ability to see how comparative advantage can be exploited. For example, take Singapore, for 200 years nothing more than a small island covered in swamp land, but now one of the economic success stories of South East Asia. No one discovered oil, or an ability to make capital-intensive manufactured goods. Rather, it was noted that Singapore would be a good place for transport ships to stop off *en route* from China to the West.

An economy based on trade developed from the simplest factor endowment of land – or, more precisely, location. Now consider Dubai, nothing but sand (and oil reserves which are almost exhausted). So how do you create trade? Simple, change the law to allow the drinking of alcohol, build an airport, world-class hotels and sporting venues. While previously rich Arab businessmen once went to Beirut for a break, they now go to Dubai. So it is not just what you have that is important for comparative advantage: it is also what you do with it.

**2**    (a) The choice point is at *G*; production and consumption are *OF* units of good *X* and *OB* units of good *Y*. We saw how this point is reached in Chapter 19.

(b) If the world price ratio is equal to the domestic ratio, then country *A* holds no comparative advantage in the pro-

duction of either good, and there is no incentive for trade to take place.

(c) With the world price ratio at *RS*, a unit of good *X* exchanges for more units of good *Y* in the world market than at home, implying that country *A* has a comparative advantage in the production of good *X*.

(d) Country *A* can now produce at point *J*, making *OH* units of *X* and *OA* of *Y*. By trading at the world price ratio, country *A* can consume at point *E*, consuming *OD* of *X* and *OC* of *Y*. In the process, the economy moves to a higher indifference curve.

(e) Country *A* exports *DH* units of *X* and imports *AC* of *Y*.

(f) *OM* represents the terms of trade when the countries are at point *W*. This can be seen to be the equilibrium terms of trade – the point where the offer curves intersect represents the point at which the offers made by the two countries are consistent.

# Chapter Thirty-four Answers

## Exchange rate regimes

### Important concepts and technical terms

| | | | | | | | |
|---|---|---|---|---|---|---|---|
| **1** | c | **4** | g | **7** | j | **10** | i |
| **2** | a | **5** | h | **8** | f | **11** | b |
| **3** | k | **6** | l | **9** | d | **12** | e |

### Exercises

**1**    (a) Managed float.

(b) Gold standard.

(c) Adjustable peg.

(d) Adjustable peg (or conceivably a managed float in which the authorities have been holding up the exchange rate for an extended period).

(e) Clean float.

(f) Gold standard.

(g) Managed float.

(h) Clean or managed float: in either case, the nominal exchange rate tends to follow the PPP path in the long run.

**2**    (a) $20.67/4.25 = 4.86$.

(b) 20 ounces.

(c) £85 converts to $510, which buys 24.67 ounces of gold.

(d) 24.67 ounces of gold is worth £104.85 at the UK price – it would then pay to repeat the exercise, selling gold in Britain, converting to dollars, and buying gold in the USA.

(e) Such a rate could hold only in the very short run because of the potential return from the sort of transactions already examined.

(f) With the exchange rate below the gold parity rate, the reverse set of transactions becomes profitable, selling gold in the USA and buying gold in the UK.

(g) *OB*: the equilibrium rate.

(h) *OC* is the rate at which everyone wants to convert into dollars, so demand for pounds falls to zero.

(i) Between *OA* and *OC* it is possible for the exchange rate to be out of equilibrium without all agents indulging in gold and currency transactions. This band arises because there are transaction costs – either brokerage or transport. It costs to ship gold about the world.

**3**    (a) Exports fall and the balance of payments moves into deficit.

(b) Aggregate demand falls and so too will output and employment if wages and prices are slow to adjust.

(c) As we have seen, the exchange rate can never move far away from the gold parity rate. The balance of payments deficit must be matched by a fall in the UK gold reserves.

(d) Domestic money supply must fall to preserve 100 per cent gold backing. This tends to push up interest rates, further depressing aggregate demand.

(e) Eventually wages and prices must adjust, and this will lead to an improvement in British competitiveness. This continues until internal and external balance are restored.

(f) Adjustment in the USA mirrors that in the UK – the balance of payments moves into surplus, aggregate demand increases, gold reserves and money supply rise, wages and prices are pushed up, and competitiveness falls as internal and external balance is restored.

**4** **(a)** The restrictive monetary policy leads to high interest rates and to an appreciation of *A*'s exchange rate.

(b) Competitiveness declines, deepening the transitional fall in output and employment.

(c) As competitiveness in *A* declines, so it rises in *B* and *C*, as their exchange rates have depreciated. There is thus some upward pressure on prices.

(d) *B*'s exchange rate now appreciates.

(e) *A*'s exchange rate now falls relative to *B* and *C*, threatening upward pressure on prices.

(f) If all three countries were to coordinate their policies, the see-saw effect on exchange rates would be avoided and there would be much more stability. There would be less speculative movement in financial capital. In this more stable environment, it may well be that the transitional cost of anti-inflation policy would be less strong and less long-lasting.

**5** (*c*) and (*f*) were features of the dollar standard, but none of the other items mentioned.

**6** Only (*a*) and (*b*) are valid under a clean float.

**7** (*c*) is a feature only of a clean float.

**8** **(a)** Arguably, the Bretton Woods system broke down because it could not cope with nominal and real strains. It has been argued that whereas flexible exchange rates did manage to cope reasonably well with the oil-price shocks, a fixed-rate scheme would have been too rigid to enable economies to ride the storm. Thus, in terms of robustness in the face of shocks, the evidence probably favours a flexible system.

(b) As far as stability is concerned, the evidence is mixed. We could argue that only the fixed-rate system offers fundamental stability, in the sense that future nominal exchange rates are known to participants in international trade. On the other hand, under a flexible-rate regime, there is potential volatility. This argument is less strong than it seems at first, for a number of reasons. First, fixed-rate regimes force any instability in markets to be accommodated elsewhere in the system: in other words, stability of the nominal exchange rate is not the only dimension of stability. Second, it is real exchange rates that are crucial in determining competitiveness, not just the nominal rates. Third, we might argue that the instability caused by exchange rate realignments in a fixed-rate system is more destabilizing than the regular small movements under a floating-rate system.

(c) Independence may not always be a good thing. One of the most powerful arguments in favour of a fixed-exchange rate system is that it enforces financial discipline upon countries and encourages policy coordination.

(d) To the extent that governments introduce protectionist measures in an attempt to bolster inappropriate exchange rates, we may view fixed-rate regimes as having undesirable effects. However, many commentators might argue that governments can always find misguided policies to adopt, and that the exchange rate regime in operation will have little influence.

## True/False

**1** False: governments bent the rules at times (see Section 34–2 of the main text).

**2** True: see Box 34–1 in the main text.

**3** True: see Section 34–3 of the main text.

**4** False: speculators were well aware that a country experiencing balance of payments deficits was liable to devalue – and could take appropriate action in anticipation.

**5** False: experience suggests that exchange rates can be sufficiently flexible to maintain PPP even in extreme conditions (see Section 34–4 of the main text).

**6** True.

**7** Not proved: see Section 34–6 of the main text.

**8** Also not proved: tariffs were substantially dismantled through GATT under the adjustable peg. In the recession of the early 1980s there were moves towards protectionism under the managed float.

**9** True: see Section 34–7 of the main text.

**10** True: but only for those members of the EMS who were also participating in the ERM.

**11** True: see Box 34–4 in the main text.

## Economics in action

**1** It is necessary to draw a distinction between the short run and the long run. In the short run it is possible that the adoption of the Euro by the UK may lead to exchange rate stability (with other Euro members). But with the loss of monetary sovereignty, the ability to control the economy independently from other Euro members may lead to output instability. But in the long run convergence of output and prices among Eurozone members may lead to long-term economic stability in output, prices and the exchange rate. The ideas associated with an optimal currency zone, discussed in Chapter 35, may lead to such a situation.

**2** With a loss of monetary sovereignty the UK would have only fiscal policy with which to control the economy. If a low interest rate in the Eurozone led to rising inflationary pressures in the UK, then the government would have to pursue fiscal tightening – i.e. increased taxes and reduced government spending.

## Questions for thought

**1** This issue lies at the heart of the 'fixed v. floating' debate – can policy harmonization be achieved without the discipline of a fixed-exchange rate regime?

**2** These headings are used in the examination of 'fixed v. floating' exchange rates in Section 34–5 of the main text. Some salient points are mentioned below:

**(a)** Flexible rates are probably better at coping with real shocks. Flexible rates also cope with nominal shocks, but a fixed-rate system may discourage the occurrence of such shocks (see (b)).

**(b)** Fixed-rate systems force financial discipline upon countries, which must adopt domestic policies that keep their inflation rates in line with world rates. The discipline is lacking with a floating exchange rate, which is able to cope with variations in inflation rates between countries.

**(c)** Fixed-rate systems by definition offer stability of exchange rates (except, of course, at the time of a devaluation), whereas under a flexible regime there may be day-to-day variability. Defenders of flexible rates point out that the volatility may find alternative expression in interest rates or tax rates.

**(d)** It is by no means clear whether protectionism is more likely under fixed or under floating exchange rates.

As far as assessing the UK's experience is concerned, we leave you to review the available evidence.

# Chapter Thirty-five Answers
# European integration

## Important concepts and technical terms

| | | | |
|---|---|---|---|
| **1** h | **4** a | **7** k | **10** g |
| **2** c | **5** e | **8** j | **11** l |
| **3** i | **6** b | **9** f | **12** d |

## Exercises

**1** **(a)** This was certainly a key part of the '1992' reforms – indeed, many EU members had dismantled all controls much earlier.

**(b)** This was also part of the reforms.

**(c)** The harmonization of tax rates was seen as a desirable aspect of a Single European Market (SEM), but politically tricky to achieve. The '1992' reforms thus made provision for progress towards harmonization of tax rates.

(d) This was part of the reforms, but some non-tariff barriers (NTBs) are subtle in nature, so enforcement could be a problem in some cases.

(e) This is the wording used in the EC 'Directives' on trade and competition policies setting out the objectives for '1992'.

(f) This also is part of the '1992' reforms.

(g) This was not part of the '1992' reforms.

**2** Option *(d)* describes a tariff; all the other items are NTBs which have been used.

**3** (a) The gradual depletion of the reserves of North Sea oil dilutes this argument.

(b) This argument disappears as other EU members dismantle controls on capital movements.

(c) The proportion of UK trade with other EU members has increased substantially since Britain's entry into the Community, so this argument becomes less powerful with time.

(d) Look at what happened to the inflation rate in 1989–90.

(e) It is argued that monetary policy is required as a short-term weapon against inflation to avoid the use of fiscal policy for this purpose. There is no definitive answer to whether this is a valid argument – it depends upon your evaluation of the consequences of fiscal management.

(f) Time inevitably must dilute this argument.

**4** Items *(a)*, *(c)*, *(d)* and *(e)* are necessary characteristics of a monetary union; the others may be.

**5** (a) Competitiveness will fall.

(b) The loss in competitiveness will presumably lead to a reduction in the demand for exported goods.

(c) Both output and employment are likely to be reduced.

(d) Adjustment will rely on the gradual restoration of competitiveness through changes in relative wage and price levels. Of course, this may take some time, and during the interim period the economy is likely to suffer from unemployment.

(e) The danger of adopting fiscal management is that it could lead to an increase in the inflation rate; this is what the Delors proposals were intended to avoid. A key question to consider is whether there are alternative ways of achieving the same objective.

(f) In the USA, an example of a monetary union, if one state suffers a temporary recession, the Federal fiscal system will provide some automatic stabilization. See Section 35–5 of the main text for the full story.

**6** (a) This is one of the benefits from the '1992' reforms.

(b) This was also part of the '1992' reforms: the hope was that transaction costs would be reduced by this move.

(c) The abolition of NTBs to trade (part of '1992') opened domestic industry up to intensified competition. Although this might be viewed as a cost in the short run if it causes unemployment, the long-run effect should be beneficial.

(d) Monetary union will bring this loss of sovereignty, but hopefully the benefits of the union will be adequate compensation.

(e) A benefit of '1992'.

(f) A benefit of '1992', although the extent to which labour mobility will be enhanced remains to be seen.

(g) This has been happening over the years in any case.

(h) Exchange rate certainty would come with monetary union – at least internally, rates would be fixed – but '1992' was also a step in this direction.

(i) An expected benefit of '1992'.

(j) Monetary union is one way of establishing this, but not necessarily the only way.

(k) This is one possible result of a monetary union – see Exercise **5**.

(l) The establishment of a common currency is one way in which a monetary union could have the effect of reducing transaction costs, but notice that in principle it is possible to have a monetary union operating without a common currency.

(m) Both '1992' and European Monetary Union (EMU) may be regarded as moves towards European integration – whether this is politically acceptable is to some extent a separate issue.

**7** (a) A rate of interest as low as $r_1$ would be required if an income level of $Y_0$ were to be realized with the *IS* curve at $IS_A$.

(b) With the ECB committed to maintaining price stability via the interest rate, it is highly unlikely that the interest rate would be permitted to fall as far as $r_1$. Given that the country is said to be a small country within Euroland, its influence within the Union will be limited, and the country is not able to have a different interest rate from other countries within the system. So, this cannot be a solution. The only exception might be if all countries in the Union were also experiencing severe recession, so that the problem was seen to be a general one.

(c) In principle, the government could try to shift the position of the *IS* curve by use of fiscal policy, but this may be outlawed within the terms of the Union.

**(d)** It is still possible that the economy will get to $Y_0$, but it may take some time. If the economy is in recession but other countries are not, then it is likely that in time wages and prices will adjust, so that competitiveness begins to be restored. As this happened, imports into our country would fall and exports would be stimulated. These effects would shift the *IS* curve to the right. Hopefully this would eventually take the country back to $IS_B$ and thus to $Y_0$. This is discussed in Section 35–5 of the main text.

**8**    See Section 35–4 of the main text for a more thorough discussion of these three alternatives. Of course, by the time you read this, events may be overtaking this question. You might then like to consider whether the best option has been selected!

**9**    **(a)**  Increased trade among EU members – true: see Section 35–4 of the main text. Increased trade among member economies is central to the development of an optimal currency zone.

**(b)**  Increased trade by EU members with China – this could be true as it would make all economies react similarly from an external shock, such as the Chinese economy moving into recession.

**(c)**  Increased rigidities in wage settlements across the EU – false, this would make wage and price adjustments much more difficult. With a lack of convergence, or synchronization across the economies, a 'one-size-fits-all' monetary policy is unlikely to deliver economic stability.

**(d)**  The rapid growth of e-commerce – if the growth of e-commerce delivers increased price transparency, then increased competition may deliver more flexible and reactive pricing structures.

## True/False

**1**    True: see Section 35–1 of the main text.

**2**    True.

**3**    Not quite accurate: the EU in 1993 had a population larger than either the USA or Japan.

**4**    False: tariffs were already outlawed before 1992.

**5**    Hopefully false: it is possible that such merger and takeover activity represents companies' attempts to restructure, so as to be in a better position to exploit economies of scale and comparative advantage in the enlarged single market. Much will depend upon the strength

and wisdom of European merger policy in the transition period and beyond.

**6**    True: see Section 35–4 of the main text.

**7**    False: Stage 3 involving EMU would have begun only in 1997 if a majority of the EU had been ready and willing to go at that time – which, of course, they were not! As you will be aware, 11 countries went ahead with the single currency in 1999.

**8**    True: see Section 35–5 of the main text.

**9**    False: the EU Structural Funds programme is not sufficient to fulfil that role.

**10**    True: see Section 35–5 of the main text.

**11**    True: see Section 35–6 of the main text. The plight of less developed countries is discussed in Chapter 36.

**12**    True: but Western governments have taken steps to reduce the burdens – for example, by the establishment of the European Bank for Reconstruction and Development (EBRD) to finance market-oriented reforms.

## Economics in action

**1**    Establishing cooperative behaviour among 25 players is difficult. There will also be the incentive for one member to cheat. This is like the success of a cartel – it is more likely to succeed when the number of members is low. However, what if the EU is a cartel of cartels? For example, Germany, France, Belgium, Holland and Spain might represent a cohesive group. So might Denmark, the UK and Ireland; or Italy, Greece and Portugal, plus the Cezch Republic, Hungary and Poland. Gaining agreement among blocs of countries would be a lot more feasible.

**2**    The new member countries have big markets which the EU would like to sell to and buy from. Enlargement will also make economic trade with Russia much easier. Funding economic development in Eastern Europe could well be a price worth paying.

## Questions for thought

**1**    This is a difficult and contentious issue, but you are now equipped to understand the economic arguments for and against. By being outside the Eurozone, the UK runs the risk of losing business and investment from foreign companies.

Evidence suggests that this might already be occurring. By being in the Eurozone the UK runs the risk of economic instability brought about by policy designed for all members and not just the UK. The UK can survive without the Euro, the real question is whether it can survive and grow better with it.

**2** Both discontent and envy probably had some part to play in the pressure for reform.

**3** We recommend that you re-read Section 35–5 of the main text, which sets out the key characteristics of an optimal currency area. As you do so, think about the extent to which Euroland meets these conditions, and the extent to which the UK would share those characteristics. This will influence your views about whether Britain should enter Euroland.

# Chapter Thirty-six Answers

## Less developed countries

### Important concepts and technical terms

| | | | | | | | |
|---|---|---|---|---|---|---|---|
| **1** | d | **4** | i | **7** | f | **10** | a |
| **2** | c | **5** | k | **8** | h | **11** | g |
| **3** | e | **6** | l | **9** | b | **12** | j |

### Exercises

**1** Population growth rates tend to stabilize in developed economies; this is probably related to a number of factors. Income levels are higher, pension systems and social security systems are more advanced. Individuals do not therefore need to have children in order to support them in the future. The infant mortality rate is also lower due to advanced medical care, leading to lower birth rates. Modern economies have generally passed through periods of industrialization and are therefore now less reliant on agriculture. Less developed economies, in contrast, still have economies which are heavily dependent upon agriculture, small farm holdings, etc. Access to clean water and adult literacy provide measures (but not perfect ones) of capital infrastructure in the economy. How good is the basic water system, and how good is the basic education system? Note many of these measures are related to health. If you cannot live a healthy life, then it is difficult to live an economically productive life.

**2** (a) Equilibrium price would have been $40 per unit and the buffer stock must buy up 75 (000) units to maintain price at $70.

(b) Equilibrium price would have been $80 per unit. The

buffer stock sells 25 (000) units to maintain price. The buffer stock now holds 50 (000) units.

(c) The net additions to the buffer stock in the five years are 0, +50, +25, –50, +100. Cumulative quantities held: 50, 100, 125, 75, 175. The total cost of operating the buffer stock over the seven years amounts to $175\,000 \times 70 = \$12.25$ million – plus the costs of warehousing and storage.

(d) Average supply over the period was 400 (000) units p.a.; a price of $60 per unit would have kept the stock stable. If the buffer stock continues to maintain the price at too high a level, stocks must build up in the long run, tying up precious resources.

**3** (a) With demand $DD_1$, equilibrium price is $OA$, revenue is the area $OAKF$.

(b) With $DD_2$, equilibrium is $OC$, revenue is $OCMH$.

(c) Quantity $OG$, revenue $OBLG$.

(d) Buffer stock buys $EG$, revenue $OBLG$.

(e) Buffer stock sells $GJ$, revenue $OBLG$.

**4** See Table A36–1.

The absolute difference between the two countries continues to widen, even though the low-income country is growing at a higher annual percentage rate.

**5** The NICs included in the list are:

**D** Singapore

**F** Hong Kong

**H** Republic of Korea.

On the basis of these figures, country C (Sri Lanka) also seems to be following this path. Country A (Brazil) seemed at one point in time to be developing rapidly, but its success was gained before the 1980s. Brazil was adversely affected during

| Period | GNP per capita | | Absolute difference in GNP per capita |
|---|---|---|---|
| | **Low-income country** | **High-income country** | |
| Initial | 380.0 | 8460.0 | 8080.0 |
| 1 | 391.0 | 8595.4 | 8204.3 |
| 2 | 402.4 | 8732.9 | 8330.5 |
| 3 | 414.0 | 8872.6 | 8458.6 |
| 4 | 426.0 | 9014.6 | 8588.5 |
| 5 | 438.4 | 9158.8 | 8720.4 |

**Table A36–1**  Relative growth in low- and high-income countries

the 1980s by debt and inflation, while the East Asian NICs continued to prosper, although even they ran into occasional problems, most notably in the financial crisis of 1997. The other countries are Côte d'Ivoire (*B*), Uruguay (*E*), Jamaica (*G*) and Chile (*I*).

**6**   (*a*), (*b*), (*c*) and (*f*).

**7**   **(a)** Clearly, comparative advantage will not lie with hi-tech manufacturing industries. More sensible might be labour-intensive activities, in particular primary production – either agriculture or mineral extraction.

**(b)** A problem with specializing in primary production is that there has been an historical tendency for the terms of trade to move against primary products, and for prices of such commodities to be highly volatile, as a result of fluctuations in either supply or demand.

**(c)** The 'infant industry' argument in favour of imposing tariffs has always been a tempting one: an LDC might hope that by imposing a tariff it would be possible to nurture new industries which would eventually be able to compete in world markets, after an initial period in which the country would save on imports. A problem has always been that the industry becomes overprotected and never fully grows up. Import substitution tends to engender an inward-looking attitude on the part of domestic producers.

**(d)** Export promotion forces an outward-looking attitude on domestic producers. It has proved very successful for the NICs, but there is some doubt about whether the same route could be followed by all LDCs, especially given the increasingly protectionist attitude adopted by the industrial countries since the recession of the early 1980s.

**8**   **(a)** It might be nice to imagine that donors act purely out of humanitarian motives, but realistically this seems unlikely. In 1997, only four OECD countries (Norway, the Netherlands, Denmark and Sweden) reached the UN target for aid as a percentage of GNP, agreed in the 1970s.

Countries such as the UK and the USA were giving a much smaller proportion in 1997 than in 1965. It seems more likely that donors are partly, if not mainly, motivated by self-interest.

**(b)** Many political motivations exist: donors may wish to preserve the ideology in which they believe, or to strengthen their own position in a region of the world. The changes in the geographical pattern of US aid flows in the postwar period are revealing.

**(c)** Much of aid is 'tied' aid. For instance, bilateral aid between countries may be based on an agreement that the recipient will purchase goods from the donor in the future, sometimes at prices above the competitive world prices for similar goods. Indeed, there is evidence that some countries regard aid as being part of trade policy.

**(d)** Political stability is important for development – and even more important for the government in power! There have been times when aid has been used to bolster the government's position. At times this has involved the use of aid for 'prestige' projects, which may improve the image of recipient or donor but do little to promote development.

**(e)** The economic reasons for acceptance of aid by a poor country hardly need stating, but one potential problem is that the recipient country may find itself in a position of dependency. For instance, it might be that aid lowers the domestic incentives for saving, or even production, such that the LDC cannot break out of its reliance on other countries.

**(f)** It has often been argued that allowing LDCs to trade on fair terms with the rest of the world would have more beneficial effects than the simple granting of aid. This may be seen in particular in terms of the incentives for the LDC economy.

**9**   All of them. Item (*c*) is worth special mention: the increasing importance of bank loans relative to official aid is a significant feature of the international debt crisis.

**10** In fact, the two countries are Sri Lanka (country *X*), and Cameroon (country *Y*). In spite of its seemingly inferior development performance on every criterion in the table, Cameroon had a GNP per capita which is more than double that of Sri Lanka ($960 as compared with $470). This reinforces the view that GNP per capita may not always be a good indicator of the standard of living achieved by the citizens of a country.

## True/False

**1** True: see Section 36–1 of the main text.

**2** True: see Section 36–2 of the main text.

**3** Sometimes true: it takes time to develop work practices and the acceptance of factory working.

**4** False: there are many problems with a heavy reliance on primary products (see Section 36–3 of the main text).

**5** False: if demand and supply are relatively elastic, then price movements will tend to be small, even in the face of large demand or supply shocks. Draw a diagram to check this out.

**6** False: this is too static a picture, which presumes that the pattern of comparative advantage cannot be changed over time (see Section 36–4 of the main text).

**7** True.

**8** True: see Section 36–5 of the main text.

**9** A bit contentious: some LDCs have claimed that structural adjustment programmes (SAPs) have been too stringent, whereas some economists argue that there are times when it is necessary to dispense unpleasant medicine.

**10** True: see Section 36–6 of the main text. Although true, however, it is also extremely unlikely.

**11** True and false: more aid is necessary but not sufficient. Freer trade is also important.

## Economics in action

**1** The problem for Africa is that there are other areas of the world that are more politically and economically important to the developed world. Africa is not well integrated into the global economy in terms of either exports or imports. Contrast this with South East Asia, or the Middle East; both are economically important to the USA and to Europe and so are of political and economic interest. Africa is perhaps a social and moral concern for the rest of the world; until it becomes a major economic concern, then the developed world's interests will remain charitable at best.

**2** Globalization could alleviate poverty in a number of ways, but it is important to think about what 'globalization' means. Does it mean globalization in product markets, financial markets or even labour markets? Product market globalization may enable greater product flows to and from LDCs, thus stimulating their economies, as might greater financial liberalization. But greater labour mobility would enable individuals from LDCs to move to more developed countries, thus reducing poverty.

## Questions for thought

**1** From the discussion of this chapter, it seems unlikely that LDCs can develop without the help (or at least the cooperation) of the rich countries. More difficult is the question of the form in which that help should come – aid, direct investment by multinationals, or freer trade? The focus of the second part of the question is on the consequences of default on international debt, which is often discussed mainly in terms of the effect on the international financial system.

**2** In exploring this issue, you will need to draw upon material from a number of different parts of your economics course. For example, one of the arguments behind the insistence that countries follow structural adjustment before qualifying for debt relief is based upon moral hazard. Countries may allow debt to build up in order to have it forgiven. Many commentators claimed that this argument had been overstated, and that six years was a long time to have to prove commitment. Others suggested that there were other ways of seeking to ensure that debt relief was channelled into appropriate policies. For example, in Uganda (the first country to qualify for relief under the HIPC initiative), funds were set aside for expenditure on primary education.

**3** As you think about this question, you will need to think back through the whole of the book. You will need to consider the causes of market failure, and whether there are forms of market failure which may affect LDCs in particular. Some discussion of this will be found in Chapter 30, where we talked about the 'convergence hypothesis' and why it might not always work. You will also need to consider the various ways in which the policies adopted by industrial economies may affect LDCs. This will include consideration of trade policy (protectionism, etc.). The pattern of the business cycle and the effects of interest rate policies may also be seen to impinge upon LDCs.

**4**    The distinction between normative and positive economics was made in Chapter 1 of the book, and it seems appropriate that we should return to it right at the end. In assessing the economic performance of different economies, and in particular in looking at the problems of LDCs, it is very easy to become emotional and to allow value judgements to cloud our view of the economic issues. Being aware of this may serve to minimize its effect.